German and Japanese Business in the Boom Years

During the twentieth century as a whole, the United States has been a reference point for industrialized economies around the world. This volume examines the American influence on two of the most important and dynamic economies in the post war period, West German and Japanese, during the so-called boom years (1950–1973).

Contributions to this volume analysis five different business sectors which played an important role as engines of economic growth and also in the development of the consumer society in both countries: automobiles, electrical engineering and electronics, synthetic fibres and rubber, consumer chemicals and retail trade. The paired case studies examine the process of introducing new technology and management methods in each company and industry with respect to the American influence. They look at possible Americanization across a wide variety of functions, including R&D, production, sales and marketing, human resources and finance. The book shows that the American models led to a transformation of existing production and management systems which subsequently became the core of the successful West German and Japanese models in the 1970s and the 1980s.

German and Japanese Business in the Boom Years makes an important contribution to the debate on Americanization from a historical and comparative perspective and will be essential reading for students and researchers of business and economic history.

Akira Kudo is Professor at the Institute of Social Science, University of Tokyo. His interests cover modern German economic and business history and business and economic relations between Japan and Germany in the nineteenth and twentieth centuries. He is the author of *Japanese–German Business Relations* (1998). **Matthias Kipping** is Associate Professor at Universitat Pompeu Fabra in Barcelona. He also teaches at the University of Reading. He has written and published extensively on the evolution of management consultancy and business education and on the American influence on European business. **Harm G. Schröter** is Professor at the University of Bergen in Norway. His main field of research is European economic history from 1850 to the present day, including the level of firms (e.g. multinational enterprise, innovation) and countries (e.g. state–industry relations).

Routledge International Studies in Business History
Series editors: Geoffrey Jones and Mary Rose

German and Japanese Business in the Boom Years

Transforming American management and technology models

**Edited by Akira Kudo, Matthias Kipping
and Harm G. Schröter**

Routledge
Taylor & Francis Group

LONDON AND NEW YORK

First published 2004
by Routledge
2 Park Square, Milton Park, Abingdon, Oxfordshire OX14 4RN

Simultaneously published in the USA and Canada
by Routledge
711 Third Avenue, New York, NY 10017

First issued in paperback 2015

Routledge is an imprint of the Taylor and Francis Group, an informa business

© 2004 Editorial matter and selection, Akira Kudo, Matthias Kipping
and Harm G. Schröter; individual chapters, the contributors

Typeset in Baskerville by Wearset Ltd, Boldon, Tyne and Wear

British Library Cataloguing in Publication Data
A catalogue record for this book is available from the British Library

Library of Congress Cataloging in Publication Data
A catalog record for this book has been requested

ISBN 13: 978-1-138-86402-3 (pbk)
ISBN 13: 978-0-415-28876-7 (hbk)

Contents

Illustrations

Contributors

Wilfried Feldenkirchen was born in 1947 in Cologne and studied history, economics and English literature. He holds the Chair of economic, social and business history at the University of Erlangen-Nuremberg. He has written numerous books and articles on business, economic and social history. A two-volume history on Daimler-Benz is about to be published.

Shin Hasegawa is Professor at the Faculty of Business Administration, Aoyama Gakuin University. He specializes in the business and economic history of modern Japan, focusing on the electrical and electronics industry. He wrote extensively in the field and co-authored *Modern Japanese Economy* (in Japanese, Tokyo, 1999).

Susanne Hilger is Assistant Professor in Economic, Social and Business History at the University of Erlangen-Nuremberg. She did her PhD on welfare policy in the German iron and steel industry before the Second World War and is currently researching business strategies in the German consumer industries after the Second World War. She has recently finished a study on the Americanization of German industry after 1945.

Motoi Ihara is Associate Professor at the Faculty of Economics, University of Saitama. His dissertation presented at the University of Tokyo analyzed the Asian strategy of Kao Corp., a leading Japanese chemical consumer maker. He has also published several papers on the same topic in *Japan Business History Review* and other journals.

Takeo Kikkawa is Professor at the Institute of Social Science, University of Tokyo. His work covers numerous aspects of business history in modern Japan. His main work is *The Development of Japanese Electricity Industry and Yasuzaemon Matsunaga* (in Japanese, Nagoya, 1995). He also co-edited *Policies for Competitiveness* (Oxford, 1999).

Matthias Kipping is Associate Professor at Universitat Pompeu Fabra in Barcelona. He also has a part-time appointment at the University of

Reading, where he was a Reader in European Management and Director of the Centre for International Business History (CIBH) until 2001. He has written and published extensively on the evolution of different carriers of management knowledge, namely business education and management consultancy. He recently edited, with Lars Engwall, *Management Consulting: Emergence and Dynamics of a Knowledge Industry* (Oxford, 2002).

Christian Kleinschmidt is Assistant Professor in the Department of Social and Economic History at the Ruhr-University in Bochum. His main research areas are economic and business history. He is the author of a study on rationalization within the iron and steel industry in the Ruhr area and recently published his habilitation thesis on the perception of American and Japanese management and production methods by German business: *Der produktive Blick. Wahrnehmung amerikanischer und japanischer Management- und Produktionsmethoden durch deutsche Unternehmer 1950–1985* (Berlin, 2002).

Akira Kudo is Professor at the Institute of Social Science, University of Tokyo. He specializes in the business and economic history of modern Germany and its relations with Japan. He recently published *Japanese-German Business Relations* (London, 1998).

Satoshi Sasaki is Professor at the School of Business Administration, Meiji University. He specializes in the history of scientific management and the productivity movement in Japan. He is currently researching the history of marketing strategy in the toiletry industry. His main work is *Development of Scientific Management in Japan* (in Japanese, Tokyo, 1998).

Harm G. Schröter is Professor of history at the University of Bergen. He has published widely on topics in German and European business history. His works include *Multinationale Unternehmen aus kleinen Staaten bis 1914* (Berlin, 1994). Currently, he is working on a book surveying Americanization in Europe.

Tsuneo Suzuki is Professor at the Faculty of Economics, Gakushuin University. His work focuses primarily on the history of the synthetic fibre industry in Japan and the analysis of the excessive competition in Japan as a necessary issue to understand Japanese business success. He recently contributed 'Industrial Policy and the Development of the Synthetic Fibre Industry', in H. Miyajima, T. Kikkawa and T. Hikino (eds), *Policies for Competitiveness* (Oxford, 1999).

Mika Takaoka is Associate Professor at the Faculty of Economics, Rikkyo University. She specializes in the business history of distribution in Japan and has published widely in the field. She is the author of 'Japan's Distribution Revolution and Chain Store Supermarkets', *Japanese Yearbook on Business History*, Vol. 15, 1998.

Hirofumi Ueda is Professor at the Institute of Economic Research, Osaka City University. He specializes in the business and economic history of the automobile and other mechanical industries in Japan, focusing on the supplier system. He has published extensively in the field. He also contributed to T. Shiba and M. Shimotani (eds), *Beyond the Firm* (Oxford, 1997).

Preface

This book is the result of the third Japanese-German Business History Conference, which took place on 24–25 March 2000 at the University of Tokyo. The first Japanese-German Business History Conference was held in 1979 in Berlin and the second one in 1981 in Tokyo. This conference therefore broke the almost 20 years' pause in Japanese-German exchange activities in business history.

When the Association of Business History of Japan was given an offer of generous support by the Taniguchi Foundation 1999, the Association and its then president Professor Hiroaki Yamazaki decided to revitalize Japanese-German cooperation and asked Akira Kudo, one of the editors, to organize a conference. Kudo accepted the offer and chose as the theme of the conference the 'Americanization' of German and Japanese firms in the post-war era. He then asked Matthias Kipping and Harm G. Schröter, both of whom Kudo knew had been interested in the topic, to co-organize a conference and they accepted. The three set up the structure of the conference in detail and asked some business historians in Japan and Germany to join the project. They are the contributors of this book.

Besides the contributors, the following historians attended the conference and some of them made comments on the papers presented at the conference: Terushi Hara, Hideaki Miyajima, Yuji Nishimuta, Reiko Okayama, Sung-Jo Park, Erich Pauer, Kin'ya Shirakawa, Kinsaburo Sunaga, Toshio Takahashi, Hiroaki Yamazaki, Hideki Yoshihara and Takeshi Yuzawa. The editors would like to thank them for their active participation, which contributed much to the revision of the papers included in this book. The editors also would like to thank Fumiki Ishizuka and Kei-ichiro Nakagawa for their administrative and secretarial support as well as Mrs Jill Turner and Mrs Carol Wright for their help with language editing. Last but not least, they would like to express their deepest gratitude to the Taniguchi Foundation for its generous sponsorship of the conference.

Akira Kudo, Matthias Kipping and Harm G. Schröter
Tokyo/Barcelona/Hamburg, May 2003

Abbreviations

AJS	All Japanese Supermarkets Association
BCG	Boston Consulting Group
BDI	Bundesverband der Deutschen Industrie
BSHG	Bosch-Siemens Hausgeräte GmbH
CNPF	Conseil national du patronat français
CP	Colgate-Palmolive
DGB	Deutscher Gewerkschaftsbund
DIPS	Denden-kosha Information Processing System
ECA	European Cooperation Administration
ECSC	European Coal and Steel Community
EPA	European Productivity Agency
ERP	European Recovery Program
FOA	Foreign Operations Administration
FORFA	Forschungsinstut für Arbeitspsychologie und Personalwesen der TH Braunschweig
GATT	General Agreement on Tariffs and Trade
GHQ	General Headquarters of the US Occupation Authorities
GMS	General merchandising store
HIS	Honeywell Information System Inc.
IC	Integrated circuit
IMF	International Monetary Fund
ISE	International Standard Electric Co.
JAPIA	Japan Auto Parts Industries Association
JUSE	Union of Japanese Scientists and Engineers
KWU	Kraftwerk-Union
LRP	Long-range planning
LRPS	Long-Range Planning Service
MCI	Ministry of Commerce and Industry
MITI	Ministry of International Trade and Industry (now Ministry of Economy, Trade and Industry)
MSA	Mutual Security Agency
MTM	Methods Time Measurement
NAM	National Association of Manufacturers

NPCs	National Productivity Centres
NTT	Nippon Telegraph and Telephone Corporation
NTTPC	Nippon Telegraph and Telephone Public Corporation
OEEC	Organisation for European Economic Co-operation
P&G	Procter & Gamble
RCA	Radio Corporation of America
REFA	Reichsausschuß für Arbeitszeitermittlung (National Committee for Work Time Determination)
RKW	Rationalisierungs-Kuratorium der deutschen Wirtschaft (Rationalization Association for the German economy)
S&H	Siemens & Halske
SE	Siemens-Electrogeräte AG
SMEA	Small and Medium Enterprise Agency
SQC	Statistical quality control
SQCM	Scientific quality control methods
SRI	Stanford Research Institute
SRI	Sperry Rand International Corporation
SSW	Siemens-Schuckertwerke
STAC	Science and Technology Administration Council
TMC	Toyota Motor Corporation
TMMC	Toyota Motor Manufacturing Corporation
TU	Transformatoren-Union
TWI	Training within Industry
UST&P	The US Technological and Productivity Program
VA	Value Analysis
VW	Volkswagen
VHSCS	Very High-Speed Computer System Project

1 Americanization

Historical and conceptual issues

Akira Kudo, Matthias Kipping and Harm G. Schröter

Introduction

Reappearance of Americanization in the 1990s

Among the most important trends in the international economy during the 1990s was the tremendous influence of the American economy, which manifested itself globally. This has led to a renewed debate about a possible Americanization.[1] The argument for Americanization has been fiercely contested with counter argument. This controversy has been linked with that on globalization, which has developed along with Americanization. The debate on convergence or divergence has also developed, arguing whether or not each nation's capitalism with its own character will change through Americanization and globalization.[2] This debate has been continuing even after the prosperity that long-persisted in the United States began to decline after 2000. In spite of the economic downturn, Americanization itself seems not to have lost its dynamics. It is interesting to ask why it persists. Moreover, its consequences are still unclear.

The word Americanization itself has a long history. One of the earliest meanings of the word was nation building in the early history of the United States. Today it is used in a variety of contexts: politics, the economy, society, culture and civilization.[3] Here, we use the word for the transfer of technology, management ideas and practices, as well as institutional frameworks from the United States. We call this influence Americanization when institutions and organizations in other countries used the United States as a 'reference' for local changes. Thus, in our view, Americanization is not a model (or several models) of values and behaviour as such, but a process. Its results are characterized by selection, transfer, change and adaptation to local, regional or national circumstances. Americanization does not mean that, after it had taken place, all organizations, institutions, values and behaviour had become identical to those in the USA, although they were definitely closer to American models than before.

During the 1990s, re-unified Germany and Japan came under considerable pressure from Americanization and globalization. They were not exceptional in this respect, but these developments had a special meaning for both countries: during the immediate post Second World War period both had already been subject to a significant US influence. Subsequently, for about two decades, during the 1970s and 1980s, they came to represent alternatives to the United States as an example of successful capitalist economies.

Americanization in Germany and Japan

After the Second World War, West Germany, to which we often refer below simply as Germany, and Japan experienced rapid economic reconstruction and high growth-rates on their way to becoming economic powers. As regional powers in Western Europe and East Asia, both countries were important as support for the Pax Americana, economically as well as politically. Moreover, during the 1970s and 1980s, German and Japanese firms and types of capitalism achieved better performance than their American competitor, counterpart and teacher. They differed characteristically from the latter in such areas as owner-manager relations, industrial relations, inter-firm relations and business-government relations. Observers argued for the advent of a 'Rhenish' model of capitalism and Japanese-style management; and they often hailed these as new, even post American models for business management and for capitalism itself.[4] The words Germanization and Japanization of business management and capitalism became fashionable. Some even argued that both countries were threatening the United States, referring to the then ongoing strategic alliance between Daimler-Benz and the Mitsubishi business group, bearing in mind the war-time alliance between the German Messerschmitt and the Japanese Zero-fighter.[5]

Ironically, from the start of the 1990s, just after the era of German and Japanese success, firms and capitalism in unified Germany and in Japan deteriorated in their performance. They then again found themselves under the influence of the United States. Taking into account the history of Americanization in both countries after the Second World War, we can call this process during the last decade of the twentieth century a 're-Americanization'. It reminds us of a process of ups and downs like the tide: Americanization became strong and weak as time passed. It is because of this that we have suggested that Americanization in the 1990s had special meaning for both countries. Germany and Japan give us ample examples in discussing Americanization. At the same time, American influences need special attention in reviewing the development of capitalism and firms in both countries.

During the 1990s, the influence of American business and capitalism extended to all functions of firms and all aspects of capitalism. At the individual firm level, it was pronounced in owner-manager relations ('shareholder value') and industrial relations (lay offs), in corporate finance, accounting practices, corporate governance, etc. Such American influences in business were closely linked to parallel influences of US-style capitalism in fields such as the finance and insurance sector, business philosophy, business education and consulting. The principal routes for these types of influences were direct investment and multinational firms, but these were not all. Trade, technology tie-ups (licensing agreements), advertising, visits, consultancies and diverse other routes exist; we may also add indirect investment, currency and financial policy, and, recently, economic policy.

The American influence on the German and Japanese economies has therefore become a topic that deserves particular attention today. As mentioned earlier, this phenomenon of Americanization of firms and the type of capitalism in Germany and Japan did not suddenly begin in the 1990s. It was visible on a large scale during the post Second World War decades, and even further back. It was at hand at the end of the nineteenth and beginning of the twentieth century, as well as in the 1920s, as will be seen later in this chapter.

While looking back at the long-term history of Americanization, the contributions of this volume will focus on the post Second World War decades, especially on the 1950s and 1960s, the period when this phenomenon reached a peak. We will try to compare the German and Japanese experiences during these years of rapid economic growth or 'boom', based on questions such as: what are the processes and routes of the respective Americanization? What was its scale in both countries? How should we assess its results? Have both types of capitalism changed as a result of Americanization? If so, how have they changed? Which country has been more Americanized, Germany or Japan? If we see any difference in Americanization of both countries, then what are the reasons for the difference?

Previous research and the focus of this volume

The reasons for this special attention to both, to a certain period and to a German-Japanese comparison, are the following. First of all, research on the history of Americanization in Germany and Japan has so far largely ignored the 'boom' years. Thus, most recent studies of Americanization have focused more on the immediate post war period, when both countries were occupied by the US army (and the other Allied powers in the German case). In this context, there has been a comparison between both of the occupied countries, Germany and Japan.[6] Second, if comparative studies exist for the era of rapid growth, they focus mainly on the level of the national economy. In Japan, research has been conducted on the comparison with Japan's former model, Germany, paying attention to a parallel history of alliance, defeat, occupation and rapid growth.[7] The

1950s and 1960s were indeed eras of rapid economic growth as well as of rapid business growth in both countries. But it is not enough to describe the rapid growth of economy and business only as phenomena under the American-centred international order or the cold-war order.[8]

It is an important task to clarify the reality of Americanization by entering into firms, the main players of this growth, and for explaining the reasons of high growth in the economy and in business. There is a large and growing number of historical studies on Americanization in each of the two countries. Comparison in the context of firm-level Americanization for the boom period, however, has so far hardly been developed.

Pioneering research on Germany has been carried out since the 1980s by Volker Berghahn.[9] Building on the work of Heinz Hartmann,[10] Berghahn suggested that German capitalism had undergone an Americanization from the 1960s onwards. He also examined the different aspects of this process. Berghahn himself concluded by highlighting the need for further work. Various aspects, such as the acceptance, rejection and revision of Americanization during the 1950s and 1960s, as well as the causes of Americanization, remained to be analyzed in more detail. Furthermore, he took heavy industry and its relations with the government as representative, while in fact other sectors were possibly more open to American influences.[11] Initially, Berghahn's book, which appeared during the period when German Rhenish capitalism was in its heyday, caused comparatively little impact. Perhaps it is not purely by chance that since the 1990s we have experienced a boom in the interest of Americanization, not only in Germany, but also in the whole of Western Europe.[12] Japan, in contrast, did not see any boom, although the discussion is now finally flourishing.[13]

However, there have not yet been any thorough attempts to look at the Americanization of Germany and Japan at the level of the firm in a comparative way.[14] It is therefore crucial to ask how German and Japanese firms showed their own features in this wave of Americanization, and whether these features imparted competitiveness and served as the driving force behind economic growth. If we pay attention to Americanization at the level of the firm, it is precisely during this period that American influence on German and Japanese business was at its strongest. During this period, management skills and technology flowed in a large stream from the United States into both countries. By focusing on the level of the firm we can demonstrate the features and advantages of the perspective of business history, especially since material from company archives about this period are more easily obtained compared to more recent periods.

The remainder of this introductory chapter has three major aims: first, it will put the Americanization of German and Japanese firms into context, by providing an overview of the different 'waves' of Americanization at the level of the firm since the end of the nineteenth century. Second, it will briefly summarize the findings from the individual chapters in this volume. And third, on this basis, it will develop some conclusions from the German-Japanese comparison.

A brief business history of Americanization in Germany and Japan

We will now outline the history of Americanization of German and Japanese firms from the late nineteenth century. In doing so, we find four large waves of Americanization before the 1990s: the first in the period from the late nineteenth century to the beginning of the twentieth century; the second in the 1920s; the third in the immediate post Second World War period; and the fourth during the 1950s and the 1960s. There is a fifth one during the 1990s, which may not yet have ended, and it seems too early to provide the specific point of view of historians on this latest wave.

The first wave: end of the nineteenth and beginning of the twentieth century

Throughout the nineteenth century, American firms accumulated investment in plant and equipment that was labour-saving and capital-intensive, against a background of an influx of funds, technology and management expertise that came from immigrants. These factors broke down old-style work-skills and gave rise to the so-called American system of manufacturing. This system had a universal character, especially in mass production and interchangeable parts, turned out with big machines, while at the same time it kept its American uniqueness.[15] This became the base for early Americanization or the first wave of Americanization.

The first wave of Americanization in Germany appeared at the end of the nineteenth and the beginning of the twentieth centuries. Large-scale, standardized, American-made machinery, including agricultural machinery and machine tools, appeared in a steady stream on the German market, and the transfer of American technology that went along with them moved ahead.[16] There was some interest in the scientific management techniques developed by Frederick W. Taylor and others. Early attempts to apply them in Germany, however, were not always successful – quite often resulting in strikes.[17] American influence was also visible in universities and research centres; the establishment of the Kaiser-Wilhelm-Research-Institute, today's Max-Planck-Institute, was a response to the American shock. The trust and merger movements in the turn-of-the-century United States also gave a considerable shock to Germany, and occasioned large scale-merger-plans, such as those by August Thyssen in steel and Carl Duisberg in the chemical industry – plans, which were not always carried out, at least not immediately. Expressions indicating American influence appeared, such as 'American invasion', 'American danger (*amerikanische Gefahr*)' and '*Amerikanismus*'.[18]

During the same period, the influence of American business also became markedly stronger in Japan, although it did not reach the same scale as in Germany. Taylor's *Principles of Scientific Management* appeared in a Japanese translation in 1913; Japan's first attempts at introducing scientific management techniques happened at about the same time as those of Germany. However, American-made machinery did not make a substantial appearance in the Japanese market. Industrialization in Japan did not reach such a level as to realize an American threat. The trust and merger movements in the United States at the turn of the century did not evoke a notable reverberation in Japan, mainly because Japanese firms, including the Zaibatsu-affiliated ones, had not yet grown sufficiently.

The second wave: the inter-war period

During the period following the First World War, American business was generating a new structure of mass production, mass distribution and mass consumption, and had developed forms of enterprise and systems of business management to conform to this structure. Ford's production system had been firmly established in the automobile sector, and General Motors's Alfred Sloan had developed his sales and business management systems. Scientific management techniques had matured. Out of these developments the second wave of Americanization was born. The American system of production and business management was seen to be of more universal character than before.

American firms stepped up their direct investment in Germany during the 1920s.[19] Led by GM, Ford and General Electric, US firms began to produce directly in Germany. This entailed Americanization: the introduction of US methods of production, organization, supervision, distribution, etc. GM's subsidiary Opel, for instance, introduced the production line format. The influence of American styles appeared not only in Opel's management: other firms tried to learn as well, especially in marketing and financial management.

The increasing direct investment of US firms, along with increasing American security investment in Germany, generated a fear of the power of the dollar. There was a fear that Americans would buy up German industry cheaply (*Überfremdung*), especially during the hyperinflation period, when the German currency became worthless. German companies developed their own form of Taylorism, 'industrial rationalization', which became the main response to the American threat.[20] Standardization continued with an eye towards establishing a mass-production system. After a certain time-lag, the shock of the turn-of-the-century American trust and merger wave was countered by a similar German one, which had its peak in the establishment of Vereinigte Stahlwerke.[21] At the same time German firms established other forms of economic concentrations, such as cartels.[22] Cartels were seen as a general answer to the American method of organization. Thus we find both the take-over of American ideas and structures and the expansion of a competing model.

In the 1920s, the influence of American business, with its established modes of mass production, distribution and consumption, became markedly stronger on Japan also. American firms also launched direct investment in Japan. Ford and GM started to assemble knock-down kits for cars, and the Ford system was transferred in part. This was one factor driving standardization in Japan. At the same time, it also provided the opportunity for GM to introduce its distribution through dealers, a system previously unknown in the country.

However, American firms' direct investment in Japan did not reach the scale of their investment in Germany. Transfer of production technology from the USA to Japan occurred primarily through technology license agreements. Experimental application of Taylor's ideas and production techniques also occurred relatively early. Regular on-site application, however, was limited to military arsenals, the railroad ministry, and some private spinning and machinery firms.[23] The response to the trust and merger movements in the USA at the turn of the century did not appear in Japan until the mid-1930s, when steel firms did finally merge to establish Nippon Steel, and Mitsubishi Chemical was established in the chemical sector. However, it can be questioned to what extent these developments were due directly to Americanization or to the influence of industrial rationalization and the cartelization movement in Germany.[24]

The period from the 1930s through to the defeat in 1945 was an era in which Americanization was interrupted and then set aside in Germany and Japan. It indicated the extent to which Americanization had advanced, as well as what happened when the process stopped. American institutions and ideas were Germanized or Japanized, sometimes to the point of becoming caricatures. Consequently, there was a renewed attempt at Americanization in the post war period.

The third wave: a new economic world order after the Second World War

In repelling Germany's second challenge for supremacy in Europe, and in repelling Japan's challenge for supremacy in Asia, the United States played a decisive military role during the Second World War. In doing so the USA deprived Britain of its leadership and established its own hegemony. In other words, the USA arrived at the position of hegemon, replacing Britain. Hegemon may be defined as a state that leads by overwhelming others not only in terms of political, military and economic power, but also in terms of capacity to enact rules and create order.

The United States established a world order with itself at the centre, Pax Americana. The main economic institutional base for this order was the Bretton Woods System: the International Monetary Fund (IMF), the

World Bank, and the General Agreement on Tariffs and Trade (GATT). The US established not just an overwhelming dominance in terms of political, military, financial and economic power, but rather established a monopolistic concentration of these, and exerted an overwhelming influence in making the rules for the world system. The existence of a second superpower, the Soviet Union, with an alternative, centrally planned macro-economic and communist political system, as well as the opposition to it, served to strengthen the leadership role of the USA.

Against the background of the emerging cold war order, both the defeated countries, Germany and Japan, became important to American regional strategy in Western Europe and East Asia, albeit important to different extents. For this reason, both received support from the US through the GARIOA- and EROA-programmes, the Marshall Plan, as well as the special procurement for the Korean War. American aid helped them to advance on the road to recovery under the aegis of the occupation powers. However, the aid was not totally free but bound to certain steps in opening up the markets to competition. For Germany, the introduction of these steps was monitored by the Organization for European Economic Co–operation (OEEC), which was set up in 1948 to coordinate the allocation of US aid and economic policies in Western Europe. Should these steps not be fulfilled, the next tranche of goods or funds from the Marshall Plan would be withheld.

These programmes became a powerful instrument of US policy in reshaping the rules of economic proceedings for firms as well as for countries. The international organizations, too, had their set of rules, without which participation was excluded. Germany, and after a time lag of a few years, Japan, joined international organizations such as the IMF and GATT and were integrated into the post war international economic order. Both countries, sometimes reluctantly, chose to apply American rules, focusing on liberalism and competition, especially in foreign economic relations.

Both countries had been placed under the power of occupation forces since 1945. The way in which that power was exercised brought about important differences. In Germany the occupation was direct while in Japan it was indirect. In fact, however, it was more important that West Germany was occupied jointly along with British and French troops, while Japan was occupied *de facto* exclusively by the USA. This point was decisive in particular for the scale of Americanization: the American coloration was less in Germany because of the joint occupation. Meanwhile, because of embryonic regional integration in Western Europe, the American influence was much weaker than was the case in Japan. The reforms brought about by the occupation forces were focused on the level of the national economy and the institutions. Americanization, including reconfiguration of the large-enterprise system, decartelization, management purges and reforms in industrial relations, proceeded decisively.[25]

The Allied Powers' occupation policy in Germany was to diminish that country as a political and military power. Reforms in the Western Zones advocated de-nazification, de-militarization and economic de-concentration. The US was most stringent on this point. Americanization in the economic system was fairly wide-ranging, from the break-up of large firms, through the relationship between enterprises and the state, to the relationship between firms. At the very least, this corrected the imbalances brought about by Nazi ideology and militarization and served to stimulate political and economic competition. The enterprise system may be viewed as typical cases of this pattern. Decartelization, in some ways, was a campaign to Americanize the German economic system from a mainly cooperative approach to a more competitive one. Labour reform was in part a recovery of the rights to organize and bargain collectively, which had been realized during the Weimar era. Overall, compared to the Japanese case, post war Germany's economic system changed less than its Japanese counterpart.

For Japan, in contrast, the Allied Powers were in fact one country, the United States, and reform brought on by US policies was a great shock. Reform was thorough, embracing not only the political and economic sphere, but also education, culture, and even the spirit. It did not stop at mere reconstruction and could hardly be characterized as a return to the Taisho Democracy era. The bulk of pre-war systems and institutions were rejected. The US attempted to transplant American systems and institutions through the dissolution of the zaibatsu, democratization of labour, land reform, and other efforts. The flip side of this attempt was that most Japanese were caught up in a deep feeling of defeat, to the extent that defeat was considered not only in military and political terms, but extended to the systems of science and technology. It was even understood as a cultural defeat. The strength of feeling of defeat corresponded to the nature of post war economic reconstruction.[26]

The fourth wave: Americanization at the firm level in the 1950s and 1960s

The central part of Americanization during post war economic reconstruction in Germany and Japan was observed on the level of the national economy. While there was also Americanization on the level of the firm, via the occupation forces or American firms, it was more or less sporadic. Once recovery had ended and rapid economic growth had begun, the focus shifted to Americanization from the level of institutions to that of enterprise. This fourth wave is obviously closely connected to the previous one.

As seen above, the predominance of American business already existed in some branches of industry at the turn of the century, even before the US position as a political hegemon had been established. This indicates that the competitive strength of American business has been the foundation for the acceptance of American rules by other countries, in other words for Americanization.[27] The predominance of American firms, and the influence it generated, tended to increase, taking the form of waves – a dynamic which had already become clear during the Second World War. Added to this was the background that the US position as hegemon was established. It is quite natural, therefore, that the fourth wave of Americanization in the post Second World War era was substantially greater than the previous ones. American influence at the level of the firm was not purely a firm-level phenomenon. To a certain extent, American business management became the model precisely because the USA was the hegemon. It was this evidence of superiority that caused managers to take American ideas into their business. The desire to learn from the United States, even in the niche of a defined enterprise and its proceedings, cannot be understood without the general and widespread idea that it was in the USA and no other country that one had to look for improvement and modern solutions.

Under US hegemony, the scale of production recovered to peace-time levels in about 1950 in Germany and 1955 in Japan. Post war economic controls were almost entirely removed. We may observe that around these years post war economic reconstruction in both countries ended. 'The post war period is already over' was the catchphrase in Japan. Up until this point in the post war economic reconstruction era, the increase in production was understood to be due to the increase in capacity with a focus on quantity. The old processes simply had to be reconstructed and started again. Raw material and machinery, energy and financial means were needed, rather than foreign advice. After this initial reconstruction, however, it became necessary to increase that part of production associated with increasing productivity. The so-called 'productivity centres' were actually established in 1950 and 1955 respectively. The focus also shifted to include quality. This called for investment in modernization, which in turn required Americanization of both technology and management at the level of the firm.

The productivity gap between the USA and both national economies, as well as in technology and management of firms, was obvious. Even German scientists, engineers and managers, insistent on tradition and confident of their own technology and management, became desperate to absorb technology and management skills from the USA. It is even easier to understand how Japanese technicians and managers were keen to absorb these, even to the point of greed. The primary routes for this introduction were the campaigns to improve productivity, direct investment, and technology tie-ups (licensing). The campaigns to boost productivity initiated in 1950 and 1955 respectively, played a leading role in Americanization.[28] In Germany this campaign was seen as a continuation of the rationalization movement in the inter-war period and was seen to be rather independent from the USA, even if many ideas in the 1920s had actually been taken over from the USA.[29] In Japan, the movement was more clear cut from its tradition and related with Americanization. In both cases, it was not only individual firms that undertook activities directed at Americanization via the route of productivity campaign; business organizations in finance and in industry, labour unions, as well as government organizations undertook them as well.[30]

Individual firms, especially large ones, aimed to absorb advanced American technology and management skills through routes including direct investment and technology tie-ups (licensing).[31] Visits to the USA by leading technical experts and managers were often an important opportunity for Americanization. In Germany, direct investment was a major route for Americanization. Germany liberalized inward direct investment as early as 1952, and also prepared its legal system. American-owned firms constituted one-quarter of foreign firms at an early date. Japan, on the other hand, did not liberalize inward direct investment until about 10 years after Germany. In contrast to its high degree of dependence on the USA in trade (approximately 40 per cent compared to approximately 10 per cent in Germany), Japan had an almost negligible proportion of American-owned firms. To that extent, the development of Americanization was more marked in Germany. On the other hand, however, American technologies were widely introduced to Japan via many technology tie-ups (licensing) in the 1950s and 1960s or in the period before capital liberalization. Moreover, many Japanese managers eagerly absorbed American management skills exploiting the chances of technology tie-ups.

Having briefly outlined the longer history of Americanization in Germany and Japan and clarified the position of the 1950s and 1960s within that history, we can reconfirm that the issue of Americanization on the level of the national economy was supplemented and complemented by that of Americanization on the level of the firm. The survey even suggests that Americanization on the latter level became more important and lasted longer than that on the former level.

The contribution of this volume

This reconfirmation gives rise to a number of questions. For example, what level of technology and management techniques did German and Japanese firms introduce? In other words, were they cutting-edge technologies or just mature ones? In such cases, with what perception, intent and strategy did German and Japanese firms make such choices? How did they perceive the American enterprise system that was itself under transformation in these decades?[32] What, and how, did German and Japanese firms try to learn from American ones? What was the relationship of those introduced with technology and management skills existing within the firm? How successful were firms at learning the technology and management skills that had been introduced? Did German and Japanese businesses have sufficient learning capacity and, moreover, sufficient learning desire? What did they select from the American 'offer'? What were the conduits that were used for the learning process? To what extent were American solutions changed and adapted to local needs?

In this volume, we are taking up five key industrial sectors: automobiles, electrical machinery and electronics, synthetic fibres and rubber, consumer chemicals and distribution. These sectors were growth sectors and modern ones at that time. We can therefore expect a readiness for change as well as a desire for learning in those sectors. We also look at the channels for the dissemination of American ideas in two introductory chapters.

The individual case studies will clarify the entire process of introducing American technology and business management techniques; they will focus particularly on acceptance and resistance in that process and the question about the extent to which Americanization was implemented by German and Japanese managers. They will examine actual Americanization across a variety of firm functions, such as production technology, research and development, employment, distribution, sales and finance. Where possible, the case studies will also look at each of these functions in detail. Finally, they will engage in a debate about whether introduction of American techniques resulted in the establishment of a type of German and Japanese production system and business management that differed from the American. We are, in short, tracing Americanization in German and Japanese firms during its high point in the 1950s and 1960s from a comparative, historical perspective. Through this process we aim to contribute to the understanding of the historical phase of Americanization in the 1990s.

Chapters 2 and 3 look at the different channels for Americanization in Germany and Japan from the 1940s to the early 1970s, corresponding to the third and fourth waves identified above. For the German case, **Matthias Kipping** argues that, contrary to a widely held belief, many of the American management models were 'imported' rather than 'exported' to Germany. This means that German companies and their representatives actively searched for new ideas and practices in the United States. Until the mid-1960s, much of this activity was conducted through a few semi-public as well as associative institutions. In general, the former went back to the inter-war period, whereas the latter were founded in the late 1940s or early 1950s. Due to their near monopoly in the importation of foreign, American management models, these institutions had a considerable influence on the selection and interpretation of these ideas and practices. Only from the mid- to late 1960s onwards did US multinationals and consulting companies of American origin become more active and influential as carriers of management models. They increasingly displaced the earlier associative channels, most of which only survived in certain 'niches' of the emerging market for management knowledge.

In his Chapter 3 on the different channels for the diffusion of technology and management techniques and ideas from the United States to
Japan between the latter half of the 1940s and the 1970s, **Satoshi Sasaki**
also highlights that different channels dominated at different stages. At
first, under the American occupation, American management systems
were introduced through personal exchanges between the occupation
authorities (GHQ) and Japanese superintendents with technological
knowledge and experience. Technology transfer, especially related to electrical machines and electronics, became important during this, and even
more so during the subsequent, stage. Since the Japanese government
strictly controlled foreign capital and foreign exchange, many Japanese
companies were eager to introduce advanced American technology. In a
third stage, the Japan Productivity Centre, founded in 1955, promoted the
productivity movement, including the dispatch of many inspectors,
foreign and domestic training, and the invitation of foreign specialists to
Japan. At about the same time, management associations also became
increasingly important, often playing a consulting role for companies.

The next two chapters deal with the US influence on technology, production, marketing and supplier relations in the German and Japanese
automobile industries. In Chapter 4 **Christian Kleinschmidt** examines the
Americanization of the West German automobile industry between the
late 1940s and the late 1960s, focusing mainly on the case of Volkswagen
(VW). The German car industry as a whole had followed the American
model since the 1920s. Volkswagen pursued a similar strategy from its
foundation in the late 1930s. After 1945 it maintained and even expanded
its orientation towards the American example, regarding production
technology, but also marketing, sales and advertising. Until the 1960s, the
success of VW was based on mass production and marketing of the famous
'Beetle', which became a symbol for the emerging consumer society in
West Germany and also sold well in the United States itself. But the story
of the Beetle also shows how too rigid a focus on the US model and the
American market could prove counterproductive. In West Germany, Volkswagen struggled to change its one-product-strategy when sales of the
'Beetle' started to decline from the late 1960s onwards. At the same time,
the car was no longer competitive in the American market, because a
tightening of safety and exhaust emission standards significantly increased
production costs.

For the Japanese case, **Hirofumi Ueda** shows in Chapter 5 how the car
producers developed a specific Japanese method of mass production. At
the beginning of the reconstruction process of the Japanese automobile
industry, car manufacturers realized the necessity of Americanization in
business and production systems to ensure rapid growth of production
levels and to realize high productivity as in advanced Western countries.
They understood that Americanization meant mass production. Their
Americanization, however, was Japanese. That is, they established Japanese

style assembler-supplier relations for mass production with less investment. Japanese automotive carmakers achieved mass production differently from US makers, who produced many parts in-house in large plants. The chapter examines in detail the cases of Toyota and Mitsubishi. It begins with the so-called Keiretsu Diagnosis in the early 1950s, which analyzed the lessons productivity missions took from their observations in the USA in the 1950s, and identifies differences between assemblers and part-suppliers. It then clarifies how the specific Japanese-style supplier relations emerged when mass production began in the late 1950s and the early 1960s.

The following two chapters focus on the drivers and limits of Americanization in the German and Japanese electrical and electronics industries. Based on the Siemens case, **Wilfried Feldenkirchen** argues in Chapter 6 that it would be erroneous to speak of an Americanization of the West German electrical industry. Rather, in the extremely difficult period following the Second World War and during the years of the country's economic miracle, Siemens, like many other West German companies, sought targeted support to compensate for the lack of know-how and competencies. The detailed study focuses on company organization, human resources policy, sales and marketing, as well as key fields of technology such as nuclear energy, semiconductor research and data processing. It shows how outside factors, such as the occupation, economic and industrial policies of the USA after the war, and domestic factors, such as the generation change in management in the 1950s, led to an orientation towards American structures and operational methods in parts of the West German electrical industry. In the end, this led to a mixture of American and German elements in the industry.

In his Chapter 7, **Shin Hasegawa** examines the effects of Americanization on Japanese electronics firms from the 1950s to the mid-1970s. He looks in particular at the general-purpose computer and semiconductor technologies. While most of the firms in these industries cooperated with American companies from the early 1950s onwards, there was a relatively large discrepancy among their absorptive capacity for the new technology. Thus, in computers the results of these technology partnerships varied significantly for each Japanese firm due to the understanding and policies of top management, as well as the conditions of human resources within the firm. In some cases the products of the American firms did not match the demands of the Japanese market, which drove their Japanese partners to produce small- and large-scale computers to complement the US firm's offerings. In the mid-1970s, Japanese firms introduced a variety of computer series to compete with IBM's machines. It was at this time that the Japanese computer firms were able to catch up in terms of accumulated hardware technology and software skills. In semiconductors, Japanese firms also started to absorb American technology beginning in the 1950s. In the 1960s, they successfully introduced a limited scope of independent research and development, even if American firms remained the predominant players in the worldwide market. Only during the 1980s did Japan come to dominate certain segments. The basis for their relative success in both industries during this period, the chapter argues, was laid in the 'Japanization' of technologies originating from America during the preceding decade.

Chapters 8 and 9 look at the reaction of several companies in the artificial fibre and, for the German case, rubber industries. **Christian Kleinschmidt** examines three German chemical firms, Hüls, Glanzstoff and Continental, which had played a leading role in the fibre and rubber industry worldwide up to the Second World War. The three companies had cooperated for example in the production of car tires: Hüls produced the raw material 'buna' (artificial rubber), Glanzstoff produced tire cord and Continental completed the tire manufacturing. All three companies had been successful internationally but lost their ability to compete during the war and were overtaken by their American counterparts. After 1945 they therefore depended on American aid to produce 'nylon', which proved to be superior material in the fibre and tire sector. While the adoption of US technologies was necessary to recover their former strength, the orientation towards the American model was less pronounced in the field of industrial relations. These companies tried to introduce American-style human relations, but the German model of co-determination, involving management and worker representatives, proved resilient.

In his Chapter 9, **Tsuneo Suzuki** examines the reaction of the Japanese artificial fibre industry to the American challenge, focusing on the major producer Toray. He shows how changes introduced in four areas enabled the company to acquire a distinctive competitive advantage during the 1950s and 1960s. In most of these cases, Toray struggled with, resolved and assimilated the American model. The first area concerns efforts made by the top management of Toray to exploit the intervention of the occupation forces, which aggressively introduced American business practices into rayon factories in Japan. The second area is the SQC (statistical quality control) movement, which deeply penetrated into Toray and, together with job analysis, was applied in the chemical company to maintain the manufacturing process. The third area is marketing, which the top management of Toray saw as one of the most successful business practices in the USA. Toray managers dispatched their subordinates to the USA to collect information which could be applied to the Japanese market. The fourth area is Toray's introduction of nylon patents and know-how from DuPont to consolidate its development from the late 1930s. By investigating these different but related areas, this chapter uncovers the relation of 'new technologies' at the time in the world and the attitude of Toray towards them.

The two following chapters also look at chemicals, but consumer chemicals, especially detergents based on the cases of Henkel in Germany and

Kao in Japan. In her Chapter 10, **Susanne Hilger** argues that the German company, which was one of the biggest players in the European consumer chemical industries since pre-war times, embraced Americanization after 1945 only rather reluctantly. She sees as the main trigger for this change the massive expansion of Anglo-American competition into the West German and European markets. After the Second World War the big American 'soapers' Colgate and Procter & Gamble, as well as the Anglo-Dutch Unilever group, restarted their pre-war business with tough profit considerations and aggressive marketing strategies. In the view of the Henkel executives, these companies showed no respect for the 'culture' and traditions of the European business world. The Henkel management reacted at first to maintain the traditional way of dealing with competition, i.e. the conclusion of market regulating arrangements. Against the background of increasing competitive pressure, however, Henkel had little choice but to establish new strategies. These included the diversification into new product areas (e.g. cosmetics or food), the implementation of new organizational structures and planning instruments, as well as the adoption of modern American marketing techniques.

In Chapter 11, **Akira Kudo and Motoi Ihara** demonstrate a profound American influence on the Japanese consumer chemicals producer Kao Corporation. This concerned the introduction of American technology and management techniques; these were transferred by various modes, including visits of managers and engineers to the USA, product analysis, and also competition, and covered a wide range of business activities, such as marketing, production technology and labour management. The company, however, was not only an imitator. American firms, from Procter & Gamble to other firms, were both teachers and rivals to Kao. Through its relations with American firms, Kao widely introduced American practices, adapting them to the Japanese environment, especially to the lifestyle and taste of Japanese consumers. The authors argue that this explains how Kao became competitive in the Japanese market in the 1950s and 1960s, and then after the 1970s also, in overseas markets.

The final two chapters of the volume focus on distribution. In his Chapter 12, **Harm G. Schröter** shows that the US example had a profound impact on the West German distribution system, especially on retail trade. In his view, it seems justified to speak about a 'revolution' since everything changed: rules, organizations, sites, relationships, values and behaviour. In terms of retail concepts and formats, the major change concerned the introduction of self-service. Other American innovations, such as supermarkets, chain stores and discount-markets, were also adopted. A key issue in this respect was the use of cars for shopping, which became a common feature in West Germany during the 1960s. In some areas, for example frozen food, Americanization took quite some time to take hold. In others, namely processed food, it only happened towards the end of the boom period. The author also shows that the process of Americanization

in the German distribution system was a reflected one. West German consumers discovered the advantages or disadvantages of the US innovations
fairly quickly. By contrast, store owners and managers needed more time
to become Americanized, mainly because of the mental changes required.
They had to learn to think in terms of sales rather than supply, to offer
choices rather than necessities to their customers, to compete rather than
cooperate with each other.

For the Japanese case, **Mika Takaoka and Takeo Kikkawa** focus in
Chapter 13 on the changes in the supermarket system from the 1950s to
the 1970s. They divide the growth process of the system into two phases:
an Americanization process in the 1950s and 1960s, and a Japanization
process in the 1960s and 1970s. In their view of the process of Americanization, the following two facts were most significant: the appearance of
supermarkets following American models, and the application of chain
operation theories. In the subsequent process of Japanization, the following three factors stood out: first, the unique financing technique based on
wholesalers activities; second, the development of general merchandise
stores; and third, the system innovation in perishable food sales. Their
analysis finds that, on the one hand, the impact of American trends on the
Japanese distribution industry after the Second World War was large. On
the other hand however, in almost all individual cases the Americanization gave rise to Japanization, which was a process of adaptation of American techniques to the unique conditions in Japan.

Of course, more research has to be done, both on Americanization and
on the comparison between the different processes of Americanization in
Germany and in Japan. However, some preliminary thoughts and results
of the comparison, based on the studies in this volume, can be suggested
here.

Preliminary conclusion: commonalities and differences

We have summarized the findings from the detailed case studies under
four headings: periodization, the scale of the American influence, the
Americanization process and, finally, results.

Periodization: Americanization in the 1950s and 1960s

As explained above, there have been several waves of Americanization in
both countries. We decided to concentrate on the fourth one in the 1950s
and 1960s, considering it to be more substantial than the previous ones.[33]
The chapters in this volume have clearly confirmed this hypothesis. They
show that during the earlier wave, the initial phase of reconstruction
immediately after the Second World War, no special advice from the USA
was necessary or even desirable, since the old processes of production and
distribution were best known by those who ran them. At the beginning it

was more important for Germans and Japanese to reorganize everyday life, to reconstruct transport lines, to rebuild plants and to restart production. Firms and managers were confronted with American rulings such as the dissolution of cartels, zaibatsu, or large firms as well as the purges of top managers.

In addition, initially the Americans were not welcome in either country in 1945, although the hostility was less in Japan than in Germany. Their forces came as victors and occupants. True, in both countries the old systems of behaviour and values were shaken to the core, and many economic actors looked for a reorientation. Obviously the USA appeared to command a superior system for economic life, but still there was reluctance on the side of the losers to accept it. Initially, defeat did not mean a preparedness to learn. Moreover, the USA ordered without consultation. Where new systems were pressed upon the vanquished with political or military threat, they lasted only as long as the threat lasted, because a precondition of all learning is the positive attitude of the actor, and Americanization is just another type of learning.[34]

The overall attitude towards the United States in West Germany changed only gradually. Public opinion definitely shifted during the blockade of Berlin, when in 1948 Soviet troops blocked all land transport to the capital, and the Americans supplied the Western parts of the city by air. In Japan, the antagonistic feeling against the victor was not as great as in Germany and, moreover, it diminished as early as the beginning of the US occupation.

With respect to firm-level Americanization, demand for a new orientation emerged after the immediate reconstruction of war damages, together with the qualitative change of improvement in production, distribution, management, industrial relations and the enlargement of firms. The productivity gap compared to the USA was found to be very wide and, thus, much could be learned. Now advice was sought after, and it was quite easily obtained. The Americans not only offered their expertise but also the means for the process of selection and transfer through the productivity campaign. Businessmen, labour union representatives and administrators were invited to travel to the USA and were shown around the sites the Americans wanted them to see. At the same time, in many reports the invited experts not only admired what they could learn, but also underlined the access and the openness with which their questions were met. Coming from more closed societies, they had expected much less.

Thus, a massive transfer of technology and management ideas and practices, although of course always selected and adapted, took place through the various channels mentioned above. In both countries, the bulk of such transfers cumulated in the 1950s and 1960s, first in Germany and then in Japan. Together with the economic boom, mass consumer markets emerged, first in Germany and then in Japan. Mass markets entailed issues that were unknown before in both countries, such as self service, discount markets, shopping by car, and here again the USA acted as a place from which to learn. Last but not least, a new generation of managers, no longer connected to the war-economy, but eager to modernize and more open to learn from abroad, entered the field of decision making from the second half of the 1950s onwards. This situation could obviously not last forever. It was quite natural that this wave of Americanization began to ebb after the transfer process had been accomplished and a learning and transformation had taken place in both countries.[35]

Breadth and depth of Americanization: reasons for the differences

In the century-long history of Americanization Germany was ahead of Japan. Even if we limit our sights to the period after the Second World War, Americanization started earlier in Germany, whether on the level of the national economy during the post war recovery period or on the level of the individual firm during the era of rapid growth in the 1950s and 1960s. But the scale of post Second World War Americanization, both at the level of the firm and the level of the national economy, was both broader and deeper in Japan than in Germany. The shock of American supremacy was far greater in Japan than in Germany.

Again on the level of the firm, both German and Japanese managers relaunched their businesses under the same initial conditions of defeat and occupation. In Germany the desire to introduce technology and management techniques from the USA was more limited, and the partial introduction often stalled at the point of trials. Japanese managers, by contrast, showed a desire to fully accept American technology and business management techniques. Both German and Japanese managers had a high capacity to learn or relearn from the USA, but Japanese managers clearly had a stronger desire to learn.

Germany's Americanization was not so thorough in the field of the productivity movement as in Japan. Links to tradition remained important. The attitude was to build on indigenous technology and management techniques and to add from the USA those that were necessary or seemed desirable. The Japanese productivity movement stood in contrast to this attitude. While it is certainly possible to confirm their continuity with prewar campaigns, the extent of such continuity was not as great as in Germany. Japanese campaigns were filled with the desire to introduce American technology and management techniques. This desire existed to a degree not seen in Germany. The productivity movements in Germany and Japan both yielded remarkable results, but their processes differed, particularly concerning the scale of Americanization and the control that indigenous institutions exercised over the selection and interpretation of US management ideas and practices, which was much higher in Germany than in Japan.

At the same time, German companies were subject to much stronger

American competition and immediate challenges, mainly through direct investment by American firms. As mentioned above, Germany had liberalized inward direct investment in 1952. Direct American investment in Germany was thriving from that year on, and American ideas, technology and management techniques were also introduced via this route. Having said that, while many aspects of the on-the-ground situation are not well known, it appears that the scale of Americanization was not necessarily that great. This was true even in the cases of American firms' German subsidiaries, such as German Ford and Opel.[36] By contrast, American firms did not invest actively in Japan during the 1950s and 1960s. Inward direct investment was still regulated, and capital liberalization did not occur before the 1970s. American firms were still not regarding Japan as an important region for investment.[37] During the boom years, the primary route for Americanization in the sphere of technology was licensing. Technology tie-ups covered practically the whole range of industries and were concluded in large numbers. In the case of technology tie-ups most Japanese firms tried to introduce American technology and management to the full. Moreover, Japanese firms entered into licensing agreements in large numbers and across a broad range of fields. Technology tie-ups thus became the primary route for Americanization in Japan.

The differences between Germany and Japan in the scale of Americanization were caused by differences in the preparedness of learning as well as in the differences in the principal routes for the phenomenon. Among the major causes for the differences in the scale of Americanization is the difference in the magnitude of post war reforms during the occupation and recovery periods. In Germany, the United States' ideas to reform the country met with resistance from German business managers. Germans partly successfully played the occupation forces against each other; for example, in the area of industrial relations where the USA had very different ideas for Germany compared to the British Labour Government. Furthermore, with the start of the cold war the international environment changed during this period. Germany became a major field of confrontation and contest. This again enlarged the German room for manoeuvre against US policy.

Reforms were realized, but inconsistently, in comparison to Japan. The break-up of firms ended in a partial and inconsistent state, and some, such as the large banks, successfully started to reassemble from the first day. Germany also basically maintained the legislation on enterprise, so that, for example, the authority of the supervisory board was as strong as it had been before. The post war reforms were in part a return to the Weimar system of the 1920s. The old generation of managers remained active to such an extent that Japan's case was not even comparable, although a new generation of managers also partly emerged as mentioned above. Some of them were the very embodiment of managerial control, while others were constrained by owners. Traditional family control remained over a broad range of firms. As a result, reluctance or even resistance to introduce American ideas, technology and management seems to have been much greater than it was in Japan.

In Japan, the United States implemented its reform plans relatively intact, partly because the USA carried out a single-handed occupation. Resistance on the part of political actors, managers included, was quite weak, and change did not occur in the East Asian political environment until relatively late. This fact caused the delay in Americanization in East Asia in comparison to Western Europe. Reforms in Japan were thus implemented in a thorough fashion. The break-up of firms was thorough, and the occupation authorities swiftly executed their plans for eliminating excessive economic concentration. Legislation on business was also drastically revised following the American model. While there was some degree of continuity between the pre-war and post war periods, Japan implemented post war reforms using the USA as a model. A new generation of managers grasped the reins of power as the old generation was swept away. Reforms extirpated family control and instituted wide-ranging managerial control. Japanese managers' resistance to the introduction of American technology and business management techniques was weaker as well as different from that in Germany.

The gap between Germany and Japan in technological and business development must be cited as another cause of the difference between the two countries in the scale of Americanization. Germany had already gained a prominent position during the Second Industrial Revolution as a leader in heavy, chemical and electrical industry. By 1950, the country had arrived at the mature stage in those industries. Germany was also entering the era of full-scale mass consumption. Through the 1950s and 1960s, technology and business management were quite literally rebuilt. In contrast, Japan in and around 1950 could not stop at mere rebuilding. Japan had to take on right away the task of heavy and chemical industrialization. The age of mass consumption had not yet arrived. For these reasons, technology and business management required substantial reform. This large gap in the development of technology and management gave rise to the different degrees of Americanization.

That Japan, through the 1950s and 1960s, also chose Germany as a subject for study in the productivity movement, and that Japan introduced various technologies from Germany chiefly through licensing agreements, shows how large the gap was between the two countries. The final reports of the studies conducted by the United States Strategic Bombing Survey after the end of the Second World War underlined the existence of this gap. The reports expressed awe for the level of technology Germany had attained and for its productive potential in principal industries, including aircraft, shipbuilding, chemicals and petroleum. At the same time, it clearly expressed its evaluation of the low level that Japan had reached relative to Germany.[38]

The process of Americanization: between rejection, selective learning and wholesale adoption

Even German managers and technical experts, who took pride in their own management and technological skills, recognized the gap between their own and the American expertise and were willing to absorb the latter. This absorption, however, was ultimately based on and filtered through their own command of technology and management. Thus, it represented the addition of American techniques and proceedings to their own, not a build-up from scratch. There were limits to the desire for Americanization; at a certain stage managers and technical experts felt they had learned enough.

In contrast, most Japanese technical experts and managers were desperate to introduce advanced American technology and management practices as a whole, for a moment even to the point of denying previous achievements and traditions. Learning and relearning became a firm-wide move, whether it occurred in the productivity movement or in licensing agreements. Managers and technologists aimed for the broadest and deepest introduction possible. But at the same time Japanese managers and technical specialists did not completely discard the technology and management standards their own companies had achieved. Through the process of introducing (learning and relearning) American technology and management techniques, they did not fully set aside their own firms' technology and management styles. The desire to revitalize their own technology and to act according to their own style of management was never completely denied.

If we turn to the level of society or the national economy, the difference between Germany and Japan in their acceptance or rejection of American technology and management practices was both a matter of degree and of style. There were pro- and anti-introduction factions among managers in both countries, just as there were factions within organized labour for and against changes in the American direction. This is the case even if we assume that the rejection faction was stronger in Germany than in Japan. If we look at the level of the individual firm, however, Japanese enterprises, which showed a hunger to introduce technology and management practices from the USA, at the same time showed strong resistance towards doing so. In other words, a strong desire to introduce technology and a strong resistance to doing so co-existed at the same time within the same firm. The strong desire shown by the total introduction of American technology and management practices was accompanied by resistance, which was stubbornly backed by the firm's own technology and management practices.

This acceptance-rejection antinomy dogged Japan's Americanization far more than that of Germany. Resistance also appeared in Germany, but the manner in which the acceptance-rejection antinomy manifested itself was different than in Japan. The clash of values between the adherence to tradition, on the one hand, and reform, on the other, was more pronounced in Japan. The strains, which enveloped Japan during the 1950s and 1960s, were exceptional even in terms of modern Japanese history. Those strains appeared most strongly at the level of the firm. Managers' desire not only to introduce technology and management practices from the USA, but also to make those things their own, was quite fierce. This differs from the German pattern of adding American technology and management techniques to one's own. And even while it was imitation, it often went beyond imitation. At certain times imitation itself failed, while at other times improvement led to innovation. Thus, while Japanese managers and technical experts tried to be good pupils of their American teachers, they were sometimes bad students at the same time. Opinions about the introduction of technology and management practices were not clear-cut along the lines of autonomous technology versus introduced technology. Thus, the policy formulation process concerning that choice ought not to be explained solely in terms of backwardness of a certain economy. It rather should be explained from the perspective of learning and relearning.

How can we explain the differences between Germany and Japan in their acceptance or rejection of Americanization? Differences in the scale of Americanization or in the necessity for it are each likely factors, but are probably not sufficient explanations in themselves. An alternative suggestion would stress the different paths Americanization took in the respective countries: associative channels and foreign direct investment in the case of Germany and technology tie-ups in form of licensing agreements in the case of Japan. Other explanations worth examining include business-nationalism on the part of Japanese technical experts and managers or the formation of business groups. These developments, though, are not likely to be the decisive factors that explain the unique shape of acceptance and resistance in Japan. Rather the decisive factor is to be found in the continuity and discontinuity of management.

Historians of science and technology long ago established that any substantial transfer of technology and management techniques is bound to a transfer of culturally specific values. This includes basic and universal characteristics of American modes of thinking and ideas. It is because of these traits that resistance to technology and management practices arose at the same time as they were accepted. Such a transfer of values occurred through a German or Japanese filter. In the process of transfer of technology and management practices the most powerful filters were, of course, the managers themselves.

In post war Germany, although such filters temporarily thinned, making them more permeable, they regained their solidity and capacity relatively quickly. As a result, connections with tradition in Germany were relatively clear.[39] Post war Japan experienced the same thinning of its filter, but in the case of Japan it was decisive. While occupation policy also purged managers in Germany, the purge was implemented more strictly in Japan. In the latter case, recovery from the purge took relatively longer, and the new filters differed from the old. They were executed by a new generation of salaried managers.[40] Thus, if we compare both countries, we find that the continuity of management and managers' values in Germany was much more profound than in Japan. Such values were characterized by the survival, on the one hand, of the old generation of managers and, on the other, of family control in a large sector in Germany.

Results: emergence of new types of capitalism

Notwithstanding the breadth and depth of the differences of Americaniza-tion, the performance of the national economy and business management in both Germany and Japan was similarly favourable. That both countries, after experiencing defeat and occupation, showed a performance superior to all those who won the war, was certainly no accident. However, to what extent this superior performance during the boom period up to 1973 was due to Americanization is a subject for speculation.

The difference in performance between the German and Japanese national economies and firms can partially be explained by the gap in the stage of development between firms and economies in the two countries. More precisely, Japan had the space in which a more powerful late devel-oper's advantage could work. This space was equivalent to the difference in the scale of Americanization. However, the connection might not be as straightforward as has been suggested above. We have to consider what connection exists between Americanization and the performance of a nation's economy and firms. This entails the suggestion that differences in economic performance may be connected to different degrees of Ameri-canization. This would lead to the formula: the more Americanization, the better the performance, which, we underline again, can be understood only as a research-stimulating hypothesis. This hypothesis should be evalu-ated together with another, somewhat competing one: not the extent of Americanization, but the challenge of and response to the whole of the US model (or models) would explain the remarkable fact that both losers of the war economically performed better than the winners.

Let us assume for the moment that good performance occurs when there exists simultaneously both a strong desire to introduce and a strong resistance to introduction. This would correspond to both the German and Japanese cases. Management education serves as an example of resis-tance. American-style business schools were not popular either in Germany or in Japan, and so Americanization of management education did not appear on a large scale in either country. This fact led to an avoid-ance of 'Wall Street syndromes', such as short-termism, and to both coun-tries' showing better performance than the USA.[41]

Especially after the large wave of economic Americanization had ebbed, German and Japanese characteristics became manifest in business management and technology in both countries. Own types of business management and systems of production technology, different from those of the USA and from the previous indigenous ones, established themselves. They emerged together with different types of political as well as industrial relations. Thus, after a period of incorporating American ideas, behaviour and values, their own and new types of capitalist systems took shape, during the 1960s in Germany and during the 1970s in Japan. These types of capitalist systems include the one later known under the brand name of Rhenish capitalism in the case of Germany, which entered into serious (possibly terminal) crisis after the reunification of the two German states in 1990 and in the following decade. This later became famous as a Japanese style of management, which also lost its way, in the case of Japan, in the so-called bubble economy before the long stagnation in the 1990s. Of course these types could not be viewed merely as a return to tradition. These German and Japanese versions were largely a transformation of American models. They emerged under the impact of, as well as in contest with, American models. And this is exactly the meaning of Americanization.

Notes

1 A. Kudo, 'Americanization or Europeanization? The Globalization of the Japanese Economy', in G.D. Hook and H. Hasegawa (eds), *The Political Economy of Japanese Globalization*, London: Routledge, 2001, pp. 120–136.
2 See for example R. Whitley (ed.), *The Changing European Firm: Limits to Convergence*, London: Routledge, 1996 and D. Held *et al.*, *Global Transformations. Politics, Economics and Culture*, Oxford: Polity Press, 1999.
3 H.G. Schröter, 'What is Americanisation? Or About the Use and Abuse of the Americanisation-Concept', in D. Barjot, I. Lescent-Giles, M. de Ferrière le Vayer (eds), *L'Américanisation en Europe au XXe siècle: Économie, culture, politique. Americanisation in 20th Century Europe: Economics, Culture, Politics*, vol. 1, Lille: CRHEN-O, Université Charles de Gaulle-Lille 3, 2002, pp. 41–57.
4 M. Albert, *Capitalisme contre Capitalisme*, Paris: Seuil, 1991; Y. Fukada and R. Dore, *Nihongata shihonshugi nakushite nanno nihon ka* (What Japan without Japanese Style of Capitalism?), Tokyo: Kobunsha, 1993. Dore later modified his tone in his book: *Stock Market Capitalism: Welfare Capitalism. Japan and Germany versus the Anglo-Saxons*, Oxford: Oxford University Press, 2000.
5 K.S. Molony, 'Japanese and Germans as Business Partners: Should America Care?', *USJP Occasional Paper* 94-07, Harvard University, 1994.
6 See, for example, D. Yui, M. Nakamura and N. Toyoshita (eds), *Senryo kaikaku no kokusai hikaku: Nihon ajia yoroppa* (International Comparison of Reform under Occupation), Tokyo: Sansei Do, 1994.
7 See, for example, K. Demizu, *Nichidoku keizai hikaku ron* (Comparative Studies on Japanese and German Economy), Tokyo: Yuhikaku, 1981.
8 See, for example, A. Forsberg, *America and the Japanese Miracle. The Cold War Context of Japan's Postwar Economic Revival, 1950–1960*, Chapel Hill: The University of North Carolina Press, 2000; L. Lindlar, *Das mißverstandene Wirtschaftswunder.*

Westdeutschland und die westeuropäische Nachkriegsprosperität, Tübingen: Mohr Siebeck, 1997.

9 V.R. Berghahn, *Unternehmer und Politik in der Bundesrepublik*, Frankfurt am Main: Suhrkamp, 1985; *The Americanisation of West German Industry 1945–1973*, Leamington Spa: Berg, 1986; V.R. Berghahn and D. Karsten, *Industrial Relations in Germany*, Leamington Spa: Berg, 1987; V.R. Berghahn, 'Wiederaufbau und Umbau der westdeutschen Industrie nach dem Zweiten Weltkrieg', *Tel Aviver Jahrbuch für deutsche Geschichte*, 1990, vol. XIX, pp. 261–282; 'Technology and the Export of Industrial Culture: Problems of the German-American Relationship 1900–1960', in P. Mathias and J.A. Davis (eds), *Innovation and Technology in Europe: From the Eighteenth Century to the Present Day*, Oxford: Blackwell, 1991, pp. 142–161; 'Deutschland im "American Century", 1942–1992. Einige Argumente zur Amerikanisierungsfrage', in M. Frese and P. Michael (eds), *Politische Zäsuren und gesellschaftlicher Wandel im 20. Jahrhundert. Regionale und vergleichende Perspektiven*, Paderborn: Schöningh, 1996, pp. 789–800.

10 H. Hartmann, *Authority and Organization in German Management*, Princeton: Princeton University Press, 1959; *Amerikanische Firmen in Deutschland*, Köln: Westdeutscher Verlag, 1963.

11 W. Link, *Deutsche und amerikanische Gewerkschaften und Geschäftsleute 1945–1975. Eine Studie über transnationale Beziehungen*, Düsseldorf: Droste, 1978.

12 M. Kipping and O. Bjarnar (eds), *The Americanisation of European Business. The Marshall Plan and the Transfer of US Management Models*, London: Routledge, 1998; M.-L. Djelic, *Exporting the American Model. The Postwar Transformation of European Business*, Oxford: Oxford University Press, 1998; H.G. Schröter and E. Moen (eds), 'Americanization as a Concept for a Deeper Understanding of Economic Changes, 1945–1970', *Entreprises et Histoire*, 1999, no. 19, pp. 5–13; J. Zeitlin and G. Herrigel (eds), *Americanization and its Limits. Reworking US Technology and Management in Post-War Europe and Japan*, Oxford: Oxford University Press, 2000; M. Kipping and N. Tiratsoo (eds), *Americanisation in 20th Century Europe: Business, Culture, Politics*, vol. 2, Lille: CRHEN-O, Université Charles de Gaulle-Lille 3, 2002.

13 J. Hashimoto (ed.), *Nihon kigyo shisutemu no sengoshi* (Japanese Enterprise System since 1945), Tokyo: University of Tokyo Press, 1996; J. Hashimoto, S. Hasegawa and H. Miyajima, *Gendai nihon keizai* (Modern Japanese Economy), Tokyo: Yuhikaku, 1998.

14 A first interesting attempt was made for the steel industry by G. Herrigel, 'American Occupation, Market Order, and Democracy: Reconfiguring the Steel Industry in Japan and Germany after the Second World War', in Zeitlin and Herrigel (eds), *Americanization and its Limits*, pp. 340–399; see also for the similarities between Germany and Japan, compared to France and South Korea, on the one hand, and the USA on the other, M. Kipping, 'How Unique is East Asian Development? Comparing Steel Producers and Users in East Asia and Western Europe', *Asia Pacific Business Review*, Autumn 1997, vol. 4, no. 1, pp. 1–23.

15 D.A. Hounshell, *From the American System to Mass Production, 1800–1932: The Development of Manufacturing Technology in the United States*, Baltimore: The Johns Hopkins University Press, 1984; N. Suzuki, 'Universal and Specific Character of Mass-production System: With Special Consideration of American Automobile Industry', in University of Tokyo, Institute of Social Science (ed.), *20 seiki shisutemu: 2 keizai seicho I kijiku* (The 20th Century Global System: 2 Economic Growth I Core System), Tokyo: University of Tokyo Press, 1998, pp. 122–156.

16 F. Blaich, *Amerikanische Firmen in Deutschland 1890–1918. US-Direktinvestitionen im deutschen Maschinenbau*, Wiesbaden: Steiner, 1984; *Der Trustkampf (1901–1915). Ein Beitrag zum Verhalten der Ministerialbürokratie gegenüber Verbandsinteressen im Wilhelmischen Deutschland*, Berlin: Duncker & Humblot, 1975; H. Kiesewetter, 'Beasts or Beagles? Amerikanische Unternehmen in Deutschland', in H. Pohl (ed.), *Der Einfluss ausländischer Unternehmen auf die deutsche Wirtschaft vom Spätmittelalter bis zur Gegenwart*, Stuttgart: Steiner, 1992, pp. 165–196; R. Koda, *Doitsu kosaku kikai kogyo seiritushi* (An Emergence History of German Machine Tool Industry), Tokyo: Taga Shuppan, 1994; W. Fischer, 'American Influence on German Manufacturing before World War I: The Case of Ludwig Löwe Company', in Barjot *et al.* (eds), *L'Américanisation en Europe*, pp. 59–70.

17 H. Homburg, *Rationalisierung und Industriearbeiterschaft: Arbeitsmarkt, Management, Arbeiterschaft im Siemens-Konzern Berlin 1900–1939*, Berlin: Haude & Spener, 1991.

18 G. Feldman, 'Foreign Penetration of German Enterprises after the First World War: the Problem of "Überfremdung"', in A. Teichova, M. Lévy-Leboyer and H. Nussbaum (eds), *Historical Studies in International Corporate Business*, Cambridge/Paris, 1989, pp. 87–110; S.A. Marin, 'L'américanisation du monde? Étude des peurs allemandes face au "danger américain" (1897–1907)', in Barjot *et al.* (eds), *L'Américanisation en Europe*, pp. 71–92; Kiesewetter, 'Beasts or Beagles?', pp. 166–167.

19 For American direct investment in Germany in the inter-war period, see M. Wilkins, *The Maturing of Multinational Enterprise: American Business Abroad from 1914 to 1970*, Cambridge, Mass.: Harvard University Press, 1974; T. Abo, *Senkanki amerika no taigai toshi: Kin'yu sangyo no kokusaika katei* (American Foreign Investment in the Inter-war Period: The Process of Internationalization of Finance and Industry), Tokyo: University of Tokyo Press, 1984.

20 Berghahn, *The Americanisation*, pp. 146–149; R. Koda and M. Ito, 'The Development of Scientific Management in Germany', in T. Hara (ed.), *Kagakuteki kanriho no donyu to tenkai: Sono rekishiteki kokusai hikaku* (Introduction and Development of Scientific Management: an Historical International Comparison), Kyoto: Showado, 1990, pp. 161–181; M. Kipping, 'Consultancies, Institutions and the Diffusion of Taylorism in Britain, Germany and France, 1920s to 1950s', *Business History*, October 1997, vol. 39, no. 4, pp. 67–83.

21 It remains an open debate, however, whether these large German combines ever achieved the same level of integration as their US counterparts, see T. Welskopp and C. Kleinschmidt, 'Zu viel "Scale" – zu wenig "Scope"'. Eine Auseinandersetzung mit Alfred D. Chandlers Analyse der deutschen Eisen- und Stahlindustrie in der Zwischenkriegszeit, *Jahrbuch für Wirtschaftsgeschichte*, 1993, vol. 2, pp. 251–297.

22 On cartelization see A. Kudo and T. Hara (eds), *International Cartels in Business History*, Tokyo: University of Tokyo Press, 1992; M. Kipping, *Zwischen Kartellen und Konkurrenz*, Berlin: Duncker & Humblot, 1996; H.G. Schröter, 'Cartelization and Decartelization in Europe, 1870–1995: Rise and Decline of an Economic Institution', *Journal of European Economic History*, 1996, vol. 25, no. 1, pp. 129–153.

23 On the introduction of the Taylor system into Japan, see S. Sasaki and I. Nonaka, 'The Introduction and Development of Scientific Management in Japan', in Hara (ed.), *Kagakuteki kanriho*, pp. 235–238, 241–245, 258; S. Sasaki, *Kagakuteki kanriho no nihonteki tenkai* (Japanese Development of Scientific Management), Tokyo: Yuhikaku, 1998, chaps. 1–3; W.M. Tsutsui, *Manufacturing*

28 Kudo, Kipping and Schröter

Ideology: Scientific Management in Twentieth-Century Japan, Princeton: Princeton University Press, 1998.

24 J. Hashimoto and H. Takeda (eds), *Ryotaisen kanki nihon no karuteru* (Cartels in the Inter-war Japan), Tokyo: Ochanomizu Shobo, 1985.

25 The anti-cartel law in Germany met resistance from managers and politicians; see Berghahn, *Unternehmer und Politik*, pp. 155–181; Schröter, 'Cartelization and Decartelization in Europe'. In Japan, it was early in enactment, although it was revised as early as in 1953; Committee on the Compilation of a History of International Trade and Industrial Policy (ed.), *Tsusho sangyo seisaku shi* (A History of International Trade and Industry Policy), vol. 5, Tokyo: Tsusho Sangyo Chosa Kai, 1989, pp. 243–347 (written by H. Miyajima). Management purges seem to have been more rigorous in Japan than in Germany; see Berghahn, *Unternehmer und Politik*, p. 17; P. Erker and T. Pierenkemper (eds), *Deutsche Unternehmer zwischen Kriegswirtschaft und Wiederaufbau. Studien zur Erfahrungsbildung von Industrie-Eliten*, Munich: Oldenbourg, 1999; H. Joly, *Patrons d'Allemagne, Sociologie d'une élite industrielle 1933–1989*, Paris: Presses de Sciences Po, 1996; H. Miyajima, 'Establishment of professional managers', in H. Yamazaki and T. Kikkawa (eds), *'Nihonteki' keiei no renzoku to danzetsu* (Continuity and Discontinuity of 'Japanese' Management), Tokyo: Iwanami Shoten, 1995, pp. 96–105.

26 For reforms in Japan during the occupation period in general, see R. Miwa, *Nihon senryo no keizai seisakushi teki kenkyu* (Historical Studies of Economic Policy in Occupied Japan), Tokyo: Nihon Keizai Hyoron Sha, 2002; for the dissolution of large enterprises in particular, see Mitsui Bunko (ed.), *Mitsui jigyo shi: Honpen dai 3-kan ge* (History of Mitsui Business Activities: Main parts, vol. 3, no. 2) (written by K. Suzuki), Tokyo: Mitsui Bunko, 2001, chap. 3.

27 See, for example, P. Kennedy, *The Rise and Fall of the Great Powers: Economic Change and Military Conflict from 1500 to 2000*, New York: Random House, 1987.

28 See for Germany A. Kudo, *20 seiki doitsu shihonshugi: Kokusai teii to daikigyo taisei* (The 20th-Century German Capitalism: International Orientation and Big Business System), Tokyo: University of Tokyo Press, 1999, III, chap. 2; for Japan, Sasaki, *Kagakuteki kanriho*, chap. 5; K. Sunaga, 'American Technical Assistance Programs and the Productivity Movement in Japan', *Japanese Yearbook on Business History*, 1995, vol. 12, pp. 23–38; S. Sasaki, 'The Emergence of the Productivity Improvement Movement in Postwar Japan and Japanese Productivity Missions Overseas', ibid., pp. 39–71; T. Saito, 'Americanization and Postwar Japanese Management. A Bibliographical Approach', ibid., pp. 5–22.

29 See M. Kipping, 'Consultancies, Institutions' and also his chapter 2 in this volume.

30 M. Kipping and N. Tiratsoo, 'The "Americanisation" of European Companies, Consumers and Cultures: Contents, Processes and Outcomes', in Kipping and Tiratsoo (eds), *Americanisation in 20th Century Europe*, pp. 7–23.

31 H. Kiesewetter, 'Amerikanische Unternehmen in der Bundesrepublik Deutschland 1950–1974', in H. Kaelble (ed.), *Der Boom 1848–1973. Gesellschaftliche und wirtschaftliche Folgen in der Bundesrepublik Deutschland und in Europa*, Opladen: Westdeutscher Verlag, 1992, pp. 63–81.

32 For the case of automation in the car industry, see D.A. Hounshell, 'Planning and Executing "Automation" at Ford Motor Company, 1945–65: The Cleveland Engine Plant and its Consequences', in H. Shiomi and K. Wada (eds), *Fordism Transformed: The Development of Methods in the Automobile Industry*, Oxford: Oxford University Press, 1996, pp. 49–86.

33 The most recent wave in the 1990s might have been more important, but we lack both the historical distance and sufficient evidence to make a qualified assessment about it.

34 A parallel case, Sovietization pressed upon East Germany (GDR), showed the same mechanisms and the same ends, see H.G. Schröter, 'Zur Übertragbarkeit sozialhistorischer Konzepte in die Wirtschaftsgeschichte. Amerikanisierung und Sowjetisierung in deutschen Betrieben 1945–1975', in K.H. Jarausch and H. Siegrist (eds), *Amerikanisierung und Sowjetisierung in Deutschland 1945–1970*, Frankfurt am Main: Campus, 1996, pp. 147–165.

35 A longer lasting flow of Americanization was to be observed only in those branches of industry where the USA kept its position ahead of the rest of the world.

36 See D. Granick, *The European Executive*, London: Weidenfeld & Nicholson, 1962.

37 On American firms in Japan, see M. Mason, *American Multinationals and Japan. The Political Economy of Japanese Capital Controls, 1899–1980*, Cambridge, Mass.: Council on East Asian Studies, Harvard University, 1992.

38 For Germany, see Summary Report (European War), 30 September 1945; Overall Report (European War), 30 September 1945; Statistical Appendix to Overall Report (European War), February 1947. For Japan, see Summary Report (Pacific War), 1 July 1946, National Archives, Washington, D.C.

39 Berghahn, *Unternehmer und Politik*, pp. 249–251; Hartmann, *Authority; Amerikanische Firmen*.

40 Berghahn, *Unternehmer und Politik*; Miyajima, 'Establishment'.

41 This argument was made most forcefully by R.R. Locke, *The Collapse of the American Management Mystique*, Oxford: Oxford University Press, 1996.

2 'Importing' American ideas to West Germany, 1940s to 1970s

From associations to private consultancies

Matthias Kipping

Introduction

In terms of management ideas and practices the United States acted as a kind of 'reference society' for the capitalist world during most of the twentieth century.[1] Much of the recent research on this phenomenon, often referred to as 'Americanisation', has focused on the period shortly after the Second World War, when the US government made considerable efforts to spread the 'gospel of productivity' and to convert Western European (and East Asian) countries to the American creed of mass production, competitive markets and a sharing of productivity gains with workers. Driven partly by the availability of archival material, a significant part of this research has concentrated on the political dimension, examining, on the one hand, the motives of the US efforts and highlighting, on the other hand, the actual pressures exercised by the Americans in countries which they occupied after the war.[2]

Certain channels involved in the dissemination of the American management ideas and practices during the 1950s and 1960s have also been examined. This is the case of the European Productivity Agency (EPA), which was meant to stimulate and co-ordinate the relevant activities of the participating countries – but largely failed to do so.[3] The considerable efforts of the Ford Foundation – namely in promoting US-style management education in Western Europe have also been examined in some detail.[4] For the West German case, Volker Berghahn has highlighted the crucial role of 'Americanised' individuals, such as Otto A. Friedrich of the tire producer Phoenix, in changing the attitudes and mentalities of the German business community towards American capitalism.[5] On the receiving end, the reaction of governments and economic interest groups, namely business associations and trade unions, has also been examined.[6] Last but not least, there are a growing number of in-depth case studies, looking at the reaction of European and Japanese industries and individual companies to American technology and management. These studies focus on their efforts to 'translate', 'transform' or 'rework' these ideas to make them fit into their own context.[7]

While negating neither the American exportation efforts, the European transformation of ideas from the United States, nor the important role of Americanised individuals, this chapter will focus on the *organised* attempts in West Germany to import and diffuse management knowledge from abroad. Its main aim is to give an overview of the different channels involved on the West German side in these dissemination efforts during the boom years from the 1950s through to the 1970s. The chapter is structured broadly along chronological lines and consists of three sections. The first section focuses on the 'official' German institutions involved in the American 'productivity drive', namely the Rationalisierungs-Kuratorium der Deutschen Wirtschaft (RKW) and the Verband für Arbeitsstudien (REFA). Both of them had been founded during the inter-war period. This section gives a brief overview of their origins and their activities before 1945 and then discusses why they managed to survive major political and economic upheaval, and continued to thrive after the Second World War. It will also discuss some of their major activities during the 'productivity drive'.

At the same time, as the second section will show, RKW and REFA did not fully monopolise the importation and diffusion of new management knowledge during the first post-war decades. In addition to the efforts of individuals and companies, a number of further channels emerged, sometimes alongside and sometimes in open competition with the existing associations. With respect to the selection and interpretation of what they 'imported' from the United States and other countries, this section demonstrates that American ideas and practices were usually not transferred 'as is', but were used either as a negative example to justify existing practices or as a positive contrast in order to highlight the need and possibilities for improvement in West Germany. The third section will show how the official channels RKW and REFA started losing importance from the 1960s onwards and were gradually relegated to a secondary role by private consultancies – often of US origin. At first sight this seems surprising, since the associative channels had a number of inherent advantages, which meant that they achieved a higher speed and extent of knowledge diffusion. This section therefore provides some – preliminary – reasons why the consultancies became so important during the 1970s.

The 'official' dissemination channels: RKW and REFA

As noted above, the so-called 'productivity drive' constituted a systematic effort to export the American model of economic and managerial organisation to Western Europe and East Asia during the 1950s. It has to be seen in the context of the European Recovery Program, which was announced by the US Secretary of State George C. Marshall on 5 June 1947. The declared intention of the Marshall Plan was, in the short term, to remedy acute shortages in the countries devastated by the Second World War and to provide means for reconstruction which, in the medium to long term, would make Europe and – after the outbreak of the Korean War also – East Asia independent of US assistance. But its instigators soon realised that material and financial help was not sufficient and, in 1948, initiated the technical assistance and productivity programme, which tried to convert European business leaders to the American creed of mass production and consumption. It relied to a large extent on study trips of Europeans to the United States and visits of American business people, academics and, to a lesser extent, consultants to Western Europe.[8]

Already from the early 1950s onwards, the Americans considerably tightened their control over the programme. Thus, in order to qualify for further funding, participating countries had to establish National Productivity Centres (NPCs), which were to co-ordinate the national efforts. This made it possible for the US authorities to have one point of access and allowed them to influence – to a much greater degree than before – the objectives and contents of the different initiatives and the selection of participants in the productivity missions, etc. The creation of these NPCs obviously constituted an important intervention in the institutional framework of the receiving countries. In this respect, West Germany was a very special, even unique case, because the German productivity centre was not a new, but an existing institution.

Existing institutions as productivity centres in West Germany

In the Federal Republic of Germany the 'productivity drive' relied largely on institutions founded during the inter-war period, namely, the Rationalisation Board RKW (Rationalisierungs-Kuratorium der Deutschen Wirtschaft). The RKW had been established in 1921 under the name National Efficiency Board (Reichskuratorium für Wirtschaftlichkeit), based on a joint initiative of representatives of industry, government and academia.[9] While receiving public funding, the RKW was controlled and administered by big business – with Siemens playing a particularly important role. During the 1920s, it developed a number of initiatives to promote efficiency or, as it was called in German *Rationalisierung*, aiming at the renewal of German industry after the First World War. These efforts were not carried out in isolation. German industrialists and academics also visited other countries, especially the United States, and the RKW reported extensively on the rationalisation efforts abroad. This was done mainly through a monthly newsletter, which was published from 1927 and reached a circulation of 12,000 by 1932. For the first time in 1930, the RKW also edited a handbook on rationalisation, which was updated and reprinted regularly. Thus, already during the inter-war period the RKW became an important channel for the dissemination of foreign, namely American management ideas.[10]

In addition to its own activities, the RKW acted as an umbrella organisation for a large and growing number of institutions in the German rationalisation movement. One of the most important RKW affiliates with respect to management methods was the National Committee for Work Time Determination REFA (Reichsausschuß für Arbeitszeitermittlung). It had been established in 1924 by the employers in the metal working industries, but soon enlarged its activities to most other manufacturing sectors. REFA developed its own method for the calculation of standard piecework times as a basis for the 'fair' remuneration of workers. It disseminated this method through a detailed handbook, published for the first time in 1928, and, more importantly, the training of engineers. By 1933, its courses had already attracted over 10,000 participants from the whole spectrum of German industry.[11]

The RKW and its affiliated institutions expanded their activities considerably during the Nazi period. After some initial hesitation due to their proclaimed hostility towards rationalisation, the new rulers soon recognised the usefulness of these institutions for the rearmament and war efforts. Replacing some of the existing leadership, they brought both RKW and REFA under their control and subsequently expanded their role considerably. Thus, during the Nazi period the RKW vastly increased the number of industry surveys which it had originally started in 1929 in order to provide efficiency benchmarks for enterprises in a given sector. By 1940, 100 branches of the economy and about 900 companies had been covered. The RKW also promoted the use of standardised management accounting, as well as the systematic identification and elimination of technical, organisational and human errors. REFA, which changed its name to National Committee for Work Studies (Reichsausschuß für Arbeitsstudien) in 1936, trained an additional 30,000 engineers between 1933 and 1945.

Both institutions survived the German defeat in the Second World War and the subsequent de-nazification. The RKW re-emerged initially at a regional level in the Western occupation zones and, in 1950, at the level of the Federal Republic. In the same year it became the German productivity centre.[12] REFA was also re-established at the federal level in 1951 as Verband für Arbeitsstudien and continued to expand its activities. Membership in the organisation increased to 13,000 by 1955 and 25,000 by 1961. During the 1950s, over 140,000 people attended its courses. REFA also published a newsletter every 2 months and disseminated translations of selected articles from foreign management journals in another publication called *Arbeitswissenschaftlicher Auslandsdienst.*[13]

It is not clear why the German government, unlike its European counterparts, opted to entrust the National Productivity Centre to an existing institution. Perhaps it wanted to draw on the considerable previous experience of the RKW and its well developed regional structures. It might actually have been very difficult to bypass the RKW and its affiliates, because of the strong following and regional base. The business community probably preferred an institution where it exercised a certain influence to a purely government-controlled department – even if it also set up its own structures, as we will see below. In addition, after the Second World War the RKW also comprised union representatives, which responded to an important concern of the Americans.[14]

Whatever the reason for the decision to give the RKW a key role in the German productivity drive, this choice had important implications both for the channels and the contents of the management knowledge imported into West Germany at the time. First of all, the RKW (and REFA) were very strong in terms of membership and well embedded in the German institutional framework. This meant that it was likely to be very difficult for new initiatives, new organisations to escape its control and institutional embrace. Second, because of their experience, they could also exercise a considerable influence in determining the contents of what was being transferred and the ways in which this was done. This meant that to a large extent they could select and interpret the possible management ideas and techniques introduced in West Germany after the Second World War.

The attempted monopolisation of knowledge dissemination

There is ample evidence to support the view that the RKW and its affiliated institutions tried – and to a certain extent actually managed – to control the productivity movement and the dissemination of new management models in West Germany. Like the productivity centres in most countries, the RKW organised study trips of German groups to the United States, published their reports and also organised the visits of American consultants and experts to West Germany.[15] In the German case, these efforts appear to be more respected and less contested by the different economic actors than in many other European countries, such as Britain or France. In the former, the British Productivity Centre and its efforts were to a large extent ignored by the business community and in the latter, there were continuous conflicts between different government departments and the employers' organisation and various business associations about the control over the productivity drive and its different aspects. In both countries, many of the productivity initiatives therefore proved rather short-lived.[16]

During the 1950s, the RKW not only carried out the activities initiated by the Americans as part of their productivity efforts, it also developed new initiatives, based on its own previous experience and insights. Thus, building on the industry-wide benchmarking efforts carried out during the Nazi period, in the post-war period, it promoted short visits by independent experts and consultants to individual companies, in order to identify sources of problems and suggest possibilities for improvement.[17] On 1 July 1956, the RKW formed a specific department for the promotion of consultancy services, which aimed at convincing companies to accept the help of outside advisers in their rationalisation efforts. This activity received a major boost 2 years later when the RKW obtained public funding to provide incentives for small and medium-sized companies to employ consultants. The RKW usually sent one of its own employees for a short diagnosis. They subsequently recommended an appropriate 'approved' consultant to carry out a more thorough examination – the cost of which would be subsidised with public funds allocated by the RKW. Between 1 April 1958 and 31 December 1965, the RKW had already carried out more than 4,000 such visits (*Betriebsbegehungen*).[18]

The dominant, even over-powering role of the existing institutional channels can also be seen in the case of REFA. Before and during the Second World War, its major activity consisted of the training of work study engineers. After the war, a possible competitor arose in the so-called Training Within Industry (TWI) programme, which had been developed in the United States during the war in order to alleviate acute shortages in qualified shop floor supervisory staff. After 1945, the Americans exported it abroad to the occupied countries. It appears that it was quite well received in Japan, where it had a lasting influence.[19]

In Germany, the occupation authorities also introduced TWI. In September 1948, they organised a training course for staff trainers (*Mitarbeiterunterweisung*) which was held by the head of training at the US department store chain Gimbel Bros.[20] Interest in the programme spread initially in the US zone and then also to other parts of the country, carried by a number of enthusiastic individuals and supported by a few companies such as Bosch in Stuttgart. A specific feature of these efforts was that they explicitly tried to promote harmonious relations in the workplace and addressed both management and employee representatives. By mid-1953, a total of 160 sessions of the trainers' courses had taken place in West Germany, most of them (97) in staff training. It was estimated that these trainers had already held a total of about 8,000 courses with approximately 80,000 participants.

This success did not pass unnoticed among the other institutions involved in similar efforts. The available evidence suggests that there were quite a few tensions between TWI and REFA despite public declarations about their complementary nature and efforts to collaborate at a local and regional level.[21] In the long run, REFA clearly proved stronger. In the mid-1950s, it formally incorporated the TWI efforts, which soon after vanished into its different training programmes. It should be highlighted here that the efforts of REFA to control the different shopfloor-oriented training programmes in Germany should not be equated with a defence of the status quo. The activities of REFA evolved over time, usually based on a careful observation of foreign, especially American practices. Thus from the early 1960s, it broadened the scope of its training programmes from work study to 'industrial engineering', which also encompassed training in basic management and human relations skills. To reflect the continuing evolution of its activities, REFA also changed its name several times during the post-war period.[22]

The selection and control of knowledge contents

Because of their importance as dissemination channels, RKW and REFA also had quite an important influence over the actual content of the management knowledge that was disseminated in Germany. Quite obviously, this control was far from being absolute. During the productivity missions organised by the RKW, its participants could observe the US 'reality' with their own eyes.[23] Subsequently, their – as far as we know – uncensored views found their way into the reports disseminated also by the RKW. A rather unsystematic examination of their contents suggests that most of the German missionaries had a certain admiration for the American achievements, but remained fairly sceptical regarding the possibility of their wholesale adoption in Germany.

Where these institutions had a significant degree of control over the import of foreign management know-how to West Germany was in two areas. One concerned the transfer of specific management techniques, the other the translation of foreign management articles into German. Concerning the transfer of new management techniques to Germany, the fate of the so-called Methods Time Measurement (MTM) system is very instructive. The MTM system was one of the advances made in work study in the United States during the 1930s and 1940s.[24] It did not rely on direct observation of the workers on the shop floor, but determined standard times under laboratory conditions and used these to set rates. At least in theory this was more objective, because it left less room for cheating or errors during the measurement. MTM was probably the most well known, but by far not the only system of this kind.

After the Second World War, REFA examined a number of these systems, including MTM and the so-called Work Factor system. Their relative advantages and disadvantages were debated at length in the association's newsletter. REFA finally decided in favour of the Work Factor system and acquired the licence for its distribution in Germany.[25] But it apparently never became very popular, and REFA probably did little to promote it against its own system, which was constantly being updated and improved. As a result, these techniques never made major inroads into German industry, unlike other countries, such as Sweden for example, where the consultancy of MTM inventor H.B. Maynard had a considerable success in selling the system to Swedish companies, including for example Volvo.[26]

REFA exercised a similar control over the import of new management ideas when it came to the translation of publications from foreign management journals in its *Arbeitswissenschaftlicher Auslandsdienst*, later renamed *Fortschrittliche Betriebsführung und Industrial Engineering*, which was published every quarter.[27] At the time only very few German managers, especially among those at a middle management level, had a sufficient knowledge of the English language to read the originals. At the same time, the German market was not perceived to be sufficiently important yet for Anglo-American publishers to translate their journals or books themselves. The selection of the different articles therefore enabled REFA to define what was considered modern or 'up-to-date' management.

An examination of the tables of contents of the *Auslandsdienst* for the 1950s reveals two interesting details. First, the titles of the articles and the journals from which these were taken show that the transferred ideas not only concerned efficiency improvements on the shopfloor or productivity in a narrow sense, but also general management issues. Thus, among the most frequently used journals were *Supervisory Management, Factory Management and Maintenance*, but also broader ones like the *Harvard Business Review* or *Advanced Management*. Second, the most frequently translated author was not American, but British. It was Lyndall Urwick – probably the most prominent European management thinker since the inter-war period, when he had been Director of the International Management Institute in Geneva. Urwick played an especially important role in disseminating (a) the views of Henri Fayol on general management and (b) the ideas on human relations preached and practised by a part of British management.[28]

Thus, due to their long tradition and their semi-official status, RKW and REFA dominated the dissemination of US management ideas and practices during the 1950s and 1960s to a considerable extent. But their role should not be overestimated. On the one hand, many West German businessmen went to the United States without using the official channels – both before and after the official start of the productivity programme. They came mainly from larger companies and aimed at renewing contacts and exchanges which they had had with American companies on a regular basis until the outbreak of the war. On the other hand, even at the level of business organisations, RKW and REFA did not hold a complete monopoly.

Establishing alternative associative channels

There were a number of other 'power centres' in the German business community. These included the chambers of commerce and industry, which had been re-established at local and regional levels almost immediately after the end of the war, and the Federation of German industry BDI (Bundesverband der Deutschen Industrie) which was formally (re)founded only in 1949/50.[29] Both probably viewed the participation of government and especially union representatives in the semi-official institutions with a certain suspicion. In any case, soon after the end of the war they developed a number of initiatives for the renewal of German management and its legitimacy through the importation of foreign ideas and practices.

The chambers of commerce and the Wirtschaftspolitische Gesellschaft

Businessmen linked to the chambers of commerce in the British occupation zone, soon joined by those from the American zone, were at the origin of another organised effort to disseminate the US management model in West Germany. On 9 August 1947 some of them met in Frankfurt to establish the 'Wirtschaftspolitische Gesellschaft von 1947 e.V.'.[30] Most of the founding members had long-established relations with the United States. For example, Rudolf Mueller, its first president, had been to the US as an exchange student and, as CEO of the chemical producer Röhm & Haas, had also been involved in (cartel) negotiations with American companies. Its vice-president Kurt Pentzlin from the cookie producer Bahlsen had stayed in the US in the late 1920s to study rationalisation. The other founding members were Ernst Deissmann of IG Farben, Alfred Petersen of Metallgesellschaft, Hubert A. Sternberg, an entrepreneur from Heidelberg, and the future West German Economics Minister and 'father' of the social market economy, Ludwig Erhard. They were soon joined by other influential personalities from all reaches of society including academia, politics, the church, and the media, but mainly the business community. By 1949, the association already counted 3,000 members.

The creation of the Wirtschaftspolitische Gesellschaft has to be seen primarily against the background of the German defeat and the widespread criticisms of the – alleged – support of the business community for the Nazi regime. The association aimed at improving the image of business and businessmen in German society and at making business an influential economic and political actor again. What is important in our context is the fact that it used the United States as a reference point and a model in most of these efforts. This concerned the role of free markets and competition in order to achieve the highest possible living standard for the whole population. But the association also promoted a more socially conscious role of management. It advocated close, trust-based cooperation between top managers (*Unternehmensleitung*) and worker representatives to ensure social peace. But at the same time it stressed that ultimate responsibility for decision-making had to remain with management. It should be noted that the American occupation authorities actually provided funding for the association in its early years, when membership contributions were insufficient to cover costs.

Most of its activities aimed at educating both the societal elite and the general public in West Germany. The association contributed to the creation of the business friendly daily newspaper *Frankfurter Allgemeine Zeitung* in 1949. While quite influential during the late 1940s and at the begin-

ning of the 1950s, the association subsequently lost some of its importance. As soon as their position in politics and society had improved sufficiently, certain parts of the German business community appear to have
hardened their stance towards labour participation in decision-making
and towards the US model of a socially responsible management. The
Frankfurter Allgemeine Zeitung, for example, took an increasingly negative
attitude in this respect, which led to its break with the association in the
early 1950s.

But at least during the formative stage of the Federal Republic the
Wirtschaftspolitische Gesellschaft has to be seen as an important channel
for a possible Americanisation of German business and society, namely
through its newsletter, the so-called *Beratungsbrief,* which was addressed to
high-level managers.

Contrasting German and American management styles

The Wirtschaftspolitische Gesellschaft made considerable efforts to disseminate foreign management thought in its *Beratungsbrief,* which was
published weekly.[31] Its editor Herbert Gross usually summarised and commented on foreign publications and experiences, mainly from the United
States, but also from some other Western countries. Occasionally, the
Beratungsbrief also contained articles from invited authors. A detailed
analysis reveals that all of these contributions were selected in order to
support the association's vision of a socially oriented, but free market
economy. Thus, many of the articles concerned competition policy, public
relations of businesses, the role and responsibilities of managers in their
companies and society as a whole. The role of the manager, which the
newsletter tried to promote, was clearly inspired by the US example. It
repeatedly and consistently highlighted a number of elements as 'typically
American': the partnership between the employers and the workers in
companies, the importance of the human element for productivity, and
the position of managers in society.

This was done in three major ways. First, the newsletter presented the
views of US 'authorities' on what constituted good, modern management.
Many of these views emanated from Harvard and usually stressed the fact
that the responsibilities of managers extended far beyond their own office
and company. Second, the *Beratungsbrief* repeated the critiques made by
American journalists, businessmen and academics about German and
European management practice. These critics highlighted, for example,
that (i) most European executives still thought that high wages and high
profits were mutually exclusive and were not willing to share higher
profits with their workers, and that (ii) businessmen in the United States
enjoyed a much higher level of social recognition and reputation than
their European counterparts. Last, but not least, the *Beratungsbrief* also
reported from American management practice, in order to show how

these ideas were actually implemented, highlighting for example employee share ownership as a way to create partnership within companies.

The *Beratungsbrief* not only presented the American views and practices, it also made suggestions on how these could be implemented in Germany. Thus, it promoted different techniques to improve human relations and create a partnership between managers and workers in companies, especially the so-called Rucker plan from the United States. Even when presenting new management tools, for example regarding more accurate costing systems, the editor of the newsletter always highlighted that most scope for efficiency improvements could be found in better human relations. The *Beratungsbrief* also insisted on the necessity to develop further management training, For example, it published a summary by Ludwig Vaubel of his experiences in the Advanced Management Programme at the Harvard Business School (see also below) and fully endorsed his view that similar efforts should be made in Germany.

Two remarks are in order here. On the one hand, from other research we know that the ideas and practices reproduced and summarised in the *Beratungsbrief* are not a full and 'true' reflection of management ideas and practice in the United States. They actually reflect the thinking of a small, but influential group of businessmen who had come to dominate public policy and discourse during the New Deal and the US productivity drive after the Second World War – at least in its initial stages.[32] On the other hand, we have already seen that many West German and European managers were not entirely convinced that American models could be easily applied in their countries. Only further, in-depth case study research can therefore show to what extent these ideas actually found their way into management practice in West Germany (and Europe).

One of the lasting changes concerned the introduction of American style executive education. It was introduced in Germany under the stewardship of the peak business association, Bundesverband der deutschen Industrie (BDI).

The BDI and the Baden-Badener Unternehmergespräche

The Federation of German Industry BDI was involved from the outset in the productivity drive in Germany. It was actually a member organisation in the RKW, alongside the Trade Union Federation DGB (Deutscher Gewerkschaftsbund). But it also had direct connections with the Americans, participated actively in the discussions regarding the possible transfer of the US economic and management model to West Germany and developed its own initiatives, namely with regard to US-style management education.

Thus, for example, the BDI and its president played an important role in the discussions regarding the adoption of a German anti-trust law. They were opposed to the original, relatively strict proposal drafted under American influence and managed to slow down the legislative process in the German parliament and to soften the provisions of the federal cartel law, which was only adopted in 1957.[33] At a European level, the BDI collaborated closely with its French counterpart, the CNPF (Conseil national du patronat français), to prevent the insertion of strict anti-cartel and merger control clauses in the Treaty establishing the European Coal and Steel Community (ECSC), based on the French proposal of 9 May 1950 to pool the European coal and steel resources. In this instance they were less successful, because Jean Monnet, the actual instigator of the French initiative, successfully overcame their resistance with the help of the steel-using industries in France and the American occupation authorities in Germany.[34]

But the BDI did not only try to block Americanisation. It actually became involved in an important initiative to introduce further management education in Germany, inspired largely by the US example.[35] At its origin were, on the one hand, the need to train qualified management personnel to replace the wartime losses and, on the other, the recognition that managers were not only born, but also required some kind of training. German business leaders realised quite early on that the American experience of post-entry level education could serve as an example for similar efforts in Germany.

Ludwig Vaubel of the Wuppertal-based artificial fibre producer Vereinigte Glanzstoffwerke AG played an especially important role in this respect.[36] In the fall of 1950, he participated as the 'first and only' German in the 13-week advanced management programme at the Harvard Business School. Subsequently, he reported extensively and very positively about his experiences, for example in the article in the *Beratungsbrief* (see above) and in a small booklet published in 1952.[37] Several German productivity missions also highlighted the contribution of management education and training to the American economic superiority. Possibly even more important as a model for the subsequent German efforts were the so-called Industrial Management Seminars – short events held in Europe, where American managers acquainted large groups of businessmen with the latest managerial know-how from the United States. In 1951 and 1952, two such events regarding operational management (*Betriebsführergespräche*) took place in Baden-Baden.

As a result of all these impulses, in 1953 the BDI set up a working party to consider 'whether and how German business leaders should get involved in the promotion and training of successors who fulfil the high expectations in terms of numbers, competence, prior education and experience'. It was placed under the direction of Wolf-Dietrich von Witzleben, chief executive of Siemens during the war and now vice-chairman of its supervisory board. The working party studied a number of foreign examples, including the Harvard Business School and the Administrative

Staff College in Henley. In the end, they decided not to copy any of these institutions, but to find a specifically German method for the transmission of knowledge – an exchange of views between two generations of German top managers.

The first of these entrepreneurs' talks (*Unternehmergespräche*) took place on a trial basis in 1954. Several large companies sent younger managers – usually in their forties – with leadership potential and significant practical experience to Baden-Baden for a seminar of 3 weeks' duration. Here they met actual business leaders to make their acquaintance, i.e. network, and exchange views on a variety of topics, including the role of managers within their own companies and within the wider economic, political and cultural context. The declared intention of these talks was not to improve the specialist knowledge or expertise of the participants, but 'to widen their horizon beyond their own company and give them a feeling for their wide-ranging responsibilities as business leaders'.

After two successful trials, the BDI decided to organise these seminars on a regular basis twice per year. In 1955, the association created an institutional framework to ensure the necessary financial and organisational support. Firms who wanted to send their managers to these talks had to become members. Their fees paid for a small permanent secretariat, which organised these events. The Baden-Baden talks also served as a model for other initiatives for the further training of managers in Germany during the 1950s. Based on a suggestion of von Witzleben, representatives of the different institutions met in Wuppertal in 1955 to discuss a closer co-ordination of their activities. They decided to create a loose working group known as 'Wuppertal Circle' (Wuppertaler Kreis), headed by Ludwig Vaubel. From 1956, it published several times per year a list of courses offered by its members. Around the same time, a number of large German companies, with Siemens most prominent among them, also created in-house training courses and institutions along similar lines.

All of these initiatives and institutions had a lasting influence on the training of German managers during the boom years. Their importance only started to wane somewhat from the 1990s onwards with the emergence of private business-oriented universities and the rise of internationally oriented executive MBA programmes. But even in this new context, the Baden-Badener Unternehmergespräche retained their pre-eminent role. Their hundredth meeting took place in the spring of 1997.[38] They had become an almost obligatory passage towards top management in Germany. Among the approximately 2,500 alumni at that point, about one-third had reached the highest management level, the executive board, and between 10 and 15 per cent even became chief executives. These include the heads of many large German companies such as Jürgen Schrempp of DaimlerChrysler.[39]

Sidelining the associations: the rise of consultancies

Thus, in addition to the initiatives developed by certain large companies and influential individuals, organised efforts played a mayor role in the German productivity movement. A number of institutions for the diffusion of new management ideas and techniques emerged in the immediate post-war period, usually backed by either the chambers of commerce or the Federation of German Industry. Some of them, namely in the area of executive education, had a long-lasting influence and existence. Nevertheless, during the 1950s and 1960s, the RKW and its affiliate associations such as REFA continued to play a dominant role in the dissemination efforts – by organising and co-ordinating the official productivity programme, by developing new initiatives, such as the Betriebsbegehungen and, occasionally, by absorbing other, competing initiatives, such as TWI.

The predominance of these associations as a conduit for the dissemination of new management methods was only reduced from the 1960s onwards, with the arrival of a new generation of American management consultants, focusing on advice to top-level management in questions of corporate strategy and organisation. At first sight, this is surprising. So far consultancies had made little inroads into Germany in comparison with other countries, such as Great Britain where they played a major role in the dissemination of new management methods from the inter-war period. Until the 1950s, their major focus had been on improvement in shop floor efficiency. Among the dominant consultancy firms at the time were those founded by Harrington Emerson, Charles Bedaux and Wallace Clark. While some of them were also active in Germany, their activity remained marginal in comparison with the near monopoly of REFA in the introduction of these methods.[40]

The effectiveness of the associative channel

The dominance of REFA found its explanation not in the superiority of the system it promoted, but in the inherent advantages of the associative/ organised channel for the diffusion of new management ideas and practices. This was highlighted again and again by the German engineers involved in these efforts. Thus, for example, at the 1939 annual meeting of REFA one of the presentations made a comparison between the REFA and the Bedaux systems of work study. The speaker highlighted the fact that the consultancy treated the intricacies of its system as 'business secrets'. For this and other reasons, he characterised the co-existence of both systems as 'unhealthy' and argued for an exclusive use of the REFA system in Germany.[41]

A group of German REFA engineers, who visited the United States in the spring of 1951 as part of the productivity programme, came to similar, albeit less virulent conclusions. One of the participants summarised his impression as follows: 'Anyone who feels competent or sees a commercial opportunity, develops his theories, his methodology and, which is the worst, his own terminology. [...] Because of this situation, those American engineers who are involved in our field out of interest are envious of our REFA organisation.'[42] A study conducted in the United States at the end of the 1920s showed indeed that there were at least three competing work study systems used by American companies at that time: Bedaux, Halsey and Emerson.[43] The Bedaux system was used by more than three times as many workers (33,177) as each of the other two systems (with 9,953 for Halsey and 9,252 for Emerson). It should be noted that, in any case, these numbers are very small compared to the total of almost 800,000 workers covered in the survey.

There are clear indications that the use of the associative channel in Germany led to a much higher penetration of work study methods in Germany than in most other industrialised countries. A representative survey carried out by the Munich based IFO Institute in March 1956 showed that an overwhelming majority of German companies (71 per cent) considered work study as indispensable and that 78 per cent had their own internal work study department. And among those companies which applied work study, over 80 per cent used the REFA system.[44] While we have no comparable data for the US for this time period, the available statistics from British industry reveal that a few years earlier less than 30 per cent of all workers were paid using some system of work study. It appears that most of these were actually working under straight piece rates rather than more sophisticated payment-by-results systems such as Bedaux or REFA.[45]

There are several reasons for this.[46] First of all, sheer numbers: by the mid-1950s REFA counted 13,000 members and had trained about 100,000 internal work study engineers. At the same time the number of consultants in Britain hardly came close to 1,000, not all of whom were actually involved in the implementation of work study. While these consultants acted as a kind of multiplier, they could never achieve the same penetration in British industry as the REFA engineers did in Germany. Second, the fact that the vast majority of work study engineers in Germany used the same methodology and terminology made it much easier to compare and exchange experiences. It also made it possible for improvements to spread quickly through this network and REFA publications. Last but not least there are some indications that 'insiders' such as the REFA engineers usually found it easier to overcome the suspicion and a negative reaction from the workers in comparison with 'outsiders' like consultants.

If the advantages of institutions for the dissemination of management knowledge were so important and rather obvious, why then, we have to ask, did other countries not espouse them to the same extent and why did they lose influence and importance in Germany from the 1960s onwards. The answer to the first question probably revolves around the importance

of trust-based relationships within a given economy. Chandler has characterised German capitalism as co-operative.[47] While he referred mainly to
the co-operation of German companies in the form of cartels compared to
the – alleged – predominance of competitive markets in the United States,
this also applies to the exchange of information. Along similar lines, a
comparative study has highlighted the importance of long-term trust relations between buyers and suppliers in Germany – compared to short-term
oriented power-based relations in the British case.[48]

The trust-based relations formed the basis for a sharing of information,
which proved to be of mutual benefit. At the same time, these long-term
relations became an obstacle when competitive conditions changed and
required a rather rapid and radical reaction – which is what happened in
Germany during the 1960s.

The expansion of US consulting firms in West Germany

As noted above, from the late 1950s onwards, a new wave of consultancies
of US origin expanded to Western Europe. They focused on questions of
corporate organisation and strategy rather than the productivity on the
shopfloor or in offices. Among the leading consultancies in this wave were
firms such as Booz Allen & Hamilton, McKinsey & Co., A.T. Kearney and
Arthur D. Little. Founded earlier, based on diverse services including contract research, psychology and management accounting, they had taken
off in the United States during the 1930s and 1940s. The reasons for their
success included (i) the fast growth of American corporations such as
DuPont, General Motors or US Steel, who therefore required assistance
with organisational rather than shop floor issues,[49] and (ii) the legal separation of commercial and investment banking which opened new
opportunities for independent advisers.[50] As Table 2.1 shows, during the
1960s they also expanded to Western Europe.

Most of these consultancies opened their first European office in
London, due to the presence of American multinational clients in the
United Kingdom and the similarities of language and – allegedly –

Table 2.1 Expansion of US consultancies to Western Europe during the 1960s

	Offices in Europe		No. of consultants		European revenues	
	1962	*1969*	*1962*	*1969*	*1969 (m$)*	*% of total*
Booz Allen	1	2	70	111	5	9
Arthur D. Little	1	4	30	53	6	16
McKinsey	1	6	15	160	8	35
A.T. Kearney	0	5	0	60	2	15

Sources: See Kipping, 'American Management Consulting Companies', p. 210.

culture. But they soon expanded to the European continent and especially to West Germany where they encountered little competition due to the absence of domestic consultancies. From the 1970s onwards, McKinsey was the largest service provider on the German consulting market.[51] It also provided a kind of role model for the domestic consultancies, who tried to imitate the 'McKinsey look of successful young professionals'. Its attributes apparently included a Porsche sports car, a house in a fashionable suburb, skiing as the favourite sport and regular visits to art galleries.[52]

Many of the successful German consultancies were spin-offs from the American consulting firms. This is the case of the company founded by Roland Berger in 1967, which remains until today the largest service provider of German origin. Berger had originally worked for the Boston Consulting Group (BCG), itself founded by a former consultant of Arthur D. Little. Following the success of the new wave of the so-called strategy consultancies, the few existing German consulting firms also changed their services, focusing more on issues of organisation and human relations rather than on shop floor efficiency. This is, for example, the case of the firm founded by the engineer Gerhard Kienbaum in 1945, which became one of Germany's leading HR and recruitment consultancies from the 1960s onwards.[53]

Pending further research, one can only speculate about the reasons for the rapid penetration of the American consultancies (and their local emulators) into the West German market for management ideas and 'fashions'. One of the major drivers seems to have been the changes in the competitive conditions. During the 1960s the opening of the Common European market and the massive arrival of US multinationals on the European continent led to a much higher degree of competition in Germany. In this context, RKW, REFA etc. could not provide the knowledge necessary to confront the new challenge. Since this knowledge was not available within the German economy itself, the mechanisms for the exchange of information between companies also proved ineffective. Up until then, many German – and European – enterprises were used to agreeing market shares rather than compete for them. Faced with new, more aggressive competitors, they decided to fight fire with fire and hire American consultancies.[54] An additional reason for the rapid rise in consultancy use during the 1960s and 1970s was probably the fact that the well known service providers such as McKinsey could also provide legitimacy with respect to the different stakeholders, e.g. governments, employees, and – more recently – investors. These stakeholders had become more important following the repeated oil crises and subsequent business failures (leading to government bail-outs), the widespread introduction of co-determination at the supervisor board level, as well as the liberalisation and globalisation of financial markets.[55]

In any case, the expansion of McKinsey and the other American consultancies provided a serious challenge for the RKW and its affiliates. Unlike in the 1950s, they could no longer claim to be a kind of 'authorised' carrier of American management know-how. In addition, the necessary know-how had also evolved from shop floor productivity to corporate organisation and management, where RKW, REFA etc. had close to no experience. While losing their former importance as a result, they tried to adapt – but with limited success. As seen above, REFA had already from the early 1960s onwards expanded the scope of its training programmes to include more elements of general management and human relations. The RKW withdrew into a kind of 'niche', targeting its activities largely towards small and medium-sized enterprises. For example, it has been organising co-operations between German and South East Asian SMEs, and promoting new initiatives to develop innovative products.[56]

Conclusion

This chapter has shown that during the 1950s and 1960s the German productivity movement evolved around a small number of organisations and associations, most of which had been formed during the inter-war period. Among them, RKW and REFA played a particularly important role in the importation and dissemination of foreign, mainly American management ideas and practices. The former became the German productivity centre in 1950 and as such organised study trips to the United States, publication of their reports and visits of US experts to Germany. REFA examined and discussed advances made in work study methods in the United States during the war and also published translation of selected articles from foreign management journals. In addition, these institutions also developed a number of new initiatives, for example the *Betriebsbegehungen* in the case of the RKW, which were based on their own experience rather than the US example.

However, despite the rather organised and centralised nature of the productivity movement, these semi-official associations never achieved total control over the dissemination efforts. Many of the major German companies bypassed the RKW etc. and rebuilt their own relationship with American companies – often dating back to the pre-war period. The other power centres in the German economy also set up their own channels for the import and diffusion of new management ideas. The chambers of commerce became the seedbed for an association, the Wirtschaftspolitische Gesellschaft, which aimed at 'modernising' German management along American lines. And the Federation of German industry participated actively in the establishment of further management training education inspired by the example of the Advanced Management Programme at the Harvard Business School.

Like the semi-official channels, the other associations also had quite a high level of control over the selection and interpretation of the US management models they imported. Thus, in its newsletter the Wirtschaftspolitische Gesellschaft presented the image of a socially conscious American management as a mirror and example to follow for German managers. This image only corresponded partially to the reality of management in the United States. But it was promoted actively by and also served the purposes of certain German business circles in the immediate post-war period, who wanted to improve the reputation and standing of business in German society.

These associative channels had a number of intrinsic advantages over other ways to import and diffuse management know-how, namely consultancies. In the case of work study, the training programmes offered by REFA were less costly than the employment of outside consultants. Also, since the REFA engineers were 'insiders' rather than outside consultants, there was usually less resistance from those concerned directly by the new methods. From the point of view of the economy (and society) as a whole the associative channel also had a number of advantages. It made sure that managerial innovations were circulated to a larger number of companies in a shorter time. Equally importantly, the predominance of a single institution ensured the uniformity of the terminology and approach used, both of which could therefore be updated relatively easily.

During the 1950s and 1960s the productivity movement in West Germany was rather special and quite unique, due to the fact that it relied mainly on associations and institutions as carriers for the dissemination of new management ideas and practices. But when the competitive and institutional framework changed from the 1960s onwards, these organised efforts proved no longer adequate and German companies resorted to other channels for the importation of new ideas and the legitimisation of their practices. As a result, the associations gradually lost their influence, being replaced by other carriers, especially management consultancies, which had already played an important role in the United States and most other countries. The existing institutions did not disappear completely, however, but concentrated their activities on specific niches, namely the knowledge transfer to small and medium-sized enterprises. Overall therefore, during the post-war boom period West Germany seems to have become increasingly similar to other industrialised countries with respect to the channels for the importation and diffusion of management knowledge.

Acknowledgements

Earlier versions of this chapter were presented at the Third Japanese-German Business History Conference in Tokyo on 24–25 March 2000, and at a seminar in the Institute of Economic Research, Hitotsubashi University in July 2000. The author would like to thank the respective organisers, Akira Kudo and Tamotsu Nishizawa, and the participants of both events for helpful comments and suggestions. The usual disclaimer applies.

Notes

1 The term 'reference society' was coined by M.F. Guillén, *Models of Management. Work, Authority, and Organization in a Comparative Perspective*, Chicago: The University of Chicago Press, 1994, p. 290. For an overview of the American influence in the twentieth century see the introductory chapter of this volume. It should be noted that similar attempts were also made in Eastern Europe. There, the reference was not the United States, but – voluntarily or involuntarily – the Soviet Union.

2 See for the former the summaries of the literature in C.S. Maier (ed.), *The Marshall Plan and Germany. West German development within the framework of the European Recovery Program*, New York: Berg, 1991, or J. Killick, *The United States and European Reconstruction, 1945–1960*, Edinburgh: Keele University Press, 1997; for the latter in particular M.-L. Djelic, *Exporting the American Model. The Postwar Transformation of European Business*, Oxford: Oxford University Press, 1998, who also stresses the role of a small elite of 'modernizers' in these countries, supporting the American exportation efforts. Cf. also V.R. Berghahn, *The Americanisation of West German Industry 1945–1973*, Cambridge: Cambridge University Press, 1986.

3 B. Boel, *The European Productivity Agency: Politics of Productivity and Transatlantic Relations, 1953–61*, PhD dissertation, University of Copenhagen, 1998.

4 Namely by Giuliana Gemelli, see for example her edited volume on *The Ford Foundation and Europe (1950s–1970s)*, Brussels: European Interuniversity Press, 1998.

5 V.R. Berghahn and P.J. Friedrich, *Otto A. Friedrich, ein politischer Unternehmer. Sein Leben und seine Zeit, 1902–1975*, Frankfurt/M.: Campus, 1993; cf. also C. Kleinschmidt, *Der produktive Blick. Wahrnehmung amerikanischer und japanischer Management- und Produktionsmethoden durch deutsche Unternehmer 1950–1985*, Berlin: Akademie-Verlag, 2002.

6 See, among others, W. Link, *Deutsche und amerikanische Gewerkschaften und Geschäftsleute 1945–1975. Eine Studie über transnationale Beziehungen.* Düsseldorf: Droste, 1975; A.B. Carew, *Labour Under the Marshall Plan. The Politics of Productivity and the Marketing of Management Science*, Manchester: Manchester University Press, 1987; N. Tiratsoo and J. Tomlinson, 'Spreading the Gospel of Productivity: US Technical Assistance and British Industry, 1945–1960', *Business History Review*, 1997, vol. 71, no. 1 (Spring), pp. 41–81.

7 See the contributions in M. Kipping and O. Bjarnar (eds), *The Americanisation of European Business. The Marshall Plan and the Transfer of US Management Models*, London: Routledge, 1998; J. Zeitlin and G. Herrigel (eds), *Americanization and Its Limits. Reworking US Technology and Management in Post-war Europe and Japan*, Oxford: Oxford University Press, 2000; M. Kipping and N. Tiratsoo (eds), *Americanisation in 20th Century Europe: Business, Culture, Politics*, vol. 2, Lille: Centre d'Histoire de l'Europe du Nord-Ouest (Université Charles-de-Gaulle Lille 3), 2002.

8 For an overall summary, see International Cooperation Administration, *European Productivity and Technical Assistance Programs. A Summing Up (1948–1958)*, Paris: ICA, 1958; cf. J. McGlade, *The Illusion of Consensus: American Business, Cold War Aid and the Reconstruction of Western Europe 1948–1958*, unpublished PhD dissertation, Washington, D.C.: George Washington University, 1995.

9 See for this and the following H.W. Büttner, *Das Rationalisierungs-Kuratorium der Deutschen Wirtschaft*, Düsseldorf: Droste, 1973; M. Pohl, 'Die Geschichte der Rationalisierung. Das RKW 1921–1996', in *Rationalisierung sichert Zukunft. 75 Jahre RKW*, Eschborn: RKW, 1996, pp. 85–115; J.R. Shearer, 'The Reichskuratorium für Wirtschaftlichkeit: Fordism and Organized Capitalism in Germany, 1918–1945', *Business History Review*, Winter 1997, vol. 71, no. 4, pp. 569–602.

10 For the US influence in Germany during the inter-war period see also M. Nolan, *Visions of Modernity. American Business and the Modernisation of Germany*, New York: Oxford University Press, 1994.

11 For this and the following see M. Kipping, 'Consultancies, Institutions and the Diffusion of Taylorism in Britain, Germany and France, 1920s to 1950s', *Business History*, 1997, vol. 39, no. 4, pp. 66–82.

12 See *RKW Jahresbericht 1951/52*, pp. 21–32. All the RKW material used in this chapter can be found at the RKW Library in Eschborn, near Frankfurt.

13 See '10 Jahre REFA-Bundesverband. Die Entwicklung von 1951 bis 1961', *Refa-Nachrichten*, December 1961, vol. 14, no. 6, pp. 221–226; L.J. Harper, 'Work Study in Germany. A Report of the Activities of REFA', The College of Aeronautics, Cranfield, Note no. 32, June 1955; REFA-Verband für Arbeitsstudien und Betriebsorganisation e.V., *Methodenlehre des Arbeitsstudiums*, Teil 1: *Grundlagen*, Munich: Hanser, 1984, pp. 28–33; all of these can be found in the REFA Library, Darmstadt.

14 The corresponding American legislation stipulated that in order to receive US funding the National Productivity Centres had to promote 'free enterprise' and associate 'free', i.e. non-communist, trade unions with their efforts, cf. Boel, *The European Productivity Agency*.

15 For an overview of the German study trips see *Internationaler Erfahrungsaustausch, Zusammenstellung der Studienreisen und deren Teilnehmer im Bereich der gewerblichen Wirtschaft*, Berlin: Beuth, 1957.

16 See, for the UK, Tiratsoo and Tomlinson, 'Spreading the Gospel of Productivity'; for France, M. Kipping and J.-P. Nioche, 'Politique de productivité et formations à la gestion en France (1945–1960): un essai non transformé', *Entreprises et Histoire*, June 1997, no. 14, pp. 65–87; and, in general, Kipping, 'Consultancies, Institutions and the Diffusion of Taylorism'.

17 See *RKW Jahresbericht 1952/53*, p. 26.

18 *RKW Geschäftsbericht 1965/66*, pp. 24–26. See the earlier annual reports for a detailed development of these activities. These activities have served as an example for similar efforts in many other countries, cf. Organisation for Economic Co-operation and Development, *Boosting Business Advisory Services*, Paris: OECD, 1995.

19 A.G. Robinson and D.M. Schroeder, 'Training, Continuous Improvement, and Human Relations: The U.S. TWI Programs and the Japanese Management Style', *California Management Review*, Winter 1993, pp. 35–57.

20 See Stuttgarter Arbeitskreis zur Förderung innerbetrieblicher Arbeitsbeziehungen e.V. (ed.), *Die Deutsche TWI-Arbeit. Ein Tagungs- und Arbeitsbericht*, Frankfurt/Main, 1953, pp. 5–13.

21 Ibid., pp. 46–52.

22 Today it is called REFA Verband für Arbeitsgestaltung, Betriebsorganisation und Unternehmensentwicklung e.V. and offers a wide variety of training, coaching and consulting services regarding shopfloor management, plant organisation and company development (see <http://www.refa.de>).

23 It should be stressed here that the US authorities made quite a considerable effort to present selected aspects of American management philosophies and practices, in tune with the overall message they wanted to convey to the Europeans, cf. M. Kipping, ' "Operation Impact": Converting European Business Leaders to the American Creed', in Kipping and Bjarnar (eds), *The Americanisation*, pp. 55–73.

24 See, for the MTM system H.B. Maynard, G.J. Stegemerten and J.L Schwab, *Methods-Time Measurement*, New York: McGraw Hill, 1948; for an overview of the different systems, B.W. Niebel, *Motion and Time Study: An Introduction to Methods, Time Study, and Wage Payment*, Homewood, Ill., 1958.

25 '10 Jahre REFA-Bundesverband', here p. 223.
26 For the success of H.B. Maynard in Europe, see M. Kipping, 'American Management Consulting Companies in Western Europe, 1920 to 1990: Products, Reputation and Relationships', *Business History Review*, Summer 1999, vol. 73, no. 2, 190–220, here p. 205; for its – difficult – application at Volvo, H. Glimstedt, 'Americanisation and the "Swedish Model" of Industrial Relations', in Kipping and Bjarnar (eds), *The Americanisation*, pp. 133–148.
27 Copies of this journal can be found in the REFA Library, Darmstadt; cf. for its importance also H. Hartmann, *Amerikanische Firmen in Deutschland. Beobachtungen über Kontakte und Kontraste zwischen Industriegesellschaften*, Cologne: Westdeutscher Verlag, 1963, p. 29.
28 See, for a summary of his ideas, among others, D.S. Pugh and D.J. Hickson, *Great Writers on Organizations. The Omnibus Edition*, Aldershot: Dartmouth, 1993, pp. 131–133; for his role in the IMI, C.D. Wrege *et al.*, 'The International Management Institute and Political Opposition to its Efforts in Europe, 1925–1934', *Business and Economic History*, 1987, vol. 16, pp. 249–265; for his post-Second World War thoughts and activities also M. Roper, 'Killing Off the Father: Social Science and the Memory of Frederick Taylor in Management Studies, 1950–75', *Contemporary British History*, Autumn 1999, vol. 13, no. 3, pp. 39–58.
29 See G. Braunthal, *The Federation of German Industry in Politics*, Ithaca: Cornell University Press, 1965; and W. Bührer, *Geschichte des Bundesverbandes der Deutschen Industrie*, Paderborn: Schöningh, forthcoming in 2004.
30 See for this and the following K.D. Schulz, *Unternehmerinteresse und Wirtschaftssystem: Beiträge der Unternehmer zur politischen Entwicklung der Bundesrepublik Deutschland*, Frankfurt/M.: Haag und Herchen, 1986.
31 See for the following in more detail M. Kipping, 'Managers and their social responsibilities: Debates and changes in Germany after 1945', paper presented at the annual meeting of the Business History Conference, Palo Alto, California, 10–12 March 2000.
32 See, among others, C.S. Maier, 'The Politics of Productivity: Foundations of American International Economic Policy after World War II', *International Organization*, 1977, vol. 31, pp. 607–633 (this article has been reprinted in several volumes edited by its author); and J. McGlade, 'From Business Reform Programme to Production Drive', in Kipping and Bjarnar (eds), *The Americanisation*, pp. 18–34.
33 For more details see Berghahn, *The Americanisation of West German Industry*, pp. 155–181.
34 For the relations between the BDI and the CNPF and their position vis-à-vis the cartel question see M. Kipping, 'Welches Europa soll es sein? Der Schuman-Plan und die deutsch-französischen Industriebeziehungen', in A. Wilkens (ed.), *Deutsch-französische Wirtschaftsbeziehungen 1945–1960*, Sigmaringen: Thorbecke, 1997, pp. 249–271; for more detail on the ECSC and the role of Monnet A. Wilkens, *La France et les origines de l'Union européenne, 1944–1952: Intégration économique et compétitivité internationale*, Paris: CHEFF, 2002.
35 For details about the following see M. Kipping, 'The Hidden Business Schools. Management Training in Germany Since 1945', in L. Engwall and V. Zamagni (eds), *Management Education in Historical Perspective*, Manchester: Manchester University Press, 1998, pp. 95–110.
36 His role is examined by M. Kipping and C. Kleinschmidt, 'Ludwig Vaubel and the Renewal of Management Education in Germany after 1945', in A.-M. Kuijlaars, K. Prudon and J. Visser (eds), *Business and Society*, Rotterdam: Centre of Business History (CBG), 2000, pp. 521–530.
37 L. Vaubel, *Unternehmer gehen zur Schule. Ein Erfahrungsbericht aus USA*, Düsseldorf: Droste, 1952.

52   *Matthias Kipping*

38 J. Bertsch and P. Zürn (eds), *Führen und Gestalten. 100 Unternehmergespräche in Baden-Baden*, Berlin: Springer, 1997.
39 Interview with the former Executive Director of the Baden-Baden seminars, Dr. Peter Zürn, on 24 September 1996.
40 For an overview of the different 'generations' of consultancies see M. Kipping, 'Trapped in their wave: the evolution of management consultancies', in T. Clark and R. Fincham (eds), *Critical Consulting: New Perspectives on the Management Advice Industry*, Oxford: Blackwell, 2002, pp. 28–49; for a comparison of their role in Britain, France and Germany see Kipping, 'Consultancies, Institutions and the Diffusion of Taylorism'.
41 F. Schlund, 'Das Bedaux-System', in *Refa und Leistungssteigerung. Vorträge der Refa-Jahrestagung Gotha 1939*, Berlin: Beuth, 1940, pp. 46–67.
42 A. Ernst, 'Leistungen in Amerika', presentation at the Siemens work study meeting on 9 and 10 December 1952, pp. 85–94, Siemens Archives, 64/Lm103. Cf. the official report *Das Arbeitsstudium in den USA. Bericht einer deutschen Studiengruppe*, Munich: Hanser, 1955, esp. pp. 8 and 16.
43 National Industry Conference Board, *Systems of Wage Payment*, New York: NICB, 1930.
44 See *Refa-Nachrichten*, September 1956, vol. 9, no. 3, pp. 91–94.
45 See *Proportions of pieceworkers in the last pay-week in October, 1949* and Ministry of Labour and National Service, *Wage Incentive Schemes, Industrial Relations Handbook*, Supplement No. 4, London: HMSO, 1951, Modern Records Centre, Warwick University, MSS.200, B/3/2/C1045, pt. 1 and 2.
46 For a more extensive discussion of the following, see M. Kipping, 'British Economic Decline: Blame It on the Consultants?', *Contemporary British History*, Autumn 1999, vol. 13, no. 3, pp. 23–38.
47 A.D. Chandler, Jr, *Scale and Scope. The Dynamics of Industrial Capitalism*, Cambridge, MA: The Belknap Press of Harvard University Press, 1990.
48 C. Lane and R. Bachmann, 'The Social Constitution of Supplier Relations in Britain and Germany', *Organization Studies*, 1996, vol. 17, no. 3, pp. 365–395.
49 A.D. Chandler, Jr., *Strategy and Structure. Chapters in the History of the Industrial Enterprise*, Cambridge/Mass.: MIT Press, 1962.
50 C.D. McKenna, 'The Origins of Modern Management Consulting', *Business and Economic History*, Fall 1995, vol. 24, no. 1, pp. 51–58.
51 For the development of the German consulting market, see in detail M. Kipping, *The Management Consultancy Business in Historical and Comparative Perspective*, Oxford: Oxford University Press, forthcoming in 2004. Only during the 1990s, in Germany, as in most other industrialized countries, McKinsey and other second wave consulting firms, were displaced from their leading positions by a new generation of service providers focusing on information systems and technologies. The most prominent firms in this new wave are Accenture (formerly Andersen Consulting), Cap Gemini Ernst & Young and IBM Global Services; see Kipping, 'Trapped in their wave', and 'Jenseits von Krise und Wachstum. Wandel im Markt für Unternehmensberatung', *zfo (Zeitschrift Führung + Organisation)*, 2002, vol. 71, no. 5, pp. 269–276.
52 'Diener vieler Herren', *Wirtschaftswoche*, 2 August 1974, p. 72.
53 See *Kienbaum und Partner. Geschichte einer Unternehmensberatung 1945–1995*, Gummersbach, 1995.
54 G.P. Dyas and H.T. Thanheiser, *The Emerging European Enterprise. Strategy and Structure in French and German Industry*, London: Macmillan, 1976. See also Chapter 10 by Hilger in this volume.
55 Incidentally, similar reasons, namely increasing competition and pressure from institutional investors, seem to have driven the expansion of the Japanese consulting market during the 1990s; see M. Kipping, 'Why Management Consult-

ing Developed So Late in Japan and Does It Matter?' (in Japanese), *Hitotsu-bashi Business Review*, Autumn 2002, vol. 50, no. 2, pp. 6–21.
56 To reflect these changes, in the late 1990s the RKW modified its name to Rationalisierungs- und Innovationszentrum der Deutschen Wirtschaft e.V. (see <http://www.rkw.de>).

3 Paths to Americanization in postwar Japan

Satoshi Sasaki

Introduction

This chapter considers the process of Americanization in management methods used in Japanese companies in the postwar period. Such a process can be divided into three distinct paths of diffusion. Each of these paths represents a different combination of the roles played by American and Japanese governments, private businesses, industry organizations and professional organizations. They also differ in the extent to which initiative and leadership were located on the side of the provider or the recipient of information and technology.

The first path was through the General Headquarters (GHQ) of the Supreme Commander of Allied Powers (SCAP) which was responsible for implementing policy in occupied Japan. In this case, the starting point of the path and the main actor in the process is the American government and GHQ. The recipients, or the ends of the path, are consulting organizations, companies and individuals in Japan. In this path, Japanese consulting organizations played a significant role in disseminating information and in internalization. In many ways, these organizations effectively functioned as an intermediary to strengthen the channel that tended to be weak due to lack of information and recognition. The second path was the Japan Productivity Centre (Nihon Seisansei Honbu), founded in the 1950s. The establishment of this umbrella organization resulted from both a suggestion of the American government and the influence of the productivity improvement movements in Europe. With the support of the Japanese government, business leaders and some labour organizations, this path became a strong and steady channel of Americanization. The third path was direct technology transfer by individual Japanese companies since the 1950s. This path represents a proactive effort on the part of Japanese companies to remedy their shortcomings in technology.

The first path: introduction of management methods by GHQ

Introduction of formalized training methods

GHQ introduced management methods such as Management Training Program (MTP), Training within Industry (TWI), and other human resource development. MTP was modelled upon the Supervisory Training (ST) system developed by the Far East Air Force to train Japanese supervisory staff. It was a training method using forty charts and worksheets in discussions, completed in 40 hours. The Ministry of International Trade and Industry (MITI) began to promote its use in Japanese industry after 1950. TWI was a system designed for the training of plant foremen and consisted of sections on job instruction (JI), job methods (JM) and job relations (JR). GHQ recommended its adoption to the Ministry of Labour, which began to promote it toward the end of 1948.[1]

Since these formalized training systems were developed in the United States to deal with low levels of literacy and the lack of English language skills of immigrant workers, some expressed scepticism in the applicability of such systems to Japan. Aoki Takeichi, who later became a specialist in education and training, later stated that GHQ recognized a need for such a training system based on the poor work habits of workers at a construction site managed by the GHQ. He also noted that GHQ underestimated the ability of the Japanese workers, many of whom were downtrodden with the defeat in the war. The training provided in leading discussions in MTP was merely leading the discussion toward predetermined answers, and the content of the answers was fairly simple-minded. Masami Doi, who then worked for Mitsui Mining, also expressed reservations regarding MTP, given the high rates of completion of compulsory education. However, his supervisor, who advised him on the introduction of this method, noted that this method was more analytical in its approach, in comparison to the spiritual exhortations of the Industrial Patriotism Movement of the prewar period.[2]

MTP was revised several times in subsequent years. According to Shin'ichi Takezawa, who took part in the development of the Japanese edition of MTP at the Far Eastern Air Force Logistics Command, there were eight major features in the revisions.

1 The content was improved through the inclusion of materials on which MTP was originally based.
2 Some revisions attempted to include descriptions of the Japanese situation and cases from Japanese experience.
3 Some revisions attempted to remove all Japanese content in order to keep the material as close as possible to the original.
4 Later developments in American management theory were incorporated.

5   A shortened version of MTP for white-collar workers was developed.
6   Different versions of MTP tailored to specific companies and organizations were developed.
7   As the work of middle and upper management became increasingly complex, a version of MTP was developed to include middle and upper level managers.
8   Some revisions attempted to include the service sector.

Of these revisions, the second type, which took place after 1955, was the only type that made an explicit attempt to adapt MTP to Japanese circumstances. In other words, most Japanese participants wanted information on American management, despite the misgivings of Aoki and Doi.[3]

Thus, managers in Japanese companies expressed a strong interest in a scientific analysis of American-style management, despite the scepticism regarding simple-minded formulaic teaching and the underestimation of Japanese workers' abilities. At this stage, the process of Americanization might be characterized as passive. However, this passive Americanization became the foundation for later active Americanization.

Role of management consulting

In the first path to Americanization, Japanese management consulting played a large role in the application and assimilation of the American style management. This section, therefore, reviews some of the major individuals and organizations involved in management consulting.

Consulting activities of Japan Management Association

The Japan Management Association (JMA, Nihon Noritsu Kyokai) was formed in 1942 through the merger of the National Association of Efficiency Societies (Nihon Noritsu Rengokai), a private sector organization, and the Japan Industrial Association (Nihon Kogyo Kyokai), a quasi-governmental organization. After the end of the war, GHQ advised the Japanese government to withdraw all governmental funding. Thus, the Japan Management Association established a policy of fiscal independence, and began to charge fees for membership and research consulting to fund its activities.[4] Thus, the organization took the first step in moving away from a quasi-governmental body under the control of the prewar Ministry of Commerce and Industry toward an independent private sector organization performing consulting activities.

JMA conducted its first factory analysis on a for-fee basis in January 1946.[5] The first factory analysis was conducted at Kinki Railway Car Company in January 1946, followed by similar analyses at other railway car factories. Other analyses performed during the same year include a project commissioned by the Ministry of Communication on administrative rationalization, factory analyses of communication equipment manufacturers such as Iwasaki Communication Equipment, and coal mines such as Aso Mining.[6] GHQ designated these three industries as priority industries for recovery, and these industries received guidance on increasing production and process management. These policies, however, were implemented with the knowledge and human resources accumulated prior to and during World War II.[7] The scope of analyses and guidance subsequently expanded so that the number of factory analyses increased from 35 in 1946 to 44 in 1947, and 73 in 1948. In 1949, there was a slight decrease to 61 cases, but with the outbreak of the Korean War in 1950, the number of analyses increased dramatically to 135. Within JMA, a programme to educate and certify consultants was also implemented. The number of consultants increased from 12 in 1946 to 55 in 1950.[8]

New knowledge was also incorporated in the process. In May 1949, JMA introduced statistical quality control methods at ten factories, including that of Daido Weaving, under the guidance of Eizaiburo Nishibori, who had been researching statistical quality control methods since the prewar period.[9] In 1951, JMA implemented the work factor method, introduced from the United States after the war, in the packaging process at Ajinomoto's Kawasaki Factory and the sewing process for athletic shoes at the Urawa Factory of Fujikura Rubber. Both of these factories showed significant improvement in effectiveness.[10] Thus, the Japan Management Association used the knowledge and human resources accumulated in the prewar period as the foundation upon which to build an independent consulting organization in the private sector. In the process, JMA contributed toward the diffusion of management methods introduced from the United States.

Establishment of new organizations

Around the time that the Japan Management Association was reorganized as a consulting organization in the private sector, many other new organizations in the consulting business were also established. These organizations came to play significant roles in the introduction and diffusion of American management methods.

In December 1945, shortly after the end of the war, the Japanese Standards Association was established with the purpose of promoting industrial standards. The Union of Japanese Scientists and Engineers (JUSE), which became the leader in the quality control movement, was established in May 1946. Both of these organizations have roots that may be traced back to the wartime period,[11] but in the postwar period, they both became leaders in the promotion of scientific management. In November 1949, the All Japan Federation of Management Organizations (Zennihon Noritsu Renmei) was founded as an overarching organization of all management organizations in Japan, with Yoichi Ueno as its first president.

The federation inherited the spirit of the former National Association of Efficiency Societies (Nihon Noritsu Rengokai);[12] like its predecessor, the purpose of the reorganized federation was to provide links between organizations in the private sector as well as quasi-public organizations. Ueno himself imagined the new federation to be a 'reincarnation of the old National Association of Efficiency Societies.'[13] Since its inception, the federation has organized annual conventions at major cities throughout Japan, and has facilitated the exchange of information through lectures and discussions.

Around the time of the establishment of the All Japan Federation of Management Organization, the Japanese business community began to develop conditions amenable to the introduction of new management systems, and the reintroduction of Western management methods proceeded. These developments affected the activities of both the Japan Standards Association and JUSE. With respect to industrial standards, GHQ recommended that the Japanese government exchange information with member countries of the International Organization for Standardization (ISO, founded in 1947). As a result, in July 1949, the Industrial Standards Law was enacted. This law replaced the prewar Japanese Engineering Standards (JES) with the Japanese Industrial Standards (JIS), and provided for programmes to promote the new standards throughout the country.[14]

On issues concerning the Union of Japanese Scientists and Engineers (JUSE), staff from the Civil Communication Section of the GHQ organized a series of lectures on management in Tokyo between September and November 1949, and then in Osaka from November 1949 to January 1950. Homer M. Sarasohn and Charles W. Protzman, among others, served as instructors, and they covered topics such as management strategy, organization, production control and operations. The section on production control included lectures on quality control. Shortly thereafter, in August 1950, JUSE sponsored an 8-day course taught by W. Edwards Deming on quality control. Deming had served as an advisor on sampling techniques at the United States Office of Management and Budget. He was invited to Japan by the Economic and Science Section of the GHQ to provide instruction in the completion of the preliminary sampling study of the Japanese population census. As soon as JUSE learned that Deming was coming to Japan they wrote to ask if he would deliver some lectures on quality control. The result was the 8-day course of lectures, which were later published under the title 'Dr. Deming's Lectures on Statistical Control of Quality'; Deming donated the royalties on the book to JUSE. JUSE, in turn, established and funded the Deming Prize with the donation. The first Deming Application Prize was awarded in September 1951. Deming attended the ceremony and delivered a commemorative lecture.[15] On leaving Japan, Deming offered the following observations:

Intelligent use of statistical techniques in all phases of manufacture, from the testing of raw materials to the marketing of the finished products, can help to build for Japanese industry a reputation for uniformity and dependability of product that will stand up to competition. The future reputation of Japan's industry, and the foundation for the peace, happiness, and prosperity of Japan's people many years to come, is being built now.[16]

This was indeed a prophetic statement, foreseeing the spread of company-wide quality control programmes and the resulting economic growth in Japan.

In addition to JUSE, some major organizations concerning management were formed between the immediate aftermath of the war and the establishment of the Japan Productivity Centre, or between the 1940s and the late 1950s. They included the Central Japan Industries Association (Shadan Hojin Chubu Sangyo Renmei, established May 1948), the Nippon Omni-Management Association (Shadan Hojin Nihon Keiei Kyokai, June 1949), the Japan Consulting Institute (Shadan Hojin Kokai Keiei Shido Kyokai, August 1952), the Japan Small and Medium Enterprise Management Consulting Association (Shadan Hojin Chusho Kigyo Shindan Kyokai, October 1954), the Association of Management Consultants in Japan (Shadan Hojin Nihon Keieishi Kai, originally founded in September 1951 and incorporated in January 1955), the Japan Productivity Centre (Shadan Hojin Nihon Seisansei Honbu, March 1955), Japan Industrial Training Association (Shadan Hojin Nihon Sangyo Kunren Kyokai, October 1955), the Institute of Research on Enterprises (Shadan Hojin Kigyo Kenkyu Kai, March 1956), the Sales Promotion Bureau (Shadan Hojin Serusu Puromoshon Byuro, January 1958), and the Japan Management School (Shadan Hojin Nihon Manejimento Sukuru, August 1959).[17] These organizations each had their own area of expertise, and worked independently to promote improved management techniques. At the same time, many of these organizations also maintained cooperative or complementary relationships with each other. Taken as a whole, these organizations served as a major pipeline for the diffusion of American management techniques.

Development of independent consultants

Along with the formation or reorganization of organizations focused upon management consulting, the number of private consultants also increased after the war. These consultants were primarily concerned with improving business management of medium and small enterprises. They were experts in the improvement of business management, and provided individualized consulting tailored to specific enterprises. These consultants were previously known as 'efficiency experts' in the prewar era, and Yoichi

Ueno and Toichiro Araki were leading examples of individuals who had continued their practice into the postwar period.

In August 1951, the Economic Stabilization Board took the initiative to call a meeting for the institutionalization and modernization of these 'efficiency experts' as 'management consultants'. As a result of this meeting, the founding meeting of the Association of Management Consultants in Japan (Nihon Keieishi Kai) was held on 25 September 1951, and the formal foundation ceremony was held on 25 October. The first slate of officers included central figures from the National Association of Efficiency Societies in the prewar period and the Japan Management Association. Masao Kamo was elected the first president, with Toichiro Araki and Kakuzo Morikawa as vice presidents. Other officers included Yasutaro Hirai, Yoichi Ueno, Takehito Ueda, Toru Okada, Torao Nakanishi, Hironori Ono, Tsuguo Ouchi, Koichi Inoue, Riichi Sonoda, Choji Kuramoto, Seitaro Toyama and Kanzo Kiribuchi .[18] This represented the first national organization of individual management consultants in Japan. The term *keieishi* referring to individual management consultants was established at this time.

The second path: development of the productivity improvement movement

Dispatch of productivity missions

The Japan Productivity Centre, established in March 1955, played a central role in the development of the productivity movement in Japan. The establishment of this Centre was influenced in part by the productivity movement that had been promoted in Europe by the United States as a part of the Marshall Plan. The Japan Productivity Centre was the fruit of cooperation of American and the Japanese governments and the support of the Japan Committee for Economic Development and other business organizations as well as some labour unions.[19] Reflecting the desires of the American government, the Japan Productivity Centre put most of its energy into organizing overseas observation missions. This section traces the history and the fruits of these missions.

The first mission took place from 31 May to 1 August 1955 and observed the steel industry. The American government funded the travel expenses of these missions under a technology cooperation programme through 1961. During these years, 393 teams with a total of 3,987 participants took part in overseas observation missions organized by the Japan Productivity Centre. From 1962, participants were required to cover their own expenses except in a few extraordinary circumstances. Between 1962 and 1966, an additional 182 teams with a total of 2,220 participants were sent out. Thus, during the 11 years of the programme, a grand total of 575 teams with 6,207 participants took part in the programme.[20]

The missions experienced a gradual change over the 11 years. From around 1958, there was an increase in missions consisting of participants from small and medium enterprises and missions including leading members of labour unions in various industries. The increase in the number of participants from small and medium enterprises was due in part to Japanese government encouragement. But in addition, the fact that companies that sent participants to the early missions subsequently experienced actual improvements in productivity proved to be a strong incentive. The mission on the automobile parts industry organized in the first year of the programme was a good example of this pattern. This team spent approximately 6 weeks, from 28 January to 10 March 1956, visiting American automobile parts manufacturers and studying their technology and production processes. The participants in this mission included members from a number of small and medium enterprises that later experienced rapid growth and became large-scale manufacturers of automobile parts. Among them were Yazaki Densen Kogyo (a manufacturer of wire harnesses for electrical equipment, later Yazaki General Industries), Nippon Denso (now Denso), Nippon Piston Ring (a major producer of valves and other engine parts), Nihon Tokushu Hatsujo (associated with the Morimura group, now NGK Spark Plug), Nihon Bane (the world's largest producer of springs), Press Kogyo (the largest producer of automobile press parts, primarily for Isuzu), Akebono Sangyo (Akebono Brake Industry in 1960) and Daido Metal Industries (largest producer of metal for bearings). These companies exhibited significant increases in productivity and growth, and their experience became a major factor behind the increase in participation by medium and smaller enterprises.

On the other hand, the increased participation by representatives of labour unions reflected the desire of the United States. It also reflected an international trend in the productivity movement for the active participation of labour. In 1961, the labour unions in the General Council of Trade Unions in Japan (Sohyo), which had previously been critical of the productivity movement, sent its first delegation on an observation mission. In the first year alone, participants affiliated with the Council accounted for fifty of the 124 labour union participants in the programme.

It is possible to divide the observation mission into three types: top management missions consisting of members from top companies and industries, missions organized according to type of industry, and missions organized by area of expertise. During the course of the programme, missions of experts increased between 1957 and 1959, although the industry-based teams began to increase thereafter. One reason for this pattern is that as participants in the expert missions returned and shared what they had learned, it created a strong desire for more industry-specific practical knowledge.[21] However, between 1960 and 1962, missions consisting of only technical experts were avoided, as technology transfer programmes had shown significant effects. By this time the Japanese level of technology had risen and facilities had been modernized considerably. After this point, the observation missions focused more on business management and less on technology, in accordance with the wishes of the American and European host nations.[22]

Results of observation missions

This section examines the results of these inspection missions based on surveys of participants completed after each team returned to Japan.[23]

Useful knowledge and publicity activities

Of 345 respondents of the survey, the largest number, 100 respondents, pointed to production control as the most useful information gained from the mission. It was followed by labour management (77 respondents) and marketing (52 respondents). Dividing the responses by the type of mission, in the industry specific missions, the most useful area was production control (72 out of 142), and for specialization based groups, 32 out of 203 respondents mentioned marketing as the most useful. The survey showed that the majority of participants (65 per cent) worked for large companies with 1,000 or more employees, and their interests were in the areas of production control, labour management and marketing. The overall responses reflected the interests of the participants from large companies due to their number.

Regarding the activities of participants upon their return, 188 respondents out of 196 held meetings in which they reported on their observations. It is quite remarkable that 128 had held at least six such meetings. Furthermore, 143 participants submitted written reports, while 179 submitted written recommendations or proposals. From these figures, it is clear that a large number of participants shared their experiences and participated in information dissemination activities both inside and outside their own companies in a variety of formats.

Implementation and results

Next, the implementation of what had been learned on these observation missions will be considered. First, 126 of 196 respondents in the survey stated that some organizational structure focused on productivity improvement was formed at their company upon their return from the observation mission. As for the format of these organizations, a committee of specialists was most common. The survey result also confirmed that the larger the company, the more likely it was to have set up such a special committee.

The degree to which the findings of these delegations were implemented was surveyed according to different fields. This survey reported a total of 669 examples of knowledge gained from these missions being put to practical use. These examples covered a wide range including accounting, production, labour relations and marketing, among others. The largest number of practical applications, 222, was reported in the area of production, and of these the greatest number, as might be expected, concerned production control, quality control and logistics. As with reporting activities and organization creation, the larger the company, the greater the likelihood that some form of practical application had been made. Most significant improvements were made in the areas of productivity, production facilities and management theory.

Although these surveys only cover the early period of the overseas observation mission programme, one can see from the survey responses that the missions produced significant results. These survey results were made public in October 1958, and it is quite clear that the positive results described in the survey served as a stimulus to observation and trainee delegations that followed in subsequent years.

Dispatch of long-term overseas trainees

In addition to the overseas observation missions, the Japan Productivity Centre implemented a second programme through which learning took place: long-term overseas traineeship. The programme began in the third year of Japan Productivity Centre's activities, and in the 5 years between 1957 and 1961, 163 trainees in 51 groups were sent to Europe and the United States. Of these, over 60 per cent were sent to the United States.[24] These trainees were employees of government ministries or business-related organizations, university professors or employees of private corporations. They spent 3 months to a year taking courses at universities and undergoing practical training at factories and offices. The purpose of their training included the development of consultants to work with small and medium enterprises as well as industrial engineering and marketing in general.

Invitation of experts

The third route by which the Japanese learned about American-style management was through the visits of experts from overseas. These visits included lecturers for the 'top management seminars' aimed at senior management and lecture series focused on specific problems or particular areas of specialization. In addition, experts were invited as consultants to visit companies and inspect plant operations and to offer advice and guidance at plant level. Experts in the latter category were much larger in number than those for the former.[25] As for the seminars focusing on specific themes, the most common subject was industrial engineering. American experts were invited to explain the basic concepts of industrial engineering, and to discuss the current circumstances in the United States. Stimulated in part by these seminars, domestic observation missions were organized in March 1957 in order to promote the exchange of information among practitioners. Takeo Kato, who had taken a leading role in the introduction of scientific management methods at the Kobe Works of Mitsubishi Electric since the prewar years, was the central figure in this movement. These domestic observation missions contributed to the mutual learning of Japanese experts and practitioners.

The third path: technology transfer under the foreign capital law

Number of transfers and the resulting production and export values

In 1949, Foreign Exchange and Foreign Trade Control Laws were enacted, followed in 1950 by other laws regulating foreign direct investment in Japan. Within the framework of Japanese government regulations based on these laws, Japanese firms took their own initiative for effecting any technology transfer. This process may be characterized as voluntary Americanization under the guidance of the Japanese government.

As Table 3.1 demonstrates, by 1961 the Japanese government had approved 1,670 Class I Technical Assistance Contracts, bringing advanced technology to Japan.[26] The number of transfers showed a rapid increase in 1956, but dropped off thereafter. It began to rise sharply again after 1959 as companies recognized the need to increase their competitiveness prior to the impending trade liberalization. The largest number of transfers occurred in 'miscellaneous machinery' industry (machinery other than electrical machinery and transportation equipment). The electrical machinery industry and the chemical industry followed in second and third place, respectively.

As shown in Table 3.2, the United States was the most common source of technology, with 1,045 contracts, or 62 per cent of the total. This figure represents a significant increase in dependence on the United States for new technology in the postwar period, since only 40 per cent of prewar technology transfer came from the United States.[27] In terms of payments made for technology transfer, Japanese companies paid 11.8 million dollars in 1956. This amount is comparable to payments to West Germany.[28]

Table 3.3 summarizes the production value resulting from the technology transfer. As the table indicates, the total value of production using transferred technology in 'miscellaneous machinery', the industry category with the largest number of transfer contracts, was 24.0 billion yen in 1955. This amount increased five-fold to 128.2 billion yen by 1960. Examining these figures more closely shows that motors accounted for a large proportion and, in particular, technology relating to boilers accounted for substantial production value.

Table 3.1 Number of approvals for Class I technology transfer by industry, 1949–61

	1949/50	1951	1952	1953	1954	1955	1956	1957	1958	1959	1960	1961	Total
Electrical machinery	5	11	24	43	22	17	20	29	26	39	99	59	394
Transportation machinery	1	6	8	6	7	8	12	2	6	6	17	24	103
Other machinery	9	33	38	19	14	16	20	25	23	31	71	101	400
Metal and metal products	1	9	16	8	4	7	18	11	12	25	19	27	157
Chemical industry	8	23	16	14	22	17	46	30	11	33	77	59	356
Textiles	0	4	5	7	8	1	12	7	3	7	8	23	85
Petroleum products	0	1	14	0	0	3	5	2	5	4	7	5	46
Rubber and leather	1	6	3	0	2	1	5	7	2	3	12	8	50
Construction related	0	1	2	4	0	1	2	3	0	1	0	1	15
Glass and ceramics	1	2	2	2	3	0	2	0	1	3	7	7	30
Paper and pulp	0	4	2	0	0	1	1	1	1	0	4	5	19
Electricity and gas distribution	0	1	2	0	0	0	0	0	0	0	0	0	3
Entertainment and amusement	1	0	0	0	0	0	0	0	0	0	1	0	2
Printing and publishing	0	0	1	0	0	0	1	0	0	1	1	1	5
Food products	0	0	0	0	0	0	0	1	0	0	4	0	5
Total	27	101	133	103	82	72	144	118	90	153	327	320	1,670

Source: Kagaku Gijutsu Cho (Science and Technology Agency), Showa 37-nendo kagaku gijutsu hakusho (Science and Technology White Paper 1962), Tokyo: Okura Sho Insatsu Kyoku, 1962, p. 41.

Note
The original table gives the number of cases for petroleum products in the 1961 fiscal year as four, but the row and column totals suggest that the correct figure is five.

Table 3.2 Number of approvals for Class I technology transfer by country of origin, 1949–61

	1949/50	1951	1952	1953	1954	1955	1956	1957	1958	1959	1960	1961	Total
United States	21	74	88	72	58	44	85	61	63	92	200	187	1,045
Switzerland	5	16	8	11	6	2	6	10	8	9	18	22	121
West Germany	0	0	12	6	5	9	11	7	6	16	45	40	157
France	0	2	5	4	1	4	6	4	1	7	5	10	49
United Kingdom	0	1	3	3	1	3	11	3	2	7	10	16	60
Italy	0	0	1	1	8	0	10	3	1	1	8	1	34
Canada	0	0	8	4	1	2	3	2	2	2	2	7	33
The Netherlands	0	0	1	0	0	1	2	18	0	9	7	7	45
Sweden	0	6	5	1	0	1	1	2	2	3	8	8	37
Panama	0	2	1	1	0	4	4	2	1	1	7	8	31
Denmark	1	0	0	1	0	0	0	0	2	1	0	2	8
Norway	0	0	0	0	0	0	1	3	0	1	1	3	9
Venezuela	0	0	0	0	0	0	0	3	1	1	5	5	15
Austria	0	0	0	0	0	1	2	0	0	0	2	0	5
Liechtenstein	0	0	0	0	0	1	1	0	1	1	3	1	8
Australia	0	0	0	0	0	0	1	0	0	1	2	0	4
French Morocco	0	0	0	0	1	0	0	0	0	0	0	0	1
Belgium	0	0	0	0	0	0	0	0	0	1	2	2	5
Bahamas	0	0	0	0	0	0	0	0	0	0	2	0	2
USSR	0	0	0	0	0	0	0	0	0	0	0	1	1
Total	27	101	133	103	82	72	144	118	90	153	327	320	1,670

Source: Kagaku Gijutsu Cho (Science and Technology Agency), *Showa 37-nendo kagaku gijutsu hakusho* (Science and Technology White Paper 1962), Tokyo: Okura Sho Insatsu Kyoku, 1962, p. 42.

Note
The original table gives the number of cases for French Morocco in fiscal year 1954 as zero, but the column and row totals suggest that the correct figure is one.

Table 3.3 Production values, export values and technology payment values resulting from technology transfer in the machinery industry

Classification	Sector total	Engines and motors				Mining and civil construction equipment	Metal-working machinery	Metal processing machinery (2)	Textile machinery	General machinery (3)	Office equipment
		Sub-total	Boilers	Steam turbines (1)	Internal combustion engines						
1955											
Production value from technology introduction (¥100 million)	240.0	138.4	64.3	15.8	41.2	10.5	1.3	6.3	12.5	50.6	80.0
Percentage of overall production value (%)	6.5	26.4	62.2	(29.4)	13.0	7.4	3.3	3.1	2.9 (40.5)	5.5	23.0
Export value from technology introduction (¥100 million)	22.0	14.5	0.4	2.1	11.4	0.3		1.6	1.7	2.1	1.0
Technology payment value (¥100 million)	11.9	5.8	1.9	0.6	2.2	0.9	0.1	0.2	0.9	2.4	0.3
1960											
Production value from technology introduction (¥100 million)	1,282.2	675.6	379.7	104.9 (139.0)	133.7	94.0	43.8	62.0 (498.0)	34.0	276.7	22.3
Percentage of overall production value (%)	9.1	31.6	62.0	26.5	13.4	10.8	8.3	6.8 (29.3)	3.8	6.9	12.4
Export value from technology introduction (¥100 million)	73.3	41.8	5.5	6.3	29.4	5.9		0.1	10.1	10.9	0.8
Technology payment value (¥100 million)	62.6	28.1	13.2	3.4	5.4	62.0	2.7	3.7	2.3	12.9	1.1

Source: Kagaku Gijutsu Cho (Science and Technology Agency), *Showa 37-nendo kagaku gijutsu hakusho* (Science and Technology White Paper 1962), Tokyo: Okura Sho Insatsu Kyoku, 1962, p. 46.

Notes

1 Number in brackets includes both gas turbines and hydropower turbines.
2 Number in brackets is primarily rolling mill equipment.
3 General machinery includes pumps, compressors, ventilators, freight elevators, motive power transmission equipment, chemical machinery, industrial furnaces, etc.

The production values for electrical machinery, in which the second largest number of technology transfers occurred, is summarized in Table 3.4. In 1955, technology transfer generated 63.7 billion yen in production, an amount far greater than that for 'miscellaneous machinery'. By 1960 the value of output had increased by more than 6.4 times to 410.2 billion yen. The detailed breakdown for this year indicates that the output of televisions, radios, electronic tubes and semiconductors had increased greatly as a result of imported technology. In these areas, imported technology accounted for a large percentage of the overall output; for example, 92 per cent of the total production value of television sets derived from imported technology. These four products also contributed significantly to the increase in the value of exports derived from transferred technology in the same 5-year period from 1956 to 1960. In particular, over half of the production value due to technology transfer for radios was exported. In electronic tubes and semiconductors, 12 per cent of the production value attributed to technology transfer was exported.

Managerial awareness and export performance

Transistor radios represent an interesting case study in managerial strategy in technology transfer and exports. Masaru Ibuka of Sony, who participated in Japan Productivity Centre's fourth senior management mission in 1958, reminisced that although Sony had exported only a small number of sample transistor radios in 1956, the number had jumped to 200,000 units in 1957 and 1.5 million units in 1958. Ibuka reported that this rapid growth caused distress among American manufacturers.[29] Moreover, Ibuka predicted that American dependence on Japanese transistor radios would continue to increase in the future for several reasons. Among his reasons were the low cost and high level of production technology of Japanese transistor radios; the superiority of Japanese technology for miniaturization of products; finger dexterity of Japanese workers; and the ease of transporting and shipping small items. He also pointed out that the United States had given priority to supplying transistors for military industrial complexes, which meant that the supply of transistors for use in radios would be low.[30]

In fact, there were approximately thirty manufacturers of transistors in the United States around this time. But, as Ibuka discovered, even at leading manufacturers like Texas Instruments, which he had visited, 90 per cent of their transistor production was for purposes other than radios. He was told that the market for radio transistors was completely inundated with cheaper Japanese imports. Motorola, a major radio manufacturer, was able to reduce their price of transistor radios from 39 dollars each to 29 dollars each by using Japanese transistors.[31] The pattern of production and export of transistors in the 10-year period between 1957 and 1966 corroborated Ibuka's prediction. Sales volume increased from 3.259 billion

Table 3.4 Production values, export values and technology payment values resulting from technology transfer in the electrical machinery sector

Classification	Sector total	Rotating electrical machinery			Transformers	Switchboards	Cable equipment	Radio communications equipment	Radio	Televisions	Electronic tubes and semiconductors
		Sub-total	General power equipment	Electric motors							
1950											
Production value from technology introduction (¥100 million)	637.1	42.8	26.5	15.5	34.0	33.9	36.2	17.1	94.0	88.4	70.0
Percentage of overall production value (%)	25.4	13.9	27.1	8.3	20.4	12.9	27.5	27.7	75.6	92.7	74.5
Export value from technology introduction (¥100 million)	11.6	1.1	0.9	0.1	0.9	1.3	0.5	0.2	2.1	0.03	1.47
Technology payment value (¥100 million)	15.5	1.4	0.9	0.4	1.3	0.8	1.7	0.3	0.5	1.1	2.4
1960											
Production value from technology introduction (¥100 million)	4,102.0	156.7	95.8	59.0	122.8	146.5	148.3	115.8	531.0	1,516.5	470.3
Percentage of overall production value (%)	33.3	13.4	34.2	8.4	21.5	12.8	29.3	56.1	73.4	92.5	67.8
Export value from technology introduction (¥100 million)	415.2	10.3	5.8	4.0	6.2	4.1	5.7	13.3	267.0	12.6	56.9
Technology payment value (¥100 million)	85.4	3.6	2.1	1.4	3.1	3.7	4.7	3.1	24.0	23.1	19.2

Source: Kagaku Gijutsu Cho (Science and Technology Agency), Showa 37-nendo kagaku gijutsu hakusho (Science and Technology White Paper 1962), Tokyo: Okura Sho Insatsu Kyoku, 1963, p. 45.

yen to 35.597 billion yen, and export value skyrocketed from 5 million yen to 4.413 billion yen.[32]

Roles of industry organizations and government

It should be noted that unity within the electronics industry as well as the support of the Japanese government played a significant role in the success of technology transfer. Key industries established industry organizations that served as the intermediary for negotiation with the government as well as foreign companies. The case of television manufacturing, which accounted for more production and export output than from any other imported technology, represents a good example of the relationships between industry organizations, the government and individual companies. In order to produce television sets it was first necessary to obtain licenses for patents for deflection circuits and horizontal synchronization circuits from RCA of the United States, for signal synchronization circuits from EMI of England and for inter-carrier technology from Phillips of the Netherlands. When television broadcasting first began in 1953, there was a sharp rise in applications for licensing contracts with RCA. In response to this increased demand, the Foreign Exchange Commission, which was concerned about the depletion of foreign capital reserves, took the policy of giving priority to companies with a good track record. In September 1953, the Commission approved the applications of thirty-seven firms, including several kit manufacturers.[33] Thereafter, the companies involved established the Television Promotion Association (Terebijon Shinko Kyokai), which took over negotiations for a collective contract with RCA. This contract was approved on 19 February 1957.[34]

In the field of wireless communications, Wireless Communication Industry Association (Musen Tsushin Kogyo Kai), its industry association, formed a patent strategy committee in 1955. Rather than having individual companies negotiate licensing contracts with patent holders, this committee took the leading role for negotiating collectively with patent holders for those of general interest. This committee was also instrumental in negotiating reductions in licensing fees, which was accomplished at the urging of the Ministry of International Trade and Industry.[35]

Conclusion

This section summarizes the major findings of this chapter. First, in the years immediately after the end of the war, the process of Americanization was heteronomous, and the initiative was on the part of the Americans. During this period, formulaic training methods were introduced, in part to increase the productivity of the Japanese labour working for the American Occupation. Some of those involved in the diffusion of such training methods were sceptical of their applicability, given the differences in the nature of the Japanese and American workforces. However, efforts to adapt these methods to Japanese business circumstances were only rarely made. Rather, these methods were appreciated for their American style and for introducing scientific analysis into business phenomena. These inclinations of the early postwar years served to develop widespread respect for American management and technology, and later fuelled active learning on the part of the Japanese.

The second path to Americanization was the productivity improvement movement. One might characterize this path as a path of cooperative Americanization, which was actively supported and led by the United States. The main focus of this movement was the dispatch of observation missions. These observation missions resulted in progress in a wide variety of fields, most prominently in production control. Study tours of model plants within Japan and programmes to exchange information among Japanese companies were also implemented. Acquisition of knowledge, especially in industrial engineering, proceeded further with the dispatch of long-term overseas trainees and observation missions of experts. It should be noted, however, that the rapid pace of Japanese industrial development caused the American hosts to become more cautious in the later periods of these programmes.

The third path to Americanization might be characterized as autonomous Americanization, and proceeded through the acquisition of industrial machinery, electric machinery, chemical and other advanced technologies primarily from the United States by Japanese companies largely on their own initiative. These efforts, however, took place within the regulatory framework of the Japanese government. The electrical machinery industry benefited the most from such technology transfer. In particular, the use of imported technology was critical in the production of television sets, radios, electronic tubes and semiconductors. In the field of semiconductors, Japan had made such progress by the late 1950s that it was already beginning to surpass its teacher, the United States.

Thus, Americanization in postwar Japan was accomplished through a number of different paths. The development of these paths corresponds roughly to the political development of postwar Japan from the Occupation to independence as well as the recovery and subsequent development of the Japanese economy following the war. It is not entirely coincidental that the development of the second and third paths to Americanization, which placed more emphasis on initiative and leadership by the Japanese, took place as Japan regained its independence and direct control of the United States lessened. In each of these paths, the eagerness of the Japanese to learn contributed toward achievement of results far greater than Americans had originally anticipated.

Acknowledgement

The author acknowledges the assistance of Azumi Ann Takata of the University of Michigan in translating and editing this chapter.

Notes

1 Regarding the introduction and diffusion of MTP and TWI, see Japan Business History Research Institute (ed.), *Keiei to rekishi (Management and History)*, 1987, vol. 10.
2 A. Iki, *Shogen sengo nihon no keiei kakushin (Testament on Management Innovation in Postwar Japan)*, Tokyo: Nihon Keizai Shinbun Sha, 1981, pp. 28–31.
3 *Keiei to rekishi*, 1987, p. 18.
4 Nihon Noritsu Kyokai (Japan Management Association) (ed.), *Junenkan no kiseki (Ten Years' Trajectory)*, Tokyo: Nihon Noritsu Kyokai, 1952, p. 56.
5 Nihon Noritsu Kyokai (Japan Management Association) (ed.), *Keiei to tomo ni (Together with Management)*, Tokyo: Nihon Noritsu Kyokai, 1982, p. 55.
6 *Junenkan no kiseki*, pp. 56–57.
7 *Keiei to tomo ni*, pp. 222–223.
8 Ibid., p. 52.
9 *Junenkan no kiseki*, p. 61.
10 Ibid., p. 65.
11 The Japanese Standards Association was an amalgamation of the Standards Section of the Dai-Nippon Aviation Technology Association (established in May 1942 under the supervision of the Institute of Technology) and the Standards Division of the Japan Management Association. The Union of Japanese Scientists and Engineers succeeded the Dai-Nippon Technology Association of the wartime era. This association, in turn, was established in November 1944 from the merger of the Industrial Policy Society (founded in 1918), the Japanese Association for Technology (founded in 1935), and the All Japan Unified Society for Science and Technology (founded in 1940). See chapters by I. Nonaka in T. Hara (ed.), *Kagakuteki kanriho no donyu to tenkai: Sono rekishiteki kokusai hikaku (The Introduction and Diffusion of Scientific Management Methods: An International Historical Comparison)*, Tokyo: Showado, 1990, pp. 268–271. For further details, refer to Nihon Kagaku Gijutsu Renmei (JUSE) (ed.), *50-nen no ayumi (Fifty Year History)*, Tokyo: JUSE, 1996, pp. 61–78.
12 All Japan Federation of Management Organizations (ed.), *Shadan-hojin Zen-Nippon Noritsu Renmei (Zennoren) Goannai (Guide to the All Japan Federation of Management Organizations)*, Tokyo: All Japan Federation of Management Organizations, 1996, p. 2.
13 T. Saito, *Ueno Yoichi: Hito to gyoseki (Yoichi Ueno: The Man and His Achievements)*, Tokyo: Sagyo Noritsu Daigaku, 1983, p. 131.
14 On the process of enacting the Japanese Engineering Standards Law and initial standardization programmes, see material by S. Sasaki in Committee on the Compilation of a History of International Trade and Industrial Policy (ed.), *Tsusho sangyo seisaku shi (A History of International Trade and Industry Policy)*, vol. 7, Tokyo: Tsusho Sangyo Chosa Kai, 1996, pp. 251–277.
15 Information concerning Deming's activities and the Deming Prize are primarily taken from JUSE, *50-nen no ayumi*, pp. 14–16. The winners of the first Deming Application Prize were Showa Denko K.K., Tanabe Seiyaku Co. Ltd., Fuji Steel Co. Ltd., and Yahata Steel Co. Ltd. See Hara, *Kagakuteki kanriho no donyu to tenkai*, p. 272.
16 JUSE, *50-nen no ayumi*, p. 16.

17 Nihon Keieishi Kai (Association of Management Consultants in Japan) (ed.), *Nihon no keiei konsarutanto* (*Japanese Management Consultants*), Tokyo: Nihon Keieishi Kai, 1991, pp. 133–135.
18 On the Association of Management Consultants in Japan see ibid., pp. 1–3 and pp. 25–26. There were fifty names on the membership list of the association at the time of founding, but this figure had reached 3,600 by 1991.
19 S. Sasaki, 'The Emergence of the Productivity Improvement Movement in Postwar Japan and Japanese Productivity Missions Overseas', *Japanese Yearbook on Business History*, 1995, vol. 12.
20 Nihon Seisansei Honbu (Japan Productivity Centre) (ed.), *1955–61-nendo jigyo hokokusho* (*Reports on Activities for Fiscal Years 1955–61*), Tokyo: Nihon Seisansei Honbu, 1955–1962.
21 Nihon Seisansei Honbu (Japan Productivity Centre) (ed.), *1960-nendo jigyo hokokusho* (*Report on Activities for Fiscal Year 1960*), Tokyo: Nihon Seisansei Honbu, 1961.
22 Nihon Seisansei Honbu (Japan Productivity Centre) (ed.), *1961-nendo jigyo hokokusho* (*Report on Activities for Fiscal Year 1961*), Tokyo: Nihon Seisansei Honbu, 1962.
23 Nihon Seisansei Honbu (Japan Productivity Centre) (ed.), *Kaigai shisatsu dantai wa dono yo na seika wo osameta ka* (*What Did the Overseas Observation Missions Accomplish?*), Tokyo: Nihon Seisansei Honbu, 1958.
24 Nihon Seisansei Honbu (Japan Productivity Centre) (ed.), *1957–61-nendo jigyo hokokusho* (*Reports on Activities for Fiscal Years 1957–61*), Tokyo: Nihon Seisansei Honbu, 1958–62.
25 Nihon Seisansei Honbu, *1955–61-nendo jigyo hokokusho*.
26 Class I (Koshu) technical assistance contracts were based on legislation concerning foreign direct investment, with contract duration or payment duration in excess of one year, and payable in foreign currency. In contrast, Class II (Otsushu) technical assistance contracts, which were based in foreign exchange and foreign exchange control legislation, included contracts under one year in duration or contracts of any duration payable in yen. Instances of technology transfer made under Class II technical assistance contracts numbered 1,845 by 1961. See Kagaku Gijutsu Cho (Science and Technology Agency) (ed.), *Showa 37-nendo kagaku gijutsu hakusho* (*1962 White Paper on Science and Technology*), Tokyo: Okurasho Insatsu Kyoku, 1963, p. 39.
27 Ibid., p. 40.
28 Ibid., p. 42.
29 Nihon Seisansei Honbu (Japan Productivity Centre) (ed.), *Dai 4-ji toppu manejimento shisatsu dantai hokoku* (*Report on the Fourth Top Management Observation Mission*), Tokyo: Nihon Seisansei Honbu, 1959, pp. 178–179.

Ibuka also praised Japanese engineering ability, saying, 'putting aside the question of creativity, Japan has developed technical ability to acquire quite sophisticated technology in a short period of time when the technology is well defined in its form. We are fortunate to be so well endowed with engineers of such high ability.' But at the same time, he was also cautious in his appraisal, pointing out that 'the electronics industry in many countries is certainly not asleep, but is constantly struggling to improve the transistor. We should reflect on how Japan has reached the position it currently enjoys, and realize that we must work today to prepare for the future.' Ibid., p. 182.

Ibuka was not the only business leader to foresee the future development of transistor production. Shotaro Kataoka of Kataoka Electric (now Alps Electric), who participated in the electrical communications equipment industry expert observation mission in 1957, later noted that he had gained two important lessons from the mission. The first came from seeing that the American electronic component manufacturers had the strength to sell products that they themselves had designed and manufactured to their assembler customers. This convinced him that it ought to be possible for Japanese component manufacturers to become independent in their operations. The second was to realize the possibility of exporting components, particularly transistors, to the United States, given the projections for expanding demand for transistor radios. See Denshi Kikai Kogyo Kai (Electronic Industries Association of Japan) (ed.), *Denshi kogyo 20-nen shi* (*A 20 Year History of the Electronics Industry*), Tokyo: Denshi Kikai Kogyo Kai, 1968, p. 368. Ibuka's comment on the rapid growth of transistor radio exports, quoted earlier, corroborates Kataoka's latter observation. In terms of the former, a number of component manufacturers who made efforts to develop their own technology eventually managed to establish their autonomy.

30 Ibid., p. 180.
31 Ibid., pp. 180–181.
32 Nihon Denshi Kogyo Shinko Kyokai (Japan Electronic Industry Development Association) (ed.), *Denshi kogyo no choki hatten* (*Long Term Development of the Electronics Industry*), Tokyo: Nihon Denshi Kogyo Shinko Kyokai, 1968, pp. 74–77.
33 A. Hiramoto, *Nihon no terebi sangyo* (*Japan's Television Industry*), Kyoto: Mineruva Shobo, 1994, pp. 23–24. A few of the thirty-seven companies later encountered managerial problems, and the number of companies was subsequently reduced to thirty-five. Ibid., p. 63.
34 Electronic Industries Association of Japan, *Denshi kogyo 20-nen shi*, p. 311.
35 Ibid., p. 301, and Hiramoto, *Nihon no terebi sangyo*, p. 24.

4   Driving the West German consumer society

The introduction of US style production and marketing at Volkswagen, 1945–70

Christian Kleinschmidt

Introduction

In recent years the question of the influence of the USA on German society and the Germany economy in the twentieth century has often been raised.[1] Aspects range from the spread of consumer society[2] to the adaptation of technology or culture,[3] or indeed the adoption of American methods of management and production within German firms.[4] These phenomena are commonly subsumed under the term 'Americanization'. However, this chapter will argue that 'focus on America' or 'the American model' are preferable descriptions to the term 'Americanization'.[5] They focus more strongly on the perspective and the actions of the otherwise commonly neglected protagonists on the German side. Models represent ideal forms and are examples to be followed while never being achieved. Models have a formative influence. Within companies, they provide orientation and a way of projecting a vision as a comprehensive solution to technical and organizational difficulties. They do not define the reorganization in detail but point in the right direction. The targeted ideals do not have to correspond entirely with reality. Models can channel information about which aims are desirable, and which are feasible. Language and metaphors play an important role. Metaphors and the images they create can provoke emotions and associations.[6] 'America' can be understood as one such metaphor. It represents technical progress, rationalization and modernization: a successful economic model.

In the following, the 'American model' will be explored in the case of the most successful postwar German car manufacturer, the state-owned company Volkswagen GmbH (VW). Given the continuity in terms of organization and staff, Volkswagen is the sole German car manufacturer which can illustrate the function of the American model over decades – aside from the subsidiaries of Ford and General Motors (Opel). First, an outline of the American influence on the German car industry in general and the early company years under National Socialism, will provide a backdrop to developments at VW. It will be shown how VW was strongly orientated towards the American model and the Ford River Rouge plant in particular.

On this basis the influence of the American model on two important personalities in the postwar period will then be explored: Heinrich Nordhoff and Carl H. Hahn both had a decisive influence on policy at Volkswagen. It will be illustrated how the American model became manifest in both their ideas and actions. Second, the importance of the American model will be examined in relation to engineering and production methods – in other words, whether the 'vision of a German River Rouge' kindled under National Socialism came to fruition in West Germany after 1945. Third, the methods by which Volkswagen aimed to move towards an American style consumer society will be examined. It will be shown that America not only played a crucial part in the rise of Volkswagen in the 1950s, but can also be linked to the company crisis at the end of the 1960s. Thus the close focus on American developments had a mixed effect and was no guarantee for success.

America and the German car industry before 1945

After the First World War, and perhaps earlier, some branches of German industry followed the strategies of American companies closely: within the car industry this was most certainly the case. While cars were first constructed in Germany, the 'first revolution within the car industry' took place in the USA. Primarily it involved mechanization and the organization of the production process.[7] At the turn of the century the American car industry had still lagged behind European technical standards but already before the outbreak of the First World War the transition had been made from a craft-based work organization to mass production, a division of labour, standardization and scientific management – that is to say a form of production associated with Ford's Model T.[8]

In contrast, the German car industry needed a further 20 years to complete this transition. The late transition to mass production and the delay in mass motorization was mainly due to Germany's underdeveloped domestic market and lower consumer spending power. Amongst those companies following the American model, Opel was an exceptional example. A leading German car producer, it was taken over by General Motors at the end of the 1920s. Nevertheless, aside from those companies following 'American principles', numerous German firms such as Daimler-Benz, Horch, Adler, Brennabor, Dürrkopp, Stoever or Wanderer remained faithful to 'German principles'. The specialized mass production of only a limited range of models was rejected in favour of the small series production. This had been merely the first step towards mechanization at Opel before the First World War. During the 1920s, Opel was the first German company to introduce assembly line production.[9]

Despite the attempts of some German car producers to catch up during the 1920s, American companies retained their leading international position. America in general, and Henry Ford in particular, were examples to be upheld, not only in the opinion of German entrepreneurs but also in the eyes of numerous trade unionists. Indeed, the latters' visits to American car producers during the Weimar Republic seem to have taken the form of pilgrimage.[10] What they saw was the transition of the car to a mass consumer good. In a country of huge distances, with a low population density and small railway network, the car swiftly became produced for farmers, businessmen and self-employed. Low costs for fuel and car maintenance, the construction of long-distance roads and motoring infrastructure allowed the USA to become a one-market economy. Here the car was 'the last element which had been missing after the railway boom. Now a big domestic market could be created which made the USA the most important international economic power in the first quarter of the 20th century.'[11] By the 1920s German companies had identified this potential not only in the car industry, but in the consumer market in general as a model to be emulated.

After 1925 opportunities to expand the car market increased in Germany too. Falling car prices opened up new markets and drew in new consumer groups, and the development appeared comparable to the American experience. Overall however great differences in infrastructure remained. The low car density made the German market attractive for American investors. Between 1926 and 1928 eight American car manufacturers set up assembly works in Germany. In 1929 General Motors acquired Opel and between 1929 and 1931 Ford set up a new plant in Cologne. German companies responded to this 'American threat' with rationalization programmes and mergers, in effect emulating the American model. In 1926 the merger between Daimler and Benz followed the example of General Motors. After the Great Depression the German car manufacturers Audi, Hoch, DKW and Wanderer merged into the Auto-Union.[12]

The National Socialists also picked up on American models of production and consumerism in relation to the car industry. In order to strengthen buying power they introduced tax exemptions for cars and motorbikes and expanded the motoring infrastructure. Another notable impulse given to the promotion of mass motorization in Germany was the planning and construction of a VW plant near Fallersleben. Despite the new political situation, America was still an important point of reference. Quite in the sense of 'reactionary modernism',[13] the ambitious National Socialist project to achieve mass production also followed newest American technological developments. Even the construction of the factory buildings was carried out along American lines, being based on the Ford plant in River Rouge. The relevant ground plans were sketched out by American experts who had 'defected' from the USA. The same was true of the plans for other parts of the plant, such as for the press shop, bodywork and mechanical workshops, and even those for the blast furnace itself, steel production, and the rubber and glass factory. American developments even dominated plans on both the automation of production and material flow and the design of social facilities.[14]

As one of Henry Ford's greatest admirers, Hitler believed that the construction of the VW plant would overcome the technological gap between the USA and Germany. However, at the end of the 1930s these plans had already been substantially modified, while during the war it became apparent that the machinery set up for peacetime production was unsuitable for the conversion demanded by war. As a result, the volume of car production did not meet initial expectations.[15] Only 630 vehicles for civilian use were produced between 1940 and 1945 and the production of vehicles for military use failed to meet original plans. Nevertheless, while the dream of a 'German River Rouge' was only partially realized under National Socialism,[16] America remained a fixed point of reference at Volkswagen after 1945.

Volkswagen and the American model after 1945

As the outline of developments prior to the end of the Second World War has shown America represented a 'reference society'[17] for the German car industry in general and for Volkswagen in particular. This focus remained despite the political changes under the Weimar Republic, National Socialism and the setting up of the Federal Republic. Immediately after the war the most urgent necessity for the company was its survival. Between 1945 and the currency reform in 1948 Volkswagen was faced with numerous problems, ranging from the threat of dismantlement, the insufficient provision of raw materials to the high fluctuation and absentee rate in the workforce. In terms of survival, production for the British occupying force was of fundamental importance. Business with major clients – the postal system, the national railways and the coal mining industry – then gave Volkswagen a decisive initial advantage against its competitors.[18]

Over and above these factors it was the continuity in following American developments which was conducive to Volkswagen's postwar success, as illustrated by the role played by Heinrich Nordhoff (who came to Volkswagen from General Motors and Opel) and Carl H. Hahn, who, working with him, was an up-and-coming Volkswagen manager (who also spent an intermediate period at Continental). This constellation also reveals how business attitudes were passed on from one generation to the next. Moreover, it shows how the rapid spread of American management methods within German industry was not only based on the vertical lines of information within one company, but also on the horizontal transfer of know-how between different businesses. What Heinrich Nordhoff and Carl H. Hahn achieved at Volkswagen between the end of the 1940s and

1960s in terms of management innovation was substantially based on the American model: above all it involved a push towards a stronger focus on the market to achieve necessary sales, in other words sales, marketing and advertising strategies.

The protagonists: Heinrich Nordhoff and Carl H. Hahn

Heinrich Nordhoff was born in 1899 as the son of a bank clerk. He studied naval and mechanical engineering at the Institute of Technology in Charlottenburg before starting work as a constructor of aeroplane engines at BMW. It was Georg Schlesinger's lectures that first introduced Nordhoff to the methods involved in American mass production and large-scale series production. Initially Nordhoff's hopes of working for an American car producer were thwarted when in 1929 Nash-Motors rejected his application. Turning to the idea of at least working for an American company even at a German location, he finally started work in Opel's customer service department in Rüsselheim. On several occasions he visited General Motors, Opel's parent company, in the USA in order to learn about American methods of sales and production. He represented Opel's interests in the project on the construction of a German 'people's car' ('Volkswagen') before transferring to the Opel plant in Brandenburg. Here, production of the Opel 'Blitz' was being carried out on American lines in one of the most modern truck production plants in the world. In 1942 and as head of the Opel plant in Brandenburg, Nordhoff joined the board of the Adam Opel AG, which was once more an entirely German company. After the war, this step in his career was to cause problems. The US military government blocked Nordhoff's return to Opel after the company's reintegration into the American firm. Despite being cleared by the denazification committee and several statements in his defence, including one from General Motors' vice president, he was regarded as a leading figure of the wartime economy.

While Nordhoff's hopes of being employed by an American car producer were thwarted for a second time, his experience of America and his intense interest in American developments remained. These were to be of great advantage while working for his next employer, Volkswagenwerk. At the suggestion of the British Control Commission he took on the post of general manager on 1 January 1948. Around the same time the decision was made to continue Volkswagen as an independent German company and not, as had been planned, as a subsidiary of General Motors or Ford. In March 1948 Nordhoff had met up with Henry Ford in order to discuss the possibility of a Ford takeover, but these discussions were blocked by the veto of the Allied Property Control Branch.[19] The year 1948 was significant for Volkswagen, not only because the independence of the company was maintained, but also because currency reform provided an important basis for future economic success.[20]

In Nordhoff's opinion the currency reform was one of the most important factors behind Volkswagen's rise. While the need for mobility was
large, the demand for cars and consequent investment opportunities
required foreign exchange. As a result Volkswagen remained closely
linked to the American economy. In order to secure foreign currency,
more cars had to be sold than was possible in the comparatively weak
German market. Nordhoff identified the USA as a potential outlet. Travel-
ling to the USA as one of the first German managers in 1948, he aimed to
assess the market for the export of Volkswagen cars. In addition he aimed
to buy the technological know-how Volkswagen needed in order to
reduce, if not eliminate, the gap between the German and American car
industries.

Thus, at Volkswagen Heinrich Nordhoff had a decisive influence on
postwar developments and represented the continuity of the American
model within the German car industry after 1945. While he had not previously belonged to Volkswagen, he brought a wealth of experience which
he had gained at General Motors and Opel. As a follower of Henry Ford
and his one product strategy, he worked on product and sale strategies at
Volkswagen until he retired in the 1960s.

Carl H. Hahn was the son of the co-founder of the Auto-Union of the
same name (Carl Hahn). In the early 1950s he started working for one
importer of the American car producers, Nash, and was then a trainee at
Fiat in Turin, during which he gained first-hand experience of American
methods of production and management. In 1953 he worked for the
European Productivity Agency (EPA) in Paris for a short time. Amongst
other activities, he made American contacts for European companies. A
year later Hahn joined Volkswagen as Nordhoff's young assistant and
within 4 years he had become head of Volkswagen of America (VWoA).

The combination of his knowledge and experience of America with
high adaptability soon made him 'even more American than a lot of his
American staff'.[21] Hahn learnt English quickly, was interested in marketing and the introduction of computers, and paid great attention to advertising, working together with Helmut Schmitz, his advertising assistant
whom he had brought over from Germany. Although Hahn also assumed
that Volkswagen would sell well in the USA even without advertising,
stronger American competition within the American small car market was
clearly looming. The first American small car came on the market in 1959.
In response VWoA immediately set up an advertising committee. At the
same time Hahn got into contact with Doyle Dane Bernbach (DDB), a
young American advertising agency, which had gained a reputation for its
use of humour and originality. Within German businesses at the end of
the 1950s, such a move was still extremely unusual. In employing a professional agency Hahn again adopted American practice.

Thus, while Nordhoff had focused on US production, technology and
customer service, Hahn took on board other elements of the American

model, namely in advertising and more generally, marketing. This was partially due to their differences in background and age, but also a result of the changing environment of the company. While Nordhoff had to deal with reconstruction and initial expansion in a sellers' market, Hahn was faced with growing competition, both at home and abroad.

The model I: production and technology

By May/June 1945, production at Volkswagen was already back in operation. By the end of the year the company had manufactured 1,785 vehicles for the Allied occupation forces and for the postal service. In 1946 production increased to roughly 10,000 vehicles, but in the early 1950s materials flow was still subject to bottlenecks which prevented further expansion. Severe shortages hit the supply of raw materials, bodywork panels and machine tools. The technological superiority of the American car industry was largely based on the USA's leading role in the machine tool market. Top management at Volkswagen thus had two reasons for being interested in importing American machine tools. Aside from reviving production itself, there was the aim of regaining international standing. The import of American machine tools was partly organized as Marshall Plan Aid. The specialist department for iron and metalworking under the Economic Administrative Office informed the Volkswagen plant in the spring and summer of 1949 that it would be allocated 724,000 dollars in two instalments for the import of American machine tools.[22]

In the meantime, in 1948, Heinrich Nordhoff had travelled to the USA for the first time since the Second World War. He was now especially interested in the acquisition of American machine tools. At the same time he examined the possibility of Volkswagen sales on the American market. In conjunction with the forecasted expansion of the German domestic market, he believed this factor would be decisive for Volkswagen's recovery. 1948 was also the year Nordhoff came into office and the year of the currency reform; the latter was of fundamental importance. While the demand for cars increased rapidly, the lack of foreign currency was an obstacle to carrying though necessary investment programmes. Thus the reasons for working closely with the USA were manifold. The accumulation of foreign exchange – dollars – was the immediate necessity. While expansion of the German domestic market was slow so long as mass consumer power was underdeveloped, Nordhoff looked to the USA as a possible sales market for Volkswagen.[23]

In the following years these contacts with America were intensified. Volkswagen's technical reorganization had much of the characteristics of a 'systematic technological transfer' from the USA.[24] In 1952 a research group for hardening technology visited over twenty American companies and research institutes in Volkswagen's name, bringing numerous suggestions back home. Whilst visiting various American plants Volkswagen managers showed interest in machining operations, automatic transport mechanisms and press shops: at the machine tool exhibition in Chicago they examined foundry techniques for crankshafts. Further trips to America in the mid-1950s and 1960s accelerated the introduction of mass production and continuous operations, replacing the single-item production which still dominated a production technology far removed from American standards. Finally, American specialists and special purpose machines were also involved in improving the automation in the press shop, work flow in the paint shop, the hardening and plating shop and in bodywork construction. The 5-year report for 1951–55 could thus conclude that the increase in car production was, in international terms, only surpassed by the USA.[25]

The postwar technical reorganization, automation and introduction of 'Fordist mass production' in the mid-1950s made a modification of work organization necessary.[26] Again Volkswagen followed the American model. The core departments within production dealt with chassis, bodywork and maintenance. Whilst introducing this reorganization, managers at Volkswagen referred to insights gained in the USA.[27] Unlike many American car manufacturers, however, Volkswagen did not adopt the American model in its entirety. Neither primary production stages involving raw materials, nor the supply of intermediate products, were drawn into the production process: cost advantages and difficulties were not expected. So already at this point it became clear that the Volkswagen factory did not reach the depth of production common to its American counterparts after the Second World War. It was not a German 'River Rouge' despite the strong influence of the American model and American style factory practice on the reorganization of production.[28]

Indeed, one of the secrets behind Volkswagen's success was the selective approach towards the American model. As Heinrich Nordhoff declared on a trip to the USA in 1962 on the occasion of the production of the millionth Volkswagen: 'One of the rules of the Volkswagen organization is that wherever we go, when we find a technique that is good, we adopt it.'[29] This strategy was so successful in relation to the USA that by the mid-1960s Nordhoff could proclaim that production technology at Volkswagen was 'right on the same level as American car manufacturers.'[30] During this period Volkswagen then started to put their own highly mechanized transfer lines for bodywork construction into operation and was thus able to loosen up the rather too close orientation towards American developments.

During the 1970s a similar development can be seen relating to the use of robots at Volkswagen. The development of industrial robots began in the mid-1960s in the USA. General Motors played a leading part here. In 1950 robots of the brand 'Unimate' were used in a welding transfer line. One year later a Unimate robot had already been tested for the spot welding of body shells at Volkswagen. Basically it was thought at Volkswagen that the use of robots would provide the solution to the need for increased flexibility demanded by more frequent modifications to existing models.[31] Dissatisfied with the pace of change, Volkswagen decided in 1972 to work on the development of robot technology itself. By the mid-1970s, nineteen industrial robots had already been developed which were used in spot welding, in the press shop, in the foundry and in body shell construction. By 1979/80 the use of robots had increased to 240 units. Now Volkswagen had become a leader in process technology in the car industry.[32]

Volkswagen continued with this approach to automation across all production areas and the use of modern information control systems throughout the 1970s, thus remaining caught by the 'old logic of Fordist rationalization' and omitting to carry out the necessary structural changes. These were postponed until the 1980s and 1990s following the impact of Japanese success. The new strategies focused on the comprehensive qualification of employees, the cutting down of hierarchies, group work and Japanese models of lean production, quality circles and the just-in-time principle.[33]

The model II: marketing and advertising

Next to technical know-how and production, the question of sales and marketing techniques was the other main issue in Volkswagen's postwar recovery. Again Heinrich Nordhoff's American know-how provided the fundamental impetus.

Marketing and advertising are the classic areas in which German companies followed the American example.[34] American efforts within the US Technical Assistance and Productivity Program (UST&P) under the Marshall Plan had already had an influence.[35] In the early 1950s a substantial number of businessmen travelled to the USA, assisted by the Mutual Security Agency (MSA) and the Foreign Administration Organization (FOA), and by the Rationalization Council for the German Economy (Rationalisierungskuratorium der deutschen Wirtschaft, RKW). There they hoped to get to know the latest methods in marketing and advertising. At a German-American conference on the 'new direction in sales', Curt Becker from the national federation of industry (Bundesverband der Deutschen Industrie, BDI) commented on the deficits in German business' sales practice: 'Given our fundamental interest in all technological change, we keep expecting to achieve industrial progress solely through the modernization of technical operations.' But in line with American developments, the aspects of consumer demand, sales and marketing needed far greater attention within German industry: 'Basic industry is not the key. The consumer holds the key to the economy. The success of the American economy is based on this conviction.'[36]

During this period those German corporate strategies which focused on markets and sales varied greatly in character. While it was often noted that conditions were changing in the early 1950s as the consumer took over the sellers' market, branches and individual companies reacted differently to the challenge. Even within single companies the assessment of sales, marketing, advertising and consumer questions could vary. In the mid-1960s marketing and advertising were still only of secondary interest within heavy industry. By contrast, top management paid far greater attention to marketing in the chemical and artificial fibre industries, as illustrated by Hüls and Glanzstoff in the mid-1950s. At Volkswagen intensive efforts to develop a long-term sales policy were made already at the end of the 1940s. The car industry seemed to be more than suited to play a leading role in the establishment of a West German consumer society. The car turned into a symbol of wealth and of national recovery. The Volkswagen ideal of the early 1930s to create a car for everyman had been interrupted by National Socialism. Now it could become reality.[37] In order to achieve this aim, customers and consumers had to be won over quickly.

Noting competition with Opel, Karl Feuereissen, head of customer services, took up plans to expand his department and establish regular market analysis as early as 1946/47.[38] Given that Nordhoff's earlier work at General Motors and Opel had involved questions of sales and customer service, it is no surprise that he continued this policy at Volkswagen. At the same time he was well aware of the fact that the American sales market would be of great importance to Volkswagen during the following decade and that the American experience would be relevant to the situation in Germany.

Initially the currency reform of 1948 boosted Volkswagen's expansion and in the early 1950s the annual growth rate remained at around 25 per cent. Despite these positive signs, it was clear that the company had to anticipate future change and especially the expectation that 'Volkswagen will also no longer simply have something to distribute, but will have to sell'.[39] Both Feuereissen and Nordhoff were convinced of the necessity of an early expansion of comprehensive sales and customer services. In 1947 Volkswagen's sales organization incorporated only 10 central distributors, 14 dealers and not a single authorized repair shop. Two years later it already had 16 central agencies, 31 wholesalers, 103 dealers and 84 authorized repair shops. By the mid-1960s this network included over 2,000 authorized repair shops.[40] At the same time Feuereissen and Nordhoff placed a great emphasis on the expansion of a broad customer service. American developments were again the point of reference. As was explained in 1955: 'We are convinced that this development will not remain limited to the USA, but that it will one day reach Europe. We want to be ready in time; this is why we're working on increasing production and creating a strong sales and customer service organization not only at home but also abroad.'[41]

While Nordhoff concentrated on expanding customer services, advert-

ising continued to be limited. He believed that satisfied customers were
the best advertisement Volkswagen could have, so that big advertising
campaigns were unnecessary.[42] Volkswagen's ambitions for the American
market were to prove that the opposite was the case. The introduction of
the VW van to the American market was slow, and measures needed to be
taken to increase sales. New corporate strategies are often linked to
particular individuals. At Volkswagen, Carl H. Hahn was behind the
launch of a new advertising offensive in the mid-1950s. However, although
it was an everyday occurrence in the USA, this did not mean that top management in Germany automatically accepted this move. At headquarters
in Wolfsburg the question was asked why VW had to spend so much
money on advertising, which, for example, involved just a large white
poster and a caption saying 'We won't have anything to show You in our
new models'.

In Wolfsburg, acceptance of the quality of American advertising and
the adoption of these methods developed only slowly. Doyle Dane Bernbach (DDB), with whom Carl H. Hahn had made contact in the 1950s,
opened a branch in Düsseldorf in 1961 as the base for its advertising campaign in Germany. DDB's American strategies were not simply copied, but
the form, picture composition, typology and humour were adapted to
Germany. One of the best known examples is the slogan '... und läuft,
und läuft, und läuft ...', which translates roughly as 'it goes on and on
and on ...'.[43] The name 'Beetle' ('Käfer' in German), later known all over
the world, made its first appearance in an advertisement. The case of VW
and DDB illustrates just how strong the American influence on German
companies' advertising strategies was. The use of slang and humour had
been previously unknown in the rather conservative form usual to
German advertising. Indeed, in Carl Hahn's opinion, Volkswagen first
'learnt' all about advertising and marketing in the USA.[44] Such a transfer
was dependent on individuals such as Hahn having an open mind and
being prepared to defend new methods in the face of initial opposition
such as in Wolfsburg.

The first TV advertising for VW was broadcast in 1960 and advertisements were also placed in various magazine and TV guides. These were
accompanied by PR-measures, such as an open day, advertising films or
road safety films for school children. Advertising, sales promotion and customer service were thus integral to VW's 'marketing' strategy, known as
such in the mid-1960s. Standardized marketing plans were developed
which laid down which measures should be employed to reach the set
sales goals. Advertising was standardized on an international scale and a
global 'corporate image' was developed to guarantee VW and its organization a modern image throughout the world.[45]

Carl H. Hahn's role in all these areas was substantial. During the 1950s
and 1960s Hahn and Nordhoff each had, in their own way, a decisive
'Americanizing' influence on VW's corporate strategy. While Nordhoff,

who lacked a feel for advertising, concentrated on the area of sales and customer service, Hahn focused on this area in particular, having gained crucial experience at VWoA. These complementary strategies are an expression not only of co-operation, but also of a corporate learning process which bridged the generational gap. This double-edged strategy with Nordhoff-Hahn on the one side and involvement with the German and American market on the other came off at the end of the 1960s. 'The United States is of tremendous importance to us in Wolfsburg', Nordhoff had commented in the early 1960s while talking to staff at VwoA:

> Twenty per cent of our total production is shipped to the United States. One day every week our employees go to work for America. . . . I hope, all of you are grateful to those workers in Wolfsburg who are making it possible for you to have such a company as this. . . . Together we are strong and together we have a great future.[46]

The result: rebirth and death of the Beetle

At first Nordhoff's strategy seemed to be vindicated by success. Volkswagen did play a fundamental role in the motorization of West Germany, in other words in economic growth and in the expansion of a consumer society. While in the early 1950s the car industry represented 1.7 per cent of GNP (1952), it had reached 8.9 per cent by the end of the 1960s (1968). Productivity in the German car industry reached annual growth rates of 9.4 per cent between 1953 and 1962. This was twice as high as the rate of overall economic productivity which, at the time, grew at an annual rate of roughly 5 per cent. With wages rising in real terms, the demand for cars continued to rise steadily within West Germany. In the early 1950s, the first step towards motorization often still involved the purchase of a motorbike, but by the mid-1950s the car had been transformed from a luxury article to a utility good.[47] The significance of the car developed from being 'a businessman's car to being the private car regardless of class, for driving to work or for a family day out.'[48] The number of new registrations exploded between 1951 and 1963, from 178,330 vehicles to 1,271,000 – seven times as many. Unlike under National Socialism, the Volkswagen vehicle now was certainly a 'Volks-Wagen', a car for everyman. During the 1950s, Volkswagen continuously represented more than 30 per cent of the West German car market (Table 4.1).[49]

A further explanation for Volkswagen's success is to be found in the American market. As Table 4.2 illustrates, the figures of VW exports to the USA seem to tell 'a story about a country of unbounded possibilities'.[50] While in 1950 the company had exported only 328 vehicles to the USA, by the mid-1950s exports increased to over 30,000 vehicles and by the early 1960s over 200,000 had been delivered. In 1950 only 1 per cent of Volkswagen's exports were allocated to the USA; by 1962 it was 31 per cent

Table 4.1 The West German automobile market in the 1950s

	1951	*1953*	*1955*	*1957*	*1959*
Volkswagen	33.7	39.3	34.0	31.0	30.2
Opel	16.7	19.1	16.9	18.1	16.9
Ford	10.1	8.3	6.9	7.8	9.1
Daimler-Benz	15.9	9.4	8.3	7.4	6.5
Autounion	7.4	7.7	6.1	4.8	4.8

Source: Wellhöner, *Wirtschaftswunder*, p. 74.

which represented 21 per cent of VW's domestic production. Twenty-five per cent of Beetle production alone went to the USA. Its market share expanded consistently within a few years from 1.7 per cent (1958) to 3.0 per cent (1961).[51]

The success of Beetle sales on the American market had been based on the idea of establishing a small car for the 'two-car household'. At the same time the VWoA's extremely successful advertising and marketing strategy also had a vital part to play. The favourable exchange rate between the dollar and the DM provided another strong argument. Success was possible on the basis of a reorganized production process: here again American developments in automation and assembly line production were pioneering.[52] New methods of production and marketing were interlinked and guaranteed success on both the American and the German market.

The export figures give an indication of how large a part the American market played in Volkswagens' postwar success. Indeed, not only the rise

Table 4.2 VW exports into the USA

	Cars	*Vans*	*Share of cars in %*	*Growth of US exports in %*
1950	328	2	99	
1951	367	50	88	26
1952	887	93	91	135
1953	1,139	75	94	24
1954	8,068	827	91	633
1955	32,662	3,189	91	303
1956	45,614	7,375	86	48
1957	55,802	19,118	74	41
1958	61,623	25,036	71	16
1959	99,862	32,133	76	52
1960	131,194	35,697	79	26
1961	163,056	22,754	88	11
1962	200,857	32,514	86	26

Source: Wellhöner, *Wirtschaftswunder*, p. 218.

but also the fall of the Beetle was linked to developments on the American market – at a time when questions of safety became dominant. In the early 1960s the USA had a pioneering role in questions of driving safety and accident research. All German producers aiming to export to the USA had to fulfil these high US standards. Despite Nordhoff's attempts to continually improve the Beetle and to thus avoid Henry Ford's mistakes, sales started to suffer towards the end of the 1960s. In addition to the pressure created by new American safety standards, new exhaust emission standards and stipulations on the size of indicators, rear lights and windscreen design exacerbated the problem. While Volkswagen reacted to these American regulations by launching a new model, the 'Super Beetle', in 1973, the costs were so high that, as a VWoA board member commented, they in fact signalled the 'death of the Beetle'.[53] Macro-economic factors, such as the US government's decision to float the dollar, also played a part in the decrease in sales. The Deutschmark's increase in value further worsened Volkswagen's export hopes.

At home too, VW's share in new car registrations fell from 32.5 per cent in 1965 to 19 per cent in 1973. Both the 'one-product-strategy' which was based on the Beetle and a centralized corporate organization so successful in Nordhoff's day proved to be a handicap in changing conditions. On Nordhoff's retirement in 1968, the company faced new challenges which could only be met by new, more open and more flexible mechanisms. In 1972 Carl H. Hahn left the company for the Continental AG which was suffering a similar crisis, but he returned 10 years later to Volkswagen as the chairman of the board. In the meantime the world market had fundamentally changed. The Americans had been overtaken not only in the car industry but also in tire production. The 'American challenge' had been superseded by the 'Japanese challenge'. In the 1980s and 1990s, German companies increasingly started to focus on Japan and no longer on the USA.

Conclusion and outlook

The American car industry was a world leader and as such it was the model which was followed by the German car industry after 1920. Under National Socialism and in the sense of a 'reactionary modernism' (Jeffrey Herf) Volkswagen planned a 'German River Rouge'. Not only the planning itself, but construction and the technical standard of plant equipment were designed accordingly. A 'one-product-strategy' was adopted and adhered to successfully until the end of the 1960s. After 1945 the focus on America was maintained, embodied in the figures of Heinrich Nordhoff and Carl H. Hahn. It now included marketing, sales and advertising.

After the Second World War Volkswagen followed American developments in production and engineering – Fordist mass production, assembly line production and automation – while specific know-how, as in the form of machine tools and industrial robots for example, was adopted. Unlike some American car manufacturers, however, VW did not set about integrating primary production stages or raw materials flow. Thus, the description 'German River Rouge' does not really fit for the period after the Second World War either.

Close observation of American technological achievements was accompanied by a strong focus on the American experience of a consumer society. This was reflected not only in the adaptation of American advertising and marketing strategies but also in Beetle sales on the US market. These strategies were not a reflection of a comprehensive Americanization pushed through from the American side, but were primarily based on a selective approach on the German side. Such a US orientation depended on the actions of individuals within their own company organization: it was a source of both great opportunity and great risk.

On the basis of their own personal experience of America, Heinrich Nordhoff and Carl H. Hahn were convinced that conquering the American market was paramount to their company's success. Indeed, until the late 1960s Nordhoff's and Hahn's strategy of concentrating on the Beetle both in Germany and the USA was vindicated by events. However, developments on the American market then, in turn, heralded the 'death of the Beetle' in Germany too. The 'one-product-strategy' was no longer tenable. Finally the 1970s saw the decline of the American car industry and the consequent loss of its exemplary role. In the early 1980s and 1990s the eyes of German car producers were increasingly to turn to Japan.

Acknowledgements

This chapter was written as part of a project financed by the Volkswagen foundation on the possibilities and limits of inter-cultural understanding (Das Fremde und das Eigene – Möglichkeiten und Grenzen des interkulturellen Verstehens) and was translated by Kirsten Petrak. See C. Kleinschmidt, *Der produktive Blick. Wahrnehmung amerikanischer und japanischer Management- und Produktionsmethoden durch deutsche Unternehmer 1950–1985*, Berlin, Akademie, 2002. Special thanks to the organizers of the 'Third Japanese-German Business History Conference' in Tokyo, especially Akira Kudo, Harm Schröter and Matthias Kipping for their comments on this chapter.

Notes

1 For a summary of publications see P. Gassert, 'Amerikanismus, Antiamerikanismus, Amerikanisierung', *Archiv für Sozialgeschichte*, 1999, vol. 39, pp. 531–561.
2 W. König, *Geschichte der Konsumgesellschaft*, Stuttgart: Franz Steiner, 2000.

3 M. Wala and U. Lehmkuhl (eds), *Technologie und Kultur. Europas Blick auf Amerika vom 18. bis zum 20. Jahrhundert*, Köln: Böhlau, 2000.
4 C. Kleinschmidt, *Der produktive Blick. Wahrnehmung amerikanischer und japanischer management- und Produktionsmethoden durch deutsche Unternehmer 1950–1985*, Berlin: Akademie, 2002.
5 On the term 'Americanization' see the introduction to this volume by Kudo, Kipping and Schröter, and my comments in Chapter 8 on the West German fibre and rubber industry.
6 M. Dierkes, U. Hoffmann and L. Marz, *Leitbild und Technik. Zur Entstehung der Steuerung technischer Innovationen*, Berlin: Sigma, 1992, pp. 16, 42; A. Kieser, 'Über die alltägliche Verfertigung der Organisation beim Reden. Organisieren als Kommunizieren', *Industrielle Beziehungen*, 1998, no. 1, pp. 57–59.
7 M. Stahlmann, *Die erste Revolution in der Automobilindustrie. Management und Arbeitspolitik von 1900–1940*, Frankfurt: Campus, 1993.
8 Ibid., pp. 22, 30; more recently R. Flik, *Von Ford lernen? Automobilbau und Motorisierung in Deutschland bis 1933*, Köln: Böhlau, 2001.
9 A. Kugler, 'Von der Werkstatt zum Fließband. Etappen der frühen Automobilproduktion in Deutschland', *Geschichte und Gesellschaft*, 1987, vol. 13, pp. 304–339; Stahlmann, *Die erste Revolution in der Automobilindustrie*, p. 71.
10 H. Edelmann, *Vom Luxusgut zum Gebrauchsgegenstand. Die Geschichte der Verbreitung von Personenkraftwagen in Deutschland*, Frankfurt: VDA, 1989, p. 69.
11 R. Flik, 'Automobilindustrie und Motorisierung in Deutschland bis 1939', in Rudolf Boch (ed.), *Geschichte und Zukunft der deutschen Automobilindustrie*, Stuttgart: Franz Steiner, 2001, p. 64.
12 Ibid., pp. 75, 78; Flik, *Von Ford lernen?*, pp. 191–236.
13 J. Herf, *Reactionary Modernism: Technology, Culture, and Politics in Weimar and the Third Reich*, Cambridge: Cambridge University Press, 1984.
14 H. Mommsen and M. Grieger, *Das Volkswagenwerk und seine Arbeiter im Dritten Reich*, Düsseldorf: Econ, 1996, p. 250; Flik, 'Automobilindustrie und Motorisierung', p. 80.
15 Mommsen and Grieger, *Das Volkswagenwerk*, pp. 285, 322.
16 M. Grieger, 'River Rouge am Mittelkanal. Das Volkswagenwerk während des Nationalsozialismus', in *Zukunft aus Amerika. Fordismus in der Zwischenkriegszeit*, ed. by Stiftung Bauhaus Dessau and RWTH Aachen, Dessau, 1995, pp. 162–173.
17 M.F. Guillen, *Models of Management. Work, Authority and Organization in a Comparative Perspective*, Chicago: The University of Chicago Press, 1994, p. 290.
18 M. Lupa, *Das Werk der Briten. Volkswagenwerk und Besatzungsmacht 1945–1949* (Historische Notate. Schriftenreihe des Unternehmensarchivs der Volkswagen AG, no. 2), Wolfburg, 1999, pp. 8–10, 88, 89.
19 Ibid., p. 79.
20 H. Edelmann 'Heinrich Nordhoff: Ein deutscher Manager in der Automobilindustrie' in P. Erker and T. Pierenkemper (eds), *Deutsche Unternehmer zwischen Kriegswirtschaft und Wiederaufbau. Studien zur Erfahrungsbildung von Industrie Eliten*, München: Oldenburg, 1999, pp. 19–52; L.-U. Kubisch, 'Ohne Blitz kein "Blitzkrieg". Heinrich Nordhoff und seine Karriere vom Opel-Rüstungsmanager zum Wolfsburger Käfer-König', in *Ich diente nur der Technik. Sieben Karrieren zwischen 1940 und 1950*, Berlin: Nicolai, 1995, pp. 41–52; V. Wellhöner, *'Wirtschaftswunder', Weltmarkt, Westdeutscher Fordismus. Der Fall Volkswagen*, Münster: Westfälisches Dampfboot, 1996, p. 104; S. Tolliday, 'Enterprise and State in West-German Wirtschaftswunder: Volkswagen and the Automobile Industry, 1939–1962', *Business History Review*, Autumn 1995, vol. 69, pp. 291, 298, 308; Mommsen and Grieger, *Das Volkswagenwerk*, p. 978.

21 A. Railton, *Der Käfer. Der ungewöhnliche Weg eines ungewöhnlichen Automobils*, Pfäffikon: Eurotax, 1985, p. 167.
22 Wellhöner, 'Wirtschaftswunder', pp. 164, 165. Due to the changes in dollar parity, which took place in the meantime, the sum was reduced to about DM300,000.
23 Railton, *Der Käfer*, p. 133.
24 Wellhöner, 'Wirtschaftswunder', p. 105.
25 Archiv Volkswagen AG, *Volkswagen GmbH Fünfjahresbericht 1951–1955*, p. 3; Wellhöner, 'Wirtschaftwunder', pp. 109–114, 126, 127.
26 Ibid., p. 69.
27 Ibid., pp. 117–119.
28 Ibid., p. 122.
29 Archiv Volkswagen AG, USA-Reise Nordhoff 1962, Remarks by Prof. Nordhoff to the Dealers Advisory Council, 19 October 1962.
30 Wellhöner, 'Wirtschaftswunder', p. 128, see also p. 122 ff.; Archiv Volkswagen AG, *Volkswagen GmbH Fünfjahresbericht 1951–1955*, p. 3.
31 H.-J. Warnecke and R.D. Schraft, *Industrieroboter*, 2nd edn, Mainz: Krausskopf, 1979; O. Mickler *et al.*, *Bedingungen und soziale Folgen des Einsatzes von Industrierobotern. Sozialwissenschaftliche Begleitforschung zum Projekt der Volkswagen AG, Wolfsburg: Neue Handlungssysteme als technische Hilfen für den Arbeitsprozeß*, March 1980, p. 134 ff.
32 Ibid., pp. 145–146, 169 ff.
33 Th. Haipeter, *Vom Fordismus zum Postfordismus? Über den Wandel des Produktionssystems bei Volkswagen seit den siebziger Jahren*, in Boch, *Geschichte und Zukunft*, p. 227.
34 See Chapter 12 by H. Schröter in this volume.
35 See my Chapter 8 on the German chemical and rubber industry and Chapter 2 by M. Kipping in this volume.
36 C. Becker, *Absatzwirtschaft. Betriebsführung auf neuen Wegen. Gespräche in Baden-Baden und Bad Neuenahr*, München: Hanser, 1955, pp. 119, 128.
37 N. Stieniczka, 'Vom fahrbaren Untersatz zur Chromkarosse mit "innerer Sicherheit" – der Wandel der Nutzeranforderungen an das Automobil in den 50er und 60er Jahren', in Boch, *Geschichte und Zukunft*, p. 181.
38 Lupa, *Das Werk der Briten*, p. 54.
39 Archiv Volkswagen AG, *Volkswagen-Informationsdienst Nr. 7*, 16 December 1949 and 1 September 1949.
40 Archiv Volkswagen AG, 'Kundendienst/Verkauf', speech by Dr. Feuereissen/VW-Verkaufsleiter.
41 K. Feuereissen, 'Wir freuen uns über den guten Geist, der jeden einzelnen und alle gemeinsam beherrscht', *Volkswagen-Information Nr. 21*, February 1955, p. 27.
42 Railton, *Der Käfer*, p. 138.
43 Ibid., p. 170 ff.
44 Interview with Carl H. Hahn on 20 February 1998.
45 'Modernes und neues Auftreten des … VW-Konzerns und seiner Organisationen in der ganzen Welt', Archiv Volkswagen AG, *Jahresberichte Verkauf und Kundendienst. Jahresbericht 1960*, pp. 38, 44; *Jahresbericht 1962*, p. 18; *Jahresbericht 1966 und 1968*.
46 Archiv Volkswagen AG, *USA-Reise Nordhoff 1962*, p. 4.
47 H. Edelmann, *Vom Luxusgut zum Gebrauchsgegenstand*; Wellhöner, 'Wirtschaftswunder', p. 71.
48 A. Andersen, *Der Traum vom guten Leben. Alltags- und Konsumgeschichte vom Wirtschaftswunder bis heute*, Frankfurt/New York: Campus 1997, p. 158.

49 Wellhöner, '*Wirtschaftswunder*', p. 74.
50 Ibid., p. 217.
51 Ibid., pp. 217, 222.
52 Ibid., p. 219; Railton, *Der Käfer*, p. 167.
53 Railton, *Der Käfer*, p. 206; N. Stieniczka, *Vom fahrbaren Untersatz zur Chromkarosse*, in H. Edelmann, *Heinz Nordhoff und Volkswagen*, Göttingen: Vanderhoeck und Ruprecht, 2003, p. 48. Boch, *Geschichte und Zukunft*, p. 195.

5   Americanization with the Japanese supplier system in the Japanese automobile industry, 1950–65

Hirofumi Ueda

Introduction

Since the beginning of the twentieth century the US has been the largest automobile manufacturing country. Japan's car makers set out to adopt the American mass production system when they began to produce automobiles before the war. To establish mass production systems, they had to introduce advanced technology from the US and also had to invest heavily in order to modernize their production facilities. Americanization, which almost equalled mass production for Japan's car makers, was their target once they launched automobile production in the 1930s and subsequently when they restarted automobile production after the Second World War.

When using the term 'mass production', we should consider three stages. First, mass production in relation to the country, with strong links to culture, consumption, society, industrial policy, education and so on. Second, mass production in relation to the company or the company group, which can effectively achieve a reduction in overhead costs such as management or R&D costs throughout the company.[1] Third, mass production on the level of the plant, which is often regarded as important initially by countries or companies who start up automobile production. In the Japanese automobile industry, plant level mass production was more important than company level production when car makers restarted car manufacturing after the Second World War, because market size was much smaller than that of the US. In the 1960s, the smaller Japanese car makers could achieve the same productivity and the same mass production at the plant level as the American giant car makers without realizing the same car production volume at the company level. How did the Japanese car makers introduce the mass production system in their plants? I analyze it in this chapter by considering the supplier system.

It is well known that automobile production requires the assembly of a large number of parts. For the Japanese car makers it was necessary to increase the number of parts suppliers when they increased the volume of their automobile production. Although Japanese car makers intended to establish the mass production system in their plants, they did not adopt in-house parts manufacturing. Instead they adopted the Japanese supplier system in order to achieve mass production.[2] What caused them to adopt the Japanese supplier system will be discussed in this chapter.

When considering the historical background of the relationship between car makers and their parts suppliers when mass production in Japan was being established, several points need to be taken into account. First, parts suppliers can be divided into different types, as illustrated in Table 5.1. Most of the parts suppliers are divided into four types depending on the combination of capital relations, transactional relations, corporate origins and content of production. Type 1 (Core Group Companies) consists of subsidiaries and associates (typically with the assembler being the primary stockholder) that form the core of the group. Type 2 (Keiretsu Group Companies) includes those affiliated suppliers who have a capital affiliation and close relations in terms of personnel. These tend to be formerly independent large or medium-sized companies. Type 3 (Shitauke Group Companies) is made up of those subcontractors who have no capital ties but nevertheless maintain strong business ties. Type 4 (Other Suppliers) is independent from assemblers, some of which are group members of other car makers. These independent suppliers generally specialize in specific parts or unit parts, delivering them to several car makers. In the period focused on in this paper, car makers had some suppliers whose company size was much smaller than in the 1980s.

Second, the speed with which the Japanese automobile industry grew was very high. After the Second World War, the Japanese were far behind the other countries that had already started mass production in the automobile industry, as illustrated in Table 5.2. In 1955 the output of Japan's automobile production was about 70,000, which was only 0.8 per cent of the US, 7.6 per cent of West Germany, and 5.6 per cent of the UK. Furthermore, with regard to passenger cars, Japan's production was only 0.3 per cent of that of the US. The Japanese automotive industry was trailing well behind those countries. From 1955 to 1965 the volume of vehicle production increased twenty-seven times. The high growth speed of automobile production required more parts and more parts suppliers mass producing very quickly.

In this chapter I mainly focus on the Toyota Motor Corporation and its relationship with its suppliers.[3] The reason why Toyota is focused on here is that Toyota is reputed to have maintained a good relationship with its suppliers over a long period of time.

Overview of the Japanese automobile industry and supplier relations

From pre-war to post-war recovery

At the beginning of the 1930s the largest car makers in Japan were the affiliated manufacturing companies of Ford and GM. In 1936 the Japanese

Table 5.1 Types of parts suppliers in the 1980s

Types of suppliers	Capital affiliation	Origin	Business relations	Size	Transactions with other assemblers	Type of manufacturer	No. of companies in co-op association	
							Toyota	Mazda
Type 1 (Core group companies)	Strong	Part of assembler	Strong	Med.-large	Many for large	I	13	6
Type 2 (Keiretsu group companies)	Strong	Independent	Strong	Med.-large	Many	I	14	7
Type 3 (Shitauke group companies)	Weak or none	Independent	Strong	Small-med.	Few	I or II	56	42
Type 4 (Other suppliers)**	Weak or none	Independent	Weak	Med.-large	Many	I	80	121

Source: H. Ueda, 'Subcontracting and Business Group', in T. Shiba and M. Shimotani (eds), *Beyond the Firm*, Oxford: Oxford University Press, 1997, p. 216.

Note
Of type of manufacturer, I is the manufacturer which specializes in specialized parts or components, and II is the manufacturer which specializes in a manufacturing process such as stamping, casting, machining or others.

Table 5.2 Major automobile-producing countries, 1945–65

Year	Japan			US			West Germany			UK		
	Cars	Trucks and buses	Total	Cars	Trucks and buses	Total	Cars	Trucks and buses	Total	Cars	Trucks and buses	Total
1945	–	1,461	1,461	69,532	655,683	725,215	1,293	5,512	6,805	16,938	122,467	139,405
1946	–	14,921	14,921	2,148,699	940,963	3,089,662	9,962	13,916	23,878	219,162	146,120	365,282
1947	110	11,210	11,320	3,558,178	1,239,443	4,797,621	9,541	13,802	23,343	287,000	154,670	441,670
1948	381	19,986	20,367	3,909,270	1,376,274	5,285,544	29,945	31,349	61,294	334,815	173,302	508,117
1949	1,070	27,630	28,700	5,119,466	1,134,185	6,253,651	104,055	39,528	143,583	412,290	216,373	628,663
1950	1,594	30,003	31,597	6,665,863	1,337,193	8,003,056	219,409	86,655	306,064	522,515	261,157	783,672
1951	3,611	34,879	38,490	5,338,435	1,426,828	6,765,263	276,622	97,529	374,151	475,919	257,964	733,883
1952	4,837	34,129	38,966	4,320,794	1,218,165	5,538,959	317,643	110,740	428,383	488,000	241,658	729,658
1953	8,789	40,989	49,778	6,116,948	1,206,266	7,323,214	387,895	102,686	490,581	592,808	239,967	832,775
1954	14,472	55,601	70,073	5,558,897	1,042,174	6,601,071	561,172	119,425	680,597	769,165	268,714	1,037,879
1955	20,268	48,664	68,932	7,920,186	1,249,106	9,169,292	762,205	146,537	908,742	897,560	339,508	1,237,068
1956	32,056	79,010	111,066	5,816,109	1,104,481	6,920,590	910,996	164,623	1,075,619	707,594	296,950	1,004,544
1957	47,121	134,856	181,977	6,113,344	1,107,176	7,220,520	1,040,188	172,044	1,212,232	860,842	288,253	1,149,095
1958	50,643	137,660	188,303	4,257,812	877,294	5,135,106	1,306,854	188,402	1,495,256	1,051,551	312,856	1,364,407
1959	78,598	184,216	262,814	5,591,243	1,137,386	6,728,629	1,503,424	215,142	1,718,566	1,189,943	370,484	1,560,427
1960	165,094	316,457	481,551	6,674,796	1,194,475	7,869,271	1,816,779	238,370	2,055,149	1,352,728	457,972	1,810,700
1961	249,508	564,371	813,879	5,542,707	1,133,804	6,676,511	1,903,075	243,849	2,146,924	1,003,967	460,167	1,464,134
1962	268,784	721,922	990,706	6,933,240	1,240,168	8,173,408	2,109,166	247,446	2,356,612	1,249,426	425,104	1,674,530
1963	407,830	875,701	1,283,531	7,637,728	1,462,708	9,100,436	2,414,092	253,791	2,667,883	1,607,939	403,781	2,011,720
1964	579,660	1,122,797	1,702,457	7,751,822	1,540,453	9,292,275	2,650,183	259,474	2,909,657	1,867,640	464,736	2,332,376
1965	696,176	1,179,438	1,875,614	9,305,561	1,751,805	11,057,366	2,733,732	242,745	2,976,477	1,722,045	455,216	2,177,261

Sources: Various data.

government passed the Automobile Industry Act to support Japanese companies' production by restricting imports of complete cars and knock-down sets from abroad. These restrictions severely damaged car assembly by GM and Ford in Japan because they had imported knock-down sets and most of the main parts for assembly in Japan. And 'the result was that, whereas Japan Ford, Japan GM, and other foreign companies had accounted for more than 95 per cent of new vehicle registrations between 1926 and 1935, the production share of Nissan, Toyota, and Isuzu rose nearly 57 per cent by 1938 and to 100 per cent in 1939, when Japan Ford and Japan GM ceased operating'.[4]

The 1936 Act drove the American car companies out of the Japanese market and encouraged domestic production. Domestic car production by the Japanese-owned car makers was frequently used by the army for military purposes and domestic car production also increased after the 1936 Act. Although domestic car production peaked around 1940, it then decreased because Japanese wartime policy gave priority to the aircraft industry. All the car makers and most of the parts makers were mobilized to manufacture aeroplanes or the parts for them. While a broad division of labour, or systematic specialization structure, began to be formed in the automobile industry from about 1940, the subsequent decline turned into a collapse, complicating business relationships.[5]

In the Industry Census of the Japanese Ministry of Commerce and Industry (MCI, forerunner of MITI or METI) more than 100 car producing or manufacturing factories were registered in 1939 and the number decreased to fifty-four in 1942. By the 1936 Act only three car makers (Nissan, Toyota and Isuzu) were licensed to produce cars and the other factories were supposed to manufacture three-wheeled vehicles or specialized cars. The Census also indicated that more than 4,000 parts makers, most of which employed less than ten workers, existed around 1940. The output of the parts makers was double that of the car makers in 1941. This showed that there was a larger spare parts market in Japan before the Second World War and that most of the parts makers did not have business relationships directly with the car makers at that time. These spare parts makers were established as manufacturing companies of other products or as spare parts producers for imported cars.

After the Second World War automotive production restarted, but until 1953 the volume of production remained below the pre-war peak. On the other hand, many parts makers that had been occupied by military demand shifted their capacity to the civilian demand for auto parts, and thus the original pre-war auto parts makers were joined by a host of new entrants. There were mainly three types of auto parts makers at that time:

1   those that had been occupied before the war with the production of auto parts and subsequently returned to making auto parts (including the spare parts and the parts for assembling);

2   those that had been producing the parts for other industries prior to and during the war, and had switched over to auto parts subsequently;
3   those that were founded after the war for the manufacture of auto parts, or had diversified from some unrelated industry.

In 1955 the MITI's report showed that many parts suppliers were established after 1945 (Table 5.3).

Keiretsu diagnosis

In order to restart car production, the car makers had to find and link up with suitable parts suppliers. The car makers did not have enough buildings, equipment or machines to establish stable production and increased production capacity. Although many smaller parts makers began to supply parts after the war, there were a lot of problems in the business relationships between the parts makers and the car makers which needed to be solved.

Keiretsu diagnosis was aimed at analyzing conditions and problems at both the car makers' plants and the plants or the works of the smaller Shitauke suppliers. Its aim was to improve relations between the two and point the way towards solutions to difficulties involving materials or finances at the Shitauke suppliers, and to boost the effectiveness of systematically specialized assembler-supplier relations.[6] Keiretsu diagnosis was a policy of MITI and the Small and Medium Enterprise Agency (SMEA). SMEA was established in 1948 and diagnosis for small and medium companies had been one of its main policies since then.[7]

Keiretsu diagnosis started in 1952, mainly focusing on the machinery

Table 5.3 Establishing companies of auto parts manufacturing companies

Types of parts	Period when the company was established						
	Meiji period (–1912)	Taisho period (1912–26)	1926–35	1935–45	1945–50	1950–54	Total
Electric parts		3	2	9	7	3	24
Casting parts		2	3	11	7	3	26
Forging parts		1	1	7	2	1	12
Machining parts		1	4	19	9	4	37
Finished parts	2		8	5	23	15	10	63
Accessories		3	6	10	13	4	36
Tools		3		12	7	2	24
Others		2		3	1	3	9
Total	2	23	21	94	61	30	231

Source: MITI, *Jidosha jiho (Automobile Journal)*, 1955, vol. 26.

industry in which the assembling companies had many Shitauke suppliers. Toyota and its smaller Shitauke suppliers were one of the first groups to undergo Keiretsu diagnoses in 1952. SMEA had a guideline for Keiretsu diagnosis, and a party of several people who were members of the local government technological or managerial supporting centre would visit each company. A diagnosis party also included some academics who specialized in management or technology. After diagnosis, a report which highlighted problems and made suggestions for improving productivity and relations between the two would be prepared for each company. This report was kept completely confidential.

Toyota led the way, instituting Keiretsu diagnosis from 1952 to 1953 in the three regions around Nagoya, Osaka and Tokyo. Accordingly, Toyota carried out works diagnosis at the Shitauke suppliers, learned methods for evaluating these firms and undertook changes in its ordering methods. Its Shitauke suppliers acquired competitive awareness and began to rationalize their works and plants more thoroughly. These changes had significant effects on the relationships between Toyota and the Shitauke suppliers.[8]

Other Keiretsu diagnoses were undergone by the Nissan Yokohama Plant in 1953, Daihatsu (then a three-wheeled vehicle maker) from 1956 to 1957, and the Mitsubishi Mizushima Plants (then Shin Mitsubishi Heavy Industries which was changing itself from a three-wheeled vehicle maker to a car maker) in 1961. Nissan reorganized the cooperative association of its suppliers into the Takarakai in 1957, laying the foundation for future development and expansion based on the diagnosis report. However, in comparison with Toyota, the effect of the Keiretsu diagnosis-induced control measures with regard to Shitauke works was not especially great for Nissan. In addition to issues bound up with Nissan's traditional view of outside purchasing, the timing of the major labour dispute in 1953 also had an impact.[9]

In the 1950s Japan's car makers were coming up against suppliers' problems and, to some extent, the Keiretsu diagnosis system was effective in modernizing the car makers' purchasing management and the Shitauke suppliers' works and management styles. The Keiretsu diagnosis system played an important role in some car makers by introducing the mass production system in a high economic growth period.

Spare parts market for parts makers

In the period of the developing automotive parts industry in those countries which were new to the production of automobiles, the spare parts market was very important for the parts makers. From 1945 to around 1950, the volume of the parts that were supplied to the spare parts market was estimated to be more than that assembled in the assemblers' plants. As mentioned before, in Japan a lot of parts makers entered the automotive parts market before the war as the spare parts maker for the domestic spares market which was larger, with about 100,000 imported vehicles. After the war most of the independent parts makers were to supply parts to the spare parts market and they began to supply parts for assembling, as car production expanded.

Spare parts were mainly divided into two groups. Genuine parts, which were delivered to the car makers, would be sold by the car makers' distribution channel. Car makers inspected the quality of the genuine parts because they were responsible for quality, and selected the better genuine parts makers or chose in-house production. Service parts, which were ordered and bought by the automotive parts wholesalers, were distributed through the wholesalers' routes. The quality of these service parts, which were supplied by the smaller parts makers, often mattered after the Second World War.

At the starting point of the high economic growth period, however, the parts market for assembling was not necessarily the main market for the parts makers. In the JAPIA report 50.9 per cent of the 1955 sales of the Japanese automotive parts makers was for assembly in the car makers' plants, 40.8 per cent for the spares market, and 7.4 per cent for export. 64.7 per cent of the 1955 sales of the Japanese automotive parts makers were directly supplied to car makers for assembling and for selling as genuine parts.[10]

Accordingly, as the volume of car production increased, the ratio of the parts for the spares market declined. We should notice, however, that the spare parts market was more important at the starting point of growing production. This fact showed that the car makers did not gain an advantage over the parts makers at that time. Parts makers could survive only by supplying the spare parts market in this period.

Productivity mission

Productivity mission of the automotive industry

In the 1950s some productivity missions visited the US for research on the advanced technology needed to introduce new methods of production and management. In 1955 a productivity mission of the automotive industry left for the US. After they returned to Japan, they published a productivity report in which the mission focused on the gap between Japan's plants and those US plants that they had visited.[11] A large gap between productivity and production volume existed not only on the level of country, but also on the level of plant, between the two. There were some interesting comments about the US car makers, the parts makers and the relationship between the two, see below:

- GM has a lot of parts suppliers that have had a long relationship with GM for several decades. GM's suppliers specialize in some kinds of parts that are estimated to have high reliability (p. 8).

- The parts makers do not rely on their exclusive position, but always study and improve their production methods to reduce production costs in severe competition under the principle of enterprise fairness. It is the most important characteristic of the US parts makers.
- The second important characteristic of the US parts makers is that they have gained equal position to the car makers, in that they can manage their business without a strong relationship with a specific car maker (pp. 20–21).
- One of the characteristics of the US automotive industry is that it has a strong and wide parts industry in which bigger parts makers are equipped with machines of high efficiency (p. 72).

What strongly impressed the Japanese mission were the following three points. First, the Japanese productivity mission members thought that a long and stable relationship between the car makers and their suppliers was one of the most important reasons for US competitiveness. Although a long and stable supplier relationship is now regarded as a characteristic of the Japanese automobile industry, it was not seen as Japanese style by Japanese mission members then because they were trying to establish supplier relationships for expanding car production.

Second, the parts makers' improving production methods, designed to reduce production costs, were also viewed as important. For the Japanese car makers, production costs were a big problem, especially when compared with the US and European car makers. They purchased more parts and materials from outside (generally 50–70 per cent of the total cost) and their suppliers' production costs were more critical. Third, the Japanese and scale: in the automotive parts industry, production scale in Japan was far smaller than that of the US at that time. Japanese car makers required the parts makers to specialize in supplying specific parts with advanced technology and to produce the parts on a large scale.

Productivity mission of the automotive parts industry

In 1955 productivity missions from the automotive parts industry, which consisted of eleven members, visited the US. Their productivity report, which described the US automotive parts industry and parts makers' management accurately, paid attention to the large US spare parts market and some parts makers that supplied more spare parts than original parts for assembling.[12] As mentioned before, the spare parts market was more important for Japanese parts makers and in the spare parts market, competition between parts makers and car makers was becoming more intense at that time. The mission members were also impressed by parts production on a large scale with advanced technology and excellent management systems. In the concluding chapter of the report the US parts makers were characterized as below:

1   most of the US parts makers are strong and independent;
2   they compete with each other severely with fairness and they are also complementary to each other;
3   both the car makers and the parts makers prepare for better original parts for assembling at a lower cost;
4   car makers rely on their parts makers' R&D which concentrate on a special field and both makers' engineers design in close cooperation . . .;
5   in mass production systems special-purpose machines can be developed to an unlimited extent, and general-purpose machines are used practically, improving jigs, tools and dies (p. 127).

The report indicated the importance of rapid and large car production expansion in order for the Japanese automotive parts makers to catch up with the US parts makers.[13] In 1955, as mentioned before, the volume of Japanese car production was far behind that of the US. The gap between the two countries was seen to be too large to catch up with over a short period of time.

For Japan's productivity mission of the automotive industry, interestingly, the automotive parts industry that supplied parts of better quality and of lower cost was required to achieve mass production like the US parts suppliers. For the auto parts makers, however, in contrast, introducing advanced technology to establish mass production in their plants was regarded as most important. For both of them it was necessary to change the situation in the automotive industry quite quickly.

Suppliers management – case study of Toyota

Toyota's plan to expand car production

In the period of the US occupation, Toyota's main products were trucks (Table 5.4). Toyota's volume of car production was considerably smaller than bigger car makers in the US and Europe. Toyota had only one assembly plant (the Koromo Plant, later the Honsha[14] Plant after the Motomachi Plant was organized) at that time and the volume of car production there was also smaller than that of other advanced plants.

In 1950 Managing Directors Eiji Toyoda and Shoichi Saito both visited Ford's River Rouge Plant in the US for the modernization of the Toyota Plant and its management. They studied the US car makers' production system and reported that TMC could achieve the US level by introducing American facilities and systems effectively. The Company History tells about their visits as below:

There they studied the facilities needed for mass production, production technology, and methods of production control and plant

Table 5.4 Domestic production of TMC

Year	Total production volume (A)	Passenger cars	Trucks and buses	No. of employees (B)	A/B	Notes
1946	5,821		5,821	6,463	0.9	
1947	3,922	54	3,868	6,345	0.6	
1948	6,703	21	6,682	6,481	1.0	
1949	10,824	235	10,589	7,337	1.5	
1950	11,706	463	11,243	5,504	2.1	Labour struggle
1951	14,228	1,470	12,758	5,264	2.7	
1952	14,106	1,857	12,249	5,160	2.7	
1953	16,496	3,572	12,924	5,287	3.1	
1954	22,713	4,235	18,478	5,235	4.3	
1955	22,786	7,403	15,383	5,130	4.4	
1956	46,417	12,001	34,416	5,315	8.7	
1957	79,527	19,885	59,642	5,688	14.0	
1958	78,856	21,224	57,632	5,936	13.3	
1959	101,194	30,235	70,959	7,290	13.9	Motomachi plant begins operation
1960	154,770	42,118	112,652	10,127	15.3	
1961	210,937	73,830	137,107	11,966	17.6	Decision made to adopt the TQC system throughout the company
1962	230,350	74,515	155,835	13,460	17.1	
1963	318,495	128,843	189,652	16,126	19.8	
1964	425,764	181,738	244,026	20,783	20.5	
1965	477,643	236,151	241,492	22,330	21.4	Kamigo Plant begins operation
1966	587,539	316,189	271,350	25,484	23.1	Takaoka Plant begins operation
1967	832,130	476,807	355,323	30,066	27.7	
1968	1,097,405	659,189	438,216	33,681	32.6	Miyoshi Plant begins operation
1969	1,471,211	964,088	507,123	36,581	40.2	
1970	1,609,190	1,068,321	540,869	39,814	40.4	Tsutsumi Plant begins operation

Source: TMC (Toyota Motor Corporation), *TOYOTA: A History of the First 50 Years*, Toyota: TMC, 1988.

management. ... Although a clear gap existed in production scale between Japanese and American car makers, overwhelmingly in favour of the latter, Eiji Toyoda became convinced while in the United States that TMC was fully capable of catching up technically with the Americans. ... Based on reports by Eiji Toyoda and Saito, TMC formulated a five-year plan for modernizing its production equipment in February 1951. This plan was designed to increase production capacity in a single stroke to 3,000 units a month by modernizing production facilities and production control.[15]

In 1951, after their visit to the US, Toyota made a five-year plan for equipment modernization and decided to invest in equipment to achieve car production of 3,000 cars per month in 3 years which would double the productivity of their plant. Toyota introduced advanced machines and equipment such as transfer machines, arc-welding machines, automatic multiaxis lathes and so on from abroad or domestic makers (Table 5.5).[16] Production of 3,000 cars per month was realized in 1956 and in the same year production of 5,000 cars per month was also achieved without increasing the number of employees (Table 5.4).[17] This scale of production, however, was half that of the US advanced plants. The productivity mission of the automotive industry reported that the number of assembled car units per day in one plant was about 500 (about 10,000 per month).[18] One of the reasons why Toyota could not achieve production volume in its plant to the same extent as in the US was that imbalance among manufacturing processes could not be solved by the gradual improvement and enlargement of each process.[19] Still, in order to establish mass production, several types of cars, trucks and buses had to be produced at the same plant and the same problem faced other Japanese car makers.[20] For Toyota, there was a need to build new plants specializing in cars in order to achieve mass production at the same level as the advanced US plants.

During the five-year plan Japanese car makers made technological tie ups with American or European car makers, because it was thought that Japan's car makers would not be able to compete with larger foreign manufacturers independently after the Peace Treaty was concluded in 1952. At that time the prices of imported cars produced by mass production with advanced technology were less than those of Japanese car makers in the domestic market. Nissan tied up with Austin, Hino with Renault, Isuzu with Rootes, and Mitsubishi with Willys-Overland. They introduced technology and produced foreign-brand cars in their plants under license. Although Toyota also had a plan to tie up with Ford, it never happened.

From 1955 the Japanese economy entered into a new era of high economic growth. The demand for new cars became so great that car makers had to increase their production power to respond to expanding demand. In order to increase production, car makers introduced new production

Table 5.5 Five-year plan for modernization

Planning year	Imported machines and equipment (1,000 yen)	Domestic machines and equipment (1,000 yen)	Total (1,000 yen)
1951	585,075	107,702	692,777
1952	109,574	470,683	580,257
1953	638,039	1,042,261	1,680,300
1954	201,346	1,420,941	1,622,287
1955	202,646	593,177	795,823
Total	1,736,680	3,634,764	5,371,444

Source: TMMC (Toyota Motor Manufacturing Corporation), *Toyota Jidosha 30-nen shi (The 30 Years History of TMMC)*, Toyota: TMMC, 1967.

facilities and also established new plants.[21] Toyota used both methods as shown in Table 5.4 and thereby changed to a policy of expansion without increasing the number of its employees. Toyota increased total production volume by twenty times in 10 years from 1955 to 1965. Its productivity per employee increased by five times in the same period. During this decade the Motomachi Plant and the Kamigo Plant, which were designed to produce passenger cars by mass production, began operation. The new Motomachi Plant was designed to produce 5,000 cars per month by one shift and also to use balanced manufacturing processes from its start-up.[22] In advanced car assembly plants the optimum production volume per month is generally regarded to be from 10,000 to 20,000 on one assembly line. From the viewpoint of plant productivity Toyota realized a standard level of advanced car production in the Motomachi Plant at the beginning of the 1960s, although, in 1965, the volume of Toyota's car production was less than one tenth that of GM, the biggest car maker in the world.

In the 1960s other Japanese car makers, such as the Oppama Plant (Nissan, 1962, Yokohama), also established new mass production plants for passenger cars. Japan's car makers had entered into a new era of mass production.

After the Keiretsu diagnosis

Toyota purchased parts and materials for about 60–70 per cent of its total production costs. In order to gather enough parts for assembly, Toyota increased the number of suppliers once it expanded car production in the 1950s, and as shown in Table 5.6 new members attended the suppliers' association after the war. The number of new members decreased after Toyota started full-scale mass production at the beginning of the 1960s. How did Toyota secure enough parts to achieve full-scale mass production without increasing suppliers? Why did Toyota hesitate to increase the number of suppliers?

Table 5.6 TMMC suppliers

Type	Period when the supplier started to supply for TMC						Total
	-1939	1940-44	1945-49	1950-54	1955-59	1960-64	1965-	
Type 1	1	1	7	1	1			11
Type 2	3	2	5	2				12
Type 3	14	5	7	8	3	4		41
Type 4	19	3	10	8	8	2	2	52
Total	37	11	29	19	12	6	2	116

Sources: TMMC (Toyota Motor Manufacturing Corporation), *Toyota Jidosha 30-nen shi (The 30 Years History of TMMC)*, Toyota: TMMC, 1967.

As mentioned before, Toyota and its Shitauke suppliers underwent Keiretsu diagnoses in 1952–53 during its five-year modernization plan, which effected Toyota's purchasing management and Shitauke suppliers' attitude over business. First, Toyota established staff groups which specialized in coordination between related sections, examining suppliers' conditions or production capacity, and planning for the management of suppliers in purchasing divisions after the diagnosis.[23] Toyota's purchasing division was composed not only of buyers who decided which suppliers to order from and how much the price of each part should be, but also staff who specialized in improving suppliers' ability and planning purchasing strategy.

Second, quality control by suppliers was becoming more and more important as car production expanded during the five-year plan. Toyota made rules for inspecting, expanding and improving quality control technology, and organizing suppliers to manage a 100 per cent supply of quality products without the need for inspection by Toyota after the parts had been supplied. Third, Shitauke suppliers were trying to develop their own production capacity, and positively diagnosed other public diagnosis by SMEA or local government after the Keiretsu diagnosis.[24] Although it is difficult to measure how these diagnoses affected the suppliers, we can confirm their aggressiveness to enhance their production capacity in order to achieve a better relationship with Toyota. Why did they pursue a better relationship with Toyota at that time? One of the main reasons was their geographical location, which was far from Tokyo and Osaka where other spare parts wholesalers were concentrated.[25] Although most Shitauke parts suppliers diagnosed before had no choice but to supply parts to Toyota while suffering a geographical handicap, they enjoyed expansion of orders from Toyota as a result.

Requirement for expansion from Toyota

Accordingly, as Toyota expanded its production capacity and productivity, it required its suppliers to supply more parts of more kinds because Toyota restricted investment in the plant to some extent, and relied on suppliers. In other words Toyota could reduce investment cost to achieve the same level of mass production as the advanced US plants. The Productivity Report of the automobile industry reported that the Rouge Plant produced 750 cars per day using 60,000 employees, most of whom were supposed to work in many factories on its immense site, where many kinds of parts were produced. The Rouge Plant was regarded as not only an assembly plant, but also a supply centre for Ford's other assembly plants. In contrast, the Motomachi Plant, which did not produce parts for other plants and had more kinds of parts, produced 500 cars by one shift per day with less than 10,000 employees.

Toyota's suppliers had to expand their production capacity in response to Toyota's demands by investing in plant and equipment and increasing their workforce. Sometimes, Toyota supported smaller suppliers financially if they could not obtain finance from banks. In Table 5.7 all the suppliers that were Shitauke smaller suppliers increased their employees in the 1950s. In Table 5.8 the expansion of the suppliers was based on investment in new machines or equipment over a period of several years and this investment was so large that each company had to be financed by banks. Most suppliers had no choice but to accept Toyota's request to do business with them, which resulted in their company growing in proportion to the expansion of Toyota's car production.

After the Motomachi Plant started operation, Toyota drew up a plan for investing in new plant and equipment that would enable it to produce 30,000 units per month in 1960, which would triple the volume of car production.[26] This plan was relayed to the suppliers who were asked to prepare for an increase in orders and requested to reduce production costs by 30 per cent in 3 years.

In the spring of 1963 liberalization of automobile imports into Japan was scheduled to begin, but there were still considerable differences in production costs and volume between Japanese car makers and those of the US or the FRG. To compete with these larger American and European car makers in the domestic market, it was necessary for the Japanese automobile industry to establish both mass production and cost reduction at the same time. Parts suppliers were also required to reduce costs because around 1960, the cost of procuring parts and materials was more than 70 per cent of production cost.

Some suppliers, who had accepted Toyota's demands in the 1950s, were initially reluctant to accept the new request because it was too hard for them within a short time period.[27] However, as it turned out, suppliers accepted Toyota's request to improve and enlarge their facilities, investing

Table 5.7 Employees of Toyota's suppliers

Company name	1943	1952	1958–59	1972	1985	Business start-up with Toyota	Notes
Myodo Works	100	47	92	210	223	August 1937	
Tsuda Works	32	190	555	1,020	1,114	August 1937	
Sango	27	67	219	780	1,330	August 1937	
Kojima Pressing	14	28	200	490	1,120	August 1937	
Ito Metal Works	56	22	50	143	160	August 1937	
Ohashi Works		78	139	196	235	August 1937	
Chuyo Spring	112	74	156	225	294	August 1937	
Ishikawa Works		85	250		945	August 1937	
Chuo Spring		320	486		1,273	August 1937	
Maruhachi Works	44		188	415	510	November 1937	
Sugiura Works	18	19	96	190	270	May 1939	
Chuo Seiki	33		135	506	964	August 1942	
Odai Works	17	25	154	180	790	November 1943	
Taiho Works		97	263	1,000	1,123	December 1944	
Toyota Metal		63	199	700	1,200	March 1945	
Shinkawa Kogyo		195	356			September 1945	Later Aisin Seiki
Banmo Works		51	215	430	408	May 1946	
Tokai Rika		70	630	2,140	4,763	January 1947	
Horie Metal		103	317	737	784	November 1948	

Sources: H. Ueda, 'Kodo seichoki no jidosha sangyo to sapuraiya shisutemu (Supplier System in the Auto Industry in the Early High Economic Growth Period)', *Kikan keizai kenkyu (The Quarterly Journal of Economic Studies)*, 2001, vol. 24, no. 2.

Table 5.8 Suppliers in the 1950s

Fiscal year

Company name		1950	1951	1952	1953	1954	1955	1956	1957	1958	1959
Toyota Auto Body	Output (1,000 yen)				695,151	825,188	1,047,904	1,023,221	3,083,616	4,117,603	4,041,245
	For Toyota (%)						47.2	47.7	78.6	86.9	83.0
	Investment (1,000 yen)					993	93,744	34,910	484,052	338,876	500,536
	No. of employees						763	969	745	794	870
Tokai Rika	Output (1,000 yen)			43,276	69,085	139,983	157,036	253,727	434,078	620,028	695,533
	For Toyota (%)			91.0	80.0	49.1	45.7	50.8	45.3	44.1	36.8
	Investment (1,000 yen)			433	1,138	7,669	1,139	10,969	25,805	47,235	28,290
	No. of employees			44	63	131	178	208	304	438	540
Shinkawa Kogyo	Output (1,000 yen)			101,554	183,575	168,486	258,055	291,000	766,275	1,078,392	1,156,332
	For Toyota (%)			12	33	46	52	63	74	79	90
	Investment (1,000 yen)			5,435	2,390	6,017	17,303	2,366	50,491	53,065	44,073
	No. of employees			179	189	190	223	203	288	302	356
Toyota Metal	Output (1,000 yen)					59,584	64,948	157,108	278,179	261,334	250,710
	Investment (1,000 yen)				2,684	3,482	3,998	4,543	11,468	28,157	8,277
Taiho Kogyo	Output (1,000 yen)			55,545	67,737	94,740	106,707	96,135	215,916	321,549	268,187
	For Toyota (%)			85.3	67.7	69.8	63.9	66.1	53.1	58.7	53.7
	No. of employees	82	79	139	165	180	177	229	246	236	308
Chuyo Spring	Output (1,000 yen)	16,282	18,749	50,935	64,846	67,574	164,320	191,644	165,617	292,333	334,698
	For Toyota (%)	91.0	91.0	91.0	82.7	81.0	82.0	82.0	82.0	74.4	62.7

Source: UNESCO Domestic Research Group, *Jidosha kogyo ni okeru gijutu kakusin no oyobosu eikyo* (Research Report of the Technological Innovation Influence in the Automobile Industry), confidential: 1960–61.

huge sums of money which would be recouped in the next decade of high expansion, and thereby increasing the size of their own suppliers.

Original style of the Japanese supplier system

In the 1960s Toyota's suppliers expanded their company size, thereby creating strong business relationships with Toyota. Larger suppliers tended to make a technological tie up with advanced automotive parts makers to introduce advanced technology, supported by MITI's industrial policy.[28] Medium to small-sized suppliers tended to specialize in specific parts for a specialized manufacturing process. At first they were told what to manufacture for a limited cost, but accumulated know-how about products which enabled them to suggest improvements to Toyota. Toyota introduced a VA (Value Analysis) suggestion system in 1964 to reduce production costs, enabling suggestions from suppliers to Toyota to become more important. For medium to small-sized suppliers it was important to get business with Toyota in which they could specialize in some parts which they themselves could improve and develop within their own companies. In this way Toyota could achieve mass production by manipulating the Japanese supplier system.

Late-coming car makers – the case of Mitsubishi

Three-wheeled vehicle

The Mizushima Works of Mitsubishi was established in wartime as an aircraft producing plant of Mitsubishi Heavy Industries, which was one of the largest aircraft manufacturing companies before the war and was divided into three companies in the period of occupation. After the Second World War, it began to produce three-wheeled vehicles. In Japan many companies entered the three-wheeled vehicle market after the Second World War because demand for cheaper three-wheeled vehicles, which were mainly used for export, was increasing and it was easier for manufacturing companies to produce them than cars. In the early 1950s three-wheeled vehicle production was greater than that of cars.

After 1955, however, the demand for three-wheeled vehicles declined, and the demand for cars, especially for small trucks, increased. Production of three-wheeled vehicles peaked in 1960 at 278,000, and decreased to 42,000 in 1965. Some three-wheeled vehicle makers changed to car makers, and some of them went to other industries. Mitsubishi, Daihatsu and Mazda had switched from being three-wheeled vehicle makers to car makers in the 1960s. Japan's car production expanded rapidly with these late-coming car makers that included old three-wheeled vehicle makers, and Honda which had specialized in two-wheeled vehicles.

Car production expansion

In 1961 when the Mizushima Works began to expand car production in place of three-wheeled vehicle production, the Mizushima and its Shitauke suppliers had Keiretsu diagnosis. The diagnosis report indicated a lot of problems in Mizushima's suppliers' management, and the relationship between the two. An unstable relationship especially was considered a critical point that made suppliers reluctant to invest in modernization. The suppliers were sometimes distrustful of Mizushima because orders and order-prices often fluctuated. Although most small suppliers were located near Misuzhima, they did not necessarily rely on it strongly at that time. The relationship between the two was not good.

In the 1960s, as shown in Table 5.9, the more volume Mizushima Works produced, the higher became the outsourcing percentage. The Mizushima Works established mass production with increasing outsourcing, encouraging suppliers to modernize their plants and equipment to accept its demands.[29] Supplier relationships between the two had changed drastically during the high expansion period of Mizushima.

Late-coming car makers such as Mitsubishi, however, required suppliers of special parts that had not been used so much before producing cars. They began to purchase those types of parts from Type 4 suppliers that were expanding their production capacity to meet demands from car makers. Type 4 suppliers, some of which were part of the biggest two car makers' (Toyota and Nissan) group of companies, played an important role in the co-existence of thirteen car makers which were all increasing their size from the 1960s to the 1980s.

Conclusion

Japan's car makers achieved mass production at the plant level in the 1960s by establishing new plants or improving old plants which specialized in producing cars with some parts from their suppliers. These types of plants were different from those of the giant car makers mentioned below: (1) plant scale was smaller, so that car makers could save investment on production facilities and equipment; (2) plant layout and balance among processes was coordinated for mass production. For operating these types of assembly plants car makers had suppliers who would accept their demands. Toyota had already improved its smaller suppliers' management and production in the 1950s after Keiretsu diagnosis. These smaller Shitauke suppliers (Type 3) expanded their company size to invest in newer facilities and equipment, so that they tended to specialize in specific parts about which they had more technological know-how. In the 1970s some of them established their own R&D sections so that they could create their own designs.

In Japan's automobile industry, mass production was established after

Table 5.9 Mizushima works

		Fiscal year								
	1956	1957	1958	1959	1960	1961	1962	1963	1964	1965
Units of production										
Three-wheeled trucks	7,396	9,703	11,876	8,966	5,397	3,240	1,974	712		
Four-wheeled trucks of middle size					2,900	7,977	11,450	11,295	13,624	14,056
Three-wheeled light vehicles					3,140	16,285	7,965	868		
Light cars						77	17,824	40,908	62,794	71,328
Others									2,457	2,287
Total	7,396	9,703	11,876	8,966	11,437	27,579	39,213	53,783	78,875	87,671
Output (1 million yen), (A)	2,585	4,212	5,540	4,214	4,795	9,507	15,151	19,670	26,956	29,398
Purchasing cost (1 million yen), (B)	772	1,698	1,958	1,479	2,145	4,337	7,245	10,274	16,460	18,089
(B)/(A) (%)	29.9	40.3	35.3	35.1	44.7	45.6	47.8	52.2	61.1	61.5

Source: Kikutaro Takizawa, 'Mizushima kikaikinzoku kogyo danchi chosa oboegaki (Note of Mizushima Machine and Metal Industrial Estate)', mimeo: 1966.

forming the original Japanese supplier system in the 1960s. The reasons why Japan's car makers adopted this Japanese-style mass production were as follows.

1   The leading car makers already had suppliers and studied how to use them effectively in the 1950s.
2   Expansion plans were presented to the suppliers to prepare for enlarging their production capacity.
3   Industrial policy and public finance were useful for suppliers to invest in facilities and equipment.
4   Suppliers could employ younger people who were willing to accept new technology.
5   First tier suppliers could place orders with smaller suppliers because there were many small manufacturing factories in Japan.

From the 1950s, a large expansion of car production for more than two decades had changed Japan's automobile parts industry drastically and had built up stable and long-term relationships between car makers and suppliers. Car makers did not often change their suppliers in this period and so managed fewer suppliers, and each supplier therefore got more orders from the car maker.[30] Relationships between the two were becoming stronger and production technology was increasing. The Japanese supplier system was characterized after the period focused on in this paper, as supporting more expansion of car production and strengthening the competitiveness of Japan's car makers.

Notes

1   Recently it has been suggested that multinational car makers with a production capacity of over 4 million could only survive in severe world-wide competition, by reducing the R&D cost which is being achieved by having mutual R&D resources. This view pays attention to mass production on the level of the company.
2   The Japanese supplier system is characterized in this chapter as follows:
    1   stable and long-term relationship as a criterion;
    2   car makers having their own group suppliers which have strong relationships with car makers;
    3   continuous improvement in quality and reduction of costs after, or before, production by suppliers;
    4   hierarchical multi-strata in which suppliers order smaller suppliers;
    5   larger suppliers specialized in some specific parts with technological capacity cooperating with car makers by designing drawings through continuous information exchange on technology.
    These traits often fluctuate as the condition of the automobile industry changes.
3   When I speak of 'Toyota', I am referring to the Toyota Motor Co. Ltd (TMC).
4   M.A. Cusumano, *The Japanese Automobile Industry*, Cambridge, MA: Harvard University Press, 1985, p. 7.

114   Hirofumi Ueda

5 H. Ueda, 'Subcontracting and Business Group', in T. Shiba and M. Shimotani (eds), *Beyond the Firm*, Oxford: Oxford University Press, 1997, pp. 218–222.

6 The origin of the Keiretsu diagnosis idea was supposed to be the wartime policy in which smaller works were mobilized to become suppliers for the bigger munitions plants. In order to expand wartime production, a lot of smaller plants were mobilized to supply parts, and from 1940 the Japanese government had a policy to create stable and cooperative relations between the customers and the suppliers. This wartime pattern based on cooperative relationships was not realized as planned for various reasons. Still, a large number of business relationships with the wartime suppliers were terminated after the war; see H. Ueda, 'The Subcontracting System during the Wartime Economy', *Japanese Yearbook on Business History*, 1996, vol. 13, pp. 78–85.

7 The diagnosis system of the SMEA was introduced as one of the main policies because a new SMEs supporting system which would be accepted by the US governors was required for MCI to establish SMEA under US control.

8 K. Wada, 'The Development of Tiered Inter-firm Relationships in the Automobile Industry: A Case Study of the Toyota Motor Company', *Japanese Yearbook on Business History*, 1991, vol. 8, pp. 34–36.

9 Ueda, 'Subcontracting and Business Group', pp. 224–227.

10 JAPIA (Japan Auto Parts Industries Association), Jidosha buhin kogyo no jittai (The Actual Conditions of the Auto Parts Industry), Tokyo: JAPIA, 1957, p. 42.

11 Productivity Mission of the Automobile Industry, *Jidosha seisansei chosadan hokokusho* (Productivity Report of the Automobile Industry), Tokyo: Japan Automobile Industry Employers' Association, 1956.

12 Japan Productivity Centre, *Jidosha buhin kogyo* (Productivity Report of the Automobile Parts Industry), Tokyo: Japan Productivity Centre, 1956. Most of the report was written by Mr Yasusada Nobumoto who became the president of Akebono Break, and later the president of JAPIA.

13 'We have to aim at the same stage of car production as America. All the environmental problems parts makers are meeting now will be solved if we can expand car production so rapidly and largely' (Ibid., p. 129).

14 'Honsha' means head office in Japanese.

15 TMC (Toyota Motor Corporation), *TOYOTA: A History of the First 50 Years*, Toyota: TMC, 1988, p. 113.

16 'Investment for modernization of facilities in the early 1950s tended to be done by studying foreign makers' catalogues, and ordering machinery and facilities as required. It was such a common practice that it became known as 'catalogue engineering' (ibid., p. 139).

17 In 1950 Toyota experienced a major labour dispute for decreasing the number of employees, and firing more than 2,000 workers. After that Toyota were reluctant to employ regular employees.

18 The daily production scale of Rouge Plant, Ford, was reported as 750 and that of San Jose Plant, Ford, as 500.

19 In the 1950s at the Honsha Plant some origins of the Toyota Production System were tried to coordinate this imbalance among manufacturing processes; TMC, *TOYOTA: A History of the First 50 Years*, pp. 141–144.

20 Honsha Plant was characterized as the type of plant which produced more kinds of cars by a variety of manufacturing methods such as by hand, by machine and by process automation.

21 The time required to produce one passenger car in the Japanese car making industry decreased from 136.87 hours in 1955 to 67.99 hours in 1965 (data from *Labour Statistical Annual Report* by Ministry of Labour, Japan).

22 'Up until then, TMC's investment in plant and equipment had generally been

for modernizing production facilities at each process. In contrast, the Motomachi Plant was designed from the outset as an integrated plant to mass-produce passenger cars, thus enabling high efficiency to be maintained throughout the entire production process. It was Japan's first plant designed exclusively for producing passenger cars and was furnished with the most up-to-date facilities, including various types of conveyors with a total length of 4 km, high-performance equipment and machinery, and a centralized production line control system using television cameras' (TMC, *TOYOTA: A History of the First 50 Years*, p. 146).

23 A staff section of the purchasing division separated out as the purchasing management division in 1966 after Toyota won the Deming Application Prize and made a plant to diffuse TQC to its suppliers.

24 Seventeen out of twenty-one supplier companies that were diagnosed in 1952 won a prize given by the Governor of Aichi Prefecture. Kyohokai (Suppliers' Association of Toyota), *25-nen no ayumi* (A History of 25 Years), Toyota: Kyohokai, 1967, p. 25.

25 The spare parts business was regarded as more profitable for parts makers at that time because: (1) prices of spare parts were generally higher than those of parts for assembling, and (2) in the spare parts business wholesalers generally paid in cash while car makers paid by draft, which lengthened payment times.

26 Thirty thousand per month included car production in the plants of Toyota's affiliated companies such as Kanto Auto Works, Central Motor and Toyota Auto Body; TMC, *TOYOTA: A History of the First 50 Years*, p. 147.

27 UNESCO Domestic Research Group (1960–61), *Jidosha kogyo ni okeru gijutu kakushin no oyobosu eikyo* (Research Report of the Technological Innovation Influence in the Automobile Industry), confidential, gave the reasons why suppliers hesitated to invest enough money in order to accept the demands of Toyota as: (1) suppliers had already invested large amounts of money; (2) it was difficult to gather necessary workers when the labour market was becoming tighter under high economic growth; (3) suppliers were sceptical about the car production plan of 30,000 per month.

28 'The various parts makers actively sought to improve technology, production rationalization, and quality control, and their forward-looking management policies were given support by government policy in the form of the Machinery Industry Promotion Temporary Measures Law'; Ueda, 'Subcontracting and Business Group', pp. 227–228.

29 M.J. Smitka, *Competitive Ties: Subcontracting in the Japanese Automotive Industry*, New York: Columbia University Press, 1991.

30 Car makers sometimes stopped orders for some suppliers or reorganized a supplier's system to make it effective. And late-coming car makers such as Mitsubishi increased the number of suppliers to expand production in the early 1960s as mentioned before. The number of association members, however, did not increase so much after the mid-1960s; Ueda, 'Subcontracting and Business Group', p. 232.

6 The Americanization of the German electrical industry after 1945

Siemens as a case study

Wilfried Feldenkirchen

Introduction

When speaking of the Americanization of West Germany, the phenomenon is usually associated with cultural and, above all, economic aspects. The term 'Americanization', which is most frequently equated with 'modernization', is understood as the takeover of American structures and concepts of industrial production and organization, and the assimilation of the corporate culture and corporate mentality that dominated in the United States.[1] One should, however, differentiate between individual economic sectors and industries. The American market concept of mass consumption, for example, was far more easily adapted to the sector of consumer goods than to capital goods. 'Chewing gum and Lucky Strikes, whose packaging alone symbolized the beautiful new world of modernity, were harbingers of McDonalds, corporate skyscrapers, and nuclear missiles.'[2] These symbols stood for a modern American consumerism that promised a materially pleasant existence as well as the possibility of achieving it.[3] Since there was an enormous pent-up demand for consumer goods in Germany after the Second World War, the tendency was naturally to look to America as a model. Yet American influences were also felt in other sectors of the economy. In view of America's substantial technological edge, the more advanced chemical, electrical engineering and automotive industries were highly receptive to American influences, while the older coal and steel industry changed only gradually.[4]

The thesis of Americanization, that is, the question of whether there was indeed something like an Americanization strategy, is not without controversy.[5] Volker Berghahn, who long set the tone for the discussion of Americanization with his definitive work *The Americanization of West German Industry*, claims that Germany's separate economic and technological development ended in 1945, when the country slowly began to adopt American models. Paul Erker, on the other hand, points out that 'the fact that many entrepreneurs looked to America ... should not be mistaken for a takeover and assimilation of what they saw.'[6] Some historians call attention to the rather meagre sources for backing the Americanization theory, and indicate that research is still lacking for many industries in which a relatively early Americanization is suspected.[7] However, there is general agreement that the United States exerted an influence that led to corresponding changes in structures within Germany. A study of Americanization in 1964 describes this influence as follows: 'If this is intended to mean that American ideas, attitudes and bias thereafter dominated in Europe, then the answer is no. If, however, "Americanization" means the development and spread of American or similar goods, processes and organizational forms throughout Europe, the answer is a qualified yes.'[8]

Numerous studies on the theme of Americanization focus on the late 1940s and early 1950s, during which the American impact on Germany's economy was most visible. The reorientation of the country's economy and social order in the post-war period, the enormous importance of the Marshall Plan in the reconstruction of Germany's economy, the break-up of the cartels, the question of the reintegration of Germany in the world economy, and the implementation of a multilateral world trade are inseparably linked with American influence in Europe and West Germany. According to Volker Berghahn, 'the Americanization of the West German industrial capitalism that began under the regulations of the occupation period culminated only in the 1970s.'[9]

The following case study of the German electrical industry illustrates the extent to which Americanization occurred. Following the war, Germany's electrical engineering and electronics industry developed, along with machine tools, into the country's largest industry. This development was fuelled by technical innovations and dynamic changes in industrial locations and markets, and by the opening of important sales markets for private investments and international competition. However, at the end of the Second World War, the situation for the German electrical industry – as with Germany's industry overall – was extremely unfavourable. In view of the massive material and financial losses, together with the loss of patents and know-how, many industries were faced with starting from scratch and with a fundamental reorientation. In order to catch up as quickly as possible with the advances made by international competitors during the war and to regain world market positions held before the war, industries increasingly turned to advanced developments in the United States.

This case study of Siemens will show whether – and if so, to what extent – American models and technologies were adapted or consciously not taken over by the German electrical industry in its search for solutions. The study focuses on company organization, human resources policy, sales and marketing as well as the technical fields of semiconductor research, nuclear energy and data processing. As an introduction, I would like to briefly sketch the general conditions of the German electrical industry after the Second World War.

Political and economic conditions

Framework conditions for rebuilding Germany's economy following the war were extremely unfavourable. Germany had been isolated from the world market during the war and had lost touch with international technological developments. Major American competitors, in contrast, had been able to develop without any restraints, and had expanded into the global market with growing capacities and economic power. By 1946, industrial production in Germany's three Western Zones had dropped to 30 per cent of the 1938 level. The severe scarcity of electrical power and raw materials, the catastrophic lack of food, and the desolate state of the surviving transportation infrastructure were the obvious reasons for a comparative slow economic revival in the immediate post-war years. As late as 1948, United Nations statistics indicated that industrial production in the Federal Republic of Germany was only half that of the same area in 1938, while world production had grown by approximately 50 per cent in the same decade between 1938 and 1948.

The United States and Britain, above all, were interested in a reconstruction of the German economy. Gradually the idea took shape that it would not only be advantageous to use Germany's industrial power to help rebuild Western Europe, but to institute changes in the country's legal framework and market structure, as well as in the economic practices of the rest of Europe's industry. In short, the idea to 'Americanize' Europe took form.[10]

A key factor in the economic reconstruction and strengthening of the Western Zones in Germany was the European Recovery Program (ERP), better known as the Marshall Plan, announced in June 1947. The aid programme was decisive in helping revive the economies of the Western Zones and Western Europe[11] and it ultimately served as a staunch bulwark against the socialization plans encouraged in broad circles of West Germany's society, including some of the conservative groups. Of particular importance in the Marshall Plan were the ERP loans given to West Berlin entrepreneurs beginning in the spring of 1949 under particularly favourable terms. With terms of 10 years, the loans initially had a 5 per cent interest rate and later only 4 per cent. From 1945 to the currency reform in June 1948, Siemens & Halske invested 25 million Reichsmarks, and Siemens-Schuckertwerke invested 34.5 million Reichsmarks to rebuild their Berlin factories. In the period June 1948 to June 1952, investments of DM51.6 million were made by Siemens & Halske and DM57.4 million by Siemens-Schuckertwerke. Of this sum, a total of DM65.2 million was provided by ERP loans.[12]

The Siemens situation after the Second World War

The Siemens group of companies – as with the entire German economy – had suffered enormous losses in the Second World War. Damages at

Siemens totalled approximately 2.58 billion Reichsmarks, representing four-fifths of the company's entire substance.[13]

The company's initial post-war production phase focusing on emergency products was followed by a more comprehensive period of manufacturing simple electro-technical products. The currency reform in 1948 introduced a third phase of gradual normalization, which led to a product spectrum planned for the long term and a return to the company's earlier entrepreneurial principles. After the currency reform, business developments in Siemens' West German operations were highly favourable, and once the blockade of West Berlin ended in the summer of 1949, the situation in the company's plants in West Berlin also improved. The reorganization of currency and market conditions in the course of the currency reform, along with the financial aid flowing in through the Marshall Plan, helped accelerate the rebuilding of Siemens' operations in West Germany. By 1950, the company had almost reached its pre-war production level in the western part of the country, and its reconstruction had been largely completed. Despite this extraordinary success, Siemens had only reached approximately 90 per cent of its 1936 production volume, while the production index of the German electrical industry was already at 125 (1936 = 100). Since other large electrical engineering companies in Europe and the US had in part quadrupled their production since 1939, Siemens' share of world production had declined to a fraction of its earlier size despite the company's strong growth.

Allied decartelization plans

By breaking up German cartels after the Second World War, the US believed it would be eliminating one of the major sources for the rise of National Socialism in the country. Siemens was exposed to the same threat as I.G. Farben,[14] Vereinigte Stahlwerke and major German banks: being broken up. The Allied decartelization plan[15] aimed at separating the two parent Siemens companies – Siemens & Halske AG and Siemens-Schuckertwerke AG – and decentralizing Siemens & Halske's operations in the Western Zones.[16] Economic agreements made in Potsdam called for limiting the workforces of large companies to 100,000 employees.[17]

In their correspondence and memoranda, board members of the Siemens companies pointed out to the American and British decartelization authorities that the separation of Siemens & Halske and Siemens-Schuckertwerke was economically and politically impossible. Their argument: reciprocal deliveries between the parent companies was a prerequisite for maintaining production.[18] In one of the memoranda submitted to the decartelization commission, it was argued that weakening the company by breaking it up was not only contrary to Siemens' economic mission, but in particular against the goals of the Marshall Plan.[19] The fact was that a break-up of Siemens would no longer have met decartelization regulations as early as 1947, since the number of employees in both parent companies already exceeded the prescribed upper limit at this point. The company management did not respond to Allied requests for suggestions on how to break up Siemens, nor did the decartelization commission established by the military authorities provide a viable proposal. The case of Siemens was not further pursued by the Allies, and at the end of 1948, the control of cartels was passed to the German authorities. The last 'Decartelization Branch' questionnaire was distributed in December 1949 and had no impact on the industry.[20] Ultimately, there was only a marginal restructuring in the entire electrical industry.

American influences at Siemens

Study tours to the US

One vital prerequisite for rebuilding business after the war was catching up with international developments and gaining access to vital know-how. To this end, numerous politicians, economists and businessmen, including Siemens representatives, visited the United States in growing numbers even before the founding of the Federal Republic of Germany. These visits were aimed not only at renewing old business contacts and establishing new relations, but were used as an opportunity to study the American industrial system.[21] The learning process for the West German business elite was certainly accelerated by such visits, fulfilling the hopes of the American High Commission for their long-term effects. Obviously America's prosperity and dynamic economy were impressive for visitors from war-ravaged Europe. In addition to seeking information about new technologies, the study groups focused on evaluating corporate organizational structures and management systems, on advertising and marketing, on industrial relations, and on the 'human-psychological' aspects of the industrial system on the other side of the Atlantic.[22] The reports that the delegations compiled upon their return were published or distributed within their companies.

The first indications of an intensive study of American management training could be seen as early as 1949–50 in West German visitor groups. They all reported on 'the important role played by so-called labour or human relations ... in American economic life for roughly a decade.'[23] There are indications that the concepts of human relations were adopted relatively quickly in some companies. This process was eased somewhat by the fact that there was a tradition of company psychology in Germany that reached back to the period between the wars and initially seemed quite similar to American research carried out in the 1930s. In addition to the study and adoption of American psychological methods, industrial and economic practices and organizational forms were also exported from the US to American subsidiaries in Europe. A study by Heinz Hartmann in the

1950s indicated that the export of industrial culture simultaneously meant the spread of technologies along with the culture and teachings they symbolized.[24]

Technology transfers

Siemens sought contact with the US after the Second World War primarily with the intention of catching up with the country's technical developments. A quickly growing number of Siemens engineers, physicists, businessmen and legal experts toured American laboratories and research institutions and participated in technical colloquia.[25] The company had maintained good contacts with American electrical companies before the war, and there had been numerous exchanges of patents and knowledge in that period, such as that between Siemens and Westinghouse (1924). The large American electrical companies were also generally interested in working together with foreign partners. On the one hand, German companies could contribute important know-how in certain areas despite lagging behind in general. On the other hand, the German generalist companies remained important competitors in the world market, but were not competing in their American home market, which was far more important for them. Overall, resuming the exchange of ideas and business experiences with American colleagues after the Second World War certainly eased efforts to catch up in technologies. Interest at Siemens focused on semiconductor research, nuclear energy and data processing. Major military interest had intensified research in these fields in the US, making the transfer of technologies and know-how especially interesting for German companies.

Semiconductor research

The development and application of semiconductor components had a decisive impact on technical developments in virtually all areas of electrical engineering and many other technical fields. By the 1950s, semiconductor technology had become the key for Siemens and today nearly all the company's business fields depend on it. In 1953, Siemens independently developed a process for producing pure silicon at about the same time as American researchers, providing the basis for semiconductor technology.

The high standard of American material research and the expected advances in this field soon led Siemens-Schuckertwerke to the idea of reviving the patent and know-how exchange agreement with Westinghouse that was originally signed in 1924, renewed in 1934, and finally interrupted by the war. A Siemens delegation visited the US in 1952 and put forward the idea.[26] The agreement with Westinghouse was based on an understanding that the companies would not sell their own products in their partner's home market. This agreement remained in effect until the Federal German Cartel Act was passed on 27 July 1957. Westinghouse, for its part, profited from the successes at SSW in the production of pure silicon,[27] which was needed as a basic material for communication components and transistors. A separate agreement was signed between Siemens and Westinghouse covering patents and the exchange of knowledge related to silicon. This agreement was followed 6 months later by a supplementary agreement on semiconductors.[28]

Before the war, the two partners set up special offices to handle the newly revived business relationship, organize the exchange of knowledge, and expedite general business transactions.[29] In addition, each of the companies set up a permanent representative office in the partner's facilities, staffed with engineers serving as liaison staff. Their function was to gather information, look after visitors from their own company, and generally cultivate good contacts between the partners.[30]

Nuclear energy

The consumption of electricity in Germany increased more than ten-fold in the period from 1950 to the present. The country's power supply system, including power plants, transformers, substations and distribution grids, had to be expanded to meet this steadily growing demand. These substantial power needs were met largely by building conventional fossil-fuelled power plants and, increasingly, with nuclear power plants.

In view of the long tradition at Siemens in designing and constructing major conventional power plants,[31] it was only natural for Siemens-Schuckertwerke in Erlangen, which was responsible for the power plant business, to take an early interest in nuclear technology[32] as a promising new form of power generation. It had long been obvious to the company's management that the most important tasks included catching up with technological know-how abroad and it should at least begin with basic work in nuclear physics. In particular, Carl Knott, a member of the board of SSW and head of the Central Plant Administration (ZW) had prepared the company management and its relevant departments for actively participating in the development of nuclear energy at an appropriate time. Knott assigned responsibility for the theoretical preparations to physicist Wolfgang Finkelnburg,[33] who had emigrated to the US after the war along with many German scientists and was working there in the field of atomic physics. Under his direction, a work group was established in Erlangen in August 1953.

Following the announcement of the Atoms For Peace Program in 1954, which was established to encourage the use of nuclear energy in the civilian sector, Siemens designated the field of nuclear technology, together with semiconductors and data processing – which were also classified as future-oriented high-tech fields – as core businesses. Since available publications made it clear that the greatest advances in nuclear technology were abroad, the management at Siemens-Schuckertwerke quickly thought of reviving the basic agreement signed in 1924 with Westinghouse that involved the exchange of knowledge and all patents. Carl Knott contacted Westinghouse, and negotiations were launched that quickly led to a renewal of the old cooperation agreement in 1954.[34] Because of the Allied prohibition in effect for Germany at this time, however, cooperation in the field of nuclear technology remained excluded from the agreement.

Siemens' obvious attraction to the idea of extending the historically based alliance with Westinghouse to include nuclear energy, became evident a short time later when Westinghouse – which had been operating an experimental reactor in Idaho since mid-1953 – began constructing the first large American commercial nuclear reactor in September 1954. The facility was being built for the American utility Duquesne Light Company in Shippingport, on the Ohio River in Pennsylvania.[35]

Encouraged by the eventual lifting of the Allied prohibition against nuclear research, Siemens-Schuckertwerke formed the 'Reactor Development' study group in Erlangen in November 1955.[36] The study group consolidated the sectors of reactor physics, material research, thermal technology and electrical engineering under one roof. It systematically researched various reactor types for their suitability as thermal power plants and for their technical feasibility. Taking all technical and economic factors into consideration, the team at Siemens-Schuckertwerke decided on two main approaches. One was its own design for a uranium-fuelled reactor controlled and cooled with heavy water. In parallel with this, the company began to develop an enriched uranium-fuelled pressurized water reactor moderated and cooled with light water.[37]

Initially, the technical development of the light-water moderated and cooled pressurized water reactor could only be pursued as theory, since political conditions for a transfer of nuclear technology from the US were not yet ripe. As a result, Siemens focused its interest on the Westinghouse design for light-water reactors as well as on the gas-cooled, graphite-moderated reactor type which was being developed in Britain and France.

To support its earlier decision to proceed on two parallel developments, Siemens sought to win over a suitable foreign partner for cooperation on designing its light-water reactor. By the summer of 1956, Westinghouse had already signalled its willingness to work with Siemens in the field of nuclear energy. Concrete negotiations for extending the existing cooperation agreement to include the new field were scheduled for the end of the year. Carl Knott and Finkelnburg travelled to the US in mid-December in order to participate in talks on further expanding the basic agreement, which had been renewed the previous year. In the course of the negotiations, they managed to enlarge the agreement as hoped, yet Westinghouse pointed out that the US government required the signing of a treaty between the US and the Federal Republic of Germany as a precondition for approving such an agreement.

In subsequent talks during June of the following year, Westinghouse insisted on a formal licensing agreement. Knott refused to accept the demand for fear of endangering his company's own developments. It took another year before a supplementary agreement for general cooperation in nuclear energy meeting Siemens' own requirements was ready to be signed.[38] Following the successful conclusion of the nuclear energy pact, Westinghouse granted its partner Siemens extraordinarily favourable conditions for the exchange of knowledge and patents, not least because of Siemens' valuable expertise gained through its own developments in the field. Siemens now had access to American light-water reactor technology and could incorporate it into its own designs and developments for the pressurized water reactor type. The advanced level of Westinghouse's pressurized water reactor technology became obvious when America's first nuclear power plant at Shippingport went critical for the first time with a Westinghouse reactor in December 1957 after only 3 year's construction time.

By this time, Siemens had gained valuable experience in nuclear energy with the construction and commissioning of the multipurpose research reactor in Karlsruhe (1965), partly designed on the basis of its own technologies and partly on ideas adapted from Westinghouse. This project, combined with the knowledge gained from Westinghouse,[39] enabled Siemens to design a commercial pressurized water reactor nuclear power plant. The consortium that Westinghouse wanted to form with Siemens-Schuckertwerke AG to build the plant did not materialize. Instead, Siemens decided to handle the project as general contractor. In August 1964, the company received a Letter of Intent from Kernkraftwerk Obrigheim GmbH[40] for the turnkey[41] construction of the Obrigheim nuclear power plant. Working together with Westinghouse and the customer, Siemens for the first time implemented innovative principles that were also incorporated in power plant designs being developed by Westinghouse.[42] After 3.5 year's construction time, the Obrigheim plant first went critical on 22 September 1968. With the synchronization of the turbine-generator in October 1968, the facility had the distinction of being Europe's largest light-water cooled and moderated nuclear power plant. The plant was handed over to the customer on 1 April 1969.[43]

In 1970, by mutual agreement, Siemens and Westinghouse terminated both the Technical Assistance Agreement of 1954 and the nuclear energy licensing agreement, which had been extended by an additional 10 years in 1966.[44] The exchange of patent licences was initially affected by the termination; both sides permitted the Kraftwerk-Union (KWU) and Transformatoren-Union (TU) companies formed in 1969 by Siemens and AEG to continue using the rights until 1972. The primary reason for terminating the agreement, however, was the fact that the cooperation between Siemens and AEG in the framework of KWU and TU would have allowed an indirect exchange of knowledge between Westinghouse and General Electric, which held a 12 per cent stake in AEG. Such contacts were not allowed by American cartel law. In addition, the Westinghouse agreements with Siemens had been formulated to ensure protection for each of the partner's home markets: this was also against the new cartel regulations[45] and could have been challenged.

Data processing

The increasing intermeshing of data processing and systems technology, coupled with expectations of favourable market opportunities, led Siemens to form a Telecommunications Group in 1954. Rapid technological developments in this field eventually led to the widespread use of electronic data processing.

When Siemens first decided to develop digital data processors, the US was the world's largest market for computers and exerted strong influence on the relatively small European market. Similarly, US manufacturers were leaders in the market, and IBM had already assumed a dominating market position by the late 1950s.[46] Despite the high performance capability and reliability of the first Siemens digital computer, the 2002,[47] the company could not overcome marketing problems and showed disappointing sales figures. Siemens' computer business generated sales of approximately DM10 million in the fiscal year 1961 and later stagnated at DM20 to 25 million marks in the fiscal year 1964. The situation further deteriorated when IBM announced its new 360 computer family in April 1964. By this time, Siemens had already accumulated a loss of DM70 million in its computer business.[48]

Siemens then decided to pursue a strategy of working with other companies in the field and outsourcing equipment whose development and production would exceed its own capacity. At the same time, Siemens would endeavour to supply as much as possible to other manufacturers and secure patent licensing for its developments. In 1957 and 1958, however, exploratory talks with IBM in Munich concluded without success. In November 1964, Siemens signed the 'Mutual Patent License and Technical Information Agreement between Radio Corporation of America and Siemens & Halske AG'. This agreement was subsequently extended in 1970, along with a 'Sales Agreement between Radio Corporation of America and Siemens & Halske AG'.

RCA,[49] in contrast with other American computer companies, had no customer base and thus had first to build up a marketing organization and find a partner in Europe.[50] Siemens was RCA's desired partner because of its size and what was important for the future – the company's broad basis in data processing, namely commercial and technical-scientific computing and process technology. In the very first year of the cooperation, Siemens succeeded in obtaining nearly DM100 million in orders. Six years later, in the fiscal year 1971, the last year of cooperation with RCA, the company's information systems division achieved sales of more than DM1 billion. Measured on the value of installed systems, however, Siemens was only able to raise its market share from 5 per cent in 1965 to 14 per cent in 1970.[51] The cooperation between RCA and Siemens helped the company expand its access to the South American computer business by founding two joint-venture sales companies in Brazil and Venezuela.[52]

Siemens profited mainly from the licensing rights for the production of central processing units. This production was substantially cheaper than outsourcing, and gave the company valuable know-how and experience in technologies, production techniques and development.[53] The work carried out by Siemens in partial cooperation with, or independently from RCA late in the 1960s ultimately helped Siemens continue developing its own computer business after RCA withdrew from the cooperation.

Later, price wars waged in the US strongly impacted upon the pricing situation in the European computer market. When IBM severely reduced prices for its peripheral equipment in 1971, Siemens was forced to follow suit and reduce prices by 15 to 20 per cent. A development of this magnitude had not been anticipated, and losses at Siemens were inevitable. From the first year of its cooperation with RCA in the fiscal years 1965 to 1971, Siemens' computer sales volume climbed from just below DM50 million to nearly DM650 million. However, the business generated a loss from the very beginning, starting with minus DM40 million and climbing to DM80 million loss as sales increased.

RCA's surprising withdrawal from the commercial computer business in 1971, prompted by its insignificant market share of only 4 per cent and high overhead costs,[54] was not followed by Siemens.[55] The company's business had attained too great an importance in regard to volume, market position and obligations to customers for Siemens to simply drop out.[56]

Corporate organization

In addition to focusing on the transfer of technologies and know-how, German companies were also interested in American rationalization methods and the possibilities offered by new techniques for employee management and promotion. American principles of organization thus played an important role in the reorganization of Siemens in the 1960s.

The rapid growth of all Siemens operating units after the war, together with the increasing integration of power engineering with low-voltage technology, resulted in overlapping development and production. These trends ultimately made imperative a reorganization of the company's structure, which also seemed advisable in view of the planned changes in Germany's laws governing stock corporations. In 1964, it was decided to reorganize the basic framework of Siemens.[57] The first step, taken in 1966, was to consolidate the three original parent companies – Siemens & Halske AG, Siemens-Schuckertwerke AG and Siemens-Reiniger-Werke – into a new corporate entity called Siemens AG. This move led to a far better profile of the company on the world market. However, in order to meet the challenges of rapidly advancing technological developments that were crucial for successfully competing in dynamic domestic and international markets, the company had to create manageable, separate, non-overlapping business units that were freed from their former identification as S&H or SSW units, and which could operate independently under the overall umbrella of Siemens AG's technical and business management.

On 1 October 1969, the company was reorganized into six groups, with five corporate departments[58] as well as regional offices and regional companies.[59] The restructuring followed principles of vertical or divisional organization taken over from the US. According to this system, each of the newly created Groups consisted in turn of divisions, main departments and manufacturing facilities, and made its business decisions virtually independently. Matters of basic importance for the company as a whole were handled by the corporate departments. These units also assumed responsibility for the company's overall earnings. The concept of the new organization rested on the principles of product, function and regional responsibility.

Although this principle of vertical or divisional organization had been developed in the US, was widely discussed in business and financial publications in Europe, and had a major influence on the new Siemens organization, the basic concept had actually been developed independently at Siemens until 1966 without the help of an American consulting firm.[60] Gerd Tacke, President and CEO of Siemens AG from 1968 to 1971, described this process:

> It certainly would be inaccurate to claim that this principle, which had been developed in the U.S. and flowed into Europe via a broad stream of literature, had no influence on the reorganization of the company. On the other hand, it was without deeper meaning for the concept and implementation of the company's organizational reform. The basic concepts behind the reform were actually developed independently within the company and reached maturity in 1966. . . . First, the 'model' of the major American companies could be seen as a confirmation of our own ideas; second, observations of models that had been adapted with vehemence and all consequence by some competitors also showed the limitations and weaknesses of this principle of organization.

The organizational matrix created by Siemens deviated in a number of points from the typical divisional organization used in large American corporations. The American organizational model helped restructuring at Siemens in two respects: first, it was felt that the organizational scheme of US companies confirmed Siemens' own concepts, and second, the observation of US systems that had already been implemented by competitors prior to 1964–66 gave Siemens a better understanding of the limitations and weaknesses of this type of organization.

According to Tacke, there were differences in the basic situations in the US and at Siemens that had to be considered when introducing the divisional principle. These culminated in the question: 'will it be possible to master the newly created and strongly centrifugal forces so that the unity of the company is not endangered? This was one of the reasons why we so strongly stressed the priority of the whole over the parts in our basic system.'[61] He pointed out a further difference to American models: the institution of 'Chief Executive' anchored in American corporate law. In the US, this individual possessed a virtually unlimited power to overrule. 'German law was completely different: the President and Chief Executive Officer didn't even have the right to object to majority decisions.'[62]

Human resources policy

In addition to drawing on organizational principles, the company also utilized experiences and the results from new research in America for its own human resources work. Beginning in the early 1950s, human resources policy in German companies focused on securing an adequate number of qualified employees and managers. In addition, increasingly tougher competition in the world market made it apparent that a company's competitiveness depended decisively on the quality of its employees and managers.[63] The steadily growing scarcity of young managerial talents in Germany in the 1950s led to the idea of adopting American experience with the systematic training of managers. A study group of German personnel managers, including a representative from Siemens,[64] visited a number of American companies in 1954 and focused their attention on a management development programme. In view of the forthcoming introduction of a general military draft in Germany, companies feared an even greater scarcity of young managerial talents.

Richard Meine, head of human resources at Siemensstadt in Berlin, called for an intensification of company vocational training and continuing education programmes, and a centralization of Siemens' entire training activities, based on American models. Shortly thereafter, in 1956, Siemens introduced the preparation of young talents and managers for management positions as part of its 'Seminar of the Wolf-Dietrich v. Witzleben Foundation for Young Talents and Managers of the Upper Management Level'. In 1959, the company introduced its 'Master Weeks' courses, and beginning in 1960, its 'Information Talks for Lower and Middle Management'. In the following years, these activities were consolidated in a special Office for Vocational Training and Continuing Education. In 1971, the company published its 'Guidelines for Managers', which drew on these earlier human resources experiences and the work of the 'Vocational Training and Continuing Education' work group.[65]

Siemens human resources managers conducted a study tour of the United States in October and November 1975 to examine the situation with regard to technical training and to gain new ideas for planning and further rationalization of the company's own educational policy.[66] The trends observed by the group on their tour led to the decision to intensify cooperation with universities and technical schools in the field of continuing education (so-called contact studies) reflecting practices used in the US, where such continuing education programmes for technical personnel were concisely organized and carefully coordinated between universities and industry.

During the institutionalization of company training in Germany, diverging American and German concepts of required management qualifications and skills became evident. The differing understandings of what constitutes a company were also apparent. While the Americans considered a company as 'propriety', the Germans understood it to be an 'entity'.[67] As a result, there were clear efforts within German industry to adapt American concepts of management training to their own national traditions and philosophy.[68]

Sales, marketing and advertising

In the light of growing competition, German companies had quite a way to go in order to catch up in the area of sales, marketing and advertising. Increasingly dynamic markets and tougher international competition prompted more advertising and a greater receptiveness at Siemens for modern American marketing methods, and for orienting product and sales policies to the circumstances of the markets and needs of customers.[69]

In its domestic market, Siemens increasingly lagged behind the growth rates of the electrical market beginning in the mid-1950s. While the West German electrical industry grew 11.8 per cent in 1958, for example, Siemens managed only a 3.3 per cent sales growth in the same year. The reason for this lag was the company's neglect of the consumer goods business. The company first countered this trend by establishing Siemens-Electrogeräte AG (SE) on 1 October 1957.[70] This company subsequently formed a 50-50 joint venture with the household appliances division of Bosch; the new firm was called Bosch-Siemens Hausgeräte GmbH (BSHG).[71] Shortly after BSHG was founded, SE began to analyze the electrical appliance market in the US with the goal of projecting the gathered information to the European market and opening up new possibilities for boosting BSHG's appliance business.[72]

Compared to booming sales in this sector in the US, the slumping and nearly saturated German market for household appliances caused concern at the company. While unit sales in the consumer electronics sector climbed 155 per cent from 1958 to 1967 in the US, there was a decline of 10 per cent in Germany in the same period. To boost sales volume and increase its market share, SE established a concept that incorporated US marketing practices as well as US elements of product planning, product development, production, advertising and organization. The primary focus was a concentration on small appliances, consumer electronics and on mass retailers similar to that in the US, where door-to-door business had virtually disappeared and shopping centres, chain stores, drugstores and department stores with mail-order service had become the standard.

Following American practice, Siemens also increasingly recognized the importance of professional 'advertising and sales promotion', which was handled externally by qualified agencies and used in new media such as television to a far greater extent than in Germany.[73] BSHG hoped that the methods taken over from the US market would enable the company to substantially boost its sales in a period of 2 years, or up to 1970. Bosch set a target of doubling its comparably low sales in BSHG of DM18 million (fiscal year 1968).[74]

In the 1920s and 1930s, Siemens had already made efforts to unify the appearance of its advertising, established its own main advertising department, and hired the prominent market specialist Hans Domizlaff. The advertising style created by Domizlaff dominated the company's image campaigns well into the 1950s. In the course of the 1950s and 1960s, empirical methods of communication from the US gained increasing importance in the planning and implementation of advertising and public communications work.[75] In the 1960s, for example, the results of image analyses provided the basis for formulating a contemporary advertising style and corporate identity strategies. In 1964, Siemens was the first German electrical engineering company to commission an image analysis in order to evaluate the public's perception of the company.[76]

The empirical examination of advertising phenomenon by psychologists and sociologists had already been initiated in the 1920s in the US.[77] In Germany, scientific analyses were first used for advertising purposes in the 1950s and initially by companies in the consumer goods industry. Somewhat later, advertising research also began to be used in industrial advertising.[78] When Siemens first exceeded the million-mark level in advertising costs for electrical appliances and radio in 1950, the company hired an advertising researcher to ensure a systematic control of the effects and successes of its advertising. The job was clearly defined:

> The growing importance of consumer business and the steadily growing scope of our advertising planning for the sale of mass goods

makes it necessary to follow the effects of our advertising measures more systematically than in the past. This task is being taken over by the newly 'Research and Methodology' work group.[79]

Summary

As a result of the Second World War, German industry suffered major material (property, plant and equipment, monetary) and intellectual (knowledge, patents) losses and was faced with the daunting prospect of starting again. In order to close the gap with international competitors that had grown during the war, German companies above all oriented themselves to American models. This process began after the Second World War during the post-war Allied Occupation, largely dominated developments in the 1950s and 1960s, and waned only in the 1970s.

In the fields of organization, human resources, marketing or sales, companies gathered information on American principles and practices, accepted the ideas, or utilized new scientific findings such as in marketing research – and then developed their own strategies that best reflected their historical background, culture and corporate identity. In this way, Siemens oriented itself to divisional principles developed in the US when it reorganized in the 1960s, but based its changes on the different situation in Germany and focused on preserving the culture of a unified company, giving 'priority to the whole rather than its parts', as the later President and Chief Executive Officer Gerd Tacke formulated it.[80]

While American models served as a helpful orientation in developing company strategies in the areas just mentioned, rather than being taken over directly in the true sense of 'Americanization', the situation in technical fields was different. Here, one was economically dependent on contact with foreign partners – particularly technologically leading American firms – in order to catch up with international developments through technology and knowledge transfers. Old relationships, such as those nurtured between Siemens and Westinghouse between the wars, were renewed, and new contacts were made with American partners. The focus here was on completely normal technology transfers in technical fields such as semiconductor research, nuclear energy and data processing, which have been covered. In a similar fashion, Siemens later made strategic international alliances in chip development with Toshiba, IBM and Motorola.

I therefore believe it would be erroneous to speak of an 'Americanization' of the German electrical industry. Nor was there ever an 'Americanization' model. Rather, in the extremely difficult period following the Second World War and during the years of the country's 'economic miracle', German companies sought targeted support to compensate for the lack of know-how and competencies. Outside factors – such as the occupation, economic and industrial policies of the US after the war – and domestic factors – such as the change of generations in the 1950s – led to an orientation toward American structures and operational methods in parts of the German electrical industry. In the end, this led to a mixture of American and German elements in the industry.

Notes

1 W. Bührer, 'Auf eigenem Weg. Reaktion deutscher Unternehmer auf den Amerikanisierungsdruck', in H. Bude and B. Greiner (eds), *Westbindungen. Amerika in der Bundesrepublik*, Hamburg: Hamburger Edition, 1999, p. 182. See also the definition by Harm Schröter: '. . . impact and transfer of values, behaviour, institutions, symbols and norms which were widespread in the USA into the economic sphere of other states. . . .'; E. Moen and H.G. Schröter, 'Americanization as a Concept for Deeper Understanding of Economic Changes in Europe, 1945–1970', in H.G. Schröter and E. Moen (eds), *Une Americanisation des entreprises? Entreprise et Histoire* 19, 1998, pp. 5–13, 6.

2 R. Willett, *The Americanization of Germany, 1945–1949*, London: Routledge, 1989.

3 Cf. V. de Grazia, 'Amerikanisierung und wechselnde Leitbilder der Konsum-Moderne in Europa', in H. Siegrist, H. Kaelble and J. Kocka (eds), *Europäische Konsumgeschichte. Zur Gesellschafts- und Kulturgeschichte des Konsums (18.-20. Jahrhundert)*, Frankfurt: Campus, 1997, p. 109.

4 Cf. H.G. Schröter, 'Zur Übertragbarkeit sozialhistorischer Konzepte in die Wirtschaftsgeschichte. Amerikanisierung und Sowjetisierung in deutschen Betrieben 1945–1975', in K. Jarausch and H. Siegrist (eds), *Amerikanisierung und Sowjetisierung in Deutschland 1945–1970*, Frankfurt: Campus, 1997, p. 154.

5 Cf. Bührer, 'Auf eigenem Weg', p. 181 and P. Erker, ' "Amerikanisierung" der westdeutschen Wirtschaft? Stand und Perspektiven der Forschung', in Jarausch and Siegrist, *Amerikanisierung und Sowjetisierung*, p. 145.

6 Cf. Erker, ' "Amerikanisierung" der westdeutschen Wirtschaft?', p. 145.

7 Cf. Schröter, 'Zur Übertragbarkeit sozialhistorischer Konzepte in die Wirtschaftsgeschichte', pp. 164, 181.

8 Cf. E.A. McCreary, *The Americanization of Europe. The Impact of Americans and American Business on the Uncommon Market*, Garden City, NY: Doubleday, 1964, German title: *Die Dollar-Invasion. Amerikanische Firmen und Manager in Europa*, Munich: Moderne Verl.-GmbH, 1965, p. 23.

9 Cf. V. Berghahn, *Unternehmer und Politik in der Bundesrepublik*, Frankfurt: Suhrkamp, 1985, p. 330.

10 Directive JCS 1779 of July 1947 states that the Allied military government must give the Germans the opportunity 'to learn the principles and advantages of *free enterprise*,' quoted by R. Robert, *Konzentrationspolitik in der Bundesrepublik*, Berlin: Duncker & Humblot, 1976, p. 91.

11 In the period from April 1948 to the end of 1952, around US$13.9 billion poured into Europe, of which US$1.32 billion went to West Germany initially to provide food, and subsequently to provide raw materials, machines and other goods. An additional US$2.7 billion came from other aid programmes. In the Federal Republic of Germany, the ERP Special Fund was formed from the payments that had to be made by West German importers of American aid deliveries to the ERP Current Fund. The ERP Special Fund financed reconstruction loans and subsidies. Beginning in 1951, the ERP was also increasingly employed to ensure the military security of Western Europe.

12 Cf. *Wiederaufbau in Berlin-Siemensstadt. Investierungen 1945–1952*, S&H und SSW, Berlin, 1952, pp. 11, 14.

13 W. Feldenkirchen, *From Workshop to Global Player*, Munich: Piper, 2000, p. 253.
14 SAA 7489, correspondence of SSW-ZBL regarding the Erlangen departments. Here: Report on the decartelization of I.G.-Farben and Krupp.
15 SAA 15293, *Decartelization in Germany and Decartelization in the U.S. zone of Germany*, microfilm files (National Archives, Washington, D.C.). The term 'Decartelization' as used by the American authorities was inaccurate. What was actually meant was the breaking up of large German companies that exceeded a certain size.
16 SAA 52/Lo 750, parts 41–43, on the question of breaking up Siemens, cf. SAA 7375: SSW Report No. 56–65 to the British and American Occupying Powers; SAA 7510, press clippings primarily from newspapers in the Soviet Zone and close to the SED Party.
17 Cf. F. Wittendorfer, 'Das Haus Siemens in Erlangen 1945–1955', in J. Sandweg and G. Lehmann (eds), *Hinter unzerstörten Fassaden: Erlangen 1945–1955*, Erlangen: Palm & Enke, 1996, pp. 433–457, p. 439 f.
18 SAA 7506, *Position of Siemens for OMGUS in the question of whether S&H and SSW belong together*, 11 August 1947.
19 SAA 49/Lp 262.
20 SAA 7645, *report on the negotiations between Dr. Muscheidt, Technical Office, Frankfurt a.M., and the head of the Decartelization and Deconcentration Division in the High Commission for Germany*, W. O'Haire (Frankfurt am Main).
21 Cf. L. Vaubel, *Unternehmer gehen zur Schule. Ein Erfahrungsbericht aus USA*, Düsseldorf: Droste, 1952.
22 Cf. H. Hartmann, *Amerikanische Firmen in Deutschland*, Cologne: Westdeutscher Verlag, 1963.
23 Cf. *Der Arbeitgeber*, No. 12, May 15, 1950.
24 Cf. H. Hartmann, 'Amerikanische Firmen in Deutschland. Beobachtungen über Kontakte und Kontraste zwischen Industriegesellschaften', *Dortmunder Schriften zur Sozialforschung* 23, 1963.
25 Cf. SAA VVA Hans Panzerbieter, *Elektronische Bauteile für die Vermittlungstechnik. Bericht über die Amerikareise* (January/February, 1954); SAA 15/Lb 364, report on a study tour to the US to evaluate business administration problems in the electrical industry (6 August 1955), SAA 15/Ll 834: Report on a trip to the US to study the field of industrial automation (15 January 1957).
26 SAA 8163, *Erinnerungsbroschüre für Direktor Dr. Leukert anläßlich des Besuchs einer Siemens-Delegation bei Westinghouse* (1952).
27 In the period between the world wars, the Pretzfeld Laboratory at Siemens-Schuckertwerke had developed a process to produce highly purified silicon. Cf. B. Plettner, *Abenteuer Elektrotechnik. Siemens und die Entwicklung der Elektrotechnik seit 1945*, Munich: Piper, 1994, pp. 169 f., 193 ff.
28 SAA 54/Lb 2, Semiconductor agreement between SSW and Westinghouse of 20 July 1960.
29 SAA 7394, SAA 54/Lb 2, Z Memorandum No. 93 of 27 February 1953.
30 SAA 7394, Guidelines for the Exchange of Know-how between SSW and Westinghouse Electric Corporation (December 1954 and 19 June 1959).
31 Cf. *Die Entwicklung der Starkstromtechnik bei den Siemens-Schuckertwerken. Zum 50 jährigen Jubiläum* (Berlin-Siemensstadt and Erlangen 1953); *Chronik der Kraftwerkstechnik im Hause Siemens* (special issue of Siemens Power Journal 2/97, published by the Power Engineering Group of Siemens AG, 1997).
32 Cf. W.D. Müller, *Geschichte der Kernenergie in der Bundesrepublik Deutschland*, vols 1 and 2, Stuttgart: Schäffer, 1990 and 1996.
33 Cf. L. Schoen, 'W. Finkelnburg', in E. Feldtkeller and H. Goetzeler (eds), *Pioniere der Wissenschaft bei Siemens*, Munich: Siemens-Aktiengesellschaft, 1994, pp. 139–146.

34 The agreement was also quite important for the company's later Power Engineering Group, since it enabled Siemens to take over production methods for transformer magnetic sheet steel with preferred direction of magnetization and for thermoplastic insulation for high-voltage machines. SSW also adopted the American method of using sulphur hexafluoride (SF6) as an arc extinguishing gas in high-voltage switchgear in its switchgear plant in Berlin. SSW did this on its own, without the participation of Westinghouse. The 110-kilovolt switchgear developed at the Berlin plant was marketed long before similar switchgear was offered in the US. The steadily growing capacity in European electrical grids made this new generation of high-performance and safe switchgear necessary. Until the 1930s, dead-tank oil circuit-breakers were still in use; in this old system, the moveable switch contacts were in a pressurized container of oil. So-called expansion circuit-breakers were developed at Siemens-Schuckertwerke during this period, but they required as much continuous maintenance and monitoring as the old dead-tank oil system. Siemens did not adopt the use of compressed-air circuit breakers that were used in the 1960s, but rather continued development of the American system in which the electrical arc produced when high-voltage switches separate was extinguished with a gas, rather than with compressed air or a fluid. Sulphur hexafluoride met the requirements best of all.

35 Cf. H.-H. Krug, *Siemens und Kernenergie. 40 Jahre unternehmerisches Engagement für den Aufbau einer innovativen Technologie zur zukunftssicheren Energieversorgung* (unpublished manuscript in the Siemens archive), 1998, p. 14 ff.

36 Cf. W. Finkelnburg, 'Arbeiten und Probleme der Reaktor-Entwicklung bei den Siemens-Schuckertwerken', *Siemens-Zeitschrift* 33, 1959, pp. 743–744.

37 Cf. W. Oldekop, *Druckwasserreaktoren für Kernkraftwerke*, Munich: Thiemig, 1974.

38 The bilateral agreement ('State Treaty') required by the US government for the implementation of this cooperation agreement and the related technology transfers that were subject to government approval first took effect in June 1957.

39 Westinghouse began operations of the Yankee Rowe pressurized water reactor nuclear power plant in Rowe, Massachusetts, in July 1961; this was the first facility to use the basic design that is still used by the industry.

40 With the main equity partners Energie-Versorgung Schwaben AG, Stuttgart; Badenwerk AG, Karlsruhe; Technische Werke der Stadt Stuttgart AG; Neckarwerke Elektrizitätsversorgungs AG, Esslingen; Stadtwerke Karlsruhe.

41 In the US, a number of public utilities companies or authorities such as the Tennessee Valley Authority had already developed the first turnkey power plant projects with their own teams of experienced engineers. Manufacturers such as Westinghouse or General Electric merely supplied the nuclear-powered steam generator systems. Beginning in 1967, nuclear power plant construction was usually done by calling for bids for parts of the project, and having a team of architects and engineers supervise the work. The utility operators bore technical and business responsibility for the projects. This process of having a variety of suppliers provide separate parts of the project led to an unwieldy number of external interfaces during construction, which in turn considerably lengthened project times and increased costs.

42 At this time, the development of Westinghouse's 575-megawatt pressurized water nuclear reactor at Haddam Neck was already quite advanced; the facility went online in 1968. Cf. Krug, *Siemens und Kernenergie*, pp. 113–120.

43 Cf. E. Schomer, 'Die Bedeutung des Demonstrationskraftwerks KWO für die Entwicklung und den Betrieb der Druckwasser-Reaktoren von Siemens/KWU' in *Kernkraftwerk Obrigheim GmbH. 25 Jahre Betrieb des Kernkraftwerks Obrigheim.* Symposium on 25 April 1994, pp. 41–49.

44 SAA 54/Lb 2, SSW/PLA announcement of 12 September 1966.
45 During the bidding phase for the Obrigheim nuclear power plant, Siemens decided to draw on its own developments in pressurized water reactors and their successful application in research reactors as much as possible, without the help of Westinghouse. Accordingly, the planning and construction of Obrigheim was largely accomplished without the participation of Westinghouse. Westinghouse was also no longer involved in the nuclear power plant projects Atucha-1, Borssele and Biblis A. The end of the cooperation was merely a formal confirmation of what had long been a fact: the two companies had worked on their own for quite some time. After ending the cooperation with Westinghouse, KWU signed a new technology exchange agreement with US manufacturer Combustion Engineering in Windsor, Connecticut, in the field of pressurized water reactors. This cooperation had the primary goal of allowing Siemens to closely follow the approval procedures and technology developments in the field of nuclear energy in the US. In addition, the company also was considering the feasibility of using this cooperation to take part as a bidder in the large and rapidly expanding American market. This cooperation agreement lasted until 1990, yet had virtually no significant influence on nuclear power developments at KWU.
46 Cf. H. Janisch, *30 Jahre Siemens-Datenverarbeitung. Geschichte des Bereichs Datenverarbeitung 1954–1984* (unpublished manuscript in the Siemens archive), Munich, 1988, p. 23.
47 SAA 35-77/Lp 75, special issue of *Digital-Rechner 2002, Entwicklungsberichte der Siemens AG*, October, 1959.
48 Cf. Janisch, *30 Jahre Siemens-Datenverarbeitung*, p. 39.
49 According to experts, RCA had a technical edge on IBM in the 1960s, yet had only a 3 per cent market share in the US compared to IBM's share of over 72 per cent. Cf. R. Malik, *And Tomorrow . . . the World? Inside IBM*, London: Millington Books, 1975, pp. 143–145.
50 RCA had already unsuccessfully sought to form a cooperation with Siemens in 1958 with its 501 business computer. Siemens rejected this approach, however, because of its recently developed 2002 system.
51 Cf. Janisch, *30 Jahre Siemens-Datenverarbeitung*, p. 55; cf. also SAA 54/Ll 91, ZI-Nachrichten No. 131 of 15 July 1969.
52 RCA held 49 per cent and Siemens 51 per cent stakes in the Brazilian company 'Interdata Empresea S.A. para Sistemas de Computadores Ltda.'; RCA's stake in the Venezuelan company of the same name was 51 per cent and Siemens' 49 per cent.
53 Cf. Janisch, *30 Jahre Siemens-Datenverarbeitung*, p. 65.
54 *Datamation*, 1 November 1971, pp. 42–45.
55 SAA 60/Ll 700, ZI Internal Memorandum 5/1971.
56 SAA 35-77/Lp 77, Siemens press conference of 18 September 1971. According to Siemens, the value of the installed and ordered Siemens computer systems (1,500 units) was approximately DM3.3 billion. The company held a 16 per cent market share in computer systems installed in West Germany, and had a 20 per cent share of new orders at the time.
57 In addition to technical and economic considerations, planned changes in Germany's stock laws prompted the company to make a major reorganization. Cf. W. Feldenkirchen, *Siemens. Von der Werkstatt zum Weltunternehmen*, Munich: Piper, 1997, p. 295 ff.
58 The reorganization created the following operating Groups (UB): Components (B), Data Systems (D), Power Engineering (E), Electrical Installations (I), Medical Engineering (Med) and Telecommunication (N). At the same

time, five corporate departments (Z) were established to provide consulting, coordinating and administrative services to the company: Business Administration (ZB), Finance (ZF), Personnel (ZP), Technology (ZT) and Sales and Marketing (ZV). Cf. Annual Report 1968/69, pp. 14–15.

59 The company's regional offices and foreign subsidiaries were equal partners of the operating Groups and contributed to the company's product programme and in developing business goals.

60 For a comparison of various organizational models, see G. Tacke, *Ein Beitrag zur Geschichte der Siemens AG* (unpublished manuscript in the Siemens archive), 1977, pp. 226–278. Other German firms, such as Daimler-Benz, at the time were also considering a new organizational structure. Daimler-Benz used Booz Allen and Hamilton to work out plans for a new organizational structure, but rejected them. Cf. Minutes of the Board-Meeting, 30 November 1971. At the time it was said that 'American consulting firms always wanted to sell organizational schemes that might fit American firms to European companies without taking their specific character and culture into account'. Thus the reaction at Daimler-Benz was similar to the point of view taken in 1954, when the introduction 'of an American organization' was rejected by the board, as not taking Daimler's corporate culture into account. Cf. Minutes of the Board, 30 April 1954.

61 Cf. Gerd Tacke, lecture at the Siemens Conference on 13 March 1971, SAA S 12.

62 Ibid.

63 Cf. *Dokumentation zur Personalpolitik 1950–1974* (unpublished study by the Human Resources Policy department at Siemens AG), 1974, p. 5 ff.

64 SAA VVA, R. Meine, *Das Ausbildungswesen in der amerikanischen Industrie (Beobachtungen und Erfahrungen während einer Studienreise nach den USA)*, 1955. The study tour of training systems in American industry included visits to Esso Standard Oil, Westinghouse, Bell, Alcoa, and DuPont. Cf. for the American influence on management education in Germany in general and at Siemens in particular M. Kipping, 'The Hidden Business Schools. Management Training in Germany Since 1945', in L. Engwall and V. Zamagni (eds), *Management Education in Historical Perspective*, Manchester: Manchester University Press, 1998, pp. 95–110.

65 SAA, Z Memorandum No. 10/72 of 10 December 1971, concerning guiding principles for managers at Siemens, with appendix.

66 SAA 14/Lr 492, on the continuing education of engineers in the US Report on a US tour to study production-oriented, technical training system in the US, from 20 October to 7 November 1975.

67 Cf. Bührer, 'Auf eigenem Weg', p. 194 f.

68 Ibid., p. 195.

69 Cf. O. Schwabenthan, *Unternehmenskommunikation für Siemens*, manuscript, 1995, in SAA 9871, p. 85.

70 SAA 7846, Z Memorandum on the founding of SE; SAA 9639; cf. also Feldenkirchen, *Siemens. Von der Werkstatt zum Weltunternehmen*, pp. 280 ff., 376–379.

71 SAA 68/Li 137: consortium agreement.

72 SAA 68/Li 137: Analysis of the small electrical appliance market in the US Study tour of Mr. Fromm, Mr. Prahl and Dr. Rumswinkel from 15 May to 29 June 1968.

73 Approximately 80 per cent of the company's national advertising in the US in 1967 was with TV spots; Cf. ibid., p. 9.

74 For 1968, BSHG projected total sales of more than DM100 million, of which SE would contribute DM82 million and Bosch DM18 million. Cf. ibid., p. 22.

75 Cf. Schwabenthan, *Unternehmenskommunikation für Siemens*, p. 85.
76 Cf. E. Knacke, 'Analyse des Firmenbildes. Fallbeispiel zur Kommunikations-forschung', in D. Rost (ed.), *So wirbt Siemens*, Düsseldorf: Econ, 1971, pp. 31–47.
77 Cf. H.G. Schröter, 'Die Amerikanisierung der Werbung in der Bundesrepublik Deutschland', *Jahrbuch für Wirtschaftsgeschichte* 1997/1, 99.
78 Cf. O. Schwabenthan, 'Die Werbeforschung dringt vor', in Rost (ed.), *So wirbt Siemens*, p. 301.
79 Ibid., p. 302.
80 Cf. Tacke, lecture at the Siemens Conference on 13 March 1971.

7 The Americanization and Japanization of electronics firms in post-war Japan

Shin Hasegawa

Introduction

The purpose of this chapter is to offer a study of the influence of Americanization on Japanese electronics firms from the 1950s to the mid-1970s. Looking back on the history of Japanese electronics firms, it is hard to deny the enormous influence of American enterprise. For example, the NEC Corporation was founded as a subsidiary of Western Electric in 1899, and General Electric Co. tied up with Tokyo Denki (Tokyo Electric Co.) in 1905 and Shibaura Seisakusho (Shibaura Engineering Works) in 1909.[1] The establishment of subsidiaries such as these and the signing of various technology agreements helped spur the pace of technology transfer for electro-mechanical and management technologies. Japan's electro-mechanical and electronics industry developed in no small measure through so-called Americanization.[2]

However, the 1930s saw a new Japanization of the firms that had formed cooperative relationships with American enterprises. Behind this new Japanization was an underlying sentiment for the need to bolster domestic production capabilities; at the same time, the panic of 1929 played no small part in cash-strapped American enterprises pulling out from their overseas subsidiaries, and choosing to cede management rights to local managers and local stockholders, etc. For example, ISE (International Standard Electric Co.) ceded the rights to manage its subsidiary, the NEC Corporation, to Sumitomo *zaibatsu* in 1932.

Subsequent to the controlled economy and seizure of foreign-owned assets during World War II, post-war Japan maintained strict regulations relating to foreign capital, including the inability of firms to obtain licensing, etc. if they were more than 50 per cent owned by foreign investors. The capital liberalization that started during the mid-1960s led to deregulation of foreign capital investments; however, high-tech industries, including computers, semiconductors and others, were still subject to regulation until the 1970s. Broadly speaking, this so-called Japanization continued from the 1930s through to the 1980s.[3] Finally, the 1990s brought with it another period of Americanization. Throughout the period of

Japanization, Japanese enterprises were still subject to the influence of Americanization. We see the influence and advance of Americanization in aspects of technology, organization, and management especially during the reformation period after World War II, in spite of the Japanese government's policy of strictly regulating foreign capital.

That the post-war introduction of overseas technology contributed greatly to Japan's industrial development is well known. For example, Akira Goto makes the following three points related to reasons behind the aggressive, and successful, introduction of leading-edge technologies after World War II: fierce competition in the midst of a growing market, absorptive capacity and government industrial policy.[4] Akira Goto further indicates that attractive incentives based in the market mechanism are a necessary condition for the pro-active introduction of technology, and that the absorptive capacity to import, to adapt and to use technology is sufficient condition for successful introduction.

For the analysis I offer here, I will assume the validity of these conditions, while focusing particular attention on intra-enterprise conditions, especially those of absorptive capacity. The subjects selected for analysis will be the general purpose computer, the semiconductor and the integrated circuit (IC) – technologies representing the foundation of post-World War II electronics goods. The purpose of my focusing on intra-enterprise conditions lies in the facts that market growth acts as a prerequisite condition for all enterprises, the introduction of leading technology is subject to relatively low levels of constraints, and industrial policy did not act as an immediately discriminatory phenomenon. On the other hand, we see a relatively large discrepancy among various enterprises related to receptivity of technology, as well as in the levels of business success experienced by and among them. By paying close attention to these inter-enterprise differences, I believe I can shed light on the absorptive capacity in the electronics firms. In other words, the purpose behind writing this chapter is to further clarify the Japanization of electronics firms in post-war Japan.[5]

The general purpose computer

The transfer of computer technology to Japanese enterprises

Japanese enterprises encountered a significant obstacle preventing them from embarking upon the manufacture of computers. That obstacle was the fact that IBM held basic patents relating to computers, and IBM policy at the time was to give permission to use these patents only to wholly-owned subsidiaries. Without using IBM's basic patents, the domestic manufacture of computers would be difficult at best, and the question of access to IBM's basic patents was the key to the very existence of Japanese computer enterprises.

The Ministry of International Trade and Industry (MITI) appealed to IBM to license the basic patents to Japanese companies. However, IBM rejected MITI's request, citing the long-standing policy of IBM to license patents only to wholly-owned subsidiaries. Meanwhile, IBM planned to begin production of computers in Japan through their IBM Japan subsidiary, who had to pay the accompanying patent license fees. IBM also wanted to send dividends from IBM Japan back to IBM headquarters in the US. Both of these plans required prior approval from MITI.[6]

MITI demanded that in exchange for approving the patent license agreement between IBM Japan and IBM World Trade Corporation, and for allowing IBM Japan to send dividends back to the US firm, IBM must also grant patent license agreements to Japanese computer enterprises. Ultimately, IBM gave in to the ministry demands, and in 1960 granted licenses to eight Japanese computer firms (Hitachi, Toshiba, Mitsubishi Electric, NEC Corporation, Fujitsu, Oki Electric Industry, Matsushita Electric and Hokushin Denki) allowing the firms to use IBM patented technology. In addition, IBM Japan had started to manufacture computers based on a technology transfer agreement they signed with IBM headquarters. This course of events led to eight Japanese computer firms being able to conduct computer product development without running foul of IBM's basic patents.[7]

In this case, MITI was in a position to influence the negotiations between IBM and the Japanese computer firms. The Foreign Investment Law and the Foreign Exchange and Foreign Trade Control Law gave MITI a pretext for placing itself in the middle of these inter-firm negotiations. The fact that the Foreign Investment Law required application to the government for technology agreements gave MITI the upper hand during the course of talks.[8] Although MITI's aggressive stance was partly due to the pleas of Japanese computer companies, the ministry fully understood the importance of computer technology and the need for Japanese enterprises to be able to manufacture computers domestically. Again, MITI stepped in to encourage Japanese firms to bring in technology from overseas. At the same time, Japanese firms were also aggressively pursuing tie-ups with overseas computer enterprises.

Although Japanese enterprises had secured the licenses for IBM's basic patents, Japanese firms were sorely lacking in computer manufacturing skills and know-how. Between 1961 and 1962, technical assistance agreements were formed between NEC and Honeywell, Toshiba and GE, Hitachi and RCA, Oki and Sperry Rand, and Mitsubishi Electric and TRW. Only Fujitsu was unsuccessful in securing an appropriate partner, finally choosing to pursue computer manufacturing through independent development.[9]

The two cases of NEC and OKI are chosen from the above-mentioned five firms, and are compared in the following sections. NEC succeeded in absorbing foreign technology and developed its own technology, while

OKI failed to introduce foreign technology and withdrew from the development of general purpose computers.

The NEC Corporation: from the tie-up with Honeywell Inc. to independent development

In this section, I will use the history of NEC to illustrate the influence of imported technology on computer development and computer production in the Japanese enterprise.

Koji Kobayashi was in charge of the computer division at NEC in the early 1960s. In 1960, he began his study of computer manufacturing, visiting firms in America and Europe. Ultimately, Kobayashi selected Honeywell as a partner for NEC. Kobayashi gives the reasons why he selected Honeywell in his own words:

> First, NEC Corporation did not have the wherewithal to simultaneously develop the entire range of small-, medium- and large-scale computers. But we knew that it would be imperative for us to be able to offer a family series of machines from small to large. In other words, we decided to introduce outside technology to compensate for the deficiencies in our line-up, until we were able to introduce our own innovations in a full range of machines. Second, we didn't have the software. IBM's strength was in its software technology and library of applications. On the hardware side, we had been able to develop a transistor machine on our own, so the gap wasn't that great. But we were still weak in software, so we decided to form a cooperative relationship with Honeywell to compensate for our weaknesses.[10]

What Kobayashi learned after his study in the United States was that the keys to success in the computer business were (1) large sums of capital and (2) software. Kobayashi knew that NEC at the time was deficient in its development capabilities, including that for software; therefore, NEC needed to form a cooperative relationship with an appropriate partner in the United States. With the lessons learned, the NEC Corporation began the search for an American partner, finally concluding a technical assistance agreement with Honeywell in 1962.[11] At the time, Honeywell was producing the well-received H400, a machine compatible with IBM's 1401, and Honeywell was expanding its market share in the segment. In addition, Honeywell had just announced the H200, a machine rivalling the IBM 1401 in cost performance, further expanding Honeywell's share of the US market. The favourable reputation of the H200 had even reached Japan, where NEC had just begun knockdown production of a similar machine. When IBM announced the launch of the IBM System 360 Series in 1964, Honeywell came out with its own series based on the H200. NEC engaged in knockdown production based on this H Series offering the machine to the market in Japan as the 'NEAC2200 Series'.[12]

Unfortunately, the formation of a product line-up for the Japanese market was not as simple a task as NEC had initially envisioned. Much of the difficulty stemmed from the fact that Honeywell provided the mid-scale H200 as the core series to NEC, while NEC was asking for a series of small- and large-scale machines – machines that the Japanese market was demanding at the time. As a result, NEC was forced to develop a series of machines on its own to meet the demand of the Japanese market. In 1964, NEC announced the small-scale NEAC-1210, a machine developed using parametric elements and scoring well on the cost-performance scale. In 1967 NEC introduced the NEAC-1240. This machine was a small office computer incorporating IC technology, and was a favourite among users of small- and mid-scale computers. Using independently developed technology, NEC was able to tailor a small-scale computer for the Japanese market.[13]

There were also many Japanese computer users asking for large-scale computers. As online systems were introduced during the mid-1960s, the demand for large-scale computers with online communications functions grew rapidly. In response, NEC began development of the Model 500 as the top-of-the line model in the NEAC2200 series. At the time, the development group at the central laboratory (having developed the ultra high-speed NEAC-L2) and the Computer Division development group (having experience in manufacturing the H800 and other large-scale machines) had been putting together a joint development plan for a new large-scale computer. The genesis of the Model 500 came from a request received from Osaka University to develop a computer to replace the large-scale IBM7090 at the University.[14]

In this manner, NEC was able to complement imported technology with independent development to quickly enhance their level of technological capability in the computer manufacturing field. NEC demonstrated a high absorptive capacity for technology based on their capability to build upon their independently developed large-scale hardware platforms in order to produce small- and large-scale products/product line-up tailored to meet the demands of the Japanese market.

That NEC had a high level of absorptive capacity was further illustrated as the cooperative relationship with Honeywell evolved. The IBM 360 Series and 370 Series commanded the lion's share of the computer market from the late 1960s through to the mid-1970s. This left other computer enterprises in fierce competition with each other and with IBM for market share. During this time Honeywell had been able to carve out a comfortable market niche as a producer of small- and mid-scale computers; however, NEC had long wanted to develop a full range of machines. These conflicting goals led NEC to question whether Honeywell was the most suitable partner with whom to work. At this point NEC reached a dilemma in their relationship with Honeywell. Honeywell was not able, or willing, to provide the new series of machines that NEC wanted. Meanwhile, NEC had developed the Model 700 as the successor to the large-scale Model 500, and had also independently successfully introduced a small-scale model for entry users. NEC found itself in a position of having to run its computer business, while independently developing machines to fill out the gaps in the Honeywell series that could not satisfy the Japanese market.[15]

Ultimately, NEC reached a point where it had to reconsider its relationship with a partner which could not offer NEC a new revolutionary series of computers. However, NEC had been relying on Honeywell to develop the revolutionary computer architecture. In October 1971 Koji Kobayashi, now president of NEC, held a meeting with Honeywell's president Stephan F. Keating during which it was agreed that the two companies would share the development of the byte-based machines, which was under the supervision of Honeywell's global development centre. Being impressed with the Honeywell proposal for a total computer architecture, NEC chose to continue joint development with Honeywell, rather than choosing the path of independent development.[16]

Unfortunately, during the development process, Honeywell's development capabilities fell far short of NEC's expectations. The work on the hardware and operating system software at each centre failed to progress as planned, leading to many changes and delays in the development schedule. NEC was forced to dedicate many of its own engineers to Honeywell's part of the project as well, frantically working to complete the development of the operating system for the new series.[17] This new series was called the ACOS Series, and was introduced to the Japanese market after 1976. What became apparent during the ACOS Series development process was first and foremost that NEC possessed greater hardware development capability than did Honeywell. This was especially true in the area of hardware design that incorporated the latest component technology, where NEC was every bit the equal, or better, of Honeywell. Second, NEC did not surpass Honeywell in terms of creative computer architecture conception. At the time in 1971, NEC made the decision to stake the future of their computer business on the conceptions created by Honeywell; and the result was not as NEC expected. Third, in spite of the disappointment, the process of developing the operating system for the ACOS Series allowed NEC to form the foundations for its own independent capabilities in software and computer development. By the late 1970s, NEC was fully able to develop its own computer series, without needing to rely on Honeywell.[18]

*Oki Electric Industry Co., Ltd.: the tie-up with Sperry Rand Corporation
and the withdrawal from the general purpose computer*

Meikosha, the predecessor of Oki Electric Industry Co., Ltd., was founded
in 1881. Boasting an even longer history than the NEC Corporation, this
maker of communications devices was part of the 'Den Den Family',
forging a close relationship with Nippon Telegraph and Telephone Public
Corporation (NTTPC), so-called Den Den Kosha, Oki's largest customer
at the time. Oki Electric specialized in the development and manufacturing of computer peripherals such as punch typewriters for punch-card
systems and line printers.[19]

Oki expanded beyond peripherals with the successful development of a
parametric computer, the OPC-1 in 1959, two versions of a transistor computer in 1960, the OTC-6020, which used a magnetic drum as its main
memory, and the first domestically produced computer with a magnetic
core memory, the OKITAC-5080. In 1961 Oki introduced the OKITAC-
5090A model, which was based on the technology of the OKITAC-5080.
Rather than using a magnetic drum, which was standard for main memory
at the time, this new model used a high-capacity core memory, with an
access time clocked at a cycle time of 25 micro-seconds (as against 2.0 to
3.0 milliseconds average for a magnetic drum). With a high-performance
CPU and excellent I/O interface, the OKITAC-5090 boasted superior cost
performance, and became a best-selling model with over 150 units sold to
universities (beginning with the prestigious Tokyo University), research
laboratories and other customers within 2 years of its introduction.[20]

Although Oki Electric was not one of the original pioneers of computer
manufacturing in Japan, the success of the OKITAC Series and other
products generated favourable results for the firm, which found itself a
respected and central player in Japan's computer industry. At the time,
many of the OKITAC machines were used by universities or used to run
scientific calculations in research labs run by private enterprise. The
company still had not had great success marketing computers for office
applications.[21] Oki Electric's computer business experienced a more successful start than the company could have imagined, but development on
the successor series to the OKITAC ran into delays. These delays were
caused by the cooperative relationship Oki Electric formed with the US
computer firm Sperry Rand Corporation. The following is an account of
the events leading to this cooperative relationship between Oki Electric
and Sperry Rand.

Oki Electric first received an inquiry from the Ministry of International
Trade and Industry as to whether Oki Electric was interested in pursuing a
technical assistance agreement with a foreign enterprise. Oki Electric con-
sidered their response to MITI during the managing directors' meeting in
December 1961. Before that, Oki Electric had initiated discussions with
IBM, RCA, Burroughs, Bull, GE and ICT. Of these foreign firms, Oki Elec-

tric felt that either GE or ICT would make an appropriate partner.[22] In other words, at that stage, Oki Electric had never considered the possibility of forming a relationship with Sperry Rand. In 1960, Sperry Rand had conducted negotiations with Toshiba; however, Sperry Rand's basic stance was that they would only supply technology to a firm in which Sperry Rand held a majority ownership. As the American firm refused to budge on this point, the two companies were never able to reach an agreement, and broke off talks in December 1961.[23] Spurred on by the need to find a new candidate with whom to form a partnership, Sperry Rand looked to Oki Electric.

By April 1962, Oki Electric had received a proposal from Sperry Rand, and was debating the merits of the proposal internally. According to the Sperry Rand proposal, the two firms would form a joint venture, Oki Remington Co., Ltd., for the purpose of manufacturing computers. Computer sales would be handled by Remington Univac Japan. Oki Electric's counterproposal was to have Remington license patents and know-how to Remington Univac Japan, while Oki Electric operated as a sublicense holder. Oki Electric would manufacture the computers, and Remington Univac Japan would oversee the sales.[24]

Within the same month, Sperry Rand rejected Oki Electric's proposal, holding fast to their position that sales be made under the Univac brand and that Sperry Rand should have at least a 51 per cent ownership of the venture. Sperry Rand did, however, acknowledge Oki Electric's desire to continue the OKITAC Series. The American firm also appeared to be committed to creating a successful partnership with Oki Electric. Oki Electric decided to look further into the merits of a partnership with Sperry Rand, and sent a group of engineers to the Remington Rand division, Sperry Rand's computer business. At this point, Oki Electric abandoned the idea of producing the Remington Rand computers, and began to lean more in the direction of Sperry Rand's initial proposal.[25]

In July 1962 the plan for a joint venture between Sperry Rand International Corporation (SRI) and Oki Electric began to take shape. The new manufacturing venture, Oki Remington Co., Ltd., would be 51 per cent owned by Oki, with SRI owning 49 per cent. Both companies would contribute the same number of directors, and in the future Oki would transfer 2 per cent of its ownership to SRI. What this proposal meant was that Oki Electric would retain the formal management rights to the new firm, but give those rights to SRI in the near future. As opposed to the negotiations with Toshiba, SRI appeared amenable to a proposal that would mean giving management rights to Oki Electric initially, with the rights transferring to SRI after a certain period of time.[26]

Once the basic outline of the proposal was accepted, the parties moved on to thrashing out the details. The course of negotiations included discussions about the new joint venture manufacturing the OKITAC, as well as housing a technical development team. However, the actual OKITAC production plans in November 1962 called for a gradual decrease in

OKITAC production volume.[27] The agreement establishing the joint venture was signed in October 1962,[28] and in November of the following year, Oki Univac Co., Ltd. was born.[29] In the final agreement, Oki Electric held a 51 per cent ownership in Oki Univac, versus a 49 per cent ownership by Univac – no clear provision was made for an eventual transfer of 2 per cent of ownership from Oki Electric to Univac. According to stipulations related to the board of directors, Oki Electric and Sperry Rand were to provide no less than three directors each. In addition, Suteji Kanbe, president of Oki Electric, was also named president of the new Oki Univac joint venture. As can be seen, Sperry Rand made quite a few concessions relating to management rights, allowing Oki Electric to retain the formal rights to guide the new firm.

However, the actual management of Oki Univac moved in a direction quite apart from Oki Electric's original intent. First, the assimilation of Univac computer technology, and the licensed production of computers at Oki Univac ran counter to Oki Electric's expectations. Computer production for Oki Univac began with the small- and mid-scale Univac machines. In 1965 the firm began manufacturing the mid-scale 9000 Series. Production never began on any large-scale Univac machines.[30] In the meantime (1968), Oki Electric planned to independently develop a large-scale computer, but the machine never made it into full-scale production, mainly due to the fact that the expected influx of computer technology from Univac never materialized. After reaching a peak in 1974, computer sales for Oki Univac slumped, while comparative sales for computer peripherals had been increasing.[31]

Second, the strategy to have Oki Univac take over the OKITAC Series from Oki Electric was substantively abandoned at the time the joint venture contract was formalized. The consensus among Oki Electric engineers at the beginning of negotiations was that the company should keep the independent development of the series in Oki Electric. Once the new partnership was established, the firms studied the feasibility of having the joint venture take over the OKITAC, and ultimately agreed to do so. However, when the new joint venture never actually got around to manufacturing the OKITAC, it became apparent that Oki Electric had done nothing more than abandon their development of the general purpose computer.

Comparison of NEC Corporation and Oki Electric Industry Co. Ltd.

NEC Corporation was able to successfully assimilate and digest general purpose computer technology from Honeywell and GE, fostering the ability to eventually pursue independent technological development. On the other hand, Oki Electric was unable to assimilate Univac's computer technology, which ultimately led the Japanese firm to drop out of the general purpose computer market altogether. Why, in very similar circumstances, did these two firms end up with such completely different outcomes? I submit that the differences can be accounted for in (1) understanding of the computer business, (2) policies and decisions of top management, and (3) internal technological groundwork and Human Resource.

Understanding of the computer business

I have described above how the then NEC vice-president Koji Kobayashi went to Europe and America in the early 1960s to study computer firms, met with top management at these companies and learned about the future direction of the computer business, as well as the potential dangers involved. After returning to Japan, records show that Kobayashi reported to his company that

> the computer business requires vast sums of capital. Not only does a company have to deal with the hardware, but then there's also software, the combination of which drives an enormous cost profile. In addition, software developers are a completely different type of human altogether (compared with hardware developers) ... there is no way [NEC] can even attempt to capture market share in the computer business as we are now.[32]

NEC top management learned first hand the risks of the computer business, as well as the need for software skills.

In contrast, Oki Electric's top management was aware of the need to form a partnership with an overseas firm, but they did not seem to have a complete understanding of the computer business in Europe and America. In addition Oki Electric did not send its Computer Division managers over to investigate Sperry Rand until after negotiations between the two firms had already started.

Policies and decisions of top management

In the case of NEC, Koji Kobayashi, as the person in charge of NEC's computer division, and as president from 1965, was directly involved in all major policies related to the computer business. In December 1960, NEC secured licenses for IBM's basic patents, and launched its Electronics Division, plunging headlong into the computer business.[33]

In contrast, Oki Electric seemed to lack a firm policy related to the future of its computer business. In December 1961, Oki Electric determined to follow an in-house development policy by which the firm would (1) place complete trust in its own engineers, and provide them with as much support as possible in pursuit of independent system development through their own internal efforts, and (2) send its engineers to American universities, IBM research laboratories and factories, etc. in order to bring leading edge technology into the firm. During management discussions, President Suteji Kanbe acknowledged the need to introduce new technology into the firm and, with an eye towards the important nature of the computer business, asked that all involved carefully consider the options available to Oki Electric. Opinions among top management varied. Some executives argued for the company to pursue the computer business using domestically developed technology alone; others argued for the need to form a cooperative relationship with another company.[34]

President Kanbe would later say that Oki Electrics' foray into computers was to establish the groundwork for developing electronic switching equipment. Compared with NEC, it appears that Oki Electric's top management was not as serious about the computer business itself. In addition, an executive assigned to Oki Electric from its main bank said that he was sceptical about the future of the computer business, and was generally negative about Oki Electric's involvement in computers.[35] While never reaching a solid consensus among top management, Oki Electric continued negotiations to form the Oki Univac joint venture.

Internal technological groundwork and human resource

The NEC Corporation was able to maintain and increase the type of engineers needed to continue independent technological development, even after forming its partnership with Honeywell. Since the start of knockdown production from Honeywell, the NEC engineering group that had been working on a large-scale computer had been freed from the necessity of supervising the manufacturing process, and therefore could devote its time and energy to the new development of a large-scale machine. In addition, NEC had a group in its central research laboratory that already had the successful development of a large-scale computer on its resume. Both groups joined forces to create a large-scale computer which met the needs of Osaka University.[36] This led directly to the successful development of the NEAC2200 Series Model 500.

In the course of the technology partnership with Honeywell, NEC replaced its main computer series with a Honeywell product. However, NEC maintained its own independent development group to complement the Honeywell series with small- and large-scale computers. The production of a series of computers particularly suited to the Japanese market was mainly due to the development capabilities that NEC fostered in-house, independent of their relationship with Honeywell. Furthermore, NEC was able to utilize the Honeywell and GE architecture in the development of the ACOS Series.[37] By successfully integrating this architecture and operating system, the Japanese firm built on the groundwork of advanced component development capability, and introduced a competitive new generation of computers to the market.

In contrast, Oki Electric opted to pursue the production of a general purpose computer in Japan through the Oki Univac joint venture with Sperry Rand. With the success of the OKITAC 5090, the Oki Electric Computer Division at first attempted to expand their computer business internally, but eventually abandoned the expansion of the OKITAC Series after the founding of Oki Univac. The inability to effect a substantial technology transfer from Oki Univac to Oki Electric, and the termination of general purpose computer development created a serious 'brain drain' (loss of talented engineers) in Oki Electric. As a result of their partnership with the Sperry Rand Corporation, Oki Electric Industry not only missed out on a chance to participate in computer technology development, but they were also forced to exit the market for general purpose computers, as they were unable to compete with other computer enterprises.

Taking into account the three factors discussed above, NEC was certainly more fortunate than Oki Electric. In the end, it was not the technological capacity of their partner that improved the Japanese enterprises' competitiveness. Rather, it was the level of absorptive capacity of the Japanese firm to computer technology that determined the effectiveness of the technology transfer. The enterprise showing the highest absorptive capacity was able to enhance its competitiveness in the general purpose computer market, going on to be successful in the computer business.

The semiconductor

The introduction of American technology and the development of MOS technology

About the only noteworthy contribution of Japanese enterprise to the early days of semiconductor research is the SONY discovery of the tunnel diode in 1957.[38] Without argument, American enterprise led the way in semiconductor research throughout the 1950s and 1960s, generating an impressive number of valuable inventions. Relying on technological assistance contracts, Japanese enterprises adopted American technology, endeavouring to use what they learned in bringing new products to the market. One example is an account from Minoru Ohno of the Transistor Department of Hitachi, Ltd.'s central research laboratory. Minoru Ohno recollects that his sole job in 1957 was to take the manufacturing specifications received from RCA, translate the documents, convert inches into centimetres, and redraw the plans accordingly.[39]

As Minoru Ohno says, introduction of technology at the time consisted of faithfully reproducing past technologies, which of course did not lead immediately to independent innovations. Rather, the introduction of foreign technology gave Japanese engineers the opportunity for independent development in a more indirect manner. For example, in the words of Hiroe Osafune, founder of NEC Corporation's semiconductor business,

'NEC was behind the technology curve in transistors. However, I was able to call on our close relationship with GE, Western Electric, Bell Labs and others in order to discuss future goals and technology forecasts with their engineers. These discussions really played a big role in helping me see the direction of the new silicon technology.'[40] One of the greatest benefits derived by the engineers from Japanese firms was the chance to soak up the latest information and technological concepts from their American counterparts.

While the 1950s was a period of technology assimilation, the 1960s saw Japanese enterprises contribute major discoveries, albeit in a limited scope. One of the most important such discoveries was in MOS transistor development. At the time, the US and Japan were virtually neck-and-neck in terms of MOS transistor development. Minoru Ohno provides an outline of the events surrounding Hitachi's MOS transistor development.[41]

1   In July 1958, the Transistor Department was spun out into its own department (later becoming the Musashi Factory), independent of the Central Research Lab. Ohno was placed in charge of the Development Department, overseeing development of the silicon transistor. Ohno and his team developed their own manufacturing process, succeeding in the development of the mesa-structure silicon transistor.

2   Ohno was shocked to learn of the discovery of planar transistors by Fairchild Semiconductor in 1960. The shock was all the greater because Ohno realized that he was close to conceptualizing a planar transistor himself. In the following year, Ohno spent some time training and working at RCA, where he personally witnessed the conversion from mesa-structure to a planar transistor. Upon returning to Japan, Ohno immediately embarked upon planar transistor development.

3   At the time, Hitachi was more interested in developing its own independent technology than in the planar structure. But Ohno was convinced that planar structure would be a mainstream technology in the future, and continued proactive MOS transistor research. In 1962, Ohno gave a speech to a scientific society about the planar transistor's field cooling effect, and in the following year, again gave a speech reporting on the successful test production of a MOS transistor based on this conception.

4   Neither Hitachi, nor anyone else in Japan for that matter, showed much interest in Ohno's successful test production of MOS transistors. At the time in 1964, MOS transistors were mainly used for home electronics such as radios and TVs – there was no widespread industrial demand for the transistors.

5   The general view of MOS would not change until the advent of the integrated circuit. In 1965, several managers from Hitachi travelled to RCA and conveyed back to Hitachi the interest that RCA had

demonstrated in Ohno's MOS transistor discovery, and that RCA was pursuing a MOS development project in earnest. Hitachi hastily dispatched Ohno to America, embarking on MOS IC research. When Ohno returned to Japan, everything was in place for MOS IC development. A major reason for this turnabout was that the company had received requests from other Japanese enterprises to develop a MOS IC for use in calculators, a market expected to expand dramatically in the near future. In 1966 Hitachi came out with the HD700 Series, which incorporated p-channel MOS IC.

6   In the process of developing planar transistors based on the field cooling effect, Ohno and his team discovered new truths about the fundamental structure of silicon crystals, enabling them to create methods which would improve the special properties of the MOS transistor. Successfully patenting these discoveries and methods, Hitachi was now in a favourable position to conduct patent negotiations related to MOS transistors with American and other firms.

NEC Corporation also embarked on MOS transistor development at about the same time as Hitachi. In February of 1963 the news came out that RCA had developed a MOS transistor. In July of the same year, RCA publicly announced a patent for the MOS transistor. Based on this information, NEC perfected an n-channel MOS transistor sample in December of the same year. In July of 1964, a p-channel MOS transistor was developed.[42] Several things are apparent from the circumstances surrounding the development of the MOS transistor. First, even though the research facilities and project resources were much greater in the US in the early 1960s, Japanese enterprises were able to successfully develop the MOS transistor at practically the same time as firms in the United States. Furthermore, Japanese enterprises were able to make ground-breaking discoveries related to MOS transistors independent of American companies.

Second, looking at the experience of Hitachi, it appears that American companies had a much more sophisticated ability to collect and evaluate information relating to invention and discovery than did Japanese companies at the time. On this point, Japanese firms still had a long way to go to catch up with American firms. Other factors that contributed to this gap were the fact that the market for leading technologies in the US had grown much more than that of Japan; as a result American firms were much more sensitive to new technologies. In the next section related to IC, I will further investigate the importance of the existence of markets for new technologies.

The IC development lag and the flexible enterprise organization

Many Japanese enterprises launched IC development projects in the mid-1960s. NEC established a Solid-State Circuit Section within the

Semiconductor Division in 1965. It was Hiroe Osafune and others who proposed the creation of a Solid-State Circuit Section after careful investigation of the differences between the IC and transistor businesses.[43] The primary characteristic of the IC business was the need to fully understand the devices and systems that would become end products, as well as the need to approach design with the implementation method in mind. In addition, the business called for bringing together engineers from a variety of fields including systems, circuits, devices and materials, and having them cooperate in such a way that the IC design reflected the information from those conceptualizing the devices and systems. Another characteristic of the IC business was the need to organize and create a diverse group of people who could act together when selecting the types of products that would be converted to IC designs. For example, completely separate technical teams are needed for analogue versus digital projects. To make the IC business a success, firms were forced to approach human resource and organization from a new perspective.

A flexible enterprise organization is what allowed the Japanese enterprise to overcome deficiencies in human capital. In 1965 NEC implemented a major reorganization, expanding from five to fourteen divisions, with each division being given a clear charter, and each divisional manager being given clearly defined responsibilities.[44] As a result of the reorganization, the Semiconductor Division was broken out as an independent unit. In 1966 this division began managing its business using a strategic division plan adopted from Texas Instruments. However, from an organizational viewpoint, it seems that the strategic development of the Semiconductor Division brought with it a lesser degree of independence and self-sufficiency than believed at first glance. In 1966, in addition to the Semiconductor Division, NEC created the Integrated Circuit Design Headquarters, the Semiconductor Integrated Circuit Manufacturing Headquarters, and the Thin Film Integrated Circuit Manufacturing Headquarters, which were grouped together to form the IC Division Group (which also included the Circuit Division).[45] The purpose of this organizational regrouping was to create a fusion of the semiconductor and thin film technology within the Semiconductor Division (Component Division) with the circuit technology of each device division – the consumers of the semiconductors – resulting in an all-encompassing integrated circuit technology.

Remembering the role of a headquarters manager, Atsuyoshi Ouchi, who was the manager of the Integrated Circuit Design Headquarters, said:

> My first duty was to gather together circuit engineers from all over the organization. But it wasn't that easy to do. At that time, we were quite short of engineers, and the various departments couldn't afford to let their circuit designers go. And at the time, there wasn't the same understanding of the importance of IC as there is now. I was told that

they couldn't spare the few engineers they had for the semiconductor group, and they refused to let me take any. So early on, the Integrated Circuit Design Headquarters numbered some twenty or so people, but almost all of them were only assigned to my group on a part-time basis, with their 'real' assignment being whatever group they originally came from.[46]

So with a group of mostly part-timers, the Integrated Circuit Design Headquarters assessed the needs of the device divisions, the main consumer of the integrated circuits, and designed the circuits to meet their needs. The organization was flexible enough to operate by effectively utilizing its extremely limited human capital.

In general the Japanese-style system of organization by divisions features a 'division by function' format.[47] Compared with the American-style system of divisions where a division is given a great degree of independence and self-sufficiency, the division in a Japanese enterprise lacks these traits, operating more as a functional group accomplishing a specific task such as 'development' or 'manufacturing'. Being no exception, NEC created many divisions along functional lines, including the Design Headquarters, Manufacturing Headquarters, etc. In the present case, divisions defined by function served to communicate information smoothly between and among other divisions, as well as playing a role in compensating for deficiencies in human capital. On this point, the organizational design and organizational management of the Japanese-style division defined by function does not always indicate inefficiencies in the system of organizing by divisions. In this case, I believe that this style of organization represented a choice of a more flexible organization that was able to adapt to and compensate for the resource-constrained Japanese enterprise.

Regardless of the implementation of the organizational changes mentioned above, Japan was not immediately able to demonstrate enhanced competitiveness with the US in the IC market of the late 1960s. The reasons for this had quite a lot to do with the aforementioned nature of the IC business: namely, that designing circuits reflecting the needs of the end users of devices and systems requires that such needs are specifically defined from the beginning between producer and user. Without this generally accepted definition of needs, the IC business cannot grow efficiently. With such high priorities placed on military and aerospace development, America practically had a ready-made IC market prepared to expand exponentially. In Japan, on the other hand, demand for IC products, understandably, developed at a much slower pace.

During the early stages of IC development and production, it was the user of the IC (e.g. device and systems makers), rather than the IC industry, that was more active in developing new products that required new or different IC configurations. The best example of this was the IC for the electronic calculator, and Hayakawa Electric (later known as Sharp) was the best example of an enterprise that took the initiative in development. And it was the strategic actions of director Tadashi Sasaki, who saw a vision of the future of the MOS IC, that allowed Hayakawa Electric to take the lead in the market.[48]

Sasaki commissioned the manufacturing of ICs for electronic calculators to Hitachi, NEC and Mitsubishi Electric, and requested that NEC and Hitachi produce MOS ICs. The first calculators integrating MOS IC were sold in 1967. Sasaki then asked NEC, Hitachi and Mitsubishi Electric to develop an even more highly integrated MOS LSI. Both NEC and Hitachi declined, and though Mitsubishi Electric test produced the MOS LSI, they refused to produce it in the numbers needed to make it a viable product.[49] The reason that these Japanese firms refused to undertake MOS LSI manufacturing was most likely the fact that there were still unresolved technological problems with the manufacturing of the MOS IC.

In 1968, Sasaki made a tour of American companies, asking them to manufacture MOS IC for electronic calculators, but he found no takers. Finally, Sasaki was able to close a deal with North American Rockwell, who manufactured LSI for the US military's Minuteman missile, for the manufacture of MOS LSI to be used in calculators.[50] Although American firms were at near capacity just filling military orders, they had already resolved the technological problems related to MOS IC manufacturing, and had greatly improved manufacturing yields. This made it much easier for the American firms to take on extra orders than it was for Japanese firms.

Once Hayakawa Electric had successfully concluded order contracts for MOS LSI with an American firm, the other Japanese calculator makers quickly followed suit. Until 1971, when American MOS LSI quality issues gave Japanese IC manufacturers an opportunity to win the business back, America enjoyed a pre-eminent position as the suppliers of MOS LSI for the supply of calculators to the Japanese. During this time, however, the Japanese IC firms were busy preparing for a technological breakthrough related to MOS IC, and the IC market itself showed signs of expanding above and beyond the demand for calculator ICs.

The evolution of MOS IC through the big scale project and MOS IC's global standardization

The electronic calculator was responsible for the growth of the IC market in Japan beginning in the mid-1960s. MOS IC, in this case p-channel MOS IC, was utilized to facilitate greater miniaturization. The driving force behind the change from p-channel MOS IC to n-channel MOS IC was the 'Very High-Speed Computer System Project' (VHSCS). The VHSCS project was the first project that came out of the large-scale project programme inaugurated by MITI's Agency of Industrial Science and Technology.[51] The programme began in 1966, and was planned to run until 1970.

Ultimately, the programme was extended for one more year, through 1971, with more than 10 billion yen spent on the 6-year project. The aim of the project was to 'perform research and development to produce a commercial, standard large-scale computer offering world-class performance, scale and reliability, based on domestic technology by the early 1970s'. Specifically, the goal was to develop a test production large-scale machine to compete against the IBM System 360.[52]

Incorporated within the project's goals was the development of the component parts making up major systems within the overall machine. Of the total project expenditures, 22.4 per cent were allocated to component research and development. Not long after the start of the project, IBM announced the IBM System 360 Model 85, which signalled the likely standard acceptance of IC memory in the near future. At that point, a decision was made by the project supervisors to extend the project for one additional year, with the goal of developing high-speed memory with a cycle time of 100 ns.[53] Two important points must be noted here relating to IC memory development. First, the decision was made to use n-channel MOS ICs instead of generally used p-channel MOS ICs and bipolar transistors. Second, the target for high-speed cycle time was set at 100 ns.

In connection with the decision to go with n-channel MOS IC, NEC was selected to oversee IC memory development, but the performance goals were determined by the initiative of the engineers in MITI's Electrotechnical Laboratory (successor of the Electrical Testing Laboratory), who served as the project leaders. Yasuo Tarui, who was in charge of memory development at the Electrotechnical Laboratory, said:

> We were fairly comfortable with the prospects for the MOS transistor, but there were some worries about instability. But attempting to build one using the even more problematic n-channel technology on an LSI level was something that no one could even conceive of. At the committee meeting to determine the goals for the LSI to be developed, a representative from the manufacturer (an engineer from NEC) couldn't believe what he was hearing. He said, 'We cannot have the national research targets for MOS transistors determined by someone's personal fantasy.'[54]

The fact was that the Electrotechnical Laboratory had already accumulated considerable research relating to MOS transistors, and Tarui had already formed a definite goal in his mind. It was clear that the MOS transistor was fundamentally possessed of greater speed than the bipolar structure, but could not compete with the speed of the bipolar structure using p-channel MOS IC. Accordingly, the decision to develop n-channel MOS IC was correct, when considering the question of which technology would bring the most future benefit. In 1968 NEC Corporation successfully produced an n-channel MOS IC memory with a 144 bit capacity and a 40 ns cycle time.

As for the 100 ns cycle time, the project team accepted the challenging goal put forth by Tarui. NEC Corporation was unsuccessful in achieving the stated goal, but from their perspective, 'We were able to achieve a 40 nano-second cycle time, which was a really amazing speed for the time. Truth be told, we were much faster than that, but we didn't have the capability to measure anything faster.'[55] Compared with the memory standards of the time, NEC achieved an impressive result. A manager at Hitachi, in charge of the logic circuits, pressed Tarui as to whether he had some theoretical basis that actually led him to believe the project could achieve the goal specifications.[56] NEC and Hitachi both showed hesitation when learning of the challenging goals – goals at levels they couldn't even consider to set for themselves in connection with in-house projects. But the nature of this national project, conceived upon the assumptions of the high technological standards of government research facilities, was such that nothing less than high achievement was expected, and ultimately this fostered an enhanced level of development capability in Japan's private enterprises.

The n-channel MOS IC memory developed by NEC in 1968 was, in the following year, incorporated into the large-scale DIPS-1 computer being developed by Nippon Telegraph and Telephone Corporation (NTT). This signalled the first time anyone anywhere in the world had incorporated MOS memory into a computer. The successful integration of the n-channel MOS IC served as a clear signpost to the NEC Semiconductor division about the direction of MOS IC utilization. In addition, the NEC computer business engineers who had participated in the VHSCS project began to consider incorporating MOS memory into their computers.[57]

However, it was the Intel Corporation of the United States that was the first to produce MOS memory for computers. In 1970, Intel's president Robert Noyce went to computer companies around the world, selling Intel's p-channel 1Kbit DRAM i1103, and established the p-channel 1Kbit DRAM as the global standard. Within NEC, the computer division pushed for adoption of Intel's products from a standpoint of compatibility, while the semiconductor group argued for the future prospects of the n-channel architecture. In 1972, NEC's Electronic Device Group approved n-channel memory development plans, and the firm embarked on the full-scale manufacture of 1Kbit DRAM.[58]

The acceptance of NEC's n-channel DRAM came with the advent of the 4Kbit DRAM. NEC developed a 150 ns 4Kbit DRAM PD411 for Honeywell. At the time, most computer makers were converting from p-channel to n-channel. Even Intel had begun using n-channel architecture. In one short push, n-channel MOS IC had become a global standard.[59] The acceptance of NEC's n-channel MOS IC as a global standard served as a springboard for Japanese enterprises to hold the predominant position in the DRAM market of the 1980s.

Conclusion

This chapter has addressed the process of post-war Americanization and Japanization, focusing on the role of technology absorptive capacity relating to Japanese enterprise management and organization. The subject of the investigation was the general purpose computer and semiconductor industry, both of which underwent Japanization in the mid-1970s. It is this process of Japanization that this author believes led to the international competitiveness of Japanese electronics firms during the 1980s.

In studying the development of the general purpose computer in Japan, we see that, with the exception of Fujitsu, the major Japanese computer firms formed cooperative relationships with their American counterparts. However, the results of these technology partnerships varied significantly for each Japanese firm.

1   The negotiating position of the Japanese firm was greatly affected by the understanding and policies of top management, as well as the condition of human resources within the firm.

2   In some cases, the product series of American firms did not match the demands of the Japanese market, underlining the importance of the Japanese partner's ability to produce small- and large-scale computers to complement the US firm's offerings. The level of human resources and technological resources available to the Japanese firm also had a major influence on whether the firm was able to withstand competition in the computer market.

3   Finally, in the mid-1970s, Japanese firms introduced a variety of computer series to compete with IBM's machines, attempting to overtake the US firm. It was at this time that Japanese firms were able to catch up in terms of accumulated hardware technology and software skills.

In our study of the early development of the semiconductor we see that (1) beginning in the 1950s, after building a certain accumulation of human resources, Japanese firms started to absorb American technology. In the 1960s, we see the emergence of, and success in, a limited amount of independent research and development by Japanese firms. The best example of this was in the MOS transistor field, where the Japanese semiconductor industry took its first steps on the path toward competitiveness on a world-class level. (2) However, as the IC industry began to expand rapidly, American firms were the predominant players in the worldwide market during the mid-1960s. During these years, Japanese firms were not able to respond to the market's need for MOS ICs and MOS LSIs used in electronic calculators. (3) But as Japanese firms experienced successful development of MOS memory for computers – especially in the field of n-channel MOS IC – the firms were able to significantly influence global standards for the technology. This trend led to Japan's dominance in the DRAM market in the 1980s.

As demonstrated above, Japanese firms were able to successfully 'Japanize' (especially technologically) in the fields of general purpose computing and semiconductors during the mid-1970s. Even today, Japanese electronics firms are called 'general electric' companies, and true to this description, a single Japanese electronics firm houses both computer and semiconductor divisions, directing the resulting synergies to both technological and market development. The groundwork for the remarkable international competitiveness enjoyed by Japanese electronics firms in the 1980s was laid in the 'Japanization' of the mid-1970s.

Notes

1 S. Hasegawa, 'Competition and Cooperation in the Japanese Electrical Machinery Industry', in A. Kudo and T. Hara (eds), *International Cartels in Business History*, Tokyo: University of Tokyo Press, 1992, pp. 165–186.
2 In this chapter Americanization means that the influence of American firms spreads to every field in other countries' firms: capital, human resources, technology, administration methods, and so on.
3 Japanization means that the influence of American firms retreats from every field in Japanese firms. Therefore, Americanization and Japanization are two sides of the same coin.
4 A. Goto, 'Technology Importation: Japan's Postwar Experience', in Y. Kosai and J. Teranishi (eds), *The Japanese Experience of Economic Reforms*, New York: Macmillan, pp. 289–301.
5 This chapter analyzes Americanization and Japanization by focusing on technology transfer. Therefore, the main issue is how Japanese firms adopted American technology, and how they succeeded in developing their own technology.
6 *Nippon IBM 50-nen shi* (A Fifty Year History of IBM Japan), Tokyo: IBM Japan, 1988, pp. 156–158.
7 Ibid., pp. 158–161.
8 On the policy of technology introduction, see Committee on the Compilation of a History of International Trade and Industrial Policy (ed.), *Tsusho sangyo seisaku shi* (A History of International Trade and Industrial Policy), vol. 6, Tokyo: Tsusho Sangyo Chosa Kai, 1990, pp. 416–418.
9 M. Fransman, *Japan's Computer and Communications Industry*, Oxford: Oxford University Press, 1995, pp. 137–138.
10 K. Kobayashi, *Koso to ketsudan – NEC to tomoni* (Plans and Decisions: My Years with NEC Corporation), Tokyo: Daiyamondo Sha, 1989, p. 82.
11 NEC concluded the Technical Know-how and Patent License Agreement with Minneapolis-Honeywell Regulator Company, the predecessor of Honeywell Inc., on 20 March 1962.
12 Nippon Denki Kabushiki Kaisha, *Nippon Denki Kabushiki Kaisha 100-nen shi* (A Century of Nippon Electric Corporation), Tokyo: NEC Corporation, 2002, pp. 496–498.
13 Ibid., pp. 517–518.
14 H. Kaneda, *NEC konpyuta hattatsu no monogatari* (The History of NEC Computer Development), Tokyo: NEC Creative, 1994, p. 91.
15 *Nippon Denki Kabushiki Kaisha*, pp. 503–507.
16 NEC Corporation, *NEC Corporation 1899–1999*, Tokyo: NEC Corporation, 2002, p. 166; *Nippon Denki Kabushiki Kaisha*, p. 510.

17 Ibid., pp. 510–511. The experienced software development members of NEC Corporation who had been committed to the DIPS (Denden-kosha Information Processing System) project of Nippon Telegraph and Telephone Public Corporation (NTTPC) transferred to the operating system development section for ACOS series.
18 *NEC Corporation 1899–1999*, p. 167; *Nippon Denki Kabushiki Kaisha*, p. 514.
19 Oki Electric Industry Co. Ltd., *Progressive Spirit: The 120-Year History of Oki Electric*, Tokyo: Oki Electric Industry Co. Ltd., 2002, pp. 106–109.
20 H. Aiso, H. Iizuka, K. Oshima and K. Sakamura (eds), *Kokusan Konpyuta ha koshite tsukurareta* (The Development of Domestic Computers), Tokyo: bit bessatsu, Kyoritsu Shuppan, November 1985, pp. 21–27.
21 According to OKITAC 5090 Catalogue on 13 November 1963, the number delivered and ordered OKITAC 5090 amounted to 52: 16 for universities and government offices, 6 for non-government laboratories, 7 for optical instrument makers, and 12 for other private companies. It may be inferred that OKITAC 5090 were mostly used for scientific calculations.
22 OKI Electric Industry Co. Ltd., The Minutes of Managing Directors Meetings, 12 December 1961; Historical Materials of OKI Electric Industry Co. Ltd.
23 The Editorial Committee of Toshiba Computers History, *Toshiba Denshi Keisanki jigyo shi* (A History of Toshiba Computer Business), Tokyo: Toshiba Corporation, 1989, p. 18.
24 OKI Electric Industry Co. Ltd., The Minutes of Managing Directors' Meetings, 3–4 April 1962, Historical Materials of OKI Electric Industry Co. Ltd.
25 OKI Electric Industry Co. Ltd., The Minutes of Managing Directors' Meetings, 26 April 1962, ibid.
26 OKI Electric Industry Co. Ltd., The Minutes of Managing Directors' Meetings, 10 July 1962, ibid.
27 OKI Electric Industry Co. Ltd., The Minutes of Managing Directors' Meetings, 27 November 1962, ibid.
28 Agreement to form joint venture company: OKI Remington Co., Ltd. and Technical Assistance Agreement between Sperry Rand International Corporation and OKI Remington Co. Ltd. was concluded.
29 OKI-Remington Co. Ltd. changed to OKI-Univac Co. Ltd., because the computer division Univac spun off from Remington Rand division.
30 *OUK no kiseki* (OUK Truck), Tokyo: OKI-Advanced Systems Co. Ltd., 1997, pp. 22–23.
31 Ibid., p. 42.
32 *NEC konpyuta hattatu no monogatari*, pp. 67–68.
33 *Nippon Denki Kabushiki Kaisha*, pp. 394–395.
34 OKI Electric Industry Co. Ltd., The Minutes of Managing Directors' Meetings, 12 December 1961, Historical Materials of OKI Electric Industry Co. Ltd.
35 OKI Electric Industry Co. Ltd., The Minutes of Managing Directors Meetings, 3–4 April 1962, ibid.
36 *Nippon Denki Kabushiki Kaisha*, pp. 500–501; *NEC konpyuta hattatsu no monogatari*, pp. 91–93.
37 Honeywell bought out GE's computer division, and established Honeywell Information System Inc. (HIS) in 1970. NEC concluded the technical assistance agreement with HIS in 1972 and was able to introduce GE's computer technology. See *Nippon Denki Kabushiki Kaisha*, pp. 509–510.
38 J.E. Tilton, *International Diffusion of Technology: The Case of Semiconductors*, Washington, D.C.: The Brookings Institution, 1971, p. 142.
39 J. Nishizawa and A. Ouchi (eds), *Nihon no handotai kaihatsu* (Semiconductor Development in Japan), Tokyo: The Industrial Research Association, 1993, p. 216.

40 NEC Corporation, *70-nen shi no tameno intabyu kiroku* (The Interview Record for a 70 Year History), Historical Materials of NEC Corporation.
41 *Semiconductor Development in Japan*, pp. 213–228; Y. Aida, *Denshi rikkoku nippon no jijoden* (The Autobiography of Japan as a Electronic Nation) vol. 2, Tokyo: Nippon Hoso Shuppan Kyokai, 1992, pp. 219–229.
42 T. Kurosawa, *Shirikon kotohajime* (The Origin of Silicon Business), Tokyo: NEC Creative, 1997, pp. 73–75.
43 H. Osafune, *Handotai no ayumi* (The History of Semiconductor), Tokyo: Nippon Denki Culture Centre, 1987, pp. 93–94.
44 *NEC Corporation 1899–1999*, p. 153.
45 *Nippon Denki Kabushiki Kaisha*, pp. 523–524.
46 Ouchi Atsuyoshi Tsuitoshu Kanko no Kai, *Makoto – Ouchi Atsuyoshi tsuitoshu* (Sincerity – The Memory of Atsuyoshi Ouchi), Tokyo: NEC Creative INC., 1997, p. 322.
47 T. Kagono, 'Shokuno-betsu kanri to naibu shijo' (Functional Administration and Inside Market), *Kokumin keizai zasshi*, 1993, vol. 167, no. 2.
48 *Denshi rikkoku nippon no jijoden*, vol. 2, p. 233.
49 Ibid., p. 264.
50 Ibid., pp. 264–272.
51 On the VHSCS project, see M. Fransman, *The Market and Beyond: Information Technology in Japan*, Cambridge: Cambridge University Press, 1990, pp. 32–38.
52 Tsusansho Kogyo Gijutsu In (The Agency of Industrial Science and Technology of the Ministry of International Trade and Industry), *Ogata purojekuto niyoru cho koseino denshi keisanki* (The Very High Speed Computer System development based on the large-scale Project System), Tokyo: The Foundation of Nippon Sangyo Gijutsu Shinko Kyokai, 1972, pp. 3–12.
53 Ibid., p. 31.
54 Y. Tarui, *Cho LSI heno chosen* (The Challenge to U-LSI), Tokyo: Kogyo Chosa Kai (The Industrial Research Association), 2000, pp. 93–94.
55 *Shirikon kotohajime*, pp. 104–105.
56 *Cho LSI heno chosen*, p. 94.
57 *Shirikon kotohajime*, p. 107.
58 *NEC Corporation 1899–1999*, p. 174; *Nippon Denki Kabushiki Kaisha*, p. 530.
59 *Shirikon kotohajime*, pp. 153–161.

8 America and the resurgence of the German chemical and rubber industry after the Second World War

Hüls, Glanzstoff and Continental

Christian Kleinschmidt

Introduction

In the words of Peter F. Drucker:

> The world revolution of our time is 'made in the USA'. It is not
> Communism, Fascism, the new nationalism of the non-Western
> peoples, or any of the other 'isms' that appear in the headlines. They
> are reactions to the basic disturbance, secondary rather than primary.
> The true revolutionary principle is the idea of mass production.
> Nothing ever before recorded in the history of man equals speed, uni-
> versality and impact the transformation this principle has wrought in
> the foundations of the society in the forty short years since Henry
> Ford turned out the first 'Model T'.[1]

A leading management expert of the 1950s, Drucker had already claimed
at the end of the 1940s that copying the American 'revolution' would
result in universal peace and freedom. Still of international acclaim today,
Drucker had best-sellers in both Germany and Japan. The American
model of mass production has since been understood as an expression of
a world-wide 'Americanization'.[2] Americanization can be understood as
either the conscious or unconscious adoption of values, behaviour, procedures, norms and institutions within management.[3] The relevant question
is how the transfer to corporate level occurs. In immediate terms, the
significance of compulsion and asymmetrical power relations requires
attention. More critical is the question whether, in the sense of the ending
'-ization', existing structures were indeed comprehensively influenced and
re-shaped on the basis of a taker-giver relationship. It is only on this basis
that an intensive, uninterrupted, continuous and comprehensive 'Americanization' of German business can be claimed.

The term is well suited to describe the American influence on the
German economy and German business in the 1950s and 1960s: but was it

simply 'Americanization', or more a 'Revolution made in the USA', the export of the American model, development aid or 'management imperialism'? In order to define the term 'Americanization' more precisely, the focus of research, subject matter and research period require differentiation. When the focus is turned away from the perspective of the aid-giving nation, away from American government and business, and towards the perspective of the aid-receivers, that is towards German companies, 'Americanization' seems less suited to the 1950s and 1960s, especially with regard to post-war political and economic upheaval. When companies are not regarded as a whole, but examined according to individual areas of management strategy such as industrial relations, marketing, public relations, controlling or technology, it becomes evident that the American influence on German companies could vary greatly, even within a single company.

As will be illustrated using examples from the chemical and rubber industry, both post-war economic and business relations between Germany and America moved away from a tendency of 'Americanization' to a voluntary orientation towards American achievements. Attempts to push through an actual 'Americanization' are mainly evident under Allied occupation. This mostly involved small and medium-sized companies. These profited from the US Technological and Productivity Program under the Marshall Plan. Representative examples will illustrate how German companies were basically subject to Allied policy, with little room for manoeuvre. The decision-making process was characterized by a high degree of insecurity. Correspondingly on the American side, a strong sense of mission, based on the asymmetric balance of power (Djelic), was evident in politics, economic affairs and business. Within the framework of the Technical Assistance and Productivity Program, this mainly influenced the form of industrial relations within small and medium-sized companies.

These initial Americanization tendencies gradually gave way to a voluntary orientation towards American management strategies as German companies recovered economically, as will be shown in the case of the German chemical and rubber industry. However, the question of technology transfer must first be explored. Here, the swift return of the German chemical and rubber industry to the world market was dependent on American 'development aid'.

Following American technology: Hüls, Glanzstoff and Continental

The transfer of technology from the USA was substantial. This was also the case in the chemical and rubber industry, a branch in which German companies had played a leading role in world developments up to 1939. The production of car tires involved a close co-operation between production at Chemische Werke Hüls, Vereinigte Glanzstoff Fabriken AG and Continental Gummiwerke AG. Hüls produced the raw material, buna rubber, Glanzstoff produced the tire cord and Continental completed the actual tire manufacture. All three companies had been outstanding internationally but had lost their ability to compete during the Second World War. They found themselves overtaken by their American counterparts. After 1945 they were dependent on American 'development aid' in their attempts to recover former strength.

The history of Hüls is closely linked to I.G. Farben's interests and National Socialist autarky plans during the Four Year Plan which led to the opening of a buna plant in Marl in 1938.[4] The technical know-how required drew on earlier developments of the century which were not only intensified in Germany following the formation of I.G. Farben in 1925, but also in the USA and the USSR. Between 1928 and 1935, I.G. Farben and the American chemical company Standard Oil in Baton Rouge co-operated closely on a new method of synthetic rubber production, known as the 'electric arc' process, which was put into operation in Marl once Hüls had been established.[5]

Although Allied prohibitions and dismantlement plans initially placed tight limits on production at Hüls, after 1945 great effort was made to take up buna production as soon as possible. It was clear that even if comprehensive dismantlement was avoided, the traditional method of production would no longer suffice to guarantee competitiveness on the world-market, especially in the face of American developments. As the company concluded in 1949: 'Hüls' hopes of retaining plant equipment from three polymerization lines and three processing lines are irrelevant in the face of the modern American method of producing qualitatively superior buna by cold polymerization. The plant equipment concerned is not suitable for the production of cold polymerizate.'[6] Within a decade, their technological know-how on buna production had become obsolete. German companies had lost their leading pre-war role and had been replaced by their American counterparts. Given the latter's success in both quantitative and qualitative terms during the war and their strong post-war position, German companies were now dependent on their competitors, if a return to the world market was to be successful.

In recognition of the American's technological superiority, plans at Hüls immediately aimed to take up the American 'cold-rubber' process and not the traditional 'warm-rubber' production method. The advantages of this process were a decrease in technological complexity, improvement in quality and easy access to raw materials. However, it also meant taking up petrochemistry. This involved a departure from the traditional raw material of coal and a fundamental re-orientation of production not only at Hüls but also within the whole German chemical industry. This also had repercussions for neighbouring branches of industry, such as mining and energy.[7]

Following the decision to take up 'cold-rubber' technology, Hüls sought to establish contact with American companies. As Paul Baumann, Chairman of the Board at Hüls, explained in 1954: 'Important American firms agreed to document their own experience of butadiene production, and the cold-rubber process, so that we could avoid unnecessary research and produce at a competitive quality comparable to the American tire sector.'[8] So, Hüls planned to erect an entirely new buna plant along the lines of the American cold-rubber process and was dependent on American help. Contact was established with American companies, such as the Houdry Process Corporation, Standard Oil (where good pre-war contacts instigated by Paul Baumann already existed) and Firestone. Contact with Firestone was mainly the result of efforts made by Ludwig Erhard, the federal minister for economic affairs and Chancellor Adenauer himself. He discussed plans for the buna plant during a meeting with representatives from the American government. Hüls acquired the technology necessary for the cold-rubber process from Firestone and in return offered information on the production of styrene, polyamide and PVC. As this illustrates, the transfer of know-how was not a one-sided affair, but also involved an element of exchange. Permission to erect a German cold-rubber plant was granted by the Military Security Board on 30 April 1955. Three years later Buna Werke Hüls GmbH, a joint venture between BASF, Bayer, Höchst and Hüls, started production. The construction of the plant was accompanied by intensive talks, particularly between Hüls and Firestone. The most modern and the largest cold-rubber plant in Europe, the Buna Werke guaranteed the return of the German chemicals industry to the world market. Karl Winnacker from Höchst commented that it was fundamentally important, 'a vital pre-condition for motorization in the Federal Republic'.[9]

The actual volume of technological transfer from America to Hüls is difficult to quantify. As Raymond Stokes has shown in his study on the reorganization of the German chemical industry on American lines,[10] this process can be sufficiently described without using the term 'Americanization'. In the case of Hüls, it would also be inappropriate to speak of an 'Americanized' company. As former Hüls manager Frederico Engel recollects, the technological transfer between Hüls and their American partners was not one-sided, but a two-way process: Hüls technology was also exported to the USA. Moreover, the American influence varied in intensity within different areas. Nevertheless, according to Engel, the acquisition of American technology was vital in the early 1950s. Time was a crucial factor. While similar technological progress could have been made on the basis of German research,[11] this would have taken years. Hüls' successful return to the world market would have been postponed indefinitely.

Glanzstoff's activities in the tire cord sector were of similar importance. Glanzstoff was the largest producer of man-made fibres in Germany and had a long international tradition. Founded in 1899, Glanzstoff initially produced viscose and continuous-filament cupramonium on the basis of English and French patents. During the 1930s, it turned to the production of staple fibre under the National Socialist policy of autarky and focused on the production of fully synthetic fibres. In the early 1940s, contact with I.G. Farben and their relations with DuPont made it possible for Glanzstoff to take up the production of 'Perlon', known as German nylon.[12] In the post-war period, it was increasingly used to manufacture ladies' tights, underwear, carpets and upholstered goods. Glanzstoff was also interested in producing American 'nylon'. This was partly a reaction to the American challenge on the car tire market. Nylon also proved to have more advantages than other fibres used by Glanzstoff. It had a higher melting-point, easier vulcanization and better performance at high speeds, and thus greater driving safety. After 1937, Glanzstoff had produced tire yarn from rayon and reacted quickly to American innovation in car tire production during the 1950s.

Glanzstoff's board shared the conviction that given US developments there was no time to lose, especially since tire companies at home and abroad were reaching patent agreements with American tire producers. Nylon, they were convinced, should not only be used because of its higher quality and guarantee of better driving safety: the export of German cars to the USA was a further important consideration. It was also argued that psychological factors, such as the better international reputation of 'nylon' vis-à-vis 'Perlon' were also relevant. Ernst Hellmut Vits, chairman of the board, was convinced that the most important material in future tire production would be 'nylon'. As he explained, it is

> clear that Germany will experience a similar development towards a fully synthetic tire cord, even if the speed and extent of change are not yet discernible. While the similarity of new international developments is one general indicator, a more particular indication is the fact that all significant German tire producers have agreements with their American counterparts on the exchange of know-how.[13]

Consequently the board at Glanzstoff decided to start its own nylon production, closely following the example of the American nylon and car tire markets. Given the expected demand, initial production levels of one ton per day were soon considered to be too low. Seeing the use of nylon in American tire cord production rapidly expand, Glanzstoff increased production too. Not only aspects of production and distribution were influenced by American developments, but also the design of raw materials storage and price structure. In the mid-1950s, larger customers such as the tire company Continental Gummiwerke AG, failed to see the demand for nylon cord. The decision by the Glanzstoff board to follow the American example was however vindicated only a few years later, as major car producers switched from their old rayon tires to nylon tires in order to meet the new requirements presented by higher speeds and the growing consciousness for car safety.[14]

Glanzstoff's decision to open a plant for the production of nylon tire cord proved to be right. The changes observed in the USA in the automotive industry were indeed relevant to West Germany a few years later. At the end of the 1950s, Glanzstoff produced 90 per cent of the entire national tire cord production, using mainly nylon and exporting 25 per cent of its own production volume. Overall, tire cord was now one of the main production lines at Glanzstoff. Furthermore, within Germany, Glanzstoff was the only company producing both 'Perlon' and 'nylon'.

Continental was also unable to ignore changes in the American market and they too finally turned to the production of car tires on the basis of nylon cord. As has been shown, Continental's interest in American developments was linked to both the nature of the product and its suppliers, Hüls and Glanzstoff. An openness for developments in other countries can be traced back to 1871, the year Continental was founded, whether in the form of contacts with Dunlop in England and with the French company Michelin before 1900, or with American firms such as Goodyear or Goodrich after the First World War. Soon Continental was, as Paul Erker commented, the 'most American' tire company in Germany, thus maintaining its leading position.[15] National Socialism interrupted these international contacts for many years, especially with American tire producers. Despite the National Socialist policy of autarky and the war economy, some technological progress was still made, such as in the development of tubeless tires and in the use of continuous filament yarn within the cord fabric. However, this did not prevent American companies from taking over the international technological lead. Working together with Hüls and Glanzstoff, Continental tried to catch up. These efforts were rewarded by the mid-1950s.

Beyond the sector of tire construction and manufacture, further pre-war contacts with American companies were revived, such as with General Tire, with which a co-operation agreement was reached in 1949. This gave Continental access to technology on cross-ply tires, which dominated tire production during the 1950s and was thus the basis for successful business on both national and international levels.[16] In this respect Continental managed to catch up with its American counterparts by the mid-1950s, but deficits remained in production, in methods of both manufacture and labour input. These had a negative influence on productivity which represented only a third of that of General Tire. However, engineers at Continental secured new information on aspects of plant-level material transport and automation on a business trip to the USA organized by the European Cooperation Administration (ECA) and RKW within the USTA&P and via contact with Goodyear, the American tire producer. Even though the representatives from Continental were advised 'not to unconditionally adopt all things American', their final report included twenty-five points considered advantageous to Continental. These included suggestions for introducing automatic trimming machinery for the production of the rubber diaphragm, as used at Goodyear, or continuous fabric flow in tire production.[17]

The case of Continental also illustrates the pitfalls inherent in a too inflexible adoption of American developments. By the end of the 1960s Michelin's steel radial tires had taken the technological lead in the branch, and by the early 1970s Michelin had increased its market share in Germany to more than one third. Although Continental had made the move from cross-ply to radial tires, it remained totally faithful to the nylon cord philosophy of the Americans.[18] As a result Continental spent the following years trying to catch up with Michelin.

Attempted Americanization and the voluntary orientation towards American management methods

The US technological and productivity program

The initial tendency towards Americanization, that is towards an American influence on German corporate life, was primarily an expression of both American occupation policy and economic aid under the European Recovery Program. The 'Anglo-American Productivity Council' was formed in 1948/49 as the basis for the USTA&P and initially aimed at a management transfer from America to Great Britain. This policy sought to spread the American model of a liberal and open world economy and promote the necessary growth in production and productivity in Europe. Soon the French, Italians and Germans called for the creation of their own 'productivity programmes' under Marshall Plan aid. In Asia, Japan was also a beneficiary of the USTA&P programme.

In the early 1950s, the Mutual Security Agency (MSA) took over from the European Cooperation Administration (ECA) which had supervised the European Recovery Program. In 1953, the MSA demanded more military economic aid for European states and its activities were eventually taken over by the Foreign Operations Administration (FOA), which aimed to guarantee a better co-ordination of American foreign aid and foreign economic policy.[19] In the same year, the European Productivity Agency (EPA) was established under the framework of the Organisation for European Economic Co-operation (OEEC) and the USTA&P. Based in Paris, its aim was to spread the American model of productivity within Europe. From the very beginning, EPA's activities focused less on technological issues and more on spreading values and attitudes, especially with regard to industrial relations and questions of modern management in the areas of marketing and sales:

The EPA Advisory Board has recommended that the EPA should

throughout its program plans emphasize improving human relations and changing attitudes. . . . This means, in our judgement, that projects in the areas of technology or technical industrial process should be limited and that projects in the management, marketing and labor fields should couple modern methods with the philosophy behind their use. Specifically, they should be designed to produce an understanding of the attitudes and human relations practices necessary for their employment in the drive to increase productivity and production.[20]

While the EPA and USTA&P programmes were aimed mainly at small and medium-sized companies, large companies also benefited. On the German side, the 'Rationalization Association for the German Economy' (RKW) was EPA's opposite number, involving trade unions, state agencies and business associations. Furthermore, the federal government worked together with the USTA&P through the Federal Ministry for the Marshall Plan, which had been formed in 1949 and was headed by Franz Blücher, with representatives in the ECA and OEEC. Two years later the 'German Productivity Council' was created with MSA advice. Supervised by four federal ministries – those of finance, employment, economic affairs and for the Marshall Plan – the council included six business representatives (Fritz Berg, Kurt Pentzlin, Walter Raymond, D. Haverbeck, W. Alexander Menne and Mittelsten-Scheid) and six from the trade union side.[21] In this manner the realization of American productivity programmes was secured on the German side by relevant organizations and representatives.

German companies wanting to benefit from USTA&P projects and financial aid were subjected to intensive scrutiny from the MSA or FOA, as from those German agencies they co-operated with, while the American side had the right of veto. Companies had little chance of success if the Americans were not convinced that the aspect of possible job loss after rationalization, questions of human relations or the creation of a good 'working atmosphere' had been prepared thoroughly. Efforts to increase productivity through technological aid were closely linked on the American side to the design of industrial relations as 'human relations' and the promotion of 'Training within Industry' (TWI). From the American perspective, the design of human relations within German companies was one important element of a comprehensive political aim or 'mission'. It was a form of development aid within an area of German company life held in the post-war period to have the greatest deficits and requiring the greatest attention.

Given these modalities, German applications needed the 'correct' terminology and catch-phrases to secure acceptance. Within the advisory boards they were supported by the German representatives who argued their case in the face of American criticism. This pragmatic German attitude was based on hopes of rapid economic reconstruction and often clashed with political and moralistic concerns of MSA or FOA representatives. While in formal terms their opinions and judgements were of no more value than those of their German counterparts, they proved to be decisive in practice. This is not only an illustration of how German-American relations were set by 'asymmetric dependencies', but also an indication of how in some cases the 'export of the American model' in human relations was to some extent forced. The USTA&P was in this sense very much an American development aid project for European companies, a form of 'aid to self-help' which was fundamentally dependent on the acceptance of American guidelines. The thrust of activities was clearly directed from the USA to Europe and to Germany. During the first post-war decade, Americanization attempts and actual Americanization tendencies which were mainly directed towards industrial relations, human relations and marketing were rooted in the political and economic dominance of the USA.[22]

Voluntary orientation towards the American human relations model: the cases of Glanzstoff and Continental

Large companies were themselves also interested in the American model of 'human relations'. While small and medium-sized companies were subjected to scrutiny and regimentation within the USTA&P framework, large German companies had their own tradition of exchange with American companies. They themselves could decide on whether to introduce new methods or not. Two points were relevant here: on the one hand American developments seemed to provide an attractive alternative to the German model of industrial relations which was based on strong trade-union power, especially during the early 1950s as the co-determination debate raged. On the other hand, there was an opportunity to re-kindle the German inter-war idea of the 'factory community' (Werksgemeinschaftsidee). Using a terminology reminiscent of Paul Osthold, a DINTA ideologist (Deutsche Institut für Technische Arbeitsschulung), Walter Raymond of the BDA (Bundesvereinigung deutscher Arbeitgeberverbände) concluded for the employer's side that, 'the fight for the soul of every single employee' could find 'its German character' within the American approach to human relations.[23]

More recently, Gertraude Krell has shown how in Germany the idea of the 'factory community' and received teaching on human resources in the 1920s were in fact a harbinger of some business concepts propagated in the 1980s, which initially had a US-orientation and later reflected a Japanese influence.[24] Given this history, some German companies regarded American management concepts simply as a post-war 're-import', which provided some legitimization. Against this background it seems that the ideology of the 'factory community' and the plant-level system of social expenditure and benefits (Adolf Geck) can best be understood as a reaction to the interventionist Weimar state. Similarly post-war concepts of human relations were a reaction to the FRG, as a state which was both interventionist and favoured co-determination. As Franz Goossens, the editor of the journal *Mensch und Arbeit*, commented in the early 1950s: 'the debate raging on co-determination suddenly made "human relations" a topic as relevant to economic and financial discussion, as to corporate life itself'.[25]

Aptly enough, as the debate on co-determination reached its climax in September 1950, the journal *Der Arbeitgeber* chose to publish an extract of Peter F. Drucker's 'Concept of Corporation'. In the selected passage, Drucker warned against trade unions gaining too strong an influence on company strategy:

> Such trade union attempts are without question a serious threat to a functioning industrial world. If central management does not enjoy undivided authority and share both the same criteria for success and undivided loyalty, industry can simply not function, whether in the Soviet Union or in Cleveland, Ohio.[26]

In their fight against co-determination, German business received further help from American employers' associations such as the National Association of Manufacturers (NAM), who started an advertising campaign in numerous German newspapers shortly before the bill on co-determination in the mining industry became law. The NAM saw plant-level co-determination as an obstacle to the continued development of a free market economy in Germany, a step towards socialism and the creation of monopolies which would block an effective reform of the German economy.[27] Both American employers' associations and the US government instead favoured the approach of modelling industrial relations through 'human relations' in a way which avoided any shop-floor unrest or trade union militancy.

The case of Glanzstoff illustrates the fusion of a pro-American orientation and German pre-war attitude. Glanzstoff's Ludwig Vaubel was the first German to take part in the Advanced Management Program at the Harvard Business School. He publicized his experience of America in the book 'Unternehmer gehen zur Schule' – businessmen go back to school. In Vaubel's opinion, the term 'human relations' was over-emotionalized and needed to be reduced to its functional core.[28] In the case of Glanzstoff this involved improving relations between workers and management, strengthening the trust in communication lines, increasing the information flow as well as broadening both initial training and training-on-the-job as well as fringe benefits. The link between these ideas on 'human relations' and those of the 1920s and 1930s was made explicit with the re-establishment of a plant-level service for industrial psychology, which was supported by the research institute for labour psychology and personnel management at the technical university in Braunschweig (Forschungsinstut für Arbeitspsychologie und Personalwesen der TH Braunschweig, FORFA). Founded in 1945, the American influence on FORFA was noticeable in the areas of human relations and TWI. Using methods of staff selection, aptitude tests and the development of a 'skill and performance profile' for each employee, it was planned to put 'the right man on the right job'. At the same time this policy bore similarity to inter-war practice at Glanzstoff in the tradition of 'Psychotechnik' and in the form of the 'Bedaux system'.[29] In addition, and as propagated by TWI, it was planned to improve the plant-level training of foremen. In sum, it was hoped that these measures would lead to a better working atmosphere in the company.

In this area Continental took up the idea of 'Supervisional Training' which had already been adopted at Goodyear, albeit not in every aspect. In co-operation with FORFA and with modification of the American concept, regular training courses for foremen were set up. In addition to so-called 'Meisterbesprechungen', which were intended to allow discussion of internal plant affairs, Continental established training courses for employees aiming to become foremen themselves.[30] Concepts of 'teamwork' and 'Gruppenarbeit' played an important part in the establishment of these courses within German companies such as Glanzstoff and Continental. The 'employee meeting' ('Mitarbeiterbesprechung') was, however, supposed to be neither a form of co-determination nor a normal work meeting during which employees were simply informed about plans and duties, but a forum for exchanging opinions and information. This new possibility for discussion was supposed to improve relations between employees and their superiors and kindle worker creativity.

Whether in the area of TWI, 'Meisterschulung' or 'Mitarbeiterbesprechung', two German legislative developments hindered the broad adoption of American-style human relations: the laws on co-determination (1951) and plant-level industrial constitution (1952). These marked the failure of attempts to significantly mould industrial relations in German companies along American lines. Instead, a 'German model' of industrial relations was established. It was based on law, involved trade unions and had roots in the corporatist tradition. It allowed employees far greater rights of co-determination than in the USA, even in the areas of training, wages, work safety and other questions of social benefits.[31] As Krober-Kenneth, a German expert on management issues, commented in 1953: 'The enthusiasm with which the seemingly attractive game of human relations was taken up has now totally dispersed.'[32]

Attempts to pursue Americanization whether through the USTA&P, which as such still stood for American political and economic interests, or the voluntary adoption of American lines on human relations increasingly lost force in German corporate life after 1955. German companies still remained basically interested in forms of direct communication between top management and employees in the sense of a 'plant-level partnership'. However, under the influence of the law on co-determination, a corporatist model came to dominate industrial relations in the FRG – with comparative success in the 1960s and 1970s. Indeed, within Anglo-American research this 'German model of management' has found as positive an evaluation as the successful Japanese model of corporate design. Both have been presented as alternatives to the 'American management way'.[33]

Conclusion

While a strong American influence on production and management can be identified at the end of the 1940s, 'Americanization' in comprehensive terms cannot. A broad adoption of values, behaviour, norms and behaviour and their implementation on the corporate level did not occur. These were adopted in varying degrees across the different fields of management. Given that different post-war phases need to be accounted for, this paper has dealt less with the term 'Americanization' itself as with the difference between tendencies to pursue American lines and the voluntary adoption of the American example. This was illustrated by technology transfer and industrial relations.

As the case of the German chemical and rubber industry illustrated, the transfer of American technology played a significant part in enabling Hüls, Glanzstoff and Continental to regain international stature. In this respect, a strong orientation towards American technological progress can be identified, which was indeed put into practice within vital corporate areas. Nevertheless, with regard to industrial relations, and especially human relations, the case was different. 'Americanization' tendencies are only evident within small and medium-sized companies dependent on American aid under the US Technical Assistance Program. Here, any disregard for American stipulations could have met with sanctions. In the case of large companies, such as Glanzstoff and Continental, management displayed, at most, a voluntary orientation towards American human relations models and TWI methods. Their implementation in practical terms was however severely limited by the realities of factory life under the framework of the German laws on co-determination.

As has been shown, the US-orientation was based on conscious selection which varied not only from one branch to another, but also between single companies. Working under specific local and national limitations, an individual company may have chosen to reject or to follow American developments, or indeed have chosen to mix American and German elements, producing new forms of management. While it is clear that in following developments in American corporate life closely, German companies did become 'more American', they were not actually subject to 'Americanization'.

Acknowledgements

Both my chapters in this volume (this chapter and Chapter 4 on the car industry) are based on a project financed by the Volkswagen Foundation on the possibilities and limits of inter-cultural understanding ('Das Fremde und das Eigene – Möglichkeiten und Grenzen des inter- kulturellen Verstehens') and were translated by Kirsten Petrak. See also C. Kleinschmidt, *Der produktive Blick. Wahrnehmung amerikanischer und japanischer Management- und Produktionsmethoden durch deutsche Unternehmer 1950–1985*, Berlin: Akademie, 2002.

Notes

1 P.F. Drucker, *The New Society. The Anatomy of the Industrial Order*, New York: Harper, 1950.
2 See A. Lüdtke, I. Marßolek and A. von Saldern, 'Einleitung: Amerikanisierung: Traum und Alptraum im Deutschland des 20. Jahrhunderts', in Lüdkte *et al.* (eds), *Amerikanisierung. Traum und Alptraum im Deutschland des 20. Jahrhunderts*, Stuttgart: Franz Steiner, 1996, pp. 7–33; P. Erker, ' "Amerikanisierung" der westdeutschen Wirtschaft? Stand und Perspektiven der Forschung', in K. Jarausch and H. Siegrist (eds), *Amerikanisierung und Sowjetisierung in Deutschland 1945–1970*, Frankfurt: Campus, 1997, pp. 137–145.
3 H.G. Schröter, 'Zur Übertragbarkeit sozialhistorischer Konzepte in die Wirtschaftsgeschichte. Amerikanisierung und Sowjetisierung in deutschen Betrieben', in Jarausch and Siegrist (eds), *Amerikanisierung und Sowjetisierung in Deutschland 1945–1975*, p. 148.
4 For more detail on Hüls see P. Kränzlein, *Chemie im Revier – Hüls*, Düsseldorf: Econ, 1980; R. Esser, *Diversifikation der Hüls AG im Spiegelbild wirtschaftlicher, poli- tischer und unternehmensstrategischer Interessen von der Gründung im Jahre 1938 bis 1960*, Magisterarbeit, Bochum, 1991.
5 P.J.T. Morris, 'Transatlantic Transfer of Buna S Synthetic Rubber Technology 1932–45', in D.J. Jeremy (ed.), *The Transfer of International Technology. Europe, Japan and the USA in the Twentieth Century*, Aldershot: Edward Elgar, 1992, pp. 57–89; for more detail on rubber production see G. Plumpe, 'Industrie, tech- nischer Fortschritt und Staat: Die Kautschuksynthese in Deutschland 1906–1944', *Geschichte und Gesellschaft*, 1983, vol. 9, pp. 564–597.
6 Hüls-Archiv, I-4-13/1, *Stellungnahme der CWH zum Abkommen der westlichen Mili- tärregierungen über die in Deutschland verbotene und beschränkte Industrie*, 13 April 1949, p. 143.
7 R.G. Stokes, *Opting for Oil. The political economy of technological change in the West German chemical industry, 1946–1961*, Cambridge: Cambridge University Press, 1994.
8 P. Baumann, 'Vorschau auf die neue großtechnische Kautschuksynthese- Anlage bei den Chemischen Werken Hüls', *Der Lichtbogen*, 1954, vol. 3, no. 12, p. 181.
9 K. Winnacker, *Nie den Mut verlieren. Erinnerungen an Schicksalsjahre der deutschen Chemie*, Wien, 1971, p. 267; Baumann, 'Vorschau auf die großtechnische Kautschuksynthese-Anlage', p. 181.
10 R.G. Stokes, *Opting for Oil*.
11 Interview by the author with Frederico Engel, 13 August 1997.
12 D.A. Hounshell and J. Kenly Smith Jr, *Science and Corporate Strategy. DuPont R&D, 1902–1980*, New York: Cambridge University Press, 1988, pp. 65, 89, 205.

174   *Christian Kleinschmidt*

13 Archiv AKZO Nobel Faser AG (Glanzstoff), K-13-5-8, *Denkschrift über die Errichtung einer Nylonkorf-Fabrik in Obernburg (Entwurf)*, 12 October 1955.
14 Archiv AKZO, K-13–5–8, *Notiz betr. Aussprache mit Prof. Nallinger von Daimler-Benz am 13 August 1959*.
15 P. Erker, *Wachsen im Wettbewerb. Eine Zeitgeschichte der Continental AG*, Düsseldorf: Econ, 1996, p. 29.
16 Erker, *Wachsen im Wettbewerb*, p. 48.
17 Archiv Continental AG, 6500 Zg. 2/69-A4.1, *Amerikareise Behr, Richter und Warnecke*, 17 August–17 September 1956.
18 J. McGlade, *The Illusion of Consensus: American Business, Cold War Aid, and the Reconstruction of Western Europe, 1948–1958*, Ann Arbor: University of Michigan Microfilm Publications, 1995, p. 193; G. Hardach, *Der Marshall-Plan. Auslandshilfe und Wiederaufbau in Westdeutschland 1948–1952*, München: dtv, 1994, pp. 95, 130.
20 National Archives Washington, Record Group 469, Mission to Germany. Productivity and T.A. Div. Labor Advisor, Subjects Files of the Chief 1952–1954, T.A. Work, *Program suggestions of PTA/FOA for the second annual program*, April 1954.
21 *Jahresbericht des Bundesverbandes der Deutschen Industrie 1 Juli 1951 bis 30 April 1952*, p. 26.
22 National Archives Washington, Record Group 469, Mission to Germany. Productivity and T.A. Div. Labor Advisor, Subject Files of the Chief 1952–1954. T.A. Work, *Program suggestions of PTA/FOA for the second annual program*, April 1954.
23 Quote from H. Kaste, *Arbeitgeber und die Humanisierung der Arbeit. Eine exemplarische Analyse*, Opladen: Leske & Budrich, 1981, p. 20.
24 G. Krell, *Vergemeinschaftende Personalpolitik. Normative Personallehren, Werksgemeinschaft, NS-Betriebsgemeinschaft, betriebliche Partnerschaft, Japan, Unternehmenskultur*, München: Mering, 1994, p. 26.
25 Quote from Kaste, *Arbeitgeber und Humanisierung der Arbeit*, p. 36.
26 *Der Arbeitgeber*, 1 September 1950.
27 Hagley Museum and Library, Wilmington, DE, Accession no. 1412, Box 19, NAM, *Labor Participation in management Germany, report of the NAM Mission to Germany*, March–April 1951, p. 1.
28 L. Vaubel, *Unternehmer gehen zur Schule. Ein Erfahrungsbericht aus USA*, Düsseldorf: Droste Verlag, 1952, p. 80.
29 W.E. Wicht, *Glanzstoff. Zur Geschichte der Chemiefaser, eines Unternehmens und seiner Arbeiterschaft*, Neustadt/Aisch: Schmidt, 1992, pp. 213–218.
30 Archiv Continental, 6500 Zg. 2/69-A4, *Bericht USA-Reise der Herren Birn, Hahne* 15 August–16 September and 6 October 1957.
31 On plant-level co-determination see H. Kotthoff, *Betriebsräte und Bürgerstatus. Wandel und Kontinuität betrieblicher Mitbestimmung*, München: und Mehring: Rainer Hampp Verlag, 1994.
32 L. Kroeber-Keneth, *Menschenführung – Menschenkunde. Ein Brevier für Vorgesetzte*, Düsseldorf: Econ, 1953, p. 218.
33 R.R. Locke, *The Collapse of the American Management Mystique*, Oxford: Oxford University Press, 1996, p. 55.

9 The Americanization of technologies and management in Japan and its multiple effects

The case of Toray

Tsuneo Suzuki

Multiple aspects of Americanization in Japan

The US, which dominated Japan through its occupation forces from 1945, wielded an enormous influence on Japanese attitudes towards American culture.[1] On the one hand, specialists, such as business leaders and engineers, welcomed the latest ideas and trends and access to new developments. On the other, ordinary people were impressed by American popular culture such as music, fashion and food – even simple things like Coca Cola and chewing gum. At the time, automobiles and automated technologies truly epitomized the idea of American products and American production systems. There were, however, many Japanese people who had antagonistic feelings towards the American military occupation. Regarding the Americanization of Japan during the occupation, I should refer to the feelings of the workers against American officers and those of top management who intended to exploit the new American way to increase production. These different and multi-storied effects permeated Japanese society through newspapers, magazines, radio and periodicals. Food and fashion, for common people, and the way of operating in the business world, were deeply affected.

The synthetic fibre industry, one of the most rapidly expanding postwar industries in Japan, was strongly affected by American technology in a wide range of ways from production technologies to marketing and scientific quality control methods (SQCM). Toray, a leading synthetic fibre company in Japan, exemplifies these changes. It sought to import nylon technology, and introduce SQCM through the Union of Japanese Scientists and Engineers (JUSE), a business management and training programme for middle managers. While Toray tried to install American management systems, it did not succeed in everything that it intended. It failed to persuade its workforce to accept the wage system based on jobs because they did not like this American way. It also made the workers look unfavourably on American supervisors imposing their own customs.

In this article I will outline the various feelings about and intentions of Americanization in Toray from 1946 to 1960, including the way top management exploited the above antipathy to forge factory systems that actually consolidated their business, leading to the production of nylon tire codes with Bridgestone Corp. I will also detail the results of the introduction and installation of American technology. In the second section, I outline the heavy dependence on the US, not only for exports but also for technology. Briefly reviewing the company history of Toray, I show the different feelings and attitudes of Toray towards American management systems which began at the beginning of the occupied era. In the third section, I focus on the process of introducing American factory systems and Toray's response. Regarding statistical control, one of the most impressive American management procedures, I investigate the extent to which Toray absorbed and extended its possibilities, and, in the fourth section, how Toray won the Deming Prize for such quality control improvements. In the fifth section, I show the process of launching nylon tire cords with Bridgestone. In the final section, I focus on the process of developing nylon fibre from the late 1930s to the 1960s, from a technological view point highlighting the reverse salient of Toray's engineering, effectively implementing DuPont's technology and other related methods. In conclusion, I will illustrate a wide range of Americanization in Toray and Japan generally.

The dependence on the American market and technology from 1945

Japanese economy depending on the US

It is clear that the Japanese export structure changed dramatically between pre- and post-World War II (see Table 9.1). Textile products had a long history of development from the Meiji era (1880s) and accounted for the largest export figures before and just after the war, up to the 1960s. While they were shipped to Asia before the war, after World War II they were mainly supplied to America. This shift is also true of toys and iron products. Table 9.2 shows two traits; first, export figures for America increased without exception until the 1970s. Second, it shows the continuous change in products from light to heavy and electrical goods as Japanese industry developed and gained a competitive edge in these industries. Although the change is reflected in the technologies imported from abroad, it is also based on the cumulative development and the structural change that occurred in Japanese companies from the Meiji Restoration.

It is clear that Japanese industry depended heavily on imported technologies from America to be able to improve its competitive edge, productivity and even for creating new ventures. Table 9.3 clearly shows the heavy reliance and relationship and identifies which industries aggressively introduced technology and machinery; the transport industries were the major players. The Japanese economy, therefore, had to catch up with the

Table 9.1 Top ten exporting products from Japan (in US$ million)

1934–36 Items	Amount	1950 Items	Amount	1955 Items	Amount	1960 Items	Amount	1965 Items	Amount
Cotton Fabrics	182	Cotton Fabrics	207	Cotton Fabrics	252	Steel Products	388	Steel Products	1,290
Raw Silk	123	Steel Products	72	Steel Products	167	Cotton Fabrics	352	Ships	713
Fishery	83	Rayon Fabrics	38	Fishery	74	Ships	288	Cotton Fabrics	303
Rayon Fabrics	48	Copper Products	36	Garments	56	Garments	218	Garments	287
Steel Products	43	Garments	30	Rayon Staple Fabrics	53	Radios	145	Automobiles	237
Silk Fabrics	25	Ships	26	Ships	52	Rayon Staple Fabrics	118	Fishery	231
Woollen Fabrics	17	Silk Fabrics	22	Rayon Fabrics	50	Automobiles	96	Radios	216
Pottery	14	Toys	12	Artificial Fertilizer	37	Toys	90	Synthetic Fibre	186
Cotton yarn	12	Rayon Staple Fabrics	11	Pottery	35	Foot Gear	73	Optical Machinery	179
Toys	10	Textile Machinery	10	Ply Wood	26	Pottery	68	Toys	98
Total	928	Total	820	Total	2,011	Total	4,055	Total	8,452

Source: The Study Group for Japanese Trade (ed.), *20 Years of Japanese Trading after WW2*, Tokyo: Tsusho Sangyo Chosa Kai (The Investigating Institution for Trade and Industry), 1967.

Table 9.2 Top ten destinations of export from Japan (in US$ million)

1934–36		1950		1955		1960		1965	
Nation	*Amount*	*Nation*	*Amount*	*Nation*	*Amount*	*Nation*	*Amount*	*Nation*	*Amount*
Korea	185	US	183	US	456	US	1,102	US	2,479
China	169	Pakistan	56	Hong Kong	88	Hong Kong	156	Liberia	371
US	147	Hong Kong	53	India	85	Philippines	154	Australia	313
India & Burma	88	Indonesia	46	Argentina	79	Australia	144	Hong Kong	289
Taiwan	74	Thailand	43	Indonesia	65	UK	121	China	245
Indonesia	49	Taiwan	38	Taiwan	64	Canada	119	Philippines	240
UK	43	South Africa	30	Thailand	63	Thailand	118	Thailand	219
Australia	20	UK	25	UK	61	Indonesia	111	Taiwan	217
Egypt	19	Australia	23	Singapore	59	India	109	West Germany	215
Singapore	16	Argentina	21	Australia	55	Taiwan	102	Canada	214
Total	928	Total	820	Total	2,011	Total	4,055	Total	8,452

Source: The Study Group for Japanese Trade (ed.), *20 Years of Japanese Trading after WW2*, Tokyo: Tsusho Sangyo Chosa Kai ('The Investigating Instituition for Trade and Industry), 1967.

Table 9.3 Number of agreements on importing technologies into Japan (by provider nations)

Nation	1949–54	1955	1956	1957	1958	1959	1960	1961	1962	1963	1964	1965	1966	Total
US	313	44	85	61	63	92	200	187	203	355	274	265	330	2,472
Switzerland	46	2	6	10	8	9	18	22	25	29	61	31	37	304
West Germany	23	9	11	7	6	16	45	40	46	64	60	55	66	448
France	12	4	6	4	1	7	5	10	8	25	15	21	33	151
UK	8	3	11	3	2	7	10	16	12	36	47	39	43	237
Italy	10	–	10	3	1	2	8	7	5	6	4	8	4	61
Canada	13	2	3	3	2	2	2	7	2	4	6	8	39	92
Holland	1	1	2	18	1	9	7	7	13	16	9	22	16	121
Sweden	12	1	4	2	2	3	8	8	6	6	5	3	5	62
Panama	4	4	4	2	–	1	7	2	3	1	1	2	4	47
Denmark	3	–	1	–	2	1	1	2	–	1	2	4	7	22
Norway	–	–	1	3	–	1	1	3	–	1	–	1	–	11
Venezuela	–	–	–	3	1	1	5	5	–	5	1	–	–	21
Austria	–	1	2	–	–	–	5	–	1	2	–	2	7	16
Belgium	–	–	–	–	–	1	2	2	3	4	1	4	2	19
Others	1	1	2	–	1	2	7	2	2	4	14	7	8	51
Total	446	72	144	118	90	153	327	320	328	564	500	472	601	4,135

Source: The Committee of Capital Import, A Bulletin of Capital Introduction, Tokyo: The House of Trade and Industry, 1967.

American economy, and Japanese companies gained a competitive position in the Japanese market because the Japanese government protected them from advanced countries until around 1970. After World War II, from 1946 to 1966, the figure for imported technologies is 4,135, of which 2,471, nearly 60 per cent, are from America, and 448, 11 per cent, are from West Germany. The figure, together with a dependence on the American market for exports, makes us realize the heavy reliance on America. While, according to Table 9.4, it seems that the synthetic fibre industry is less dependent on foreign technologies, we should bear in mind that many technologies in the machine industry or chemical sector also apply to the fibre industry.

Toray: a brief history

Toray, a rayon company, was founded by Mitsui Bussan (Mitsui & Co.), at Ishiyama in Shiga prefecture in 1926. As the Mitsui Trading Co. they decided to build a rayon company by obtaining a patent and relying on outside instruction. They succeeded in contracting Osker Kohorn A.G. to construct a plant. Dr Antonio Minelli, an Italian engineer and president of the Shiga factory, arrived at Ishiyama in 1926 and started supervising the project from the construction of the factory to the drawing of a filament, but unfortunately he ultimately failed due to the many and complex layers of staff who were composed of German and Japanese nationals.[2]

While Toray succeeded in drawing a rayon filament in 1927, it relied completely on Mitsui Trading Co. as its sales channel. Toray, therefore, had to improve technology to become independent. As Teijin and Asahi Chemical Co. were established in the rayon industry and dominated the market, Toray had to try to improve its rayon quality to their level and also to become innovative and create new fibres. In 1926 when Dr Staudinger first introduced fibres made from a high molecular compound, Toray started to collect information about new fibres and to test their physical quality, their nature and potential. In 1936 DuPont announced their new synthetic fibre, nylon, which had a huge impact on Toray and in academic circles, especially, Professor Ichiro Sakurada at Kyoto University. While some nylon products were sent from America through various channels into Kyoto University,[3] Toray also obtained them through the New York branch of Mitsui and Co. When the laboratory staff of Toray tested them, they immediately recognized that nylon was the best fibre they had encountered and decided to focus on it.[4]

After World War II, Toray reconstructed factories for rayon filament and staple fibre, as these materials were expected to be exportable products and necessities for the domestic market, and it started to research nylon again. While gut and string were, at first, the target for production, Toray, getting information about the new market for nylon from an

Table 9.4 Number of agreements on importing technologies into Japan (by industry)

Industry	1949–54	1955	1956	1957	1958	1959	1960	1961	1962	1963	1964	1965	1966	Total
Electrical machinery	109	17	20	29	26	39	99	59	82	122	81	80	64	827
Transportation equipment	28	8	12	2	6	6	17	24	17	4	5	10	19	158
Other machinery	113	16	20	25	23	31	71	101	95	272	202	182	207	1,358
Prime metal industry	38	7	18	11	12	25	19	27	22	16	40	34	70	339
Chemical industry	83	17	46	30	11	33	77	59	82	93	95	81	126	833
Textile industry	24	1	12	7	3	7	8	23	3	16	17	15	14	150
Petroleum industry	15	3	5	2	5	4	7	5	5	16	2	2	10	88
Rubber and leather industry	12	1	5	7	2	1	12	8	5	9	4	5	6	68
Construction industry	7	1	2	3	–	1	–	1	2	1	7	13	12	57
Glass and cement industry	10	–	2	–	3	3	7	7	12	9	10	7	20	83
Paper industry	6	1	1	1	1	–	4	5	6	4	6	4	6	48
Others	1	–	1	1	–	1	6	1	4	7	24	39	47	126
Total	446	72	144	118	90	153	327	320	328	564	500	472	601	4,135

Source: The Committee of Capital Import, *A Bulletin of Capital Introduction*, Tokyo: The House of Trade and Industry, 1967.

American company, focused on a fishing net which MITI (now Ministry of Economy, Trade and Industry) and the Ministry of Agriculture (now the Ministry of Agriculture, Forestry and Fisheries of Japan) supported financially and encouraged, so that cotton nets were replaced by synthetic fibre ones. Although this was a large and profitable market, the long-range target for Toray was the hosiery market, especially stockings. As it appeared to be impossible for Toray to establish itself without the technologies of DuPont, Toray started to get information through various channels, and eventually obtained patent rights in 1953 and from then on could produce considerably better nylon.

After licensing a polyester fibre and resin patent from ICI in 1957, Toray firmly established its foundation as a synthetic fibre company, and diversified into related products such as petrochemicals, video and audiocassette tapes, and invested in synthetic fibre factories in Asian countries. With sales in 2001 standing at 1,075 billion yen, with an operating profit of 40,866 million yen, Toray had earned a reputation 'as an excellent technological company'.[5]

The multiple effects of Americanization in the company

While Americanization in Japan is identified with economic success, it has different and multiple features once we investigate companies that have truly absorbed American influences. Asahiko Karashima and Shigeki Tashiro, top managers at Toray, expected American technology to be the way to get ahead, while Kotaro Tanemura, the chief of the Toray laboratory, decided to follow DuPont and IG Farben as well, especially in producing nylon or 'Perlon'.

Under the reconstruction of the Japanese economy backed by American aid in the years after 1946, there were some Japanese institutions that transferred American management into Japanese companies. In transferring SQCM, the Union of Japanese Scientists and Engineers (JUSE) played a key role as an agent of change and organized seminars for Dr Deming to instruct on the subject of SQCM.[6] There is another aspect of Americanization, especially for workers who were ordered to do things in an American way; some had antagonistic feelings against American supervisors who wielded extraordinary powers to control textile companies. They exerted control over the allocation of raw materials and coal, and in an extreme case could even stop factories operating. Textile companies had to accept regulations and keep their factories in line with the Americans in areas such as cleanliness.

To keep a factory clean or stop operating

Mr Crewdson and Mr Plezia: instructors or dictators?

Mr R.C. Crewdson, the chief of the silk and artificial silk sub-division of a textile division in the Economic and Science Section, visited the Shiga factory and Ehime factory in August 1947, and Mr Plezia, a member of staff of the same sub-division, visited the Shiga factory in December 1947 and the Ehime factory in March 1948 in order to inspect and advise on operations and to comment on defects. One of their objectives was to keep factories clean – a precondition for producing high quality yarn. Mr Crewdson had visited the Shiga factory ten times by February 1951 and Ehime factory four times by June 1950. Mr Plezia had visited the Shiga factory four times by April 1950, and the Ehime factory twice by December 1949, as well as visiting the Seta factory.[7]

After Mr Plezia inspected the Shiga factory for the first time in July 1948, he had lunch with the workers in the dining room. When he faced all the staff of the Shiga factory he remarked that although the factory had a good appearance, it was rather like a rotten apple, therefore the possibility of allowing its continued operation depended on whether its cleanliness could be improved. The comment shocked the top management of Toray and prompted them to immediately start keeping cleanliness and safety records in order to avoid closure. The second inspection at the Shiga factory was done over two days in May 1949 to check whether the factory was operating as previously suggested. When he saw that not enough had been done to improve things, Mr Plezia returned to Tokyo and strongly criticized the president of Toray for not doing enough and not following orders, especially not keeping the factory clean, nor improving workers' discipline. He refused to hear any accounting information and declared 'the factory might stop operating unless you follow my recommendations'. This shook up the top management to such an extent that it began improving the qualifications of workers and keeping the factory clean by introducing a campaign with the motto 'Improving Movement'.[8]

Exploiting the opportunity: top management consolidating the improvement

The 'Improving Movement' created different attitudes towards the American way of doing things. Some workers felt antagonistic about it; in the Ehime factory, workers dubbed it a 'CP Movement', apparently an abbreviation of the two American inspectors' names, while the top management exploited the situation to push ahead their aims. Mr Plezia coined the phrase 'What Toyo Rayon makes, makes Toyo Rayon', which served as the Toray motto from May 1949, and became a symbol of dictatorial methods during the occupied era. The inspectors went around many rayon companies and gave the same instructions, which succeeded in drastically changing the atmosphere and circumstances in factories.[9] Efforts to raise cleanliness, maintain safety and improve qualifications of workers continued after the inspectors left Japan. Toray's top management continued the same movement as a tool in their quality improvement programme with successive targets; to improve the quality of final goods, to reduce waste of materials and to raise efficiency. The results succeeded in improving productivity and reducing costs, which reinforced the team commitment to press on.

Research and development of nylon and the introduction of technologies

Deciding to produce nylon

Synthetic fibres were not widespread until after World War II when Americanization flourished throughout industry. Dr Staudinger's predictions in 1926 about a natural fibre made from polymer encouraged researchers to investigate and to create synthetic fibres in the 1920s and 1930s. The prediction stimulated scientists and chemical companies to search amongst many candidates for monomer and to polymerise in order to create a new synthetic fibre. Among the companies in the forefront of this research were IG Farben and DuPont. They had different strategies; the former intended to create a new fibre by polymerization, the latter by condensation. PC, a polyvinyl alcohol yarn, was made through the polymerization of vinyl alcohol by IG, as is acrylic fibre, but nylon was made through condensation of an adipic acid and hexamethilene diamine by DuPont. In Japan there were many companies and universities who tested the reports released by foreign chemical periodicals and research papers, including Toray. Researchers at Toray were convinced that nylon was the best fibre they had ever tested. They decided nylon was the best fibre to research and wanted to create it in the laboratory.

It seems the competitive edge between IG and DuPont in the synthetic fibre industry changed. DuPont became the leading manufacturer, and IG followed by discovering nylon 6, which is made by polymerization of caprolactam. Confronting a lack of such materials as stainless steel, raw materials and a comprehensive know-how to create nylon 66, Toray decided to produce nylon 6 because it was easier to make, thus following IG.

There were four steps to accomplish the production of nylon 6 starting with the identification of contents to drawing a yarn without the assistance of foreign companies; the first step, 1936–41, was to identify the contents of nylon 66 and nylon 6. Having selected nylon 6, in spite of the lower melting temperature than nylon 66, Toray engineers created a melt-spinning machine. The second step, 1942–47, was to build a small plant for preparation of continuous production for fishing nets and guts. When Toray was asked by the Japanese Navy to produce nylon chips for use as insulation for electric apparatus in airplanes in World War II, it established a pilot plant for nylon chips and supplied them, although the chips produced were of lower quality than the Navy had expected. The third step, 1948–51, was to set up a new division in order to launch the nylon business in the Nagoya and Aichi factories, and the fourth step was a fully fledged era of producing nylon products such as stockings by introducing the technology of DuPont in 1951.[10] Toray could not produce nylon 66 because of a lack of necessary materials, but it had accumulated experience of nylon 6, especially a melt-spinning technology that was the same as nylon 66. Through trial and error and the accumulation of technology and know-how, Toray acknowledged that it needed more time to overcome reverse salience[11] before it could enter the hosiery market.

Improving the quality of nylon by Toray's engineers and by the introduction of DuPont's technologies

In 1949, when Toray hurriedly consolidated a base in the nylon business, the Japanese government supported it by limiting companies producing synthetic fibres in order to avoid excessive competition and to raise profits. In effect, for several years, the government allowed Toray to become the only company to officially produce nylon. After establishing a nylon branch to concentrate its resources, and expanding the plant at Shiga, Toray succeeded in drawing a nylon yarn in October 1949 by batch production. While Toray was able to draw a nylon yarn there remained drawbacks in the melt-spinning process. As Toray controlled the temperature by applying an electric heater, it was very hard to maintain the same temperature continuously. Therefore it could not control quality among the different spinning machines. In the extreme case, nylon chips became cemented together due to a lower temperature, and impaired the process as a whole. Although Toray improved the process, it could not resolve all the problems until it introduced the melt-spinning machine. It was the first and the worst reverse salient.

As Toray acknowledged that Amilan, the trademark of Toray's nylon 6, did not have the appropriate quality, it had to find an expanding alternative market and finally found this in fishing nets and guts.[12] Toray exploited fishing guts and gained a huge profit not only due to quality but also scarcity, and also exploited the market for fishing nets backed by the Japanese Government.[13] Although nylon fishing nets and guts were the largest production items and raised a huge profit, it only proved that the quality was not good for hosiery.

In the Aichi and Nagoya factories constructed in 1951, Toray started to draw a nylon filament after resolving the particular problem of making ammonia nitrite. The 5-ton plant per year factory expanded at the end of 1951 and Toray produced nylon filament (110 denier and 250 denier) and staple fibre, but had to resolve another difficulty – gum like elasticity. For weaving nylon filament into cloth, the Katsukura company was selected because Toray appreciated its skill and expected it to be able to overcome the difficulties. Although the Katsukura company had excellent rayon weaving skills, it failed to weave nylon because nylon stretches over one and a half lengths when woven on the same machine as rayon, and at the same time during weaving, it generates a static electricity which prevents continual operation and consistent quality.[14] As Toray recognized that elasticity was the main problem, it struggled to refine a drawing machine to stabilize the quality of the yarn to enable continuous weaving, only succeeding when it introduced a drawing machine made by Whiting Co. This is the second reverse salient.

The introduction of DuPont patents and technologies

The most urgent issue regarding the introduction of DuPont nylon patents was to avoid a situation in which another company dominated the Japanese market by introducing a sole right to produce nylon. This would undermine the experience and effort accumulated for more than 15 years and destroy the opportunity to launch nylon products as a first mover. Unfortunately, there are no documents or witnesses that can decisively explain the reason why DuPont agreed to offer the nylon patents only to Toray among the many Japanese companies in the running. There are two main factors to consider: the first is that the Shiga factory had already produced a nylon filament as reported in the Rose Mission Report (1946), an American Mission overview of Japanese rayon companies;[15] the second factor is the early and ardent efforts of Shigeki Tashiro, the president of Toray, who was able to negotiate directly with the relatives of DuPont thanks to his ability to speak good English. Together with the ambition and speculation of engineers who almost succeeded in producing nylon filament by themselves, DuPont decided that Toray was the best company to produce nylon.

In investigating the technologies of DuPont, Toray declared that it needed three technologies in order to completely succeed in the nylon business. The first was to implement a melt-spinning system with the Dowtherm boiler, corresponding to the first reverse salient;[16] the second was to import a draw-twister, corresponding to the second reverse salient; and the third was to transplant the chimney cooling system in order to improve productivity. After contracting nylon patents with DuPont in March 1951, Toray imported the draw twister, made by the Whiting Co.,[17] which offered the possibility of spinning a fine yarn for hosiery and improved nylon quality especially in the unification of a denier that Toray's engineers had unsuccessfully struggled to overcome for a long time. This, together with the completion of the Nagoya and Aichi factories in setting up a melt-spinning system, enabled Toray to expand production to include items such as raincoats, shirts, blouses, a neckerchief and linings. Having resolved the difficulty of weaving caused by elasticity Toray created new and large markets with a fine and high quality yarn for garments. The chimney cooling system which Toray desired to introduce enabled faster spinning than ever, and also enabled the enlarged spinneret which had more holes to spin, to work better by controlling the air condition surrounding yarns just after spinning.

It appears Toray introduced from DuPont two categories of change: the first was to improve the quality of nylon yarn to produce a fine, unified denier; the second was to raise productivity. And from the viewpoint of the nylon business, Toray went into the black in 1951. While these technologies turned Toray into the leading synthetic fibre producer, the last one, the chimney cooling system, was not introduced into Toray factories even after it was operational, because Toray was more interested in developing quality rather than productivity at the time. Therefore Toray took on the cooling chimney system after it succeeded in producing high quality nylon.

Winning the Dr Deming prize: introduction of statistical management

Shigeki Tashiro, the president of Toray, initiated new management policies

After attending a lecture of Dr Deming, in August 1950, Shigeki Tashiro decided that he should start SQCM in Toray to synthesize cleanliness and quality control, because he had not previously always necessarily applied scientific methods. The centre for research and development started to apply SQCM informally, because it was accustomed to statistics. It organized a study group of SQCM in Toray in August 1950, and thereafter it gradually expanded the number of staff and employees involved until September 1951 when Dr Deming was invited to give a lecture to the senior staff. The lecture stimulated them to implement SQCM in Toray and, as a result, in October 1951, a month after Dr Deming's visit, a committee of SQCM was formally established, responsible for applying SQCM and charting progress. The committee dispatched engineers to gather information about scientific control, and set up sub-committees in every factory in order to promote the system. Although every factory accepted an application and engineers established a control chart, difficulties arose in changing processes and handling procedures. The collection of samples and how to analyze them caused further problems. It appeared that workers and engineers were less able to manage SQCM in order to maintain high-quality operations, because they did not know exactly how to bridge making control charts and keep the process on the right track. Many situations remained out of control on site, and the problems remained because no one knew the right procedure to identify causes and implement solutions.

It was JUSE who had the responsibility for diffusing a statistical control movement in Japan. In Toray, Dr Eizaburo Nishibori, a delegate of JUSE, lectured on the application of control charts and binomial probability distribution, and on how to exercise process analysis and gave hints on improving amelioration, which stimulated Toray to establish a sampling procedure, and to inquire into the relationship between causes and results by applying the control charts. While SQCM was at first mainly arranged for engineers, the next step extended it to superintendents and shop floor management. By observing every motion of workers in order to establish job specifications, Toray created a standard job activity list of over 30,000 in March 1953,[18] and created a check list for the superintendents on sites. The list showed standard job activities and clearly demonstrated demarcations and responsibilities. After introducing standard job activities and exercising statistical control for the superintendents, unstable process conditions among the different teams were reduced.

Winning the Dr Deming Prize

Toray won the Dr Deming Prize, along with two other companies, in November 1954. According to the comments on the Prize, there are four conditions:

1   to establish an effective and reliable connection with suppliers of raw materials;
2   to enforce good process analysis and to apply it to operations;
3   to promote measurement procedures to keep a good track record at every step; and
4   to have enthusiastic activities initiating and improving SQCM.[19]

Along with introducing SQCM on site, Toray started to train middle and top management to improve their capability through lectures backed by Nikkeiren (Japan Federation of Employer's Associations). These activities aimed to raise the quality of middle managers, to instruct workers, to advise on improvements and to provide training, and propagate new procedures. Such movements spread amongst top and middle management, and even into lower management and foremen, who specialized in such issues as how to instruct the rank and file, how to treat them and how to improve conditions on site. With improved physical control methods, Toray developed labour relations, and then boosted productivity and secured the long-term commitment of labour to production.

While SQCM contributed to the improvement of productivity and quality of products, it did not solve other problems. One of these problems was the lack of a way to define exactly how to obtain a sample to approve quality. As there was no procedure to test spinning on site, the workers were allowed to maintain given conditions by making adjustments themselves. When viscose rayon is spinning in a bath containing sulphuric acid, quality of a filament depends on the density of the sulphuric acid, but there is no strict manual for shop workers to maintain the density within a given range. This practice leads to different quality levels among the three teams who operate in rotation on one day, and, in an extreme case, the thread is broken, and production has to stop.

Although standard motion is set for the operators, it depends on their expertise rather than on chemical engineering insights, because there is no systematic procedure for checking the different density of the sulphuric acid circulating in a spinning bath. This suggests that standard motion and job analysis for pay is not based on scientific knowledge of processing, but on the physical action. In Toray, SQCM goes beyond standard motion to a process analysis in order to unify employees' operations, and reduces differences between three teams.

Advancing to the next step: Kaizen

While SQCM gave impressive results in maintaining conditions in some areas, Toray was less adept at applying scientific control as a tool to resolve difficulties caused in processing. After Toray won the Dr Deming Prize it organized a small committee whose members were responsible for the resolution of any further problems. When the committee considered the problem of yarn breaking, it investigated the causes of deteriorating quality or breaking the yarn, and tested the suppositions in order to identify the real cause. Eventually, engineers on the committee found that when a pulp containing a lesser alpha cellulose was put into operation, the main problem was the spinneret that weakened the yarn. Initially, although they invented many types of spinneret to which inorganic material did not adhere, they succeeded only moderately in reducing yarn breaking, even after applying SQCM. Therefore, they changed their focus from the spinneret to adding a material that reduced adherence, and finally discovered a cation solvent that dramatically reduced the problem. This raised productivity because of less breaking and also increased the quality of the yarn by introducing a cyclical replacement.[20]

It is not instructors, but workers and engineers operating on site, who play the most important role in establishing SQCM, resolving difficulties and improving productivity and quality. It seems SQCM was of more help in maintaining better quality and sustaining continuous operations than even the top management had expected.

Creating nylon tire code and diversifying into plastics

Developing nylon tire filament for tire cords in cooperation with the Bridgestone Corp.

In 1951, Bridgestone Corp., the largest tire company in Japan, knew that nylon cords were replacing rayon cords in aircraft tires in the US because nylon tire cords were tougher for the impact of landing. It obtained nylon 6 from Toray in 1951, and started joint research in developing nylon tire cords with Toray from 1952.[21] After making a presentation at the International Rubber Conference held at Copenhagen in 1953, Shojiro Ishibashi, a president of Bridgestone, visited the US in order to observe nylon tire cords and to collect information about their prospects. The experience stimulated Bridgestone to develop nylon tire cords. It obtained nylon cords made of nylon 66 from the Goodyear Tire and Rubber Co. to start tests. While, in 1955, it started to create nylon cords for aircraft tires and in 1956 for trucks and buses, it recognized that it had to build up a base for the nylon tire business by making and supplying nylon cord facilities itself.

In this situation, as Bridgestone knew that Toray was producing nylon, it proposed joint development of nylon tires. As Toray produced nylon 6, with a lower melting temperature than nylon 66, it had to improve it for use in tire cords. As Toray succeeded in creating a tenacious nylon yarn, Type 350, for nylon tire cords in 1958, Bridgestone began producing and selling tires with nylon cords for trucks and buses in 1959.[22] As a result, in the tire market, nylon cords gradually replaced rayon cords. The trend continued steadily because nylon tire cords were durable for heavy weight vehicles and withstood impact, and also improved fuel efficiency. Toray, identifying the nature of the trend, decided to stop producing tenacious rayon cords for automobiles in 1961, and scrapped the facilities in February 1963.[23]

Diversification into plastics: the keyword is 'polymer science'

After Toray consolidated the nylon business in hosiery, it gradually shifted its strategic product from rayon to synthetic fibre. At that time, in 1955, nylon sales were the largest item in Toray, and together with the polyester business introduced from ICI in 1956, Toray became one of the largest synthetic fibre companies in Japan. While many rayon and cotton spinning companies such as Kanebo, Asahi Chemical Co., Teijin and Kureha (now Toyobo) entered the nylon market in 1964, Toray kept its No. 1 ranking and also diversified into plastics in the 1960–70s.[24] Toray integrated into the petrochemical industry to stabilize its raw material supplies and diversified into new products such as fine chemicals, films, carbon fibres and engineering plastics. With the increasingly strong yen and rising oil prices in the early 1970s, Toray invested in factories in Thailand, Malaysia and Indonesia in order to shift its strategic plants from Japan to Asia. It focused its resources on high-value plastics and fibres with the key word being 'polymer science'.

Conclusion

Americanization is not an entirely clear concept when we focus on the manufacturing industry in Japan. Therefore I will focus on three areas: the first is the antagonistic feelings of workers against American supervisors who ordered them to operate factories as the Americans did by wielding extraordinary powers; the second is SQCM, in which not only Dr Deming but also JUSE played an important role in persuading manufacturing companies to apply the procedure effectively; and the third is the excellent products created, a reflection of the brilliant technology Japanese companies identified and introduced.

In considering these three factors, we should not separate them. It was top management who combined these issues and exploited them to consolidate Toray's base and enabled it to produce and improve nylon. The top management of Toray 'consciously aimed to create organizational subcultures that simultaneously sought to achieve and amalgamate human and corporate goals'.[25] Although factory cleanliness was modified and exploited by top management, and SQCM was applied to raise productivity, in addition, Toray was strongly affected by excellent technology. Toray, along with other chemical companies such as Asahi Chemical Co. and Teijin, followed in the wake of American chemical companies such as DuPont. Table 9.1 reflects the appreciation Japanese companies had for American technology.

American technology in, for example, the creation of nylon, is not the sole invention of DuPont. There seems to have been a cluster of activities in which many related companies were involved. Nylon, for example, was not created in isolation by DuPont's technology but in association with the Dowtherm boiler and the draw twister of the Whiting Co. Because there was no opportunity for Toray to obtain such technologies as the melt-spinning system and the draw twister, Toray could not have produced fine nylon even if it had resolved the processing problems and invented a machine. Although Japanese companies succeeded in assimilating American technology and were able to shorten production time and costs, the dependence on American technology gradually undermined the creativity of Japanese firms. Even now when we view the history of chemical products or fibres, Japanese companies follow the products or technologies that American or European counterparts invent and succeed by their modification of process or materials.

192   *Tsuneo Suzuki*

Notes

1 H.G. Schröter, 'The German Question, the Unification of Europe, and the European Market Strategies of Germany's Chemical and Electrical Industries, 1900–1992', *Business History Review*, Autumn 1993, p. 391.
2 Toray, *70 Years of Toray*, Tokyo: Toray, 1997, pp. 35–36.
3 M. Noguchi, 'An Overview of the Japanese Textile Industry 5', *Sen'i kagaku* (*The Textile Science*), November 1968, pp. 43–46.
4 Toray Document, 'Nylon Material', in *25 Years of Toray*, Document no. 3, 1953.
5 Toray, *Annual Report*, 2002.
6 See B. Boel, 'The European Productivity Agency: A Faithful Prophet of the American Model?', in M. Kipping and O. Bjarnar (eds), *The Americanization of European Business: The Marshall Plan and the Transfer of US Management Models*, London: Routledge, 1998.
7 Toray, *70 Years of Toray*, p. 238.
8 K. Sodeyama, 'Movement for Quality Improvement', *Reien* (Monthly Periodical for Toray members), July 1948, pp. 2–3.
9 Toyobo, *100 Years of Toyobo*, vol. 1, Tokyo: Toyobo, 1986, pp. 494–496.
10 Toray, *70 Years of Toray*, pp. 206–207.
11 T.P. Hughes, 'The Dynamics of Technological Change: Salients, Critical Problems, and Industrial Revolution', in G. Dosi, R. Giannetti and P.A. Toninelli (eds), *Technology and Enterprise in a Historical Perspective*, Oxford: Clarendon Press, 1992.
12 K. Makihara, *On the Fishing Net Made of Synthetic Fiber*, Tokyo: Sangyo Shizai Chosakai (The Agency for Industrial Material), 1949, in an introduction.
13 T. Suzuki, 'Industrial Policy and the Development of the Synthetic Fiber Industry: Industrial Policy as a Means of Promoting', in H. Miyajima, T. Kikkawa and T. Hikino (eds), *Policies for Competitiveness*, Oxford: Oxford University Press, 1999, pp. 88–91.
14 Katsukura Shokufu (Katsukura Textile Co.), *50 Years of Katsukura*, Fukui: Katsukura Textile Co. (now Katsukura Co.), 1979, pp. 42–43.
15 H.W. Rose, *Rayon Industry of Japan*, Washington: Textile Research Institute Inc., 1946.
16 R.H. Boundy and J.L. Amos (eds), *A History of the Dow Chemical Physics Lab*, New York: Marcel Dekker, 1990, p. 43 ff.
17 T.R. Navin, *The Whiting Machine Works Since 1831*, New York: Russell & Russell, 1950, pp. 389–390.
18 Toray Document, *On the Publication of the Sheet of Job Organization*, Tokyo: Toray, no date.
19 JUSE, *The Report of the Deming Prize 1954*, Tokyo: JUSE, November 1954, p. 13.
20 Toray Document, *Report on the Investigation of Choking in Spinneret*, Tokyo: Toray, 1957.
21 Bridgestone Corp., *The 50 Years of Bridgestone Corp.*, Tokyo: Bridgestone Corp., 1982, p. 213.
22 Ibid., p. 219.
23 Toray, *70 Years of Toray*, p. 341.
24 T. Suzuki, 'A Synthetic Fiber industry in Japan after WW2', in S. Yonekawa, K. Shimokawa and H. Yamazaki (eds), *Sengo nihon keiei shi 1* (*Japanese Business History after WW2*), vol. 1, Tokyo: Toyo Keizai Shinpo Sha, 1991, pp. 170–173.
25 W.M. Fruin, *The Japanese Enterprise System*, Oxford: Clarendon Press, 1992, p. 172.

10 Reluctant Americanization?

The reaction of Henkel to the influences and competition from the United States

Susanne Hilger

'What should we do when the Americans come to Germany with their products?'[1] This question which was being asked by members of the Henkel management in 1952 was posed with a view to the changing competitive situation in the consumer chemical industry after the Second World War. At that time a massive expansion of international competition broke into the German and European markets, particularly by 'the big American soap manufacturers, Procter & Gamble and Colgate, but also by the Anglo–Dutch Lever combine.[2] Up to that time Henkel in Dusseldorf had been one of Germany's oldest and best known brand article firms. The development of the washing powder Persil in 1907 proved itself as a pathmaker for the growth of the company which had been founded in 1876. Before the Second World War, Henkel had already moved beyond the traditional markets for detergents and household cleaners and is today one of the major suppliers of consumer chemicals. The diversification process was at first accelerated through the affiliation of supplier industries and, later on, through the increasing competition in the original core business of the company.

With regard to the 'Americanization' of the West German economy after the Second World War, it is interesting to find out about the effects of the changing competitive situation for the corporate policy of Henkel, which, for a long time, appeared to be a 'typical German enterprise' with regard to competitive behaviour and appearance. Since it predominantly concerned Anglo-American competitors, it is necessary to examine the 'American influences' on Henkel between the 1950s and the early 1970s.[3] Americanization on a microeconomic level means 'the adoption of values, types of behavior, [...] ways of procedure, norms and institutions which were [...] widespread' in US American business management.[4] It can be communicated, e.g. by institutionalized contacts such as conferences and workshops, business trips, contracts with US American consultancies and the adoption of the competitors' strategies.[5]

Starting from Volker Berghahn there are several approaches dealing with the Americanization process. Many of them, such as Jonathan Zeitlin's idea of 'reworking' or Ove Bjarnar's and Matthias Kipping's concept of 'translation and transformation' do not interpret Americanization as a 'one way' process, but as a form of best practice with hybrid results.[6] Reinhard Neebe also stresses the 'synthesis' between modern American industrial culture and the traditional West German economic mentality and structure being the base 'for the long-lasting success of the West German economy after the Second World War' and a 'decisive prerequisite [...] that the technological delay of Europe towards the U.S. [...] could be overcome'.[7] With these concepts in mind, I will first refer to the relationship between Henkel and its Anglo-American competitors in the European market for consumer chemicals before and after 1945. Focussing on the company's competition strategies in functional areas, such as technology, marketing (sales, advertising, and communications), and corporate organization, I will discuss the 'Americanization' of a traditional German company.[8]

Henkel and its US competitors in the European markets for consumer chemicals before and after 1945

Only a few years after its foundation in 1876, Henkel & Cie established a market for detergents and washing powder in Germany. The launch of 'Persil', the first 'self-active' detergent, in 1907 brought international growth to the company which became Europe's leading detergent producer. The outbreak of the First World War endangered this market position. Up to the Second World War there had only been 'regional competition of national detergent companies', such as Henkel and Lever Sunlight.[9] Lever Sunlight was part of the Anglo–Dutch Unilever combine which had been built in 1929. The company was not only the major producer of margarine in Europe but also used fats which were obtained from the oil refining process for the production of soap. Lever had been the first to package soap and to put it on the market with a brand named 'Sunlight'.[10] Thus Henkel's main competitor was mainly engaged in the soap business, but after the First World War it tried to break into the market for detergents as well. From 1919 onwards the legal conflicts between Henkel and Unilever on the use of the trademark 'Persil' in France and the former states of the Commonwealth caused a deterioration in the relationship between the competitors.[11]

The American company Colgate-Palmolive (CP) also tried to put a foot in the traditional markets of Henkel in Germany and Europe by acquiring the German firm Binder & Ketels in Hamburg in the early 1930s. This combine, which goes back to the early nineteenth century, primarily produced soap and toiletries and, in 1909, had invented 'Palmolive', a new kind of soap which was made of natural olive and palm oils instead of tallow. The firm was renamed the Palmolive Company in 1917 and merged with Colgate in 1928. From very early on, the company used typical American marketing techniques such as discounts, coupons, free gifts and advertising campaigns.[12] The emergence of synthetic detergents in the early 1930s was the reason why Henkel and the American soap producer Procter & Gamble (P&G) entered into restricted cooperation. After its founding in 1837 Procter & Gamble had been reorganized into a joint-stock company in 1890.[13] The so called gentleman's agreement between the two companies based on the exchange of licences and technology and established spheres of interest, linked the P&G business to the US and Canada and that of Henkel to Europe.[14]

But after the disintegration of world economy during the 1930s Henkel, like other German firms, as a consequence of the Second World War lost its foreign possessions, patents, brands and licenses and became subject to allied dismantling and deconcentration measures.[15] The Henkel management was convinced that foreign competitors took advantage of these Allied restrictions against German firms. When in the summer of 1948 the partial dismantling of Henkel's washing-powder plant began, the management presumed Lever was behind this measure.[16] Yet, after the Persil production had started again in 1950, Henkel had a continually rising market turnover and a 'satisfactory financial situation'. Like other branches of the consumer goods industry, the detergent producers profited from the prosperity of the 'economic miracle'.[17] Nevertheless there was no doubt that for German companies after the Second World War the competitive conditions had totally changed because of the US-American companies which were about to capture the European markets.

As already mentioned, in the US, since well before the Second World War, the three largest detergent firms, Procter & Gamble, Unilever and Colgate-Palmolive, controlled the strongly oligopolistically-structured markets for soap, detergents and household cleaners with a market share of 75 to 90 per cent.[18] Among the 'Big Three', Procter & Gamble, whose share in the American market for detergents rose from 30 per cent in 1925 to 69 per cent in 1953, had become the largest American supplier of detergents and household cleaners as well as of bodycare products and was ahead of Unilever. P&G had profited both from an innovative product policy and an active 'brand marketing'. The launch of new brands guaranteed 'the permanent growth of profits' to the company.[19] After P&G had started its European business, it grew from the late 1950s onwards to become the strongest competitor of Henkel, although both companies were still playing in different leagues. In 1950, while P&G had a total balance sheet of 1.5 bn DM, Henkel only showed an amount of 149 million DM in 1952.[20]

The relationship between Henkel and its international competitors now fluctuated between cooperation and confrontation and was dependent on the attitude which the foreign firms showed towards market conditions and arrangements in Germany.[21] In contrast to P&G, Lever seemed to adapt well to the unwritten rules of competition and showed openness towards arrangements on pricing and advertising which still existed in Germany. Henkel also fostered a close relationship with Colgate, by the 'exchange of nationally and/or internationally protected symbols', through mutual support on matters involving customs legislation, and by way of technical cooperation.[22]

Yet, with the entry of Procter into the European market in the course of the 1950s, the 'cold war' between the detergent firms began. The company's market entry in Europe was accompanied by an aggressive product, price and sales policy. So besides product quality, marketing-know-how became a decisive factor. The competitive behaviour of P&G worried the Henkel executive management which tried hard to reactivate the pre-war agreements. Yet it all too soon became clear that Procter, with the change of generations in management, was pursuing new market interests and did not want to bind itself to old arrangements.[23] In 1953, when P&G with the soap powder 'Tide' subsequently entered the markets in Belgium, Italy and Switzerland and took a glance at the Swedish market as well, Henkel protested persistently against the 'disruption of the traditional markets of the Henkel group'. Up to the end of the 1950s the West German and Austrian markets remained untouched by Procter & Gamble, but in the summer of 1958 the company prepared for the launch of a household detergent on the West German market which promised high turnover.[24]

Up to the 1960s P&G had no production facility of its own in Germany but distributed products which came from the company's plants in Belgium. In the summer of 1960 P&G founded a German subsidiary in Frankfurt/Main. In 1965 the West German detergent producer Rei-Werke AG in Boppard/Rhine was acquired. Together with the detergent plant P&G had opened in Worms in 1964, Rei-Werke predominantly produced for the German market.[25] Seeing these obvious preparations, the Henkel management decided to make this process of market entry 'as difficult as possible for P&G'.[26] Their colleagues in the P&G headquarters in Cincinatti/Ohio could not understand this attitude. They could 'not believe' that Henkel was willing to terminate 'our exchange of experiences only because of P&G being about to enter the European markets'.[27]

In the long run, the increasingly competitive pressure of P&G selling on the German and European detergent markets exposed Henkel to a painful adjustment process and led the company to the adoption of competitive strategies which had hitherto been unknown so far. At least 'the growing number of US-American companies in Europe' and the competitive pressure contributed not only to the fact that 'the traditional ... business techniques' of German companies changed, but also that they began to take part in the international search for new markets.[28]

Taking up the 'American challenge': competition strategies of Henkel up to the early 1970s

Technology

After the Second World War the Henkel management soon recognized that 'our firm', when measured against development abroad, especially in the US, 'remained far behind', because since the middle of the 1930s technical and economic investment for modernization and repairs was no longer being undertaken. 'In order to catch up on the large lead of the foreign firms and to stay competitive', there was a need for massive effort. This meant, for example, a production change-over to synthetic full-detergents 'like in the U.S.' which required an estimated investment for the technical re-equipment of '10 million DM annually'.[29]

In fact, because of the loss of capital and know-how, Henkel's product development lagged behind in international competition for some years. 'Although it is not possible to produce something like that', after the years of isolation, German companies, only one year after the end of the war, found it 'interesting, how and by what means production abroad' developed.[30] This was the reason why Henkel directors, in 1949, restarted their study trips to the United States of America. Visits to US companies had already been undertaken by company founder Fritz Henkel Sr before the First World War and were carried on by his sons Fritz and Hugo and his grandson Jost in the 1920s and 1930s.[31] The trips were primarily 'to find out if we are at our best with regard to the technical equipment' but also to get to know product innovations, forms of packaging and new advertising concepts.[32] After the Second World War Konrad Henkel, the grandson of the company founder, travelled to the US in the company of, for example, engineers, chemists or marketing experts. From 1949 onwards Henkel sent delegations to the US every year to study the production of detergents and cosmetics or the processing of fats and oils among others, and to visit not only the chemical branches, but companies such as Colgate, Hercules Powder, Procter & Gamble, Quartz Corp., Standard Oil, Westinghouse, Whirlpool and Ford to seek cooperation in the further training of staff.[33]

Nevertheless the company showed a certain time lag in its product development activities. In 1951, after Henkel had started again with the detergent 'Persil' 'with its well-tried pre-war-quality', Lever in 1955 entered the German market with the first synthetic full-detergent in which the soap flakes were replaced by synthetic substances. Thus the market share of 'Persil' fell from more than 40 to 20 per cent. Only in 1959 when Henkel with 'Persil 59' also switched over to synthetic components did these losses gradually reduce.[34] Henkel also lost time in the production change-over to liquid products. Since the first half of the 1950s powdery wash-ups (*Geschirrspülmittel*) were replaced by washing-up liquids. In the

US, the market share of Lever's liquid product 'Liz' had risen from 25 per cent in 1953 to 36 per cent in 1954. Although in 1958 Henkel still doubted that 'the German housewife would be inclined to use a liquid cleaner', the members of the management could not shut their eyes to the market changes. Thus in March 1959 the Henkel subsidiary Böhme launched 'Pril-liquid' on the West German market, reaching a market share of 15 per cent within only 2 years and soon becoming the market leader.[35]

'Since [...] the US American literature again and again had stressed the increasing market share, i.e. of liquid synthetic detergents' the Henkel subsidiary Thompson around the middle of the 1950s supported the idea 'that [...] a firm of our group should soon enter the market with those special cleaners'.[36] But when in June 1962, the softener 'Lenor', the new liquid product of Procter & Gamble, showed a somewhat sensational start, Henkel launched a rival product just 2 years later in September 1964. But on account of 'extensive advertizing and an attractive packaging', Lenor proved itself, in the long run, to be a more successful product than that of Henkel. Thus Henkel wondered whether, in view of the required advertising expense and the sustained losses, 'it is necessary [...] to be present in this market only for prestige reasons'.[37]

In trying to find a product for core business, 'consultations with the US', that is with the US American advertising agency McCann, would reveal 'if there are possibly some other products among the [American] household cleaners' which would be suitable for Henkel's range of brand articles.[38] Cleaners for lavatories and pipes (*Rohr- und Toilettenreiniger*) turned out to be one such product. A market inquiry in 1958 assumed that almost 50 per cent of West German households could be won over 'as consumers for a product like that'. 'Potential buyers' could be convinced of the 'product's utility value' by 'appropriate marketing'. Up until then, the product 'WC Null Null' of the US producer Yankee Polish which had been introduced in 1957 in West Germany was the market leader. Because of the activities of Yankee Polish, whose advertising costs for the West German market was about 400,000 DM per year, Henkel could rely on an 'already [...] prepared field of approximately 2 million households' when entering the West German market with a new product division. But it still took some time until the subsidiary Thompson, Henkel's specialist for household cleaners, offered a toilet cleaner at the beginning of the 1960s.[39]

The importance of the US American market increased when deciding the product policy of the European consumers' chemical industry so that Henkel intensified 'the observation of the product development in the US' at the beginning of the 1970s, not only in regard to detergents, but also with regard to household cleaners and cosmetics as shown by the cooperation with Tampax or the strategic alliance with Clorox.[40]

Marketing

After the Second World War, international competition had totally changed. Henkel recognized that branded products maintained their hold on the market not only by their constitutional characteristics, such as constant quality as well as good value and appearance, but '[...] clear strategies and their utilisation in operative activities [...]' seemed to be a 'requirement for their survival and growth in a rapidly changing environment'.[41] Up to the Second World War, German producers of branded articles had put less significance on the outward appearance and marketing effects of their products than to the quality. But after the Second World War they learnt from the Americans 'that the packaging and the opening of products was gaining greater [...] importance'.[42] In 1957 P&G nearly caused a sensation with the product design of the new soap 'Camay' of which the colour corresponded to the packaging. Nevertheless in spite of large consumer successes, Henkel's general management considered many of the US marketing techniques to be unsuitable for German consumer taste. So Konrad Henkel's suggestion to use light colours when printing detergent packaging was met with scepticism since his colleagues in the Henkel executive management doubted the effect on the German consumer.[43]

As far as package sizes were concerned, Henkel also reacted only slowly to the changing consumer needs following the introduction of the electrical washing machine. When Sunlight, in the spring of 1958, brought the Sunil 'super packet' onto the German market, which soon reached 25 per cent of total sales, Henkel was hardly prepared for this 'unusual' success. On its packaging machines, the company could only produce 'marginally larger [...] boxes than those of the Persil 59'. If larger packaging units were required 'in consideration of American competition in the future', there was no way around additional investment. Not least because of lack of capital, the product policy of Henkel in the early years, ran permanently behind its competitors. The management had scarcely come to the decision to bring out the new 'Persil-Riesenpaket' in a large size when Sunlight was already about to enter the market with the next packaging innovation, the 'Sunil-twin-pack'.[44]

The marketing of scouring powder (*Scheuerpulver*) required an increasing expenditure on packaging as well. In the US, cardboard boxes had been replaced by more functional canisters made from synthetics (*Kunststoffdose*). With its product 'Ajax', Colgate was by far the market leader in this segment of household care. When Colgate introduced 'Ajax' with the new packaging in the summer of 1966, Henkel still showed a sceptical attitude towards this mode of packing because of the high capital expenditure needed for new packaging machines. This view was soon revised as the production change-over from cardboard to synthetic cans for 'ATA' was scheduled for 1968. '[W]ith regard to Colgate'

Henkel's sales and product managers were convinced that 'we have to adapt ourselves to synthetic packaging and must have a competitive scouring powder'.[45]

Similar to the product policy, the Henkel price and conditions policy moved along the conservative paths of regulated competition. Price undercutting, discount rates and free gifts, which were part of everyday business practice in the US, were categorically rejected by Henkel, because the executives of the company believed that in this way 'one would discredit the brand article'. In contrast to this, P&G felt themselves, as far as free gifts for consumers and discount rates were concerned, 'apparently tied to no usage of the German market'. Responding to this attitude Lever took the introduction of discount rates into consideration, 'in order to disturb the launching of new P&G products'. This was strongly rejected by Henkel, because the management was afraid 'that corresponding measures would be taken by other competitors too, and therefore the market and the price resale maintenance would be tangibly interfered with'. Instead of this, the Henkel management urged P&G, together with Lever as well, 'not to use any unusual sales methods in Germany' but 'to comply with certain rules of competition'.[46] The company tried hard to ensure that 'in Germany the same sales methods would not gain a foothold' as in Belgium. Here the detergent producers had promoted sales campaigns which enabled Belgium housewives 'to wash for free' for some months in the year.[47]

Instead, Henkel decided to carry on without these methods 'in that we will not be forced by our competitors' behaviour to change our attitude'.[48] Only when Henkel launched the new hair spray 'Pretty Hair', which could hardly hold up against strong competitive products, the management decided 'to follow the marketing methods of P&G and Colgate', which usually launched new products below the price level to reach a high market share in a very short time. This corresponded with the strategy of the Henkel cosmetics division, which, with regard to the maximum turnover, accepted negative results in order to achieve 'an appropriate market position'.[49] Helmut Sihler, who had been Henkel's marketing specialist since the 1960s, installed modern marketing strategies into the tradition-based company. His Anglo-American education – Sihler obtained his BA degree in Vermont, US – strongly influenced his career. This became clear with the setting up of a modern product management which was oriented towards US American models. According to Sihler marketing should be based on elements such as philosophy, organization, market research and advertising which were taken from US origins.[50]

Through cooperation with the leading US producers of brand articles, merchandisers, and sales companies, Henkel hoped to get some information about new sales methods and marketing trends. This was to establish whether 'American developments can be applied to our firms'.[51] The market position of the retailing companies was fostered by the concentration tendencies in this area which became stronger after the 1960s and were mirrored, not only in high sales volumes and the growing density of stores, but also in the increasing number of products which were sold as profitable household brands. The big US American grocery retailers like Sears Roebuck, Penny and Woolworth, which turned some products into brand articles through strong advertising, put themselves on the same level as the traditional producers of brand articles.[52]

In West Germany, the concentration among the retailers also exerted a strong influence on the structure of distribution. With distribution in mind, producers had to consider their range of products, sizes of packaging and forms of delivery. Because of German public price maintenance, brand articles were not initially offered in supermarkets which at first predominantly sold low-priced household brands and 'no-name articles'. In contrast to the manufacturers' brands which directly named the producer of the single product or product family, the household brand starts out from the distributing organization whereas no-name articles are not branded. In Henkel's opinion, all of this had a weakening effect on the protective function of a trademark. For this reason the company had blocked production for other producers and trademarks for a long time. In 1968, although Henkel had already tested this segment 'indirectly' using its small subsidiary Kossack which was to produce detergents for other firms and trade companies, 'officially' the engagement was to be 'kept away from Henkel' because the image of the brand article producer should not be discredited.[53]

Advertising and communications

It was not only in the area of applied technology, product development and sales, but also in advertising and communications, that Henkel recognized a high 'catch-up requirement' because many 'rival products have broken into the market [...] mainly through massively organized propaganda supported by large foreign firms'.[54] A communication policy with advertising and public relations is one of the main marketing instruments of a firm. Before the Second World War, Henkel had paved the way for 'modern advertising' in Germany, but during the 1950s and 1960s the company was forced to restrict its advertising activities.[55] This was because of the high costs for advertising. Paper advertisements, for example, had become five times more expensive than before the war.[56]

Direct advertising which seemed to become popular with the consumer after the war was used particularly by foreign competitors in the 1950s. On the occasion of the launch of the new soap 'Rexona' people were invited by Lever 'for dancing' and 'free consumption'.[57] In a reaction to competitors' increasing promotion activities, Henkel increased its field staff for branded products between 1952 and 1962 from 700 to 2,700 employees.[58] This proved to be farsighted because the company was now able to meet the product activities of P&G with an intensified field organization. In Autumn 1961, after P&G had achieved a distribution of 75 to 80 per cent for their products 'Fairy' and 'Camay' in the Darmstadt area, the Henkel sales staff visited all the local merchandisers and retailers 'in an additional tour [Sondertour]'.[59]

In the 1930s Henkel had spent, on average, around 10 per cent of net turnover on advertising. In contrast to this, the expenditure on advertising had clearly fallen after the war and was at about 4 per cent at the start of the 1950s. In comparison to this Henkel's international competitors spent considerably larger sums on advertising. The German Lever Sunlight, for example, in April 1952 spent around 204,000 DM just on newspaper advertisements, in contrast to Henkel who spent 12,000 DM.[60] The same goes for advertising on radio. Henkel 'realised [...] that an advertising hour on radio had a strong impact' because of 'the good response'. But in contrast to Sunlight, which in October 1952, spent almost 1 million DM for slots on 'Suwa' and 'Vim', Henkel spent 'considerably smaller amounts for slots on radio'.[61] From the beginning of the 1950s, in addition to radio, cinema advertisement was taken up again. Full-length movies which put the product in a narrative context were especially popular.[62]

Besides advertising on billboards, newspapers, radio and cinema, television advertisements appeared in the second half of the 1950s. While Unilever, in 1960, spent around 83 per cent of its American advertisement budget on this medium, the amount spent by P&G already stood at 90 per cent.[63] On their visits to the US the Henkel delegates showed a strong interest in the advertising efforts of US American companies. In autumn 1964 a number of advertising slogans which had been on US TV Channels were taken to Düsseldorf in order to submit some new ideas to the management (see Table 10.1).[64]

The number of branded products Henkel put into TV commercials rose from 67 in 1959 to 117 in 1960 and reached 264 in 1961. Although the Henkel management had tried very hard, the number of broadcasting minutes was small compared to the competitors' activities: in 1963 P&G spent around 3.5 million DM on TV slots in the second German TV Channel, whereas Henkel's expenses were around 1 million DM.[65] A rise in the advertisement budget seemed to be unavoidable because in view of 'the expected launch of Procter's Dash and the sales efforts of Camay and Fairy in Germany', Henkel had to counter strongly with advertisements in these markets as well. The additional expenditure was to come out of a surplus fund, which had been established for 'extraordinary competitive measures against P&G'. So Henkel seemed to use advertisements right into the early 1960s primarily as a defensive measure against the 'unusual advertisement endeavours' of P&G. Only in the second half of the 1960s did the company changed the 'wait-and-see-attitude' towards an offensive

Table 10.1 Advertising slogans broadcast on New York's TV channels, 1964

Product	Slogan
COMET	'goes deep and disinfects'
AJAX	'stronger than dirt'
ALL	'outcleans them all. More active cleaning power'
WHISK	'puts its strength where the dirt is'
IVORY liquid	'helps mother's hands stay like her daughter's'
WOOLITE	'cold water detergent for fine fabrics, powder or liquid'
SNOWY Bleach	'bleaches like the sun does'
DOWNY	'skin loving softness'

Source: HA 413/19, US trip of A. Müller, B. Werdelmann, J. Heinz, autumn 1964, p. 61.

marketing policy. There was no misunderstanding that the slogan of 'Persil 59', 'nothing in the world washes whiter than Persil', was addressed to P&G and intended to emphasize Henkel's 'international claim'.[66]

In the 1960s a firm's 'loud and vociferous advertising' and its 'cheap and insistent outward style' was generally considered to be 'American influenced'. With its own advertising style, Henkel did not want to evoke that impression at all. This is underlined by the 'consultation spots' (*Beratungswerbung*) which since the 1960s provided an unemotional supply of information.[67] Nevertheless the management also had to recognize the sweeping success Procter & Gamble had with its campaigns. P&G launched 'Dash' in February 1964 with the so-called 'Operation Big Lift'. This was to be the 'strongest advertising campaign one had ever seen in Germany' and was to mobilize millions of German housewives. Sixty-thousand advertising messages were broadcast up to twice a day on TV and two or three times on radio. In addition, there were full-page and double-page four-colour ads in the magazines and daily newspapers.[68]

The marketing activities of the competitor were not without consequences for Henkel's market share for soap and detergents, which decreased between 1963 and 1964 from 47 to 44.3 per cent in quantity and from 48.7 to 44.4 per cent in value.[69] According to Henkel's sales experts the strong advertising impact and the attractive product design, together with the concessions the company made to the distributors in the form of price maintenance and generous trade margins, contributed to the success of 'Dash' in the West German market.[70] Besides market research there was an additional prerequisite for successful marketing. Hence, in the Henkel marketing department a central unit was established in 1961 which was to collect 'all documentation on the appearance of new brand articles in the USA' and which instructed the different divisions of the company. The observation of competitors was thus to make 'an important contribution towards the planning of our own advertisement measures'.[71]

Public interest in the company's performance, results and strategies increased in post-war times even in Europe. From the late 1950s onwards news about Henkel came to the public's notice which did not 'fit the facts'. So the company felt compelled to correct this information and moreover to use the public interest to its own advantage as the Americans did. For a long time, and in contrast to the open-minded policy of American companies, Henkel directors had not been interested at all 'that [...] it should be recognised which firms belong to the Henkel group'. Only at the beginning of the 1970s did the management show a more liberal attitude towards the growing public interest. The local press would be informed about the activities of the company in order 'to bring Henkel more obviously into the forefront'.[72] But there were still different viewpoints among the members of the executive management because some of the directors only wanted to give 'as little as possible' to the public. In contrast to this Henkel's press officer, Erwin Stapf, insisted on 'saying something at least', so that Henkel was not regarded as 'unfriendly towards public information'. 'Especially in view of the forthcoming competition with P&G' one should reconsider its standpoint.[73]

After a visit to the US in 1964, members of the executive management recognized 'the lack of a genuine prestige publication about Henkel' which could give some 'real information on the size of the company and its position in the German and International market'.[74] Thus in the 1960s, Henkel took the step of promoting image building activities which would complement the advertising of products. Again it was Erwin Stapf, who wanted 'to give an overview to the public of those activities with which Henkel touched the consumers' markets'. For the creation of a corporate image the Stanford Research Institute recommended Henkel to combine 'brand article orientation' with high quality standards, long-term product care, and a consequent, but flexible, price policy'.[75] So the advertising of brand articles from the 1960s onwards was brought more into context with the name of the company than had been the case previously. Now, the well known name of Henkel was also used for the product marketing of the subsidiaries. After it had been discovered that consumers showed only very vague attitudes to less known subsidiaries, all branded articles subsequently bore the additional mark 'made at the Henkel works'. Also the overalls which were worn by the workers in the production areas in Holthausen were printed with the Henkel oval, in order to create a corporate identity.[76]

In 1965 the public relations department started a campaign which was to associate the name of Henkel with cleanliness in the public mind. So the exhibition 'Cultural history of washing' which Henkel promoted in Düsseldorf in November 1966, combined for the first time public relations and marketing interests with cultural engagement.[77] Studies on the corporate image of firms revealed that 'the term tradition' proved to be 'of central importance' for the public image of Henkel. In preparation for the public relations campaigns, some surveys on the firm's image had been carried out at the beginning of the 1960s. They made clear that the image of Henkel was 'more distinctive' than that of Sunlight and that consumers showed some 'emotional ties' to Henkel which were passed from generation to generation.[78] After P&G had entered the German market Henkel thus advertised using the characteristics of tradition and family. In contrast to P&G which described the size of the parent company in Cincinnati, Henkel emphasized that they were 'the largest German family firm on the detergent market'.[79] This was supported by the fact that members of the Henkel family represented the firm officially and internally and gave the impression of continuity to employees and to the public.[80]

Corporate planning

The implementation of a strategic corporate plan after the mid-1960s heralded an important new approach in the Henkel corporate policy. The necessity to come to grips with the long-term development of the company was inspired by Konrad Henkel who became Chairman of the Board in 1961. In his opinion Henkel was 'not sufficiently up to date' 'for a long-term competitive position on the highly contested market for detergents'.[81] Under his guidance, and with a view to the fact that foreign markets especially offered strong growth potentials to Henkel,[82] the company, which was mainly engaged in the German market, was transformed into an international business group. To use this potential, the group had to dispose 'a unified marketing policy and a better information policy [. . .] for a fast reaction to the trends on the single markets'.[83]

Konrad Henkel belonged to the 'new generation of top managers' which 'had experienced a significant American influence during their formative years since 1945'.[84] He was born in 1915, the grandson of the company founder, and he felt an affinity with the US as had his family for many years. Just like his uncle Hugo Henkel and his brother Jost who went to the 'new world' before the war, the United States for Konrad Henkel became the symbol of modernization and innovation. Driven by the belief that 'we have to be modern, we have to come to the top', from the early 1960s onwards he succeeded in overcoming the extremely conservative and anti-modernistic attitudes in the management team and paved the way for the americanization of the company.[85] Konrad Henke, who reestablished former contacts with US firms, recommended as a model for Henkel the corporate behaviour of the 'Americans', who had already been dealing 'with the problem of long-term company planning'[86] for a couple of years.

Long-term planning, alternate ranges of products and some organizational 'considerations on the possibilities and limits of a family enterprise, especially from a financial viewpoint' became the most important aims of Henkel's corporate strategy.[87] Therefore contact with the Stanford Research Insitute (SRI) which was brought in 'as a consultancy for the implementation of planning activities' had been made in the early 1960s.[88] Up to that time Henkel had been one of those German family-owned companies which usually shut itself off from the influence of banks, external investors, and consultants as well. So cooperation with an American consultancy from the second half of the 1960s onwards was clearly a break with the past, both in terms of its duration and its scope. One of the reasons for this decision was the expansion and the diversification of the company in the post-war period. Henkel's top management had to realize that there was a growing awkwardness within the organization, which stood in the way of a flexible market policy. As the company's 'economic environment' grew more and more complex and its business activities were increasingly transferred to the European markets outside Germany, production, marketing and financing methods had to be used which 'diverge somewhat from the traditional ones'. In this context in modern management theories corporate planning and organization at that time were specified as the basic preconditions for a 'systematic expansion'.[89]

Probably even more important for the restructuring of the company was a significant decline in the earnings of Henkel's main business which was due to the appearance of the American competitors on the German market.[90] Henkel's business in branded products relied to a large extent on brands such as 'Persil', 'Dixan' and 'Pril', and there was a growing risk 'that the market position of these three brand marks will be strongly attacked by Procter and Colgate'.[91] As a result, the company became 'aware, that the detergents market was endangered, and that is why we had to look for new ways'.[92] Thus, to become better acquainted with the modern management techniques applied by many large international corporations, Henkel decided to hire an American consulting firm. There are numerous other examples, where the pressure from US competitors led European companies to question their own practices and ask American consultancies for help.[93]

In contrast to many European companies, Henkel did not hire the American consultancy McKinsey but contacted the Stanford Research Institute (SRI) which was founded in 1946 in cooperation with Stanford University.[94] Soon after the Second World War, SRI gained some reputation for working on company strategies and the implementation of the necessary technical, administrative and organizational facilities in government and commercial business. From 1958, the institute maintained a 'Long-Range Planning Service' (LRPS), which focussed on the economic changes and their consequences for the individual industries.[95] Members of the Henkel executive board had already attended a meeting on 'company planning for industrial growth' which SRI had arranged in Düsseldorf in May 1963. As a result of this contact Henkel first issued and circulated an internal paper on the purposes and methods of long-range planning in the single corporate units, which contained detailed instructions on the analysis of plants and markets, followed by the determination of profit targets.[96] Three years later, in March 1966, Henkel authorized SRI to advise on the realization of planning activities in the company. As a consequence, a department for long-range planning (LUP) was established shortly after, which was to create planning cycles for the product markets and investment activities of the Henkel Group at home and abroad.[97] The underlying objective of these efforts was to achieve a better 'transparency' of the entrepreneurial risks. Against the background of growing competition, LUP was designed to 'recognize the market of tomorrow and its determining factors'.[98]

Corporate organization

The main result of the cooperation with SRI however was the implementation of a divisional organization in the spring of 1969. Since its founding, the Henkel corporation had grown more or less unsystematically parallel to the functional expansion of the group, as Figure 10.1 shows.[99]

Economic success can be put down to a company's 'organizational capability', that is its capability to adjust itself to changing economic conditions.[100] Above all, the so-called M-form which is seen as 'American capitalism's most important single innovation of the twentieth century' was to cover a wide production programme and a multitude of markets and was seen as an efficient base for management delegation, since each division was run as a profit centre, individually responsible for product development, production and marketing.[101] The multidivisional structure or M-form can be traced back to the 1920s, when a number of American corporations decentralized their activities along product lines ('structure follows strategy'). It is, according to Alfred Chandler, 'the American style of industrial groups'.[102] The low economic performance of the European industry was therefore put down to a lack of organizational capability within the companies.[103] With the assistance of American consultancy firms like McKinsey the M-form became a 'model for a number of Western European countries'.[104] Whereas the M-form had been almost unknown in Germany up to the 1950s, 50 out of the 100 largest German firms had already adopted it by 1970.[105]

In place of the functional structure, the new divisional organization of Henkel also proceeded in relation to product groups: Six divisions – inorganic products/adhesives, cosmetics, food/housecare products, organic chemicals, packaging and detergents, which covered the domestic and European business – were run as profit centres with responsibility for product development, production and marketing (see Figure 10.2).[106]

Divisions were set up quite easily when subsidiaries could be used as 'a frame'. The division food/housecare products e.g. based on the Henkel

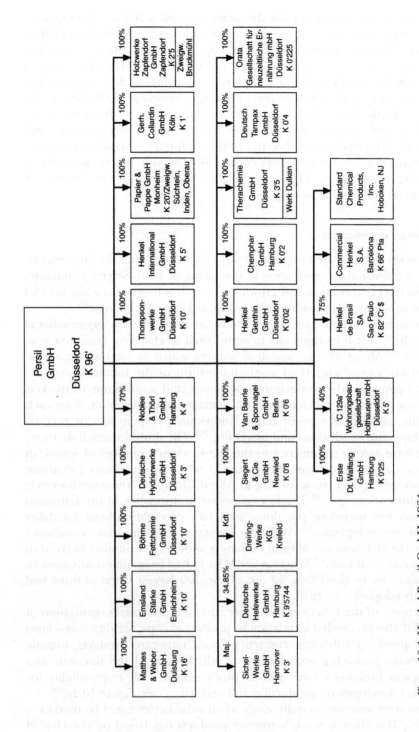

Figure 10.1 Henkel-Persil GmbH, 1964.

Source: Henkel Archives.

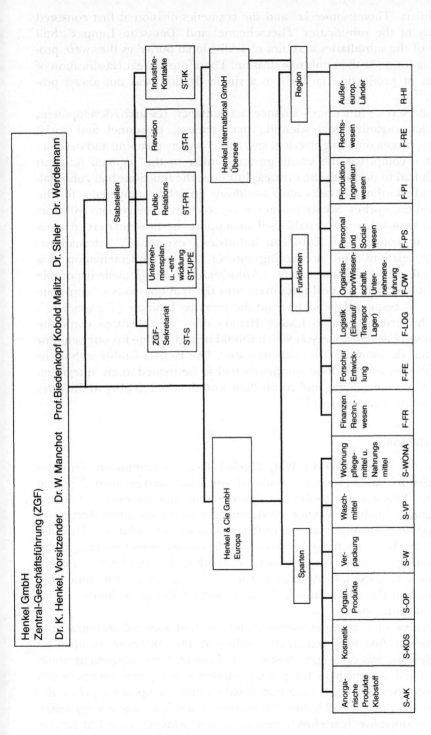

Figure 10.2 Henkel GmbH, divisional organization, 1964.
Source: Henkel Archives.

subsidiary 'Thompsonwerke' and the cosmetics division at first consisted mainly of the subsidiaries 'Therachemie' and 'Deutsche Tampax'. Still most of the subsidiaries were not of a 'divisional purity' as they were producing for more than only one division. Therefore a 'clear classification of plants or production facilities to a single division' was not always possible.[107]

Nine service functions – finance/accountancy, research/development, logistics, organizational/scientific management, personnel and social affairs, production/engineering, law, and company planning and development – comprised the whole group. Similar to the regional function which had to deal with the overseas business, the functions had consultative and coordinating tasks and a worldwide guideline competence for the related enterprises. Six staff positions in executive management with specialist knowledge were established to support the headquarters in areas such as 'contact with European industries', 'executives', 'international public relations' and 'accounting control'.[108] The implementation of a 'central executive management' (*Zentralgeschäftsführung*) made it possible for the directors 'to deal intensively with the real questions of corporate policy by being independent from the everyday business (*Tagesgeschäft*)'. For the first time in its history Henkel drew up a 'written corporate purpose (*Unternehmenszweck*) which should be a guideline for our behavior and our decisions for the years to come'. The Henkel GmbH with all its subsidiaries and portfolio companies had to be treated as an 'integrated whole' when managing and controlling, and thus had to obey to the rules of scientific management.[109]

Conclusion

After the Second World War, Henkel faced a completely different competitive situation in international and local markets than they had before. This was due to the fact that the economic recovery of German companies in the consumer goods industry meant an intensification of competitive pressure to an extent that was up to then unknown. This situation can be characterized by tough profit considerations and aggressive marketing strategies. So according to Henkel, the 'thinking in market shares and sales' was 'American style'.[110] The company was quite convinced that the competitors had 'no respect for European business practices or traditions'.[111]

Because of a strong corporate culture of tradition and conservativism Henkel at first very reluctantly embraced the American competitive 'model' and was even quite hostile to it. Instead, the management would have liked to return to the pre-war market sharing agreements, which enabled them to react to the traditional German competition policy; the latter, as in the period before the Second World War, was less aggressive than cooperative (cartelized) measures, and primarily aimed at market regulating arrangements. That was the reason why the company very soon and pro-actively sought to renew the contacts and exchange of ideas immediately after the war. But in view of the changing market conditions, which were characterized through the appearance of new international competitors on the European markets, Henkel was confronted with new technologies and new concepts in marketing and organization. As some examples of the Henkel product policy up to the early 1960s show, the management could hardly contemplate – obviously from lack of capital – the launch of new products and strategies regarding price and advertisement policy which were being implemented by their competitors.[112]

The managerial qualities of a company are shown by its ability to gain control of the various changes by flexible adaptation and permanent innovation. Through contact with American business consultancies, like the Stanford Research Institute, and through featuring specific instruments of scientific management such as planning and strategy, an adaption process appeared to be underway at Henkel. The influence of the 'American-friendly' members of Henkel's general management should not be underestimated.[113] Konrad Henkel, who opened the company to 'American influences', briefed the general management about innovations and provided inspirational ideas so that in the second half of the 1960s, Henkel had regained its hold on the market quite well. Between 1965 and 1971 the company increased its market share of detergents from 45 to almost 55 per cent, whereas that of Sunlight fell from 30 to 22 per cent and that of Procter from 19 to 11 per cent. Colgate-Palmolive was even temporarily squeezed out of the German market for detergents. The expansion of the product range seemed to be one decisive factor for the company's success as one of Henkel's main marketing strategies was to anticipate 'as far as possible [. . .] the successful products of their main rivals as a means of defending the present market share of the firm'.[114]

So Henkel's strategic competition policies continued both the maintenance of the core businesses and diversification into other production areas. The detergents' turnover which was at 80 per cent in 1938 declined to 43 per cent in 1966 and halved to 23 per cent in 1997. Thus the company soon had readily and quite sucessfully espoused American technology, management and marketing methods, with the main restriction being the available funds. It did not wait for the American soap manufacturers to come to Germany in the 1960s, but pro-actively sought to renew former contacts immediately after the war. Yet, besides the 'Americanisms' in technology, marketing and corporate organization, in public relations policy Henkel held to 'the strong effect of the Henkel name', and in doing so combined tendencies of Americanization with the tradition of a specific German corporate culture.

Notes

1 Henkel Archives (HA) 153/8, daily minutes, 9 December 1952.

2 HA 314/130, SRI report, vol. 1, July 1966, p. 64: 'The prospect of Persil/Henkel in the field of detergents and cleaning products must be seen in the light of an intensified competitive pressure. There are reliable signs that Colgate-Palmolive, as well as especially Procter & Gamble, will increase their efforts during the coming ten years. There are many European markets which are not penetrated by these two companies up to now [...].'

3 Cf. V. de Grazia, 'Amerikanisierung und wechselnde Leitbilder der Konsum-Moderne in Europa', in H. Siegrist, R. Kaelble and J. Kocka (eds), *Europäische Konsumgeschichte. Zur Gesellschafts- und Kulturgeschichte des Konsums (18.–20. Jhd.)*, Frankfurt/Main: Campus, 1997, pp. 109–137, here p. 111. Also P. Erker, '"Amerikanisierung" der westdeutschen Wirtschaft? Stand und Perspektiven der Forschung', in K. Jarausch and H. Siegrist (eds), *Amerikanisierung und Sowjetisierung in Deutschland 1945–1970*, Frankfurt/Main: Campus, 1997, pp. 137–147. R. Pommerin (ed.), *The American Impact on Postwar Germany*, Providence: Berghahn, 1995. W. Bührer, 'Auf eigenem Weg. Reaktionen deutscher Unternehmer auf den Amerikanisierungsdruck', in H. Bude and B. Greiner (eds), *Westbindungen: Amerika in der Bundesrepublik*, Hamburg: Hamburger Edition, 1999, pp. 181–201. B. Greiner, ' "Test the West". Über die "Amerikanisierung der Bundesrepublik Deutschland" ', in Bude and Greiner (eds), *Westbindungen*, pp. 16–54. A. Doering-Manteuffel, 'Dimensionen von Amerikanisierung in der deutschen Gesellschaft', *Archiv für Sozialgeschichte*, 1995, vol. 35, pp. 1–34.

4 Cf. H.G. Schröter, 'Zur Übertragbarkeit sozialhistorischer Konzepte in die Wirtschaftsgeschichte. Amerikanisierung und Sowjetisierung in deutschen Betrieben 1945–1975', in Jarausch and Siegrist (eds), *Amerikanisierung und Sowjetisierung*, pp. 147–166, here p. 148. Cf. E.A. McCreary, *Die Dollar-Invasion. Amerikanische Firmen und Manager in Europa*, Munich: Moderne Verlags-GmbH, 1965, p. 23, who understands by 'Americanization' 'the development and expansion of American commodities, proceedings and organizational forms in Europe'. See also Bührer, 'Auf eigenem Weg', p. 182: Americanization means 'the adoption of U.S. American economic structures and concepts of industrial production and organisation' as well as 'the adoption of the U.S. business culture and mentality'.

5 Cf. Schröter, 'Übertragbarkeit', pp. 148, 152. Cf. also W. Link, *Deutsche und amerikanische Gewerkschaften und Geschäftsleute 1945–1975*, Düsseldorf: Droste, 1978. H. Bude, 'Vorwort', in Bude and Greiner (eds), *Westbindungen*, pp. 7–15, here p. 8.

6 J. Zeitlin, 'Introduction', in J. Zeitlin and G. Herrigel (eds), *Americanization and its Limits. Reworking US Technology and Management in Post-War Europe and Japan*, Oxford: Oxford University Press, 2000, pp. 1–50, especially pp. 28–34. O. Bjarnar and M. Kipping, 'The Marshall Plan and the Transfer of US Management Models to Europe. An Introductory Framework', in M. Kipping and O. Bjarnar (eds), *The Americanization of European Business. The Marshall Plan and the Transfer of US Management Models*, London: Routledge, 1998, pp. 1–17, especially pp. 6–14.

7 R. Neebe, 'Technologietransfer und Außenhandel in den Anfangsjahren der Bundesrepublik Deutschland', *VSWG*, 1989, vol. 76, 49–75, here 75. See also Bührer, 'Auf eigenem Weg', p. 201.

8 In contrast to these, the human relations approach was of less importance in the business policy of German companies during the 1950s and 1960s. Cf. M.F. Guillén, *Models of Management: Work, Authority, and Organization in a Com-

parative Perspective, Chicago: University of Chicago Press, 1994, pp. 126–151. Cf. for Henkel i.e. the statement of SRI: HA 251/2b, SRI, Long term planning for Persil/Henkel, Phase II: Strategical Planning, vol. 2, July 1968, p. 302.

9 HA 153/16, daily minutes, 24.1.1961.

10 HA 333/2, paper on the Unilever combine, 7.12.1949. See also C. Wilson, *The History of Unilever. A Study in Economic Growth and Social Change*, vol. 2, London: Cassell, 1954. The growth of the margarine industry did not start before the turn of the last century. Only from 1912 onwards when the hardening of vegetable oil succeeded, did this substance become the most important raw material for the production of margarine. After the Second World War Unilever, which now showed a broad diversification from toiletries and cosmetics to fishing and meat products, ice cream and frozen food, was subdivided into two holding companies of the same name with headquarters in Rotterdam and London. The German Unilever group in 1964 held firms such as the Margarine Union GmbH, Sunlicht-Gesellschaft mbH, Elida GmbH, Kleinol GmbH, Langnese-Iglo GmbH, Deutsche Lebensmittelwerke GmbH, Norda Heringshandel GmbH.

11 W. Feldenkirchen and S. Hilger, *Menschen und Märkte. 125 Jahre Henkel KGaA*, Düsseldorf: Stürtz, 2001.

12 HA 333/2, Wohlthat, memorandum, 3 February 1956. HA O23, Henkel legal department to Board of Directors, 12 August 1957.

13 HA 153/9, daily minutes, 29 September and 13 October 1953. HA 314/130, SRI report, vol. 1, July 1966, p. 66: 'Although Unilever held the strongest position in sales on the European market Persil/Henkel's decisive competitor will be without any doubt P&G – one of the most successful companies in the world on the market for branded consumer articles. P&G is known for its outstanding marketing abilities and inconsiderate actions.' HA 153/21, daily minutes, 21 May 1963. See also HA O22, P&G – 30 years in Germany, 11 September 1990, pp. 32 f., 46. See also HA 333/2, Wohlthat, memorandum, 23 January 1955. Newly introduced products were successful because P&G advertised them for a year, spending 104 per cent of net sales value, in other words they spent more money on advertising the product than they achieved in sales revenue. From the 'American point of view' these amounts were 'investments'.

14 Except for the acquisition of the British firm Hedley in 1930, Procter kept out of the European markets for a long time. HA 153/10, daily minutes, 2.3.1954. HA 153/8, daily minutes, 9.12.1952. HA 153/9, daily minutes, 17 February 1953. HA 333/1, Wohlthat, memorandum, 23 December 1953. HA O22, Henkel & Cie. GmbH, undated report for the British military government.

15 HA 289/1127, memorandum, 8 June 1955. HA 289/1270, memorandum, 3 June 1947. The value of the East German subsidiaries was estimated at 55 million RM. Ibid., Schmelz, concerning decartelization, 20 January 1947. HA 289/1134, Henkel & Cie. GmbH, commentary on the annual account, 31 December 1944.

16 HA 273/48, report, 24 and 25 September 1945. HA 153/4, daily minutes, 25 June and 19 April 1948. Lever planned an extension of production, Henkel headquarters in Düsseldorf noticed, 'while we are dismantled because of spare capacity'.

17 HA 153/6, Board of Directors' report, 16 January and 4 April 1950. HA 153/9, daily minutes, 6 October and 7 April 1953. Similar also HA 153/29, daily minutes, 1 February 1966.

18 HA 153/8, daily minutes, 16 December 1952. HA 333/1, Wohlthat, memorandum, 23 December 1953.

19 HA 455/19, P&G Cincinnati/Ohio, Annual report of the 30 June 1965.
20 HA 153/9, daily minutes, 13 October 1953.
21 Cf. to the differing competitive behaviour of US American and West German companies A.D. Chandler, *Scale and Scope. The Dynamics of Industrial Capitalism*, 3rd edn, Cambridge, MA: Belknap Press, 1994, p. 10: 'In the United States managerial capitalism was more competitive; in Germany it became more cooperative.'
22 HA 153/11, daily minutes, 21 June 1955. HA 153/30, daily minutes, 3 May 1966. In 1966 there was a lively exchange between Colgate and Henkel on 'problems with detergents'. See also the various reports of Henkel's directors on the visits to the US, i.e. HA 458/2, K. Henkel, report, autumn 1953. HA 413/24, visit of Dr. Heinz, 10–28 June 1968.
23 Henkel noticed that the 'younger generation' of managers obviously no longer wanted to foster 'the friendly relationship, we had with P&G in former times'. HA 153/9, daily minutes, 29 September 1953. HA 153/15, daily minutes, 17 March 1959. HA 153/11, daily minutes, 25 January and 22 March 1955. Also HA 153/14, daily minutes, 15 July 1958: Henkel agreed with Lever Sunlight to defend itself against the launch of a P&G detergent on the German market. See also HA 452/11, K. Henkel *et al.*, US-visit, September/October 1957.
24 HA 333/1, Dr. Brandt, memorandum, 21 April 1958. Still in 1958, P&G's Vice President Lingle stated that P&G 'won't enter Germany and Austria' because they were seen as the 'core of the Henkel business'. Also HA 333/2, Wohlthat, meeting in Den Haag, 21 January 1955, 23 January 1955: Lever also stated that 'Germany had been postponed by P&G' for the reason mentioned above. Therefore in the 1950s Belgium was the only market where P&G and Henkel met 'in direct competition'.
25 HA 153/9, daily minutes, 29 September. and 13 October 1953. HA 153/16, daily minutes, 13 July and 27 September 1960. HA 153/18, daily minutes, 22 August and 14 November 1961. HA 153/17, daily minutes, 20 June 1961. HA 153/20, daily minutes, 9 October 1962. HA 153/24, daily minutes, 5 May 1964. HA O22, P&G – 30 Years in Germany, 11 September 1990, pp. 17, 32.
26 Henkel noticed with satisfaction that P&G's market entry in Germany progressed only slowly because of the restrictive German legislation. HA 153/16, daily minutes, 9 February 1960. HA 153/30, daily minutes, 19 July 1966.
27 HA 333/1, Dr. Brandt, memorandum, 21 April 1958.
28 HA 251/2b, SRI, Long-term planning Persil/Henkel, Phase II: Strategic planning, vol. 2, July 1968, p. 320.
29 HA 289/1127, memorandum, 8 June 1955. HA 153/31, Monopolies Commission, 'Report on the Supply of Household Detergents' in the UK, London 1966. The production of synthetic detergents increased in the 1950s when the lack of raw materials on the European markets had been overcome.
30 HA 455/104, daily minutes, 3 August 1946.
31 The reports on study trips to the US are kept in the Henkel family archives in Düsseldorf no. 92 and 101 and in HA 413/1 to 413/33, 452/1 to 452/17 and 458/1 to 458/31. In 1946, the Henkel family contacted former partners in the US such as Procter & Gamble. They hoped for their support and intervention during decartelization and denazification. HA Henkel 2, Walter Kobold, memorandum, 8 March 1946.
32 HA 101/18, Fritz Henkel Jr, Dir. Bartz, Dir. Funck, Visit to America from 31 August to 30 September 1925.
33 HA 458/2, US visiting report of K. Henkel, Otto Lind and Bernhard Klöss, Autumn 1953. HA 458/6, Visit at P&G's, 15 August–26 August 1955. Also

HA 458/8 and 458/9. HA 413/16, US trip of Dr. Sinner, Dr. Harder, washing-machines and dish washers in the USA, 9 May – 10 June 1961. HA 413/23, US trip of Dr. Berth, Dr. Harder, Dr. Werdelmann und Dr. Zoebelein, Autumn 1967.

34 H.O. Eglau, 'Wenig Clan – mehr Elan', *Die Zeit*, no. 13, 26 March 1971, 28.

35 HA 153/11, daily minutes, 14 June 1955. HA 153/14, daily minutes, 11 March and 6 May 1958. See also HA 153/16, daily minutes, 6 May and 16 August 1960. In 1960 Sunlight was the first to enter the American market with 'Lux liquid' in a plastic bottle. Cf. HA 153/17, daily minutes, 20 June 1961. Since the US American market had shown that turnover growth also resulted 'from an attractive packaging' Henkel developed a waisted bottle (*taillierte Flasche*) made from PVC for 'Pril liquid'. HA 153/32, daily minutes, 6 December 1966. HA 153/20, daily minutes, 7 November 1962. HA 153/30, daily minutes, 19 July 1966. In contrast to the usually offered discounts of 10 per cent 'Palmolive' was launched with a maximum discount of 16 per cent.

36 HA 455/8, Thompsonwerke to Henkel & Cie. GmbH, 2 August 1955.

37 HA 153/19, daily minutes, 5 June and 26 June 1962. HA 153/23, daily minutes, 18 February, 7 April and 30 April 1964. See also Helmut Sihler: 'one mistake we made [...] was to underestimate the market for softener', H. Sihler, 'Kreative Werbung und Marktforschung nicht gegeneinander ausspie-len', in J. Kellner, U. Kurth and W. Lippert (eds), *1945 bis 1995. 50 Jahre Werbung in Deutschland*, Ingelheim: Westermann, 1995, pp. 91–96, here p. 94.

38 HA 455/8, Thorbecke to K. Henkel, 28 November 1955.

39 HA 455/7, sales planning department to Kobold, commentary on the Nielsen report, 30 May 1958. See also ibid., Kobold/Stapf to Thompsonwerke, 6 June 1958, and memorandum, 24 October 1957. Henkel at first did not want to take products like these into its range of products. Cf. the cooperation with the Californian producer of household detergents, Clorox company. HA 153/53, daily minutes, 16 January and 17 April 1973. HA 153/55, daily minutes, 7 May 1974. HA 153/59, daily minutes, 18 May 1976.

40 HA 455/23, report on the meeting from, 6 March 1972. HA 455/79, memo-randum, 29 May 1972. Ibid., memorandum Szymczak to Dr. Henkel, 27 July 1972.

41 H. Schwarzer, *Behauptung des Markenartikels im strukturellen Wandel des Marktes*, Diss. Hamburg: Universität, 1990, p. 58. According to Mellerowicz brand art-icles are not only a result of modern mass production but also a consequence of modern sales and distribution methods. K. Mellerowicz, *Markenartikel. Die ökonomischen Gesetze ihrer Preisbildung und Preisbindung*, 2nd edn, Munich: Beck, 1963, p. 2.

42 HA 289/1127, memorandum, 8 June 1955.

43 HA 153/14, daily minutes, 17 December 1958. HA 153/16, daily minutes, 24 May 1960.

44 HA 153/16, daily minutes, 29 March, 5 July and 13 September 1960. HA 153/14, daily minutes, 6 May 1958.

45 HA 153/29, daily minutes, 11 January and 29 March 1966: Colgate-Palmolive launched 'Ajax' in plastic cans in March 1966. The selling price was raised by 0.10 DM to 1.10 DM. See HA 153/30, daily minutes, 2 June and 14 June 1966: To be competitive towards Colgate the Henkel sales and product manage-ment also favoured 'the launching of scouring powder in plastic packaging', but the time to switch over required a year's lead time. HA 153/33, daily minutes, 5 September 1967: In September 1967 Henkel launched the scour-ing powder 'Tenn' in 'a modern plastic can'. HA 153/32, daily minutes, 17 January 1967.

46 HA 153/23, daily minutes, 25 February 1964. HA 153/16, daily minutes, 16 August 1960. See also HA 153/17, daily minutes, 17 January 1961.

47 HA 333/1, K. Henkel, memorandum, 21 October 1960. See also HA 413/1, Report on the US trip of J. Henkel and Dir. Erbslöh in autumn 1936, p. 60 f.

48 HA 153/21, daily minutes, 19 March 1963. See also HA 153/66, daily minutes, 29 March 1966. HA 153/31, meeting from 7 December 1966.

49 HA 455/23, memorandum, 6 March 1972. See also H. Sihler on the principles of the Henkel marketing: 'An active shaping of product range and a rational and consequent use of all marketing factors. Guideline is the rise of output.' In: HA A26, Neuer Org-Anzug. Mini wurde zu klein.

50 'Kurz vorm Ziel', *Manager-Magazin*, 1979, no. 2, p. 8. According to Helmut Sihler in West Germany 'especially the 1960s was the decennium of the United States [...] from products to advertising etc.', Sihler, 'Kreative Werbung', p. 94. Cf. in general R.S. Tedlow, *New and Improved. The Story of Mass Marketing in America*, Boston/MA: Harvard Business School Press, 1996, pp. XVIII–XXX. Cf. also to the adoption of 'American marketing' in Germany: R. Bubik, *Geschichte der Marketing-Theorie. Historische Einführung in die Marketing-Lehre*, Frankfurt/Main: Lang, 1996, pp. 149–161.

51 HA 455/79, Szymczak to Dr. Henkel, 27 July 1972.

52 Cf. in general Tedlow, *New and Improved*, pp. 259–343. HA 455/57, St-UPE, The new economic power. Outline of an evolutionary process, July 1972.

53 HA 153/42, daily minutes, 12 March 1968.

54 HA 289/1127, memorandum, 8 June 1955. HA 153/9, daily minutes, 18 September 1953: Henkel's advertising was considered to be 'good but not to be modern' by the Persil sales staff. The sales representatives rather attached 'some value on the competitors' advertising'.

55 The detergents industry was one of the first industries to create brand articles by advertising. In Germany Fritz Henkel is regarded as one of the 'pioneers of modern advertising' since he used the traditional media such as leaflets, neon signs and posters 'in an innovative and vivid way with a certain instinct for their possibilities and effects and with all means of artistic and emotional impression'. The entrepreneur had his own opinion of 'flashy advertising' ['schreiende Reklame']: 'Articles of civilization are put on the market in hundreds. The public only remembers those whose name, value and function is hammered into them every day.' Fritz Ornoldi, 17 October 1936. in: HA A5. See in general the history of advertising in Germany: D. Reinhardt, *Von der Reklame zum Marketing. Geschichte der Wirtschaftswerbung in Deutschland*, Berlin: Akademie-Verlag, 1993, pp. 169–369.

56 HA 152, Dr. Winkler, report, 3 October 1949.

57 HA 153/9, daily minutes, 10 February, 28 April, 12 May and 30 June 1953. The 'Rei-Revue' was an entertaining program of 2 or 3 hours with free admission. HA 153/16, daily minutes, 13 March 1960: Sunlight combined in their so-called 'Super-shows', washing demonstrations with artistic performances which promised 'non stop entertainment' with free admission.

58 HA 153/19, daily minutes, 5 June 1962.

59 HA 153/18, daily minutes, 24 October 1961.

60 HA 22/2, market research to Kobold, 4 November 1968. HA 153/8, daily minutes, 20 May 1952.

61 HA 153/8, daily minutes, 21 October 1952.

62 This can be inferred from the positive response the Henkel movie received. HA 153/9, daily minutes, 18 September 1953: 'Our film is still played to a full house.'

63 HA 153/16, daily minutes, 2 August 1960.

64 HA 413/19, US trip of A. Müller, B. Werdelmann, J. Heinz, autumn 1964, p. 61.
65 HA 153/16, daily minutes, 18 October 1960. HA 153/21, daily minutes, 22 January 1963.
66 HA 153/27, daily minutes, 4 May 1965. The reserve fund was meant to finance 'additional marketing campaigns to which we are forced by the rough competition'. HA 153/21, daily minutes, 21 May 1963. HA 153/31, daily minutes, 22 November 1966. Cf. also HA O22, P&G – 30 years Germany, 11 September 1990, p. 32 f.
67 HA 153/16, daily minutes, 18 October 1960. HA 153/21, daily minutes, 22 January 1963. Cf. also 153/22, daily minutes, 2 July 1963. Cf. also Sihler, 'Kreative Werbung', p. 94. Cf. the 'slice-of-life-strategy' which put psychological pressure on the consumers by appealing to their bad conscience. Procter used this strategy in television slots for 'Ariel' and 'Lenor'. S.J. Schmidt and B. Spieß, 'Von der Reklame zur virtuellen Werbewelt', in Kellner, Kurth and Lippert (eds), *Werbung*, pp. 183–197, here p. 187.
68 HA 153/23, daily minutes, 4 February 1964. HA 22/2, market research to Kobold 4 November 1968.
69 HA 153/26, daily minutes, 16 March 1965.
70 HA 153/22, daily minutes, 29 October 1963. Cf. HA 153/30, daily minutes, 19 July 1966.
71 HA 153/16, daily minutes, 24 January 1961. For this more than 500 studies and reports on the trends in retailing, consumer habits and tests on new products were carried out. HA A24, report of the executive management for 1961.
72 HA A24, finance division to public information office, 17 January 1957. HA 153/16, daily minutes, 6 September 1960.
73 HA 153/17, daily minutes, 9 May 1961.
74 HA 153/25, daily minutes, 24 November 1964.
75 HA 153/14, daily minutes, 16 September 1958. HA 252/25, Henkel & Cie. GmbH, annual report 1968.
76 HA 153/20, daily minutes, 21 August 1962. HA 153/16, daily minutes, 13 July 1960. HA 153/17, daily minutes, 3 January 1961. Also HA 153/18, daily minutes, 14 November 1961. At this meeting Erwin Stapf presented a 'new corporate label' which was to be used by a single department for different products. But with regard to the complexity of Henkel's range of products, the executive management recoiled from subsequent use. So before the launch of a new soap it was to be checked to see 'if the Henkel oval is suitable to support the sale of soaps', HA 153/23, daily minutes, 7 January 1964. HA 153/19, daily minutes, 17 April 1962, HA 153/18, daily minutes, 1 August 1961.
77 HA 153/31, daily minutes, 28 October 1966.
78 HA 153/20, daily minutes, 7 November 1962. HA 153/22, daily minutes, 19 November 1963.
79 HA 153/161, daily minutes, 16 August 1960.
80 HA 153/16, daily minutes, 5 April 1960.
81 Eglau, 'Wenig Clan', 28.
82 Henkel KGaA (ed.), *100 Jahre Henkel*, Düsseldorf: Henkel und Cie., 1976, p. 152. HA 314/96, memorandum, 17 October 1968. HA 153/42, meeting with SRI, 16 October 1968.
83 HA A26, 'Henkel blickt über die Grenzen des heimischen deutschen Markts hinaus', *International Management*, February 1972, 4. For Konrad Henkel 'the standardization of marketing' was the 'most important part of the

reorganization'. The close contact with the regional markets was seen as of 'decisive importance for entering the markets for daily goods' since consumer habits were different from country to country (ibid., p. 6). In the same way as P&G always acquired a good knowledge of the living conditions in the single geographic markets, Henkel now paid more attention to regional management, O. Schisgall, *Blick nach vorn. Der Aufstieg des Markenartikel-Herstellers Procter & Gamble*, Wiesbaden: Gabler, 1985, p. 246. Also A. Lief, *'It floats'. The Story of Procter & Gamble*, New York: Rinehart, 1958; A. Swasy, *Soap Opera. The Inside Story of Procter & Gamble*, New York: Random House, 1993.

84 M. Kipping, 'The U.S. Influence on the Evolution of Management Consultancies in Britain, France, and Germany since 1945', *Business and Economic History*, 1996, vol. 25, p. 120. Cf. also HA 153/21, daily minutes, 19 March 1963; HA 321/1866, Objectives and Methods of Long Range Planning, 6 December 1963; HA A24, paper Dr. Henkel, 25 May 1966; Eglau, 'Wenig Clan', 28; V. Berghahn, *The Americanization of West German Industry 1945–1973*, Cambridge: Cambridge University Press, 1986; L. Vaubel, *Unternehmer gehen zur Schule. Ein Erfahrungsbericht aus USA*, Düsseldorf: Droste, 1952. Cf. also V.A. Berghahn and P.J. Friedrich, *Otto A. Friedrich, ein politischer Unternehmer. Sein Leben und seine Zeit 1902–1975*, Frankfurt/Main: Campus, 1993. Because of his attitude Friedrich was seen as the 'American' among his colleagues in the West German industry. H. Hartmann, *Amerikanische Firmen in Deutschland. Beobachtungen über Kontakte und Kontraste zwischen Industriegesellschaften*, Cologne: Westdeutscher Verlag, 1963.

85 HA, Interview Prof. Sihler, 26 May 2000, pp. 5 and 7. According to Sihler, the progressive elements were not 100 per cent successful. For example, the delayering of hierarchies was 'so to speak, killed by the establishment [durch den Apparat sozusagen gekillt]'. Even the company's opening since going public in the mid-1980s has been pushed forward 'against conservative forces' and was supported 'by the change of generation within the family' (ibid., p. 12).

86 'Langfristplanung im Gespräch. Neue Wege in die Zukunft', *Blätter vom Hause*, 1967, vol. 8, p. 16 f., here p. 16.

87 Ibid. Also HA 152, Dr. Winkler, report, 3 October 1949: Still at the end of the 1940s Henkel realized that one had to think not only of 'liquidity' but also of 'rentability'. For this reason other firms like Ford had long ago installed its own planning department, cf. 100 Jahre Henkel, p. 152; HA 314/96, memorandum, 17 October 1968; HA 153/42, meeting with SRI, 16 October 1968; HA 153/30, daily minutes, 2 June 1966.

88 Cf. also S. Hilger, 'American Consultants in the German Consumer Chemical Industry', *Entreprises et Histoire*, 2000, vol. 25, 46–63. SRI was affiliated to Stanford Research University in Menlo Park, California, but was financially independent. In 1966 the institute employed about 3,000 workers. Since 1958 SRI offered a 'Long Range Planning Service'. This was to prepare companies for technical, economic, social and political changes and their consequences for trade and industry, i.e. by the opening of new sales opportunities, possible competitors, raw material demands, changing service demands, and effects on private and public institutions.

89 HA 251/1, SRI, Implementation of Long Range Company Planning within the Persil/Henkel Group – Phase I, April 1967.

90 HA, Interview Prof. Sihler, 26 May 2000, p. 6.

91 HA 153/21, daily minutes, 12 March 1963.

92 HA, Interview Prof. Sihler, 26 May 2000, p. 8. Sihler underlines particularly the pressure caused by P&G.

93 Cf. B. Kogut and D. Parkinson, 'The Diffusion of American Organizing Principles to Europe', in B. Kogut (ed.), *Country Competition: Technology and the Organizing of Work*, Oxford: Oxford University Press, 1994, pp. 179–202, who underline the fact (p. 192) that at the same time 'some of the widespread imitation of American firms was driven by the attempts of European firms to compete in the United States'.

94 Cf. W.B. Gibson, *SRI. The Founding Years*, Los Altos/CA: PSC, 1986, p. 92.

95 Henkel KGaA (ed.), *100 Jahre Henkel*, p. 152; HA 314/96, memorandum, 17 October 1968; HA 153/42, meeting with SRI, 16 October 1968; HA 153/29, daily minutes, 22 March 1966; 153/43, daily minutes, 6 September 1969.

96 HA 455/8, Thorbecke to K. Henkel, 28 November 1955; HA 153/42, daily minutes, 27 August 1968. Cf. also HA 153/21, daily minutes, 19 March 1963; HA 321/1866, Objectives and Methods of Long Range Planning, 6 December 1963; HA 153/30, daily minutes, 2 June 1966.

97 HA 321/1866, Objectives and Methods of Long Range Planning, 6 December 1963; HA 153/30, daily minutes, 2 June 1966; HA 153/44, daily minutes, 7 July 1970.

98 HA 153/30, daily minutes, 2 June 1966. Cf. Kogut and Parkinson, 'Diffusion', pp. 191 ff.

99 HA 153/30, daily minutes, 27 June 1966.

100 A.D. Chandler, *Strategy and Structure. Chapters in the History of American Enterprise*, Cambridge/MA: M.I.T. Press, 1962.

101 O.E. Williamson, *Corporate Control and Business Behavior. An Inquiry into the Effects of Organization Form on Enterprise Behavior*, Englewood Cliffs/NJ: Prentice-Hall, 1970, p. 382; also R. Whittington *et al.*, 'Chandlerism in Post-war Europe: Strategic and Structural Change in France, Germany and the UK, 1950–1993', *Industrial and Corporate Change*, 1993, vol. 8, p. 529; O. Zunz, *Making America Corporate 1870–1920*, Chicago: University of Chicago Press, 1990.

102 A.D. Chandler, 'The M-Form: Industrial Groups, American Style', *European Economic Review*, 1982, vol. 19, 10; B. Kogut and D. Parkinson, 'Adoption of the Multidivisional Structure: Analyzing History from the Start', *Industrial and Corporate Change*, 1998, vol. 7, pp. 249–273; J.-J. Servan-Schreiber, *Die amerikanische Herausforderung*, Hamburg: Rowohlt, 1970, p. 194.

103 P. Drucker, *The Practice of Management*, 1st edn, London: Mercury Books, 1961, p. 42.

104 C.D. McKenna, 'The Origins of Modern Management Consulting', *Business and Economic History*, 1995, vol. 24, pp. 51–58; Guillén, *Models of Management*, p. 150; Kipping, 'U.S. Influence', p. 118; P. Drucker, *The Concept of the Corporation*, New York: Day, 1946; A.D. Chandler, *Visible Hand. The Managerial Revolution in American Business*, Cambridge/MA: Belknap Press, 1984; H. Gammelsaeter, 'Divisionalization: Structure or process? A Longitudinal Perspective', *Scandinavian Journal of Management*, 1994, vol. 10, p. 331; R.F. Freeland, 'The Myth of the M-Form? Government, Consensus, and Organizational Change', *American Journal of Sociology*, September 1996, pp. 483–526. Cf. L.G. Franko, 'The Move toward a Multidivisional Structure in European Organizations', *Administrative Science Quarterly*, 1974, vol. 19, pp. 493–506.

105 See esp. G. Dyas and H. Thanheiser, *The Emerging European Enterprise*, Boulder: Westview, 1976, pp. 29, 65–75 and 102; N. Fligstein, 'The Spread of the Multidivisional Form among Large Firms, 1919–1979', *American Sociological Review*, 1985, vol. 50, pp. 377–391. Cf. also Guillén, *Models of Management*, p. 149 f.; M.-L. Djelic, *Exporting the American Model. The Postwar Transformation of European Business*, Oxford: Oxford University Press, 1998, pp. 6 f. and 30 f.; M. Dritsas, *European Enterprise. Strategies of Adaptation*, Athens: Trochalia, 1997.

220   *Susanne Hilger*

106 HA 252/25, Henkel & Cie. GmbH, annual report 1968; HA 252/9, Henkel
     GmbH, annual report 1968; HA 252/20, Henkel GmbH, annual report 1969.
107 HA 314/96, Dr. Heise to K. Henkel, 11 December 1968 and 13 January 1969;
     HA 252/20, Henkel GmbH, annual report 1969; HA 153/43, daily minutes, 4
     March 1969. Cf. Eglau, 'Wenig Clan', 28.
108 HA 153/42, daily minutes, 16 October and 12 November 1968; HA 252/20,
     Henkel GmbH, annual report 1969; HA 252/25, Henkel & Cie. GmbH,
     annual report 1968; HA 252/9, Henkel GmbH, annual report 1968; HA
     314/96, daily minutes, 20 February 1969.
109 HA A26, Dr. Bohmert, memorandum, 10 November 1969. Ibid., The corpor-
     ate purpose [Unternehmenszweck] of Henkel GmbH, version from 1 August
     1969.
110 HA 153/6, daily minutes, 21 November 1950 and 30 January 1951, 'The
     advertising of our competitors becomes more and more aggressive'; ibid.,
     report on meeting of the Board of Directors, 29 September 1950; HA 333/1,
     memorandum, 21 April 1958.
111 HA 314/130, SRI report, vol. 1 July 1966, p. 66.
112 HA 153/31, daily minutes, 13 December 1966; HA 252/23, Henkel & Cie.
     GmbH, report of the executive management on the year 1963.
113 Schwarzer, *Behauptung*, pp. 37, 48 f.; also H. Hinterhuber, *Strategische
     Unternehmensführung*, Berlin: de Gruyter, 1977, pp. 3, 5.
114 HA 314/130, SRI report, vol. 1 July 1966, pp. 73, 87.

11 Emerging postwar-type managers and their learning of American technology and management

The consumer chemicals industry and the case of Kao

Akira Kudo and Motoi Ihara

Defining the topic

Typified by synthetic detergents, the consumer chemicals industry was one of the industrial sectors that helped advance the Second Industrial Revolution and establish a mass consumption society.[1] In Japan, the consumer chemicals sector traces its history back to the end of the ninteenth century. Its full-scale development, however, arrived only after the Second World War with the full advent of a mass consumption society in Japan. In the postwar period, especially in the 1950s and 1960s, in this industry like many others in Japan, the gap in technology and management techniques between Japan and the West, especially the United States, was very large. Consequently, the impact from the United States was overwhelming. In the Japanese consumer chemicals manufacturing industry, firms actively learned from the United States and attempted to catch up.

This chapter examines this era of full-scale development in Japan's consumer chemicals industry during the 1950s and 1960s. It will focus on one of the leading firms in the sector, Kao Soap, currently Kao, and will clarify both the firm's strategy for catching up with American industry and the firm's business activities. Since its founding in 1887 and its entry into soap manufacture in 1890, Kao has long occupied, along with its primary competitor Lion Soap, now Lion, a leading position in the Japanese consumer chemicals market. Currently, it is diversifying from soap and synthetic detergents into cosmetics, hygiene products, and so on. Even though Western firms like Procter & Gamble and Unilever have fully entered Japan, Kao continues to maintain its position. In recent years it has developed plans to expand actively into Western and Asian markets as well.[2]

In the 1990s Kao became one of Japan's outstanding firms, receiving high marks for its production technology, research and development, marketing and distribution, as well as both its management and its internal sharing and disclosure of information. In terms of information disclosure and corporate governance, Kao is regarded as riding the crest of the globalization wave. At the same time, however, the company also holds out a more singular management philosophy. The previous chairman of Kao, Fumikatsu Tokiwa, in pointing out and criticizing Japanese companies' enthusiasm for things American, most strongly insisted that Kao was a firm with a Japanese corporate identity. So, in fact, Kao also appears representative of a Japanese firm. The American influence in Kao's history, however, is apparent and may be traced back to the firm's inception. Particularly during the 1950s and 1960s, Americanization held great significance for Kao. The technology and management methods available to the present-day Kao are the products of a discordant history of accepting this massive influence from the United States, of resisting that impact, and of attempting consequently to establish its own identity. Because most observers have overlooked this history, they often tend to see Kao as a 'pure' Japanese-style firm.

While Kao was a company that thoroughly learned from American industry, at the same time it appeared completely Japanese. By recovering the history of the process and consequences of the Americanization process at Kao in the 1950s and 1960s, this chapter will attempt to clarify, from a business history perspective, this paradoxical situation.

Initial conditions and policy preconditions

Technological accumulation

The interwar period was the dawn of a mass consumption society in Japan. During this period Kao achieved major expansion in both its product development and distribution.[3] On the product development side, Kao began selling a synthetic soap equivalent to Procter & Gamble's Ivory, as well as a synthetic detergent for industrial use (household detergents remained powders). On the distribution side, the existing distribution organization was restructured to accommodate the launch of the synthetic soaps. The company also improved the efficiency of its transaction relationships with local wholesalers which had grown increasingly complicated.[4] Kao began efforts to develop its own technology in the 1930s and the first half of the 1940s. The core of this technological development was a technique for manufacturing aircraft lubrication oil by hydrogenating high-grade alcohols produced from coconut oil. As applications, Kao developed production technology for sorbitol, styrene resin, paraffin oxidation and the like. This research prepared the way for Kao's subsequent developments in surface science and polymer chemistry. Kao also launched a research council called the Research Study Group which pioneered experimenting in the management of R&D in Japanese industry. In labour management, the company eliminated the apprentice system in favour of continued training of company personnel in technology and marketing.[5]

In this process of managerial and technological development, there were influences from both German and American firms. From 1928 to 1929, Tomiro Nagase, the second president of Kao, took a study tour of Europe and the United States. The managerial and technological methods learned from Western corporations on this tour greatly influenced Kao. In the interwar period, German corporations' influences exceeded those of American companies. During the 1930s Japan imported dye adjuvants for the textile industry from Germany. Stimulated by this opportunity, in cooperation with other Japanese companies Kao undertook the joint purchase of related German patents. This project provided the basis for Kao's successful domestic manufacture of industrial synthetic detergents.

Thus, prior to the Second World War, Kao had attained a certain level of technology and management. Although not the leader within the soap market, Kao did belong to the upper group. Its own development of hydrogenation technology for aviation lubrication oil manufacture marked the highest point in technological development. Ironically, limited supplies of raw materials other than coconut and fish oils provided the primary reason for the development of this own technology. At the same time, however, there were limits to how fully such technology could be realized in mass production. Still, as described later, these experiences in experimentation at an early stage became the preconditions for the quick, decisive and thorough subsequent introduction of technology. This hydrogenation technology became useful in the postwar production of synthetic detergents. Equipped with hydrogenation facilities, the Wakayama factory arose as the driving force in Kao's postwar factory system. The technologies accumulated during the prewar period became the basis for business expansion in the postwar period.

Corporate merger

The immediate aftermath of the Second World War produced circumstances of resource scarcity and heightened demand for manufactured goods. The government implemented both controls on feedstock oils and fats and a quota system for soap. Later in the midst of the Korean war, the price of feedstock oils and fats dropped precipitously, leaving many companies that had purchased materials at high prices with severe operational difficulties. Most Japanese firms in the immediate aftermath of the Second World War experienced business difficulties or experienced profound labour conflicts; Kao fared similarly. By accelerating conversion from military to civilian goods production and by restructuring its labour management system, Kao overcame its operational problems and labour strife.[6]

Meanwhile, in 1954 Kao Soap and Kao Oils and Fats – two companies that had separated of their own volition immediately after the war – reunited. In the process of overcoming its business difficulties and uniting these two firms, the company renovated its ownership and management structure. Within the overall stock ownership profile the proportion of stocks held by the founding family drastically declined. Stock ownership became more broadly dispersed. Moreover, the founding family was driven from top management in favour of salaried managers, initially managers brought in from the outside, who took over management control.[7] Kao thus transformed – or at least began the transformation – from a family business into a managerial enterprise. Completed prior to the arrival of rapid economic growth, the merger – and the accompanying reforms of ownership and management – proved a timely event. At this point, Kao contrasted strongly with Lion. Established around the same time as Kao in 1891, Lion was Kao's longstanding competitor. The company subsequently split into Lion Abrasives and Lion Oil and Fats; their reunion only occurred much later in 1980. In the difficulties following the war, Lion's management continued to be drawn from its founding family. Similarly, the two companies undertook postwar business reduction and rationalization independently.[8]

Even during the difficult postwar period, Kao's research and development team remained very much alive. In research and development at Kao, collection of information from overseas publications played an important role. The 'PB Report', a collection of German materials on chemical technology seized and disclosed by the American military, was the most important of these. The Kao technology team made frequent visits to the Hibiya Library run by the Occupation authorities (GHQ). There they learned much from the PB Report on file there. For example, one such fruit of their study was the surfactant Levenol, coming to Japan from Germany via the United States.[9]

A supervising engineer's visit to the United States

Although Kao started learning from the United States during the prewar period, it did not proceed in earnest until after the war. The opportunity for this was a visit to the United States by one of Kao's supervising engineers.[10] Against a background dominated by a deepening cold war, GHQ distinctly changed its occupation policy towards Japan in order to aid the reconstruction of the Japanese economy. As part of this, through the Science and Technology Administration Council (STAC), GHQ sponsored a programme for Japanese firms, to dispatch first rate technical specialists and managers to American businesses, universities and other institutions. Founded in January 1949, STAC was responsible for GHQ's science and technology policy. It had authority to assign foreign exchange to fund research in specific fields and research trips to the West.

Eizo Ito, the president of Kao Soap before the merger in 1954, received news of this programme and, despite the harsh business climate, enrolled managing director Yoshiro Maruta. Prior to the war, Maruta had played a central role in the technical team developing technology for aircraft lubricant manufacture using hydrogenation. Now, Maruta was the plant chief at Kao Soap's main plant at Wakayama, the same plant that drove Kao's fortunes following the merger. Graduating from a national college of technology and being a chemist, Maruta had advanced through the company to become Ito's right hand man as a salaried manager. After the merger and Ito's rise to president, Maruta also ascended to the top management positions of president and then chairman – which suggests something of his abilities. Having such a career, Maruta, as a manager, was able to observe both from a technical and from a management perspective. Maruta toured the United States from November 1950 to March 1951. Preceding the first delegation sent by the Japan Productivity Centre by 5 years, Maruta's visit occurred very early in the postwar importation of American expertise to Japan.

From the start Maruta showed a deep interest in the American oil- and fat-based chemicals industry. For example, because non-branded bar soaps were the mainstay of the Japanese laundry soap market, there had been scant attention to quality as a basis for competition. Maruta held a critical view of this behaviour. He noted how brand name products held a large share of the United States market, how firms gained consumer support and kept market prices stable through clever marketing, and moreover how they managed to strengthen their businesses by keeping costs down through thorough rationalization and high-volume production. Based on these insights, Maruta studied trends in the United States oil- and fat-based chemicals sector, especially in the surfactant and synthetic detergent industries.

His densely scheduled observation tour of the United States demanded concentrated mental effort. At a stop in Hawaii on the way over, Maruta's observations had already begun. There, Maruta picked up a package of Procter & Gamble's synthetic detergent Tide. The product's contents interested him. Launched in 1946, Tide was a heavy-duty synthetic detergent produced mainly from petroleum-based alkyl benzenes. As such, it was representative of the synthetic detergent products then becoming more popular in the United States.[11] Maruta sent the sample back to Kao's headquarters, attaching a note detailing how Tide was capable of cleaning not only wool but cotton clothing as well, how coconut oil was used as one of its ingredients, and how this detergent could be manufactured in Japan. By the time that Maruta returned to Japan, Kao's technical team had analyzed Tide's different components and projected that Kao would be able produce it with the company's current technology. Analysis of Tide led to the development of Wonderful, a synthetic household detergent that typified the future of Kao.

Once in the continental United States, Maruta inspected not only soap and detergent companies like Procter & Gamble, Lever Brothers and Colgate-Palmolive, but also petrochemical and electrical firms as well as universities and research laboratories. Most of what he learned, however, he learned from the soap and detergent companies, especially Procter & Gamble. Maruta observed production equipment for soap and synthetic detergents (Tide) at Procter & Gamble's Cincinnati plant. The firm's high technological standards and rational business management techniques strongly impressed him. The highly automated, continuous, high-volume production equipment left an especially deep impression. For example, the moulding and packaging of soap, which in Japan still depended upon manual labour, had been automated using moulding and heat sealing machines connected by conveyor belt. Maruta learned much from Procter & Gamble, and, above all, learned about equipment modernization, automation, mass production and quality control.

Maruta also learned about business methods, such as sales techniques, from Procter & Gamble. An example of these was the '10 days 2 per cent' cash transaction system, which later enabled Kao to revise transaction practices among its existing Japanese domestic distributors. In addition, at Procter & Gamble, Maruta learned various other aspects of business management, including public relations, systematic market research and business accounting that allowed one month's profits or losses to be calculated at the beginning of the next month.[12] In this way, acting as both a supervising engineer and a manager, Maruta undertook an extremely thorough study trip by himself to the United States comparatively early. Maruta recognized America's overwhelming technological and managerial lead. This understanding became the starting point for Kao to overcome this gap. The trip provided an opportunity for Kao to develop new products in the future and a starting point for technology import from America. It was also the beginning of exchange between Kao and Procter & Gamble, exchange that became a valuable source of information for Kao. Although, after this, like many other firms, many other managers and engineers from Kao would visit the United States, there would never be a visit with quite the significance of the first.

There were a number of prerequisites to learning from the United States. First, an important initial condition at Kao itself was the accumulation of technology and the business development led to its dissolution and merger after the war from the prewar era through the postwar reconstruction era. Second, during the early 1950s, visits to the United States by leading technical experts at Kao provided the point of departure for further learning from the United States. Finally, the Japanese government's prohibitive policies on foreign capital in the 1950s and 1960s provided the policy circumstances influencing Kao's corporate activities. We cannot ignore the last condition because of its considerable regulation of Kao's attitude towards introducing technology and management practices from Western companies. During the 1950s and 1960s the Japanese government adopted foreign capital policy that strictly controlled inward direct investment. These measures continued until the Japanese government implemented capital liberalization around 1970.[13] This contrasts with West Germany. There, already in 1961, inward direct investment had been fully liberalized, and West German firms were already encountering foreign capital in their domestic markets.

During this period, Western firms gradually became more interested in the Japanese market. In the petrochemical industry, chemical engineering firms and medium-sized chemical firms specializing in certain areas were the main players moving into Japan through licensing. The West's leading large firms in the consumer chemicals field, on the other hand, had less interest in the Japanese market. In the light of the subsequent expansion of the Japanese market, this reflected these companies' effective underestimation of both Japanese firms and their domestic market. Japanese firms worked to introduce advanced technology and management practices through product analysis (reverse engineering) and licensing. Kao conducted product analysis and copied management methods as well. Kao also became one of the most active Japanese firms in the introduction of technology and management techniques via licensing, as seen below.

Development of new products

To the technical accumulation from the war period was added the fruits of Maruta's observation tour of the United States and the information collected from overseas publications. The technology researchers at Kao – comprised both of Kao Soap and Kao Oils and Fats – took up the development of new products like synthetic neutral shampoo and synthetic detergents which had not yet been marketed in Japan.

The development process for these new products reflects both the changes and constancy in the characteristics of life in Japan. In the 1950s and 1960s a mass consumption society finally emerged fully in Japan. In textiles, as cotton goods became pervasive, chemical fibres and then synthetic fibres quickly became popular. Also, electric washing machines spread into general household use; a suitable powdered or liquid synthetic detergent for such electric washing machines was needed. In terms of the Japanese diet, the consumption of fresh vegetables began to become more commonplace once the consumption of salad oil and other vegetable fats and oil began to expand. As a consequence, kitchen detergents began to become more widespread.[14] Using seminars, films, pamphlets, and advertising through radio, television, and the newspapers, Kao worked to accelerate these changes. Differences in lifestyle compared to the West, however, remained. For example, whereas in the West warm water was preferred for washing, in Japan cold water was the norm. Also, in terms of water quality, the hard waters common in the West differed from the soft water widespread in Japan. Even consumer characteristics differed; for example, Japanese hair is sensitive and easily damaged. In the consumer chemicals industry, there remained special market qualities that could not be ignored. Kao's goal was to develop products conforming to a Japanese market that continued to change even as it retained many special qualities.

Synthetic neutral shampoo[15]

When Kao developed synthetic neutral shampoos, it drew directly on American-made products and analyzed them from a variety of perspectives. It does not need repeating that Maruta's observations from the United States were an important resource in this. By analyzing products popular in the United States at the time, Kao's research and development team determined that, because they were compounded from petroleum-based alkyl benzenes, American-made shampoos were too irritating to the skin to suit Japanese tastes. Using technology that Kao itself had accumulated in the prewar era, Kao's technical team decided to use as their chief shampoo ingredient a powdered surfactant (alkyl sulfate) for industrial use, Emal, that was itself based on coconut oil. Into this they mixed an agent to prevent dirt being redeposited and to yield a new shampoo with better foaming, rinsing, anti-dandruff and anti-split end qualities. For the packaging, Kao took a cue from a product produced by the American company Colgate-Palmolive and adopted aluminum foil, which protected against moisture. Because this was the first use of aluminum foil for packaging in Japan, Kao had to make extraordinary efforts to develop the in-house technology to print onto the aluminum foil and process it into a tube.

Following its launch in October 1955, the resulting product – named Feather Shampoo – became the product that typified Japanese shampoos. Though it took American products as its model, it was developed based on Kao's existing development capabilities and thoroughly in conformity with the tastes of Japanese consumers.

Synthetic detergent[16]

At the time of Maruta's inspection tour of America, synthetic detergents were coming to the fore in the United States. Because they did not use traditional soap raw materials, they were called soapless soaps. From Maruta's perspective, these products were made using the same principles that had been used to make Excelin, a synthetic powdered soap Kao had developed before the war on the basis of German patents.[17] Excelin used as its raw materials high-grade alcohols made from coconut oil. Although American soapless soaps represented some measure of advancement in that they employed petroleum-based alkyl benzenes, one-third of the raw materials was still derived by the sulfonation of high-grade alcohols. At the time, Kao did not lead the soap industry. It was rather pushing against the

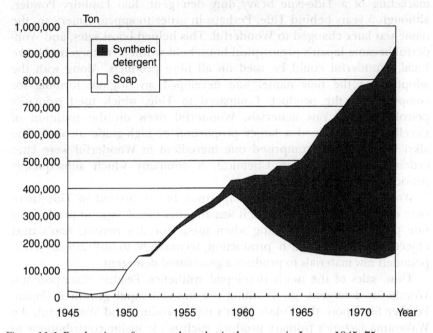

Figure 11.1 Production of soap and synthetic detergent in Japan, 1945–75.

Source: *Nihon sekken senzai kogyokai nenpo* (Annual Reports of Japan Association of Soap and Detergent Industry).

more powerful firms in the industry like Mitsuwa Soap and Miyoshi Oil and Fat. Many firms, however, had still not come to a firm conclusion whether to go with soap or detergent in the future. Kao forecast the arrival of an era of synthetic detergents and began development at once (see Figure 11.1).

Procter & Gamble's Tide detergent, the prototypical synthetic detergent or soapless soap, was chemically analyzed in detail by Kao's technology team and its make-up ascertained. At the time, electric washing machines had only recently begun to become popular and hand-washing remained the norm in Japan. There was little demand for powdered detergents.[18] Moreover, products based on higher alcohols were preferred because of the good tone and soft touch imparted to the cloth. Whether the Japanese market would broadly welcome a Tide-type synthetic powdered detergent made from petroleum-based raw materials was, therefore, a matter of some concern.

In July 1951 Kao first launched a high-grade alcohol-based synthetic detergent, Emal. This only represented a name change to the synthetic detergent Excelin that had been introduced prior to the war. Emal's applications were limited to wool, silk and chemical artificial fibres. Unlike Tide, Emal could not be used on cotton products, which limited demand for the product. In October of the same year Kao embarked on the marketing of a Tide-type heavy duty detergent, Kao Laundry Powder, although 5 years behind Tide. Perhaps in order to appear American, the name was later changed to Wonderful. This helped boost sales, and Wonderful became Japan's prototypical household synthetic detergent. Unlike Emal, Wonderful could be used on all fibre products. Along with the adoption of the new name, Kao developed an original formula for compounding the product. Compared to Tide, which used primarily petroleum-based raw materials, Wonderful drew on the tradition of Excelin and contained a larger proportion of high-grade alcohol. The alkyl benzenes that comprised one ingredient in Wonderful were later ordered from California Chemical, a company which subsequently provided technology to Kao.

Wonderful did win consumer approval, but compared to Tide there were quality problems. Because it was an 'after-blend' type of product, its fine particles caused sneezing when used. For this reason, Kao's next objective was to establish production technology to dry already compounded raw materials to produce a granulated detergent.

Thus, sales of the newly developed synthetics, Feather Shampoo and Wonderful detergent, grew, riding the wave of rapid growth in Japan. Feather Shampoo, the Tokyo plant's main product, and Wonderful, the Wakayama factory's primary product, each made major contributions to Kao's industrial performance. The success of both products matched the plan of Eizo Ito, the then vice president of the new Kao Soap after the 1954 merger, to 'move forward like Procter & Gamble at Wakayama and like Colgate in Tokyo'.[19] These products contributed to the fully-fledged development of a mass-consumption society in Japan.

Although the development of both products used knowledge that Maruta had gained in the United States, these products were not simply copies of American products. Both products achieved a certain level of quality using the existing stock of technology within the company. Also, they were developed with the aim of adapting this quality to specific Japanese consumer tastes. Nevertheless, problems remained. Compared to American products, quality was inferior. As before, the lack of mass-production technology remained a problem. In addition, the synthetic detergent industry was shifting to petroleum-based raw materials, whose price was lower and more stable. Consequently it was essential that Kao move to petroleum-based surfactants. For this reason, introduction of new technology was unavoidable. This led Kao to introduce technology from American firms.

Introducing production technology

Continuous sulfonation: introducing technology from the Chemithson Corporation[20]

In 1956 Kao undertook a large-scale capital investment plan at its main Wakayama plant, with the goal of improving the quality of Wonderful detergent and increasing production. The plan was named the 'AW Plan' from the initials 'A' for alcohol and 'W' for Wonderful. Equipment for executing the plan could be procured domestically. Kao was dissatisfied with its performance and so purchased nearly everything from the United States. Purchases included continuous sulfonation equipment from the Chemithson Corporation and spray-drying equipment made by Industrial Engineering, Inc. Chemithson's continuous sulfonation equipment was used in the sulfonation of alkyl benzenes and high-grade alcohols. Industrial Engineering's spray drying equipment was used to address Wonderful's quality problems that were described above.

Kao received technical guidance from the American firms on how to set up the equipment and conduct trial runs. There was not enough budgetary slack to allow use of outside engineering firms, however, so Kao was forced to go it alone, depending on literature information on the overall engineering of the project. Still, since the construction of the prewar hydrogenation equipment, Kao had accumulated little in the way of engineering experience. Therefore Kao hired a specialist in chemical engineering, Noboru Yasumura, from Mitsubishi Oil, and worked to foster its own engineering capacity by making him head of engineering. Kao's formula was, with the exception of civil engineering, architecture and electricity, to rely entirely on itself and in particular upon its supervising engineers. This approach called for capable supervising engineers that could largely decide plant efficiency. Great confidence resulted from the successful design, construction and testing of such comparatively high-level equipment.

This type of self-help in engineering capability led first to improvements in the technology introduced and subsequently to technological innovation. Spray dryer no. 2 was produced domestically through reference to the blueprints for spray dryer no. 1 bought from Industrial Engineering, Inc. Moreover, Kao added improvements. A little later, after efficiency and maintenance problems were noted in the sulfonation equipment from Chemithson, Kao designed improvements to the equipment. Kao solved these problems in the late 1960s by developing reaction equipment known as 'climbing film reactors.'[21]

Alkyl benzenes and lubricating oil additives: technology transfer from the California Chemical (Chevron Chemical) Company[22]

Kao introduced technology for manufacturing alkyl benzenes and lubricating oil additives from California Chemical (later Chevron Chemical), abbreviated Calchem below, a subsidiary of Standard Oil of California. Calchem was famous as a maker of lubricating oil additives. At that time it was drawing up plans to manufacture lubricating oil additives in Japan through a joint venture. Kao announced its candidacy to be a partner in the joint venture. Both sides reached agreement, and in May 1961 the joint venture, Kalonite Chemical, was established. The capital shares were: Kao 45 per cent, Calchem 45 per cent and Nomura Company, the intermediator, 10 per cent.

A broad division of responsibilities was worked out for the joint venture, with Kao in charge of overall management and Calchem in charge of technological development. Opinion was, however, divided as to production. Initially Calchem tried to have Kao manufacture on consignment; Kao objected to this arrangement, however, as it regarded production technology as critical. As a result, Calchem's production technology was installed, and an automatic control system modeled on Calchem's Oak Point plant was introduced to a new plant in Kawasaki. While Calchem was in charge of the basic design of this facility, Kao was responsible for the detailed design, under Calchem's guidance.

Various arguments went back and forth between the American and Japanese technology teams because of differences in design concepts. Understanding the difference in design concepts between Japan and the United States was in itself a form of learning for Kao. Of course, Calchem's efficient design methods based on technical standards, its management methods for project organization and so on, were not an inconsequential subject for study. Because of huge bodies of technical material and advanced engineering methods carried out at Kao, where initially the accumulated engineering capacity was poor, a passion for America spread among Kao's engineers. Through the cooperation with Kalonite, Kao's engineers had the opportunity to encounter genuine engineering practice. On the other hand, from the point of view of Kao's engineers, the design based on Calchem's technical standards appeared to raise the cost of construction materials considerably, because it assumed one size fits all applicability. The Kao team would have to consider thoroughly this point if they were to accept it.

For construction and operation, Calchem dispatched two engineers and Standard Oil of California sent one. Kao sent the manager for Kalonite Chemicals, Akira Numata, to visit the United States on an inspection tour of Calchem's factories. During construction, many engineers from Kao participated, assimilating the contents of huge amounts of technical standards, manuals, and so on. Simultaneously, to acquire operating technology, several people were dispatched to the United States.

Kalonite Chemicals reinforced its facilities after 1965. At that time the Kao technology team moved to domesticate production of its American equipment. At that point, they were provided with data on the analogous equipment at Calchem, which they analyzed and tested repeatedly. As a result, the quality of Kalonite's products garnered praise as the most out-standing among Calchem subsidiaries. Through this chain of borrowing and indigenization, the Kao technology team learned American mass-production technology and engineering techniques. The introduction of technology from Calchem was a response to the rise of petroleum-based synthetic detergents. After the introduction of this technology, it became possible for Kao to manufacture alkyl benzenes for petroleum-based sur-factants without depending on imports from Calchem any more.

Surfactants and polyvalent alcohols: borrowing technology from Atlas Chemicals[23]

Kao also introduced production technology for non-ionic surfactants, polyvalent alcohols, polyurethane and other materials from Atlas Chem-ical, which originated at DuPont. Atlas was a well-known producer of non-ionic surfactants like Tween and Span. Although Kao already possessed a stock of surfactant technology, the company was hoping to acquire from Atlas production technology for the superior non-ionic surfactants. Beyond surfactants, Kao also aimed for other production technologies for chemical products such as polyurethane.

Although Atlas had tried to initiate business in Japan through contacts with Nippon Oil and Fat, the negotiations had ended poorly. Kao was informed of the results of the contacts. In February 1962 Kao and Atlas held their first meeting and went ahead with contract negotiations. The foremost problem during the negotiation process was the product lines the joint venture would handle. Both Kao and Atlas were manufacturing surfactants. Because surfactants are quite diverse and because there was no method for classifying them perfectly, both firms found it difficult to separate their respective markets. As a last resort, in the joint-venture con-tract they agreed that the non-ionic surfactant 'scope of product' would be the 'contribution' of Kao-Atlas. Hard-to-classify products, clearly classi-fiable as non-ionic surfactants yet developed solely by Kao, came to market one after another. The cement dispersing agent Mighty, which was brought to market in the spring of 1966, was typical of these.[24] This product was recognized, on an exceptional basis, as a Kao product via an exchange of personal notes between Atlas Vice President Robert P. Barnett and the Kao technology team. Still, dissatisfaction at these limita-tions increased internally among members of the Kao camp.

Meanwhile, the Ministry of International Trade and Industry (MITI) issued instructions based on Japan's foreign capital regulations to the joint venture. The Ministry took a strict position towards Atlas. Noting that in the joint venture, the Japanese side should hold the majority of equity, MITI directed that Kao should have a 51 per cent stake. In August 1963 the licensing agreement was approved, and the joint venture Kao-Atlas was established. Kao held a 51 per cent capital stake, and Atlas 49 per cent.

The substance of the venture was 'the manufacturing and selling of surfactants, polyvalent alcohols, and polyester resins'. In February 1964 construction of facilities began at the Wakayama plant. Atlas was in charge of the basic plans and dispatched technicians; Kao was the main coordinator of the construction itself. For sales and research training Kao dispatched to the United States the five employees chosen for loan to Kao-Atlas.

How was Kao's introduction of technology from Atlas evaluated? Within the Kao technology group there were differences in this assessment. Initially, doubts existed at Kao concerning how much need there was for Atlas. When Kao-Atlas was established Kao expanded its central research and development facilities, the Industrial Science Research Laboratory, to absorb the Atlas technologies, and the research results generated at the Laboratories were almost entirely Kao's original ones. In the 10 years following the start of the joint venture, hardly any new technology came from Atlas. What of the engineering methods as well as the marketing methods demanded by technical service requirements for chemical products? For Kao, which had already learned much engineering technology through its joint venture with Kalonite Chemicals, there was little new in the Atlas engineering technology. At this point, Kao learned little from Atlas.

From the start, however, Atlas' goal had been the expansion in the Japanese market of its Tween and Span products and subsequently Atlas' corporate headquarters had entered into the British ICI group. Thus, it should not necessarily be thought that Atlas' technological capabilities had declined. The secondary effects of technology introduction cannot be ignored. First, Kao developed experience in the manufacture of other products beyond surfactants such as polyester and sorbitol. Second, it found in Atlas' particular approach to surfactants a way to expand further its technical stock. Third, by undertaking exchange with American and British firms, Kao was able to receive foreign business know-how. If we include secondary effects like these, introduction of technology from Atlas led to the strengthening of Kao's surfactant and other industrial chemicals business and, indirectly, of its raw materials base for detergents and other household products.

Thus, the first case described learning stemming from the purchase of machine equipment. The next two examples demonstrated technology introduction based on licensing. Through this series of technology transfers from US firms, Kao acquired advanced technology for surfactants and other chemicals that were raw materials for synthetic detergents. When they turned to licensing, Kao adopted the joint venture format ultimately as an expedient for introducing technology. These transfers of technology played a major role in the sudden increase in the synthetic detergent business and in the fleshing out of the chemical products business at Kao. Not only that, they enabled Kao to learn advanced methods across the management spectrum, including engineering techniques, research and development, and marketing techniques, especially those for industrial chemicals for which technical service was central.

At the same time, an opposition of interests arose between Kao and the American firms. For Kao, it was desirable for the American firms to withdraw from Japan once a certain amount of learning had been achieved. The American firms, however, intended to expand their business in Japan. What allowed Kao to realize its own goals was the fact that Kao had created a system that eliminated the need for the American companies by accumulating its own stock of technology.

Learning management techniques

Marketing methods

A cash transaction system

Kao introduced the '10 days 2 per cent' scheme, a cash transaction system that Maruta picked up from Procter & Gamble, for some products in 1960, and for their entire line in 1961. It replaced a transaction system based on credit and rebates.[25] Because the discount rate of 2 per cent every 10 days was considerably higher than even contemporary bank loan interest rates, sharp merchants actively utilized the new cash transaction system. It rendered the previous, slow-moving bill clearance system unnecessary and shortened the transaction period. By doing so, capital turnover increased, thereby increasing business efficiency and allowing greater allocations for research and the like.

The cash transaction developed further and bore fruit in the 1970s as the exclusive sales company system. The formation of the exclusive sales company system needed the implementation of an additional condition, the Resale Price Maintenance Agreement System.[26] Based on the recognition that soap, detergent, cosmetics, medicine, books, etc. were exempt from the anti-trust law, the Resale Price Maintenance Agreement System aimed to maintain the wholesale and retail prices of these goods. This differed from the American anti-trust laws. Coming from America, the cash transaction system interacted with Japan's price maintenance system to produce Kao's particular distribution system.

Procter & Gamble's basic marketing strategy was to undertake price competition without regard for profit. At the launch of a new product, Procter & Gamble invested heavily in marketing to drive its competitors from the market. This approach featured aggressive promotional campaigns with distribution of free samples. In contrast, averting from a bold strategy to promote sales in response to competition from other companies, Kao considered of primary importance the establishment and maintenance of an efficient distribution system. Partially, the influence of Japan's distribution system, designed as it was to prevent 'excessive competition', limited sales promotion.

Advertising techniques

Kao regarded an integrated marketing strategy as including not only distribution but also sales and advertising. Kao began advertising with radio spots in 1953. Around 1960, it quickly shifted focus to television. Throughout the 1950s and 1960s, advertising typically stood at approximately 10 per cent of sales.[27] As an important component of Kao's active marketing strategy, advertising was strongly influenced by Procter & Gamble.

Kao's advertisements appear at first glance extremely local to Japan, as befits something so close to the lives of ordinary Japanese people. In reality, however, they were an attempt at modern marketing, and they were strongly influenced by Procter & Gamble's techniques. Rather than giving priority to image, they clearly demonstrate the quality of Kao products to the consumer. This sort of awareness already could be seen prior to the war. For example, in a Kao Soap advertisement the characters 'purity 99.4 per cent' were reproduced on a figure of a traditional Japanese woman wearing a Japanese cook's apron. This followed Procter & Gamble's slogan '99.44 per cent pure' extolling the virtues of its Ivory soap. Kao's language paralleled Procter & Gamble's catch phrase closely.[28] In the sponsorship of radio and television shows, Kao lagged behind Procter & Gamble (which had started sponsorship) and other American firms' methods by about 5 years.

Of course, this copying did not continue forever. Procter & Gamble's television advertisements unconsciously reflected the patterns of American life. Consequently, they were sometimes incompatible with Japanese consumers' sensibility. For example, the laundry detergent Cheer was described in a commercial as 'works the same in any temperature'. Because, unlike the American and European, the Japanese usually used cold water, this copy was not effective. Although Kao continued to emphasize clearly the quality of its products, Kao organized them to agree more with the patterns of Japanese life and the particulars of the Japanese market. Since the 1970s, when Procter & Gamble entered Japan, advertising became a sort of cultural barrier to entry.

An attempt to introduce the product manager system

In the 1960s, along with its chief rival Lion and other companies, Kao attempted to introduce an American-style product manager system, including a system of brand managers with much narrower authority. This movement was broadly visible in the consumer products sector. The product manager system had been driven by the notion of product management, in which the profits for products and brands were tracked individually. Japanese firms recognized the effectiveness of product management as a response to the need to unify marketing functions – for example, advertisements and sales – as well as to attain product diversification. Procter & Gamble was viewed as the model firm typifying product management. But ultimately, at least in the 1960s, product management did not take root in Japan.

In the case of Kao, already in 1960 a goods planning department, responsible for market research and design improvements, had been established. In 1967, Kao set up a marketing department to strengthen its market research. At the same time, it introduced a brand manager system. In 1970, Kao created product managers to supervise the brand managers for each product line. With the organizational changes of 1973, however, the product managers disappeared, although the brand managers remained as they were.[29] At Kao, the exclusive sales company system took the place of product managers. With the establishment of sales companies at the start of the 1970s, the front line for Kao's sales division moved from traditional wholesalers to the sales companies. In short, as a seller Kao moved into a closer relationship with the consumer and became able to grasp market movements with a higher degree of sensitivity. Because sales companies could recognize the movements of individual brands, Kao was able to have a more fine-grained product line-up.[30]

However, despite this sort of learning, in this most American field, Kao was clearly inferior in comparison to Procter & Gamble, a company that had developed and accumulated marketing theory since the 1920s. In 1970 Maruta saw marketing, rather than research and development, production technology or distribution, as the point where there was the largest gap between Kao and the likes of Procter & Gamble and Colgate-Palmolive.[31] One reason for this was that, despite overwhelming desire to discover more, opportunities for learning were limited. One of a few exceptions was the continuing exchange of information with Procter & Gamble, which had continued following Maruta's 1951 visit to the United States, and which provided a valuable opportunity for such learning. The acquisition by Kao of a Procter & Gamble subsidiary in Taiwan provided another such opportunity.[32]

Personnel management methods

In the 1950s, American style personnel management based on ability pay was enthusiastically introduced into Japan. Although examples of an American style function pay existed, from the combination of meritocracy with Japanese circumstances, an ability-based grade system soon became widely spread.[33] Under the ability-based grade system, the employee was graded on their ability to carry out their duties and performance. The grading was used in promotion and wage decisions. As a system, the ability-based grade system was a certain kind of meritocracy. Its primary characteristic was that even though work might not change, wages could still increase. As a result, this system became a mechanism for promoting the development of capabilities in the work force.

Kao was one of the first companies to adopt the ability-based grade system. In January 1956 the company outlined the 'New Grading System'. Unlike its predecessor which was based on educational achievement, work tenure, and age, Kao implemented a grading system based primarily on workers' ability and performance to carry out their duty.[34] The nucleus of Kao's personnel system based on meritocracy was its evaluation system. Although ability, performance, character and behaviour had been important under its previous evaluation system, and was aimed at strengthening the development of employee capabilities, Kao added self development and individual enhancement plans under the new system. In 1965 Kao introduced specialist work systems and discontinued compensation by post. This raised the status of staff employees as opposed to line employees. Although Kao's personnel management based on meritocracy was pioneering, it was pioneering in that it allowed space for compromise with its previous system. Of course, in that it lacked the possibility of demotion, there were areas where this meritocracy was not always fully applied. However, in its regard for the development of capability and flat organization to name only a few characteristics, the larger structure of Kao's current personnel system was created in this period. In addition, in 1960, Kao expanded the previous management sections, establishing an integrated planning department staffed to collect external data, establish operational plans, and so forth.[35]

Thus, American companies, especially Procter & Gamble, appear to have influenced Kao strongly in various management areas. In marketing, however, because of limits on the learning process, Kao's learning was less. Instead, the company developed its own system of exclusive sales companies. In personnel management methods, consideration was given to the continued introduction of meritocracy in the previous management system.

Conclusions

Outline

In a protected Japanese market, fierce inter-firm competition developed. Kao dominated the early market for Tide-type heavy-duty detergents and also led in the process for softening detergents. (This was linked to a change in raw materials from hard alkyl benzene ABS to soft alkyl benzene LAS.) In kitchen detergents, however, in 1956 Lion released and subsequently led the market for neutral detergents. Although Lion was overwhelmingly strong in the market for toothpaste products, Kao held one corner of it.[36]

From the 1960s to the early 1970s, Kao stood at the head of the synthetic detergent market, consistently ahead of Lion in market share (see Figure 11.2). By the end of this period, Kao had acquired, along with its

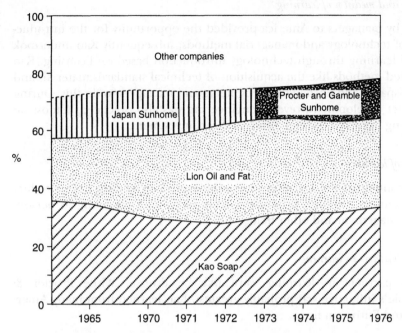

Figure 11.2 Market share of synthetic detergent in Japan, 1960–76.

Source: *Yushi (Fats and Oils)*, 1977, vol. 30, no. 13, p. 28.

Note
'Procter & Gamble Sunhome' has now been renamed 'Procter & Gamble Far East, Inc.'; similarly, 'Lion Oil and Fat' is now 'Lion Corporation', 'Kao Soap' is now 'Kao Corporation'.

chief rival Lion, the status of a leading firm in Japan's consumer chemicals industry.

Most of this success was based on Kao's ability to learn from American firms. Even in places where, looking from today's perspective, Kao seemingly felt little American influence, it is possible to discern real effects on the firm's management and technology resulting from Kao's knowledge gained from the United States. Behind this outcome lies Kao's aim, in every facet of management to copy thoroughly American corporations, beginning with Procter & Gamble.

Beginning with Procter & Gamble, what did Kao learn from the American firms? How did it learn these things? What level of American technology and management methods did Kao introduce? Alternatively, what did Kao dare *not* to learn, assuming that 'unlearning' is also a learning technique? How did the results of Kao's learning from Procter & Gamble and other American firms contribute to shrinking or eliminating the technological and management gap vis-à-vis American firms? In the conclusion to this paper, we would like to provide some answers to these questions.

Shape and medium of learning

Visits by managers to America provided the opportunity for the introduction of technology and managerial methods; subsequently Kao undertook active learning through technology introduction based on licensing. Kao adopted methods like the acquisition of technical standards materials and the dispatch and exchange of engineers and managers to do this. During product development, reverse engineering was also practiced. Almost no learning occurred through internal direct investment.

Fields of learning

The content of the learning was multi-faceted, extending from product development, through production technology and marketing to personnel management and other fields.

Their partners in learning

Kao's partners in learning were likewise diverse. While Procter & Gamble's influence was probably greatest, Kao learned from many American and European firms.

Depth of learning

The opportunity to learn from the United States saw rapid increases in the levels of technology and management methods. Good examples are product development based on reverse engineering and learning through engineering technology. Kao did not, however, simply introduce these American firms' technologies and management methods, but rather adapted them to the requirements of the Japanese marketplace and labour relations. Kao did not adopt products that would be difficult to accept in Japan. This stemmed from Kao's understanding of the Japanese market and from possession of its own stock of technology. Examples of this were the development of synthetic detergent and shampoo in product development, the introduction of the exclusive sales companies system in distribution, and the introduction of the ability-based grade system in personnel management.

Subject of learning

What sustained this kind of technological borrowing was the powerful desire of engineers and managers to learn. The salaried managers who headed Kao in the postwar era believed that, having been isolated from the technologies developed by the advanced nations during the Second World War, they found themselves technologically blinkered. For people who thought this way, the fastest way to rebuild the company was to absorb advanced foreign technology, especially from the US, even if that meant some sacrifice.

Outlook: during and after the 1970s

Despite widespread and thorough learning from the United States in the 1950s and 1960s, today Kao can be regarded as a Japanese company mainly because it carried out product development closely tied to the needs of the Japanese consumer and established its own distribution systems and advertising methods. The Japanization of these technical and managerial methods occurred in earnest in the period of capital liberalization at the beginning of the 1970s, when Procter & Gamble changed from teacher into competitor.

Having nearly completed its programme of trade liberalization from 1967 to 1973, the government changed its foreign capital policy and embarked on gradual capital liberalization. Oil and fat-based products such as soaps and detergents were marked for liberalization in the third stage from September 1970 onward.[37] Around this time, at long last, leading Western firms made clear their interest in the Japanese market. Among these firms, Procter & Gamble had the greatest presence.[38] Prior to capital liberalization and following Maruta's visit to the United States, Kao had chosen Procter & Gamble as its instructor. Kao tried to learn thoroughly American technology and managerial methods from Procter & Gamble. By allowing tours of its factories and research laboratories to Kao employees visiting America, Procter & Gamble became an important source of information to Kao for technological development. Kao also offered up information by providing factory tours and the like to Procter & Gamble personnel visiting Japan.

Prior to capital liberalization Procter & Gamble was an excellent instructor to Kao, although, at the same time, little by little both sides came to regard each other as their future competitor. Following capital liberalization, this latter aspect became clear. On the Kao side, Yoshiro Maruta, who was appointed President in 1971, saw Procter & Gamble as both Kao's best teacher and its strongest competitor.[39] In Maruta's words, one can see a love-hate relationship in Kao's relationship toward Procter & Gamble. In the spring of 1970, Procter & Gamble sounded out Kao regarding cooperating in the synthetic detergent business. This plan collapsed before the two companies had entered into earnest negotiation. Subsequently, in 1972 by making a capital investment in Japan Sunhome, Procter & Gamble formed Procter & Gamble Sunhome and entered the Japanese market for real. The company's main products were the heavy-duty detergent Cheer and the disposable diapers Pampers.[40]

Other Western firms followed into the Japanese market. Colgate-Palmolive attempted a tie-up with Kao. This cooperative relationship was to have sold Colgate products through Kao's sales companies, and it seemed that selling toothpaste and other Colgate products would have the advantage for Kao of increasing the number of products that its sales companies handled. Without an agreement about overlapping products, however, the cooperative relationship never materialized.[41] Unilever also created a joint venture with Honen Refineries called Honen Lever in 1964. In 1972, Unilever created a joint venture called Japan Cosmetic Soap between Honen Lever and Mitsuwa Soap; Honen Lever provided 70 per cent of the capital with the balance coming from Mitsuwa. It entrusted soap production to Mitsuwa Soap. In 1973, Unilever made its own independent investment with the formation of Japan Unilever. Like other Western firms, Henkel showed interest in the Japanese market. By the late 1960s there had been contacts between Henkel and Kao. They too bore no fruit. Henkel's full-scale move into Japan happened during and after the 1970s, and the partner Henkel selected was not Kao but Lion instead.[42]

Kao met this assault of foreign capital. In the face of continuing severe competition for a share in the detergent market, Kao aimed to diversify away from its core detergent business. One component of this was the launch in 1968 of the base cosmetic Nivea built upon technology imported from the West German company Beiersdorf.[43] This goal of diversification became especially strong during the 1980s.[44] Kao further promoted the development of products in response to the Japanese consumer, the construction of an independent distribution system and the development of advertising methods. Thus, since capital liberalization, at least within Japan's domestic market, Kao has resisted the onslaught of Western corporations.

Kao has also earnestly expanded its international business operations through overseas direct investment.[45] Since 1990, however, in both its increasingly internationalized domestic and its overseas markets, Kao has reportedly tough games. Because the conditions for competition have changed, using only its current competitive advantages, Kao is increasingly less able to compete. Various recent attempts at Kao to improve management reflect this problem. Although the particulars have changed, the attempts at self-reform from the 1950s and 1960s continue.

Notes

1 A.E. Musson, *Enterprise in Soap and Chemicals*, Manchester: University of Manchester Press, 1965.
2 M. Ihara and A. Kudo, 'Technology Transfer and Adaptation to Local Condition: Multinationalization of the Japanese Chemical Industry and the Case of Kao', CIRJE Discussion Paper Series F-106, University of Tokyo, February 2001.
3 For the history of Kao in the prewar period, see S. Hattori and Y. Kobayashi, *Kao sekken 50-nen shi (A 50 Year History of Kao Soap)*, Tokyo: Kao Soap Corporation, 1940; and T. Yui, A. Kudo and H. Takeda, *Kao shi 100-nen (A Century of Kao History)*, Tokyo: Kao Corporation, 1993 (subsequently referred to as Kao History).

4 L. Rubinfein, 'Ryutsu kakushin no kokoromi: Kao no kesu wo chushin ni' (An Attempt at Innovation in Distribution, with Attention to the Kao Case), in A. Okouchi and H. Takeda (eds), *Kigyosha katsudo to kigyo shisutemu: Daikigyo taisei no nichiei hikakushi (Entrepreneurial Activity and the Enterprise System: A Historical Comparison of Large Enterprise Systems in Japan and Britain)*, Tokyo: University of Tokyo Press, 1993, pp. 154–182; S. Sasaki, 'Kao ni miru senzen nihon no ryutsu kakushin' (Innovation of Distribution in Prewar Japan as Seen at Kao), *Keiei shigaku (Japan Business History Review)*, 1994, vol. 28, no. 4, pp. 28–53; 'Keshohin-sekken gyokai ni miru gijutsu kakushin: Shiseido to Kao no jirei wo chushin ni' (Technological Innovation seen in the Cosmetic and Soap Business: Focus on the Cases of Shiseido and Kao), in T. Yui and J. Hashimoto (eds), *Kakushin no keieishi: Senzen sengo ni okeru nihon kigyo no kakushin kodo (A Business History of Innovation: Innovative Activities at Japanese Firms in the Pre- and Postwar Eras)*, Tokyo: Yuhikaku, 1995, pp. 115–134.

5 S. Sasaki, 'Kao ni miru senzenki shokuinso kogakurekika no hitokoma' (An Aspect of the Trend for White Collars' Higher Education in Prewar Era seen from Kao's Case), in H. Kawaguchi (ed.), *Daigaku no shakai keizai shi (A Socio-Economic History of the University)*, Tokyo: Sobunsha, 2000, pp. 209–226.

6 Kao History, pp. 165–212.

7 Ibid., pp. 212–223.

8 Lion Corporation: Company History Editing Committee, *Raion 100-nen shi (A Century of Lion)*, Tokyo: Lion Corporation, 1992, pp. 1–7, 51–59, 202–211.

9 Kao History, p. 188.

10 For more on Maruta's visit to the United States, see Kao Corporation Historical Compilation Room Archives (subsequently referred to as Kao Archives), Y. Maruta, 'Mite kita amerika' (The America I saw), Tokyo: Kao Soap Corporation, 1951; S. Ochiai, *Ito Eizo: Sono hito to jiseki (Eizo Ito: The Man and the Evidence)*, Tokyo: Kao Soap Corporation, 1973, pp. 181–188; T. Nomura, 'Kao: Sengo no tachi-naori to saisho no amerika shisatsu' (Kao: Postwar Comeback and the First U.S. Study Tour), in Japan Business History Institute, *Keiei to rekishi (Business and History)*, 1987, vol. 10, pp. 43–47; Kao History, pp. 203–208.

11 After having marketed the first synthetic detergent Dreft in 1933, Procter & Gamble continued new product research and development and played a major role in the popularization of synthetic detergents in the United States. By 1957, synthetic detergents held over 90 per cent of the American market for household detergents.

12 This 'direct costing' method was implemented around 1962. Kao had formerly used total costing, or the so-called 'rolling formula' (see Kao History, p. 329), whereby monthly accounts were settled around the 20th of the following month. By introducing direct costing, which calculated manufacturer costs solely on the basis of variable manufacturer costs, it became possible to settle accounts on the 10th of the succeeding month.

13 On trade liberalization and the approval system for technology introduction, see Committee on the Compilation of a History of International Trade and Industrial Policy (ed.), *Tsusho sangyo seisaku shi (A History of International Trade and Industrial Policy)*, vol. 8, Tokyo: Tsusho Sangyo Chosa Kai, 1991, pp. 463–494.

14 Japan Neutral Detergent Association, *Nihon chusei senzai kyokai 20-nen shi (A Twenty Year History of the Japan Neutral Detergent Association)*, Tokyo: Japan Neutral Detergent Association, 1983, pp. 11–35.

15 For details on the development of shampoo, see Kao History, pp. 262–268.

16 For details on the development of synthetic detergent, see ibid., pp. 230–233, 246–247.

17 Ibid., p. 206.

18 On the spread of the electric washing machine and its social influence, see J. Suzuki, *Shin gijutsu no shakai shi (Social History of New Technology)*, Tokyo: Chuo Koron Shinsha, 1999, pp. 241–261; S. Partner, *Assembled in Japan: Electrical Goods and the Making of the Japanese Consumer*, Berkeley: University of California Press, 1999.

19 For details, see Kao History, p. 264.

20 Ibid., pp. 248–255.

21 Ibid., pp. 464–469. The climbing film reactor, however, was not based directly on research into how to improve the Chemithson equipment but rather was the product of a key part of the sulfonation research group's pure research and development activities at the Wakayama research lab.

22 Ibid., pp. 276–280.

23 For details, see ibid., pp. 280–283.

24 On the development of Mighty, see ibid., pp. 534–542.

25 Ibid., pp. 296–298.

26 Ibid., pp. 365–372; I. Son, 'Kodo seichoki ni okeru ryutsu shisutemu no henka: Sekken, senzai gyokai wo chushin ni' (Change in the Distribution System During the High-speed Growth Era: Focus on the Soap and Detergent Sector), *Keiei shigaku (Japan Business History Review)*, 1993, vol. 27, no. 4, pp. 32–63.

27 Kao History, p. 304.

28 S. Ochiai, *Kao kokoku shi (A History of Advertising at Kao)*, Tokyo: Kao Corporation, 1989, pp. 98–101.

29 '"Awa" to kieta Kao sekken no purodakuto maneja' (The Disappeared Product Manager at Kao Soap like 'Suds'), *Kindai keiei (Modern Management)*, December 1973, pp. 62–66; Kao History, pp. 422–427. A number of explanations have been offered for why product managers did not strike roots in Japan's consumer products sector: 1) Japanese enterprise organization was vertically divided on product lines and was not amenable to profit management for each product; 2) while in the US product changes were dramatic and the market was highly segmented, the Japanese market was homogeneous and had little necessity for product diversity. However, these explanations are rather impressionistic and cannot account for the important role that the product manager system played in the automobile industry.

30 S. Sasaki, 'Toiretari: 1960–70 nendai no ryutsu senryaku: Raion no tai kao senryaku wo chushin ni' (Toiletry: Distribution Strategy in the 1960s and 1970s: Focus on Lion's Kao Strategy), in M. Udagawa, T. Kikkawa, J. Shintaku (eds), *Nihon no kigyo kan kyoso (Inter-firm Competition in Japan)*, Tokyo: Yuhikaku, 2000.

31 Y. Maruta, *Waga jinsei kan waga keiei kan (My Life View, My Management View)*, Tokyo: Kao Soap Corporation, 1984, pp. 267–273.

32 Kao History, pp. 438–439.

33 On the ability-based grade system, see H. Sato, 'Nikkeiren *noryoku shugi kanri: Sono riron to jissen* wo yomu' (Reading Japan Federation of Employer's Association *Meritocracy Management: Its Theory and Practice*), in *Dai 42-ki Hitotsubashi Foramu 21 (42nd Hitotsubashi Forum 21)*, Tokyo: Josuikai, 2000.

34 Kao History, pp. 314–323; Japan Federation of Employers' Association Workshop of Meritocracy Management, *Noryoku shugi kanri: Sono riron to jissen (Meritocracy Management: Its Theory and Practice)*, Tokyo: Japan Federation of Economic Organization, 1969, pp. 158–162.

35 Kao History, p. 325.

36 'Kao korugeto de hamigaki ni saichosen' (Kao Rechallenges Over Toothpaste with Colgate), *Yushi (Oil and Fat)*, 1977, vol. 30, no. 3, p. 27; Kao History, pp. 506–512.

37 On capital liberalization, see Committee on the Compilation of a History of International Trade and Industrial Policy (ed.), *Tsusho sangyo seisaku shi (A History of International Trade and Industrial Policy)*, vol. 8, Tokyo: Tsusho Sangyo Chosa Kai, 1991, pp. 363–494.

38 H. Yoshihara, 'Procter & Gamble Far East, Inc. Nihon kogaisha ga inobeshon no gensen' (Procter & Gamble Far East, Inc. The Japanese Subsidiary Company is the Origin of Innovation), in Yoshihara *et al.*, *Gurobaru kigyo no nihon senryaku (Japan Strategy of Global Enterprise)*, Tokyo: Kodansha, 1990, pp. 238–282.

39 Maruta, *Waga jinsei kan waga keiei kan (My Life View, My Management View)*, pp. 186–189.

40 A. Yoshioka, 'P&G nihon shinshutsu no 10-nen de okina tenki ka?' (Decisive Change in the Ten years after P&G's entry into Japan?), *Yushi (Oil and Fat)*, 1983, vol. 36, no. 10, pp. 24–27.

41 'Kao korugeto de hamigaki ni saichosen', pp. 22–27.

42 *Kagaku kogyo nippo (Chemical Industry Daily Report)*, 23 April 1987. The business tie-up between Lion and Henkel not only occurred with Japan's domestic market but also in Europe and Asia. For the development of international competition centering on Asia, see M. Ihara, 'Kagaku shohizai sangyo no ajia jigyo tenkai: Kigyo nai gijutsu iten to genchi tekio' (Consumer Chemicals Industry's Business Development in Asia: Intrafirm Technology Transfer and Local Adaptation), unpublished Ph.D. thesis, Graduate School of Economics, University of Tokyo, 2000.

43 On the manufacturer of Nivea, Beiersdorf, see H.G. Schröter, 'Erfolgsfaktor Marketing: Der Strukturwandel von der Reklame zur Unternehmenssteuerung', in W. Feldenkirchen, F. Schönert-Röhlk and G. Schulz (eds), *Wirtschaft Gesellschaft Unternehmen. Festschrift für Hans Pohl zum 60. Geburtstag (Vierteljahrschrift für Sozial- und Wirtschaftsgeschichte, Beiheft 120)*, 1995, pp. 1099–1127. Also, see Kao History, pp. 512–517.

44 In terms of diversification, Kao trailed Henkel of West Germany. In 1966, the proportion of total product sales occupied by detergents (including soap) was 73 per cent. It was not until 1977 that this dropped below 50 per cent. In 1966, Henkel had already reached 43 per cent. Cf. Kao History, p. 337.

45 See Ihara, 'Kagaku shohizai sangyo no ajia jigyo tenkai'; Ihara and Kudo, 'Technology Transfer and Adaptation to Local Condition'.

12 'Revolution in trade'

The Americanization of distribution in Germany during the boom-years, 1949–1975

Harm G. Schröter

Introduction

Nothing short of a 'revolution in trade' happened during the boom years in West Germany and in Western Europe according to Robert Nieschlag.[1] Who was Robert Nieschlag, and why did he use such strong words? During the 1950s and 1960s Nieschlag became what Bruno Tietz had become during the 1970s and 1980s, the scientific pope of German distribution.[2] By using the term revolution, he wanted to underline the dramatic change which took place not only in the form and size of distribution systems, but in the fundamental change in the approach and understanding of it. At the beginning of this period, one of the leading economists in Germany, Burkardt Röper, wrote: 'Surprisingly small is the desire of retailers to compete with each other on prices.'[3] However, 10 years later Nieschlag established: 'While formerly a defensive attitude was widespread within retailers, there now is a remarkable change in the younger generation towards a truly traders' approach.'[4]

Before the Second World War all changes and new forms of distribution were met with disapproval by the established firms, since owners as well as employees thought such steps to be a threat against their existence. When the consumers' co-operative movement became more powerful it had to face massive hostility, including the boycott of wholesalers. During the interwar period, when the department stores became strong, the Nazi party promised to fight them, and by such propaganda successfully gained votes. With this background we can understand why the word revolution was employed when a conservative attitude such as 'we do not want any novelties!' was changed into a business-like one such as 'how can I exploit this innovation for my own business?' Openness to new ideas led to new strategies. According to Alfred Chandler, business structure follows strategy, which in this case meant the transfer of new forms of sales and sales organizations.[5] At the same time, development represented a change from a co-operative way of thinking towards a more competitive way of behaving in everyday life. Since such attitudes and forms of competitive behaviour were much more widespread in the US than in Germany, Alfred Chandler has called these two basic types of doing business competitive and co-operative capitalism.[6] The latter attitude prevailed in the distributive sector in Germany up until the 1950s.

Substantial parts of the change towards a more competitive, more dynamic approach can be understood as an Americanization. We define Americanization as the adaptation and transfer of behaviour, institutions, culture, values, decision-making strategies, organizational structures, symbols and norms, away from the USA where they were widespread, to somewhere else.[7] Through the process of transfer to another nation and by its adaptation to specific needs, traditions and circumstances, such American cultures are changed, sometimes substantially. We cannot expect such transfers to take place in the same way as the import of a piece of machinery. There are specific transfer channels, translations and transformations which are part of this process of adaptation.[8] Furthermore, all transfer of culture needs time to adapt, proceeds stepwise, is open for a backlash, etc., which means that the whole issue is, on the one hand, extremely flexible and powerful but, on the other, cannot be measured and accounted for by quantitative methods.

In 1962, Max Gloor, at that time director of the marketing division of the Swiss transnational firm Nestlé, argued at an international symposium under the headline 'Today in the USA – tomorrow in Europe?' 'Basically I could tackle my task very easily – I would not be the first – by simply saying what is going on in the USA today will be the tomorrow in Europe. But this would be a simplification and only partly correct.'[9] In other words, while there was a lot of development, and most of it resembled patterns to be found in the USA, we had not only adaptations, but failures of Americanization as well as changes on an indigenous basis. Nearly all such changes can be understood as modernization. However, the problem is that not all modernization can be explained as part of an Americanization process.[10] Below we will provide an overview of successful and unsuccessful Americanization in the West German distribution sector.

Distribution is about the transfer of goods and services from production to consumption and incorporates the following aspects: space, time, organization, quality, quantity, price, credit, assortment, mentality etc. We will concentrate on forms and organization of distribution and explore these sectors for expressions of Americanization. In size the economic sector of distribution was substantial. In 1950 trade represented 8.2 per cent of GNP (wholesale 4.3, retail 3.9) while industry represented 32.4 and transport 6.5 per cent. In 1971 trade represented 12.2, industry for 41.2 and transport for 5.5 per cent.[11] In other words, trade mattered. At the beginning of the period German households spent about 50 per cent of their income on food and drink, a figure which sank to about 30 per cent at the end of the boom. The turnover of food at the beginning represented about 15 per cent of GNP and shrank to a little less than 10 per cent in 1975. Though there was a diminishing trend, the food sector remained one of the largest in the economy. Below we will concentrate on those sectors in which we found significant changes towards American patterns; that is generally more in retail than in wholesale trade and more specifically in the mail-order business and in the distribution of food and textiles. Our evaluation cannot be fully comprehensive. Some types of Americanization took place in management, internal organization of firms, advertising, use of consultants, etc. Because of space restrictions we refer to the respective studies without taking these issues up again.[12]

Forms of Americanization

Development of self-service

Self-service was invented in the United States. Around 1912, the first trial of this new sales system took place. At first it spread only slowly, but it grew during the interwar period. After the Second World War it took off. From 1948 onwards more and more shops changed to this system and, in 1958, 95 per cent of food turnover was sold in this way.[13] In the USA, as well as in Germany at a later time, self-service was most widespread in the food sector; therefore we shall concentrate on this area.

Herbert Eklöh, a private shopkeeper, was the first to open a self-service shop in Germany in 1938. Incidentally, it was also the first one in Europe. His shop in Osnabrück, a small town in Northern Germany, was neither a great success nor a total failure. Consumers showed little interest, and during the war the shop was bombed.[14] After the war the consumers' co-operatives were heading the trend to self-service. As a first step, on 30 August 1949, the co-operative *Produktion* opened the first self-service shop in Hamburg. The expansion of this new form of marketing was slow. In 1950, 38 shops had opened; 2 years later 100, in 1954, 203 and in 1956, 738. The trend could already be seen, but compared to more than 150,000 ordinary shops, it was negligible. The majority of consumers had never seen a self-service shop. However, from 1957 onwards numbers rocketed. It was not until 10 years later, in 1968, that the number of self-service shops surpassed the number of service shops, but these were just statistics. The economic element was decided much earlier. In 1961 the number of self-service shops stood at 14 per cent, but their turnover already represented 39 per cent! 50 per cent was reached in 1963 and at the end of the boom (1975), there were 76,122 self-service shops, taking 96.6 per cent of turnover, as opposed to 17,575 service shops. Thus it took two decades to reach the respective American figures.

To what extent can this 'triumphal march of self-service' (Herbert Eklöh) be understood as Americanization? It was recognized by representatives of the distribution sector, as well as by customers, as a learning process which had transferred from the USA. Herbert Eklöh visited the USA in 1935 for the first time. He opened the first self-service shop 3 years later based on the impressions he had gained in New Jersey.[15] Expanding from his one shop in 1938, he built up a chain of shops after the war. In doing so the USA remained his focus of learning. In the German distribution system Herbert Eklöh became quite famous as a first mover. Altogether he made thirty-three trips to the USA in order to get ideas. Surely we can presume that his travel frequency was exceptional. However, such journeys by decision-makers in the distribution sector internally were called 'the pilgrimage', and the USA the 'Mecca', which was an indication of how often such trips were made and how important it was that they were taken.[16] In 1953 Max Nixdorf, director of the German REWE chain, described the difference between the USA and West Germany in the following words: 'While food retailing in Germany still shows traces of narrow-mindedness, in America it shows genuine and generous entrepreneurship combined with the spirit of a modern merchant.'[17]

At the same time the USA tried to export their standards of productivity to Western Europe in all sectors of the economy. Consequently distribution, being an important sector, was included. In 1954 the evaluation of European self-service was not encouraging. The European Productivity Agency maintained in its report *Productivity in the Distribution Trade in Europe*: 'When Europe is taken as a whole, the tendency for self-service seems to be more an experiment than a development, which takes place on the basis of conviction and generally accepted principles.'[18] It seemed that Europe was not yet ready for self-service. The report suggested obstacles to self-service, and in Germany there were many. First of all there was no tradition, and only a few people could imagine what self-service entailed. At the beginning there was no vision of new and more productive organizations, better sales, etc., but instead reservations at all levels, such as the following.

1   Shopkeepers feared theft. They thought it an invitation for shoplifting when all goods were to be taken from the shelves by the customers themselves. Consumers who were not used to taking goods into their own hands could be tempted, and indeed shoplifting was widespread. Eklöh caught twenty-one thieves in his supermarket on one Saturday alone, and he suggested that there probably had been just as many who had slipped through![19] Of course, since he mentioned this figure, it was an exceptional one. But in any case shoplifting was a problem which had to be taken into account and was more important for small shopkeepers than for supermarkets. Often shoplifting was not a problem of hunger or of poverty, but a personal problem. For a small shopkeeper this translated into: What shall I do if a regular customer lifts something? Should I turn a blind eye or lose the customer?

2   It was argued that self-service would suit the American mentality well, but not the German one.

3   Many shops were simply too small to allow self-service. During the 1950s new local shops, often no bigger than 25 square metres, were still being built.

4   The switch to self-service meant a costly reconstruction of the interior of the shop. Usually shopkeepers did not have enough capital to invest, and banks, because of the lack of tradition, and also lacking the vision of what self-service could mean, were extremely reluctant to give credit. Even the well-known pioneer of self-service, who became officially honoured as a 'Konsul', Herbert Eklöh, could not obtain credit for his shops when he asked for it.

5   Last, but not least, the wholesale trade and industry were not used to servicing self-service shops. Only a very few items were pre-packed, which is a precondition for such shops.

6   The differentiation of goods on offer was rather limited.

At the same time owners feared negative reactions from their customers. Would they not feel neglected? Would they accept the shopping basket or trolley? Indeed, it took some months to teach the customers what to do with their own shopping bags and where to put them. At the beginning customers were queuing at the entrance of the shop. One person (a male) even refused to take a shopping trolley and argued he would not behave ridiculously by pushing a cart resembling a pram.[20] But all this happened only at the very beginning, and after self-service as an institution was established and became discussed by newspapers etc., even customers in remote villages had no problems. In the end all possible problems connected with self-service were much more widespread within the retail trade than with its customers.

In 1952, in order to overcome the gap between self-service and traditional shops a combination of the two kinds of shop was invented: these were called 'speed shops' (Tempoläden, Ratio-Läden). These speed-shops were initiated by the consumers' co-operatives, which acted as pioneers for self-service in Germany. In 1953 they commanded 200 of these shops. Even in these speed shops there was still service, but common goods such as flour or sugar could be obtained pre-packed, and some of these shops had a different cash point, which meant the customer did not have to wait until the customers who had been served had paid. Ten years later, in 1962, the Association of Consumers (Arbeitsgemeinschaft der Verbraucherverbände) ordered an evaluation of the consumers' perception of self-service.[21] The German consumer was presumed to be very conservative with a mentality opposed to self-service. But the result turned out to be a surprising contrast to the initial presumption. Consumers liked self-service and drew up the following positive list: uninfluenced and undisturbed choice, open display of goods, comparison of price and quality, better information on goods, better hygiene, timesaving, easier checking of prices after purchase.

Self-service was indeed a bigger problem for the shop-owner than for the customer. For the customer the change was towards easier shopping and more freedom because no real personal contact was involved when it was not wanted. Shopping could also be done much quicker than before. If advice was sought, it could still be obtained. What the customer lost was a daily contact with other people. In contrast, the shopkeeper had to change profoundly the way his role was defined. In the service-shop he concentrated on contact with his customers. He was there not only to hand over goods and add up the bill, but to give advice. In doing so he could perhaps not only sell a bit more but – more importantly – he could bind the customer to his shop. Known customers could usually get their loaf of bread, their half a pound of sugar or their litre of milk at the back door even when the shop was closed. Advice to customers was, of course, differentiated advice; well-to-do people were advised differently from less wealthy ones. A precondition for such service was considerable personal information about the various customers. Often the shopkeeper could address his customers by name. Especially in villages and small towns, where the majority of people lived, shopkeepers used to inherit their job and their shop from their father, who in his turn had inherited it from his father. Later shopkeepers shared their tradition with their future customers. Dynasties of shopkeepers sold to dynasties of customers, knowing each other from cradle to grave. In this sector, besides know-how about products, the key to success was knowledge about people. However, with the introduction of self-service this type of knowledge was devalued and in the end became irrelevant.

In contrast, the idea of self-service is that goods should sell themselves. Therefore the presentation of goods, the windows, the interior design of the shop, packaging, etc. became important. At the same time small percentages of rebates, credit margins, the secrets of write-offs and tax reductions, and other financial issues suddenly became crucial. But all this was never taught to traditional shopkeepers. Hundreds of years of retailers' tradition became worthless during the decade between 1958 to 1968, when the share of sales through self-service jumped from 15 to 80 per cent. Under these conditions we can understand why traditional retailers reflected on their situation in a gloomy way: 'This bedevilled "triumphal march of self-service" held us in its claws.' At the same time the new generation was thinking along the following lines: 'We will adjust to the [growing – H.G.S.] speed of coming years and we will learn to swim, even in the whirlpool.'[22]

During the 1950s there was an intense debate within the distribution sector about self-service. An evaluation of the few existing self-service shops showed that with the switch to the new system, turnover jumped by 93 per cent. Sales per head of selling personnel was 51 per cent up, and turnover per square metre 27 per cent.[23] Though the basis of these figures was quite small, the figures themselves were very impressive. The discourse on self-service became so important that new institutions were set up. In 1957 the Institute for Self-Service (Institut für Selbstbedienung) was founded in Cologne, which acted as a centre. It promoted the idea of self-service among retailers, it evaluated this form of trade, it succeeded in its negotiations with industry about standard sizing of packages, and it acted as a political lobby. Its main voice was its periodical *Dynamik im Handel.* Other periodicals inspired by US-models such as *Supermarket Merchandising* or *Chain Stores Age* were launched. Even a special publishing house, Verlag Gesellschaft für Selbstbedienung, was created. However, one main difference between the American and the German model of running the economy remained. While in the US several periodicals and organizations competed with each other, in Germany everything focused on this one and only institute for self-service; all the different types of owners, shopkeepers, consumers' co-operatives, department stores, chain stores, etc. co-operated in this – their – institute.

Reservations against self-service lay, to a large extent, with investors. As usual, owners were less willing to take a risk than managers. At the same time it was much easier for managers to take such a risk because investment did not involve their own property and usually they made decisions for much larger firms, which could venture into self-service with one or two shops, but not with their entire property. Therefore up to the mid-1950s the majority of self-service shops were owned by consumers' co-operatives such as *Produktion,* and chain-stores, such as REWE, but already in 1960 the picture had changed, since at that time 75 per cent of such shops were owned by the shopkeepers.[24]

In 1957 Germany's position in Europe concerning the trend towards self-service was a middle one.[25] Sweden, Norway and Switzerland were miles ahead with 5,000, 1,300 and 1,120 self-service shops, the UK, Denmark and the Netherlands were at about the same level, while others were far behind. There was a clear North/South difference. The percentage of self-service shops in Norway were 10.1, in Germany 2.2, in Austria 0.2 and in Spain 0.003. However, 2 years later, Germany was already leading in Europe with 11.8 per cent (Norway 11.5, The Netherlands 7.4, Switzerland 7.0, UK 4.3, France 0.9, Spain 0.14, Italy 0.11). Indeed, since the 1960s, Germany led self-service in Europe (perhaps with the exception of Scandinavia).

Development of supermarkets

Self-service supermarkets were invented in the USA. They emerged during the early 1930s when, during the World Economic Crisis, production sheds, garages, etc. stood empty. Goods were put on display and no service was offered in order to keep prices low. In fact the innovation was more a discount shop than a supermarket; however, out of this initial idea the US-supermarket developed very quickly.[26] A supermarket was understood to be a shop managed on self-service lines, which combined the traditional offer of food with that of fresh meat, vegetables and fruit, and sometimes even some non-food items. A US-supermarket needed a certain minimum space, a minimum turnover of $2 million, and a car park. The idea of the supermarket was to concentrate all the requirements of everyday shopping into one shop. Thus it was the natural extension of the idea of self-service. In the USA during the early 1960s two-thirds of food turnover was being sold in supermarkets. A proverb says the better is the enemy of the good; in this case the supermarket swallowed most of the small self-service shops, a development which was related to the spread of cars. In this respect Germany followed the US pattern with a time-gap of about 15 years, still well ahead of the comparative development in Japan.[27] Compared to the rest of Europe, Germany was not a forerunner in the trend towards the supermarket. The UK, Belgium and Denmark were well ahead.[28] The regulatory framework was somewhat different from the USA, though not decisively. Opening hours for shops, which were restricted by law in Germany, were different. While in this respect there was no change – and, more astonishing, no demand for a change – a price-binding suggestion set by producers for retail trade was given up during the 1960s. Beyond these facts there was little state intervention, since the government believed in a liberal policy.[29]

The first person to invest in large supermarkets in Germany was the same person who pioneered self-service: Herbert Eklöh. And again it was the first of such shops in the whole of Europe. In 1957 he started in Cologne with a shop of 2,000 square metres with a car park for 200 cars. Others followed and in 1961 about 250 supermarkets existed in Germany. Compared to the overall number of shops, this was a very small proportion. At that time supermarkets were still a 'widespread unknown phenomenon'.[30] Up to 1958, there were only sixteen supermarkets. The Institut für Selbstbedienung set up its own organization for the promotion of supermarkets, the Internationale Selbstbedienungs-Organisation and launched the respective periodical *Selbstbedienung und Supermarkt* (which later merged with *Dynamik im Handel*, its periodical for self-service). This new institution especially promoted the supermarket, among others, by pointing out the comparisons between supermarkets and ordinary, that is relatively small, self-service shops. In supermarkets turnover per employee was one-third higher. In 1962 calculations showed that the old rule of thumb that self-service needed one cashpoint per 50 square metres did not apply to supermarkets. They could do with 84 square metres per cashpoint. Both these facts reflected the jump in productivity that the supermarket stood for. Because of this the number of supermarkets grew quickly. In 1968 it reached 1700 and peaked in 1973 with 3889.[31] After that year the numbers contracted like the numbers of self-service shops from 1972 onwards. In parallel at the end of the boom, both self-service shops and supermarkets ended their phase of expansion and entered a period of consolidation, or in other words, a phase of maturity. As with self-service, Germany headed the development in supermarkets in Europe, both in the build-up and in the consolidation process.

Of course, capital investment to set up a supermarket was substantially larger than for a traditional self-service shop. In consequence private shopkeepers were reluctant, which meant that in 1961 only 3.7 per cent of supermarkets were owned by private people, while chains represented 64 per cent and department stores 30 per cent. In this respect development can be compared to the introduction of self-service. In contrast, and like private owners, the consumers' co-operatives hesitated, even though they had enough capital to invest. They probably felt that the supermarket terminated the relationship between shop and customer, which was a precondition for the success of consumers' co-operatives.[32] With the setting up of supermarkets new principles for locations of sales were adopted from the USA. Self-service shops had, initially, replaced traditional shops at their respective locations. But supermarkets where set up not so much in the city but along main roads in suburbs. Supermarkets needed a considerable amount of space. In contrast to department stores with several storeys they used to have only one floor. At the same time they needed a car park. Such space was expensive in the city, but the idea was to drive with the car to the shop. Therefore the city was not the best place for this type of shop. With the supermarket the topographical aspect of life became important. While at first work was separated from living, now shopping became separated from it as well.

Though the idea of the supermarket was based on that of self-service, it went much further. Self-service was one step in the division of the old personal commitment between shopkeeper and customer, but in relatively small shops such a relationship could be kept up to a certain extent. In contrast the supermarket created a gap between these groups, the organization of the shop prevented any personal contact. The old European idea that the shopkeeper cared for the supply and well-being of his known customers was terminated not so much by self-service but by the establishment of supermarkets. In a supermarket the division between the management and the customer became even wider than in ordinary self-service shops. While in the latter the owner used to do all necessary work, e.g. at the cash-point, arrange goods at the display, talk to customers, etc., the manager of a supermarket had little or no contact with his customers. His task was to take care of the whole, supervise the heads of divisions (e.g. for fresh meat, non-food, etc.), ensure supplies were on time, etc.; in general, to organize. He no longer needed to be a good seller himself, his success was based on management skills. Logistics became important. With an annual turnover of 3 million DM it was calculated that 1,500 tons of goods passed through the shop. 2,800 different deliveries of goods were needed and only four people were needed in this part of the shop.[33] With the introduction of the supermarket part-time work emerged. Previously, part-time work, as such, had not been widespread in Germany, retail service was one of its pioneers. While at traditional shops full-time employment was the rule, in supermarkets half of the personnel often worked part-time. This illustrates that in order for a supermarket to be successful, a very different type of person was required compared to the traditional shopkeeper's virtues.

On their study trips to the USA, delegations and private persons were impressed by the large assortment of products in shops. The range was much bigger than in German shops and its numbers grew quickly. In 1955 a typical US-supermarket offered 2,200 different types of goods, by 1960, 4,500, 1969, 8,000 and at the end of the period in 1974, 9,000.[34] In Germany it was a deep-rooted idea to have a rather small range of goods, offering little or no choice for customers. The advantages of a small assortment were that less capital was tied up and less work was involved regarding supervision, orders, etc. The conviction was that customers would buy what was on offer and thus meet their needs. Why start competition between own goods? The German vision of a customer was of a person who would buy for his requirements. The US idea was to sell to the customer and make him happy. It took quite a long time before the German distribution sector understood that competition between offers did not lead to what was called *cannibalism* but to additional sales in quality and quantity. The first German self-service shop started with only 600 different products. During the next decades those who switched from service to self-service offered about 600 to 800 products. The average number of products in self-service shops grew from 1,086 in 1958 to 1,394 in 1961, that is by 100 per year.[35] The variety of goods in American shops was never matched in Germany. In 1988 supermarkets still sold no more than about 4,000 different products.[36]

Supermarkets by definition included fresh vegetables, fresh meat, etc. While today we simply expect such goods to be on offer, in the beginning they caused problems. In the 1950s it was questioned in Germany whether fresh meat should be sold through self-service since its nature seemed not to be compatible with this system.[37] In contrast, because of the higher standard of living in the USA, American shops did not have the same problem. All shopkeepers agreed that fresh meat acted as a 'magnet' for customers, but because a substantial amount of losses could be generated, many retailers thought it to be a 'hot iron'. While the management of some large shops thought its function of being a 'magnet' was so important that they were prepared to absorb constant losses on fresh meat, others maintained this sector had to come up with similar results as for the other sectors. However, retailers agreed that fresh meat was by far the 'most dangerous' division of all. The basic problem with fresh meat was its perishability; Monday's fresh meat is no longer fresh on Friday. The mentioned 'danger' grew out of (1) the fluctuations in demand, (2) the quality of meat sold, and (3) packaging. The problem can be explained by an admittedly extreme case.[38] On Monday turnover in meat was DM600, on Tuesday DM2,000, and on Saturday DM16,000, in other words sales on Mondays were less than 5 per cent compared to sales on Saturdays.

Even with part-time personnel such a structure of demand is difficult to meet. Part-time personnel can be used for organizational reasons and information in addition to ordinary full-time personnel. Swings up to 1:5 – but no more – could be met with service shops. Thus self-service should have been the appropriate answer to the problem. However, even for these types of sales the swing was too wide. But how could traditional butchers survive these problems? For two reasons they had different swings: first, they not only sold, but also partly produced their goods. Second, they sold not only meat but sausage etc., which was bought throughout the whole week. Third, the self-service shops attracted customers who ate meat less regularly than others.

A second problem with fresh meat in self-service was the quality of meat. The quality was lower compared to US-standards.[39] In Germany at that time demand in self-service shops was primarily for medium quality. Naturally medium quality did not look as good as top quality. However, sales went by the look of the meat. Self-service found itself trapped: better off customers bought at the butchers, therefore supermarket demand was for medium quality. But while the butcher had little problems in selling this type of quality too, it had little appeal to the eye, which is a precondition for self-service. Even those retailers who were convinced to include the offer of fresh meat in the future were reluctant. It is revealing for the situation that even pioneers like Eklöh did not find making the decision straightforward. On the one hand he exclaimed: '. . . without sufficient cooling there is no successful self-service! Refrigeration is the key to success.'[40] On the other hand difficulties in his shops made him resort to traditional thoughts: '. . . furthermore, we think it is not entirely sound and fair to the handicraft of butchers if we, as owners of large shops, use our opportunities to subsidize the meat sector above other sectors, and force down those prices on which a respected and competent profession has to live.'[41] Here the traditional approach of *do not compete too much*, but *live and let live alongside your competitor* was proposed.

A third problem was packaging. For undefined reasons, but probably because of high prices (the German currency was undervalued in order to promote exports), original US-packaging could not to be obtained. It took years until the various aims of quality, appearance, cheapness, and keeping meat fresh as long as possible could be met by packaging. In the end all these difficulties were overcome. To a certain degree problems were solved by new and better products, but more important was the rise in the standard of living which enabled people to eat meat every day and not just on Sundays. They demanded higher quality, and better appearance and thus meat was better adapted to be sold through self-service.

While fresh meat established itself as a widespread product, other groups of products followed. In the USA frozen food was first offered in the 1930s, and in spite of the economic crisis became a success. During the 1950s it became widespread as an every-day product. It entered German shops only during the second half of the 1960s. Frozen food led to another new investment, the freezer, which had the great advantage of enabling food to remain fresh for more than a couple of days. For the retailer the decision was straightforward, just a question of investment and space within the shop. In spite of this, many were reluctant to take frozen food.[42] The reason was their customers who hesitated over buying it. First of all there was no tradition of eating frozen food, second it was considered of lower quality compared to fresh food, and third only very few customers had their own freezer at home, which meant frozen food was to be consumed at once, and in view of this the majority preferred fresh food. Therefore it took some time until substantial amounts of it were consumed. The figures rose (per head and year) from 2.0 kg in 1966 to 4.8 kg in 1974.[43] Though nearly all shops (93%) offered frozen food at the end of the boom, today we are not very impressed by a consumption of 5 kilos per head. But we have to take into account the fact that the era of pizza and ice-cream at home in every household had still to come. Five kilos of frozen food was, of course, much less than consumption per head in the USA. It took one more generation before consumption patterns narrowed closer to the US-standard. Furthermore, a certain group of food never achieved the same role as in the USA: processed food. Although several attempts were made to introduce products such as peeled potatoes, frozen juices, etc., up until 1975, they never played a role in Germany.

As Mika Takaoka and Takeo Kikkawa show in Chapter 13 of this volume, the small convenience-store continued to remain a stable issue in residential areas in Japan. In contrast, this type of shop was squeezed out in Germany. Shopping at arm's length was no match for lower prices after cars became widespread. This caused a process of concentration. The supermarkets took over the small self-service shops, and they were taken over by self-service centres (SB-Centre) or self-service department stores (SB-Warenhäuser). Again these types, emerged first in the USA before they were known in Germany. Self-service centres differed from supermarkets in size and in the variety of goods on offer. Their size was between 1000 square metres and 20,000 square metres or more. While they usually sold all types of goods, the rule was the larger the centre the smaller the amount of food was sold. The difference between a traditional and a self-service department store was that in the traditional shop, cash points were scattered all over the building, while in the latter there was only one at the check-out. This made it possible to use shopping carts in a self-service department store. In contrast, in a traditional department store, customers had to carry the goods themselves. There was therefore a larger turnover per head in the new type of shops. Furthermore such centres were situated on main roads and always had a large car park. This too enhanced the amount of sales compared to old-style department stores in the centre of towns with no, or only a small, car park.

Self-service centres and self-service department stores emerged during the second half of the 1960s, towards the end of our period of investigation. In 1966 there were only 66 of these centres in Germany. After 1967 more than 100 were built annually, which increased their total to 1,137 in 1975.[44] The smaller ones with up to 2,000 square metres mainly concentrated on food, using most of their space for it (65.2 per cent) and achieving the biggest share of turnover (84.6 per cent).[45] The larger ones with more than 4,000 square metres concentrated on non-food items, using less than one quarter of their space for food (23.3 per cent). Still their turnover was two-thirds in food (66.9 per cent). For the medium-sized centres the figures were 35.8 per cent of space and 63.2 per cent of food turnover. Because earnings on non-food products used to be much higher, big centres promoted these products. But food was considered to be necessary as the so called magnet. Those who bought food often bought something else when they saw it on offer. Thus the factor habit was calculated. Customers who used to buy food in such a centre would go there first but would look for other goods as well. Thus the food-department was considered to be a necessity.

However, although self-service centres and self-service department stores were invented and expanded in the USA, Germany was gaining confidence in this market. While with self-service shops and supermarkets it was self evident that all could and had to learn from America, there was comparatively little reference to the USA to be found in the case of self-service centres and self-service department stores. It seems that during the last years of the boom the gap between the USA and West Germany had narrowed and the US model was no longer as important as it had been up to the mid-1960s.

Development of chain-stores

While self-service centres and self-service department stores no longer accepted the USA as a model for their ongoing business as they had with its introduction, the situation with chain-stores was different. When the idea of chain-stores entered Germany, common chain-stores were already widespread in the USA as well as in Germany. The chain Thams und Garfs from their headquarters in Schwerin, Northern Germany, for example, already commanded 1,184 retail shops in 1934. While this common type of chain-store owned by one person or an institutional investor was well known, the new type was the so called voluntary chain, that is a group of shopkeepers who joined such a group in order to enjoy the advantages of a chain, without selling their own shops. In contrast to co-operatives, in the USA as well as in Europe, such voluntary chain stores were usually initiated by wholesale traders. By creating such a chain wholesalers organized their own market, obtaining a group of shops which they could deliver to exclusively themselves. The shopkeeper in return promised to buy only from his chain-wholesaler.

Voluntary chains emerged in the 1920s and grew especially during the 1930s when competition was tough. The first, and up to the 1950s, the biggest, the Red and White Corporation was founded in 1921. It seemed that in the USA after the First World War the time was ripe for such an idea, since three persons from three different states, S.M. Flickinger from New York, H.A. Marr from Colorado and A.M. Scokum from Minnesota, had the same idea. Each set up such an organization, but when they learned about each other they merged to set up the Red and White Corporation. Other organizations were formed on the same basic idea. In 1940 chains represented 24 per cent of turnover in food.[46] After a period of growth their market-share shrank during the war, because of the general price-freeze. Then single retailers grew by offering additional service such as free delivery to homes. However, when the price-freeze was lifted in 1946 the chain-stores expanded again, taking 55 per cent of turnover in 1955.[47] The advantages of such chains were large. Together they could act as wholesalers, and thus could save a lot of money; they combined their efforts in marketing and advertising; they used standardized forms for calculation which offered the possibility of instant comparisons; and they combined their efforts in continuing their education.

In contrast to Japan credit was not usually given by wholesalers. It was one of the principles that the private shop-owner had to pay for his goods on delivery. Therefore the financial system had to be based on different principles. Shopkeepers as well as other small businessmen could rely on their local bank or, even more widespread, their local savings bank. It was the task of such local savings banks to channel savings from private persons to small and medium-sized business in the locality of the respective bank or branch. Thus the financial network was a local one, with no direct links to the distribution itself.

The first European voluntary chain was founded in the Netherlands by a wholesaler in 1932. In order to save costs he used the same trademark for the chain that he had already registered just for tea. In this way the SPAR chain was initiated and is well known in the whole of Europe today. *Spar* is the Dutch word for fir tree, and incidentally means 'save!' The symbol of this chain still is the fir tree, but for customers the word 'save!' was of course more appealing. Another advantage sprang up just by chance. When such chains were set up abroad, it was discovered that the word 'spar' ('save!') had the same meaning in German and in the Scandinavian languages, that is in markets which were six times larger than the Dutch one. The German SPAR-organization was founded in 1952. The Dutch did not invest but gave advice for a long time. While the

260 Harm G. Schröter

Dutch SPAR was designed after American models, the German one focused on the Dutch experience. Therefore it was in the beginning at most an indirect Americanization. However, internal rules, such as the so called 'cost-plus' system of calculation and others were taken directly from the USA, as well as all initiatives for public relations. Thus a certain Americanization was to be found within voluntary chains such as SPAR and others.

Development of discount-markets

The idea of the discount-market is to a certain extent the idea of self-service thought through to its logical conclusion. There is no service in a discount shop and all goods are presented as they came into the shop without repackaging, arranging, etc. The shop is simple both inside and out. The amount of goods on offer is very limited, it concentrates on products which will produce a high turnover. All these disadvantages for the customer are balanced by low prices. The basic idea of a discount shop was best developed in the USA by the so called *box stores*. The viability and success of such stores was measured by a set of target figures which had to be met. These were, among others: minimum purchase $50, labour-cost below 6 per cent of turnover, turnover per employee an hour $175, prices at least 15 per cent lower when compared to the average supermarket.[48]

The first German discount-markets, which were created following the US-design, came into being between 1954 and 1956. And as in the US, nearly all of them first watered down their initial idea by offering more articles, some services, etc. In the end they ceased their original form of organization but became a variation of the low-price supermarket instead.[49] In contrast, one special discount-firm which entered the market using this form relatively late had a great success. In 1946 the brothers Karl and Theo Albrecht inherited one small shop in Essen. By 1950 they already owned thirteen shops, all of which were very traditional. They concentrated on only a number of cheap goods and by doing so used one of the main ideas of discount-markets. However, they did not employ the discount-system in its pure sense until 1962, when they founded their ALDI system. It seems that while a couple of discount-firms, which quitted this segment relatively early, looked to the USA and tried to learn from the American experience, ALDI did not, but the two brothers experimented until they re-invented the discount-system for a second time.[50] Instantly they developed a similar system of target-figures to the box shops in the USA. If ALDI had looked for more international information instead of developing it from scratch, the firm would probably have saved a lot of investment.

Cash and carry markets, that is wholesale discount-markets, were taken over from the USA as well. But during the period discussed here, their success was rather limited. Their leap forward came only after the boom;

from the 1980s onwards the cash-and-carry market Metro became one of the biggest distribution firms in Europe.

In the late 1960s news about a new system of shops reached the German special journals: franchise. In 1898 it was first developed in the USA by General Motors which handed out a license to sell and service General Motors cars. It became widespread in the USA in retail trade; many chains such as Macdonald's were based on it. In the franchise system one contractor provides the investment on the site while the other gives an exclusive license to sell and serve a certain good, use the respective trademark, deal with advertising, etc. Both firms stay independent and can, after the termination of the contract, re-orientate themselves. The core idea of franchising is a long-term binding contract which can save both sides substantial amounts of capital. Though some American firms (e.g. Coca Cola) had introduced it into Germany, it was generally unknown. The basic idea of long-term contracts was rather uncommon in the retail sector. Similar contracts used to be open-ended, as in the voluntary chains. In evaluating the concept of franchise the German journal *Blätter für Genossenschaftswesen* headlined: 'Another step towards a contract-oriented market economy.'[51] This was exactly what franchise meant to the German distribution system: another step towards Americanization.

Change in language

Since Americanization is a cultural concept, it is hard to measure. However, since culture expresses itself to a large extent through language, the use of words can be taken as an indicator. In our context this is the use of American words within a German context. There are several reasons why foreign words are incorporated into another language, among others for greater precision, in case there is no equivalent, or simply to show modernity.[52] The use of American words became widespread especially during the 1950s, and instantly provoked criticism. Heinz Weinhold castigated 'the epidemic course of Anglo-Saxon foreign words'[53] and Carl Hundhausen became upset that 'the good and hundred per cent sufficient word "Absatz" [distribution – H.G.S.] or "Absatzwirtschaft" will be eliminated from our language in order to give room to another sloppiness of our German language.'[54]

Eklöh for instance, as well as many other authors, used American words for key expressions (Drug-Stores, Super-Markets), while in some cases they mixed American with German (Non-food-Artikel, Discount-Häuser).[55] Though there were German expressions, in many cases the authors used the American ones.

Marktinformationsdienst, the volume on chain-stores in the USA, had a German headline ('Kettenläden'), but in the text the American word 'chain-store' was used. The periodical *Versandhandel* published an article on 'odd-prices', translating it to 'ausgefallene Preise' but used in its text only the US-expression. During the 1960s, however, the situation became more settled. Some expressions were absorbed into German by Germanization, thus 'super-markets' became 'Supermärkte' at that time. Others were used by applying the original US-words ('non-foods') or in an American-German mixed version ('cash-and-carry Märkte');[56] a third group was used totally in German, showing no traces of a previous use of foreign words, for example since the 1960s only eccentrics refer to 'shopping centres' and not to 'Einkaufszentren', to 'food-brokers' instead of 'Handelsvertreter'. It seems that during a period of admiration, many people were ready to take over anything from the Americans, while, when the uncritical admiration had petered out, it became more obvious which expressions could be translated and which were taken into everyday use as foreign words.

Conclusion

In the West German distribution system, especially in retail trade, we traced a substantial transfer of US-everyday culture; clearly an Americanization took place. It could well be called a 'revolution in trade' since it changed everything: rules, organization, sites, relations, values and behaviour. It was, to a large extent, a reflected process, since organization, proceedings, goods on offer, etc. were obviously superior in the USA compared to Germany. The transfer was very clear in the introduction of self-service, supermarkets, chain-stores, discount-markets, etc. In some sectors, such as frozen food, Americanization took time to establish, whilst in others, such as processed food, it did not occur, at least not before the end of the boom.

During the period of the boom-years (1950–75), the various transfers speeded up the economic basis of mass consumption which started in West Germany during the 1950s. While it took Germany about 20 years to reach US-percentages in self-service, the subsequent introduction of, for example, the supermarkets took less, and that of self-service centres even less time. The reasons for the acceleration were manifold. Of course, at first the initial reservation against the former enemy of war had to be overcome. Second, during the initial years many people focused on a simple reconstruction before they reoriented their business. But a general Americanization of life helped to change the economic sector as well.[57] With Americanization, as with many other things, first steps are always the most difficult ones, while it is simpler later to continue using given structures of influence. Of course, economic growth enabled customers to diversify their demands, and conditions for consumption became more similar to those in the USA. A key issue in this respect was the use of cars for shopping, which became a common feature in Germany during the 1960s.

In contrast, while there was a speeding up of transfers during the second half of the boom-period, it seems at first glance that American influence diminished. During the 1960s there was not the same amount of admiration towards the USA compared to the previous decade. Organized information-seeking travel ended, firms compared themselves not only to the US, but to European competitors, etc. Decision-makers became more critical in general. The Germans had learned some lessons and the gap between the two different systems of distribution had narrowed. In some sectors the Germans developed even better than their former American teachers. At the end of the boom an expert exclaimed: 'American know-how in distribution governed the world for many decades. Today in this field the leading position of the USA is no longer as self evident as before.'[58]

Decisive for the Americanization of the German distribution system were less the customers than the owners or managers. While the customers discovered the respective advantages or disadvantages fairly quickly, changes in management needed time. Of course, the supply-side had to think more precisely since it was much less flexible than the demand side. The former had to act and to invest while the latter could pick the best offer without any commitment. But more important than financial considerations was the mental change. Initially, especially in the food retail trade, the German shopkeeper was thinking in terms of supply for his customers with whom he was often familiar, he had a leaning towards co-operation with colleagues, towards tradition, etc. The new way of thinking in a competitive way, e.g. in sales as in contrast to supplies, in offering choices to his customers, and not only caring for their known requirements, took some time. During the second half of the boom this new and different attitude towards business proceedings deepened. The transfer was facilitated by trade associations which offered guided tours for selected groups and afterwards provided a forum for publication of impressions. The German organization RKW (Rationalisierungs-Kuratorium der deutschen Wirtschaft), which acted as part of the American Productivity Mission played an important role in this.

In the end a somewhat complicated picture emerged of the Americanization of German distribution. It started with admiration and less reflected and less adapted transfers of American culture. Then, with the acceleration of knowledge about the American distribution methods, there were fewer open signs of Americanization, e.g. in the form of the take-over of words. However, there were better adaptations to German conditions and the American character of the transferred issue was better hidden. While the introduction of self-service openly and often reflected the American model, we do not find the same amount of open reflection with the introduction of, for example, the supermarket. But it was the supermarket, not self-service as a system, which broke down the traditional relation between the shopkeeper and his customer. While self-service was a transfer of a new form of sales, it was still a form which tolerated traditional relations of supply (with a sense of care-taking), money (even borrowing), it involved people, etc. In contrast supermarkets reduced these relations to the issues of capital, investment and turnover, leaving out any personal considerations. As a result the process of Americanization deepened, though German decision-makers became more critical. It deepened because the American values of competition in contrast to co-operation were taken over – without ever reaching true US-standards. Financial considerations became more important, personal relations were reduced. At the beginning of this process managers voiced views such as: 'We all have to learn how to get along better with each other.'[59] It ended with the feeling that competition is basically something good, not bad. Though even today (2002) German managers see competition differently from their US-counterparts, a profound change in attitude in favour of competitive behaviour took place during the boom period in Germany.

The fact that during the 1960s less admiration can be traced, less organized visits were carried out, less American words were taken over (or they became 'Germanized') is no contradiction to the process of Americanization. It is rather the result of this process. The gap between the American and the German approach had narrowed indeed. During the 1960s American values of competition had taken deeper roots in Germany's distribution system than in the previous decade. This result, that there was a more profound change during the 1960s compared to the 1950s is in tune with parallel findings on, for example, the development of thinking of business elites,[60] or how and when managers changed their views on cartels, or on the reasons for the decline of the co-op shops.[61] It is well in tune with Alfred Chandler's views on the downswing of co-operative capitalism in Germany after the Second World War.

Notes

1 R. Nieschlag, 'Strukturwandlungen im Handel', in H. König (ed.), *Wandlungen der Wirtschaftsstruktur in der Bundesrepublik Deutschland*, Berlin: Duncker & Humblot, 1962, pp. 493–524.
2 As a professor Nieschlag taught the economics of trade at the High School in Nuremberg. He was engaged in setting up one of the first scholarly marketing institutions in Germany.
3 B. Röper, *Die vertikale Preisbindung bei Markenartikeln. Untersuchungen über Preisbildungs- und Preisbindungsvorgänge in der Wirklichkeit*, Tübingen: J.C.B. Mohr, 1955, p. 42.
4 Nieschlag, 'Strukturwandlungen im Handel', p. 499.
5 A.D. Chandler, *Strategy and Structure*, Cambridge: MIT Press, 1962.
6 A.D. Chandler, *Scale and Scope*, Cambridge: Harvard University Press, 1990.
7 H.G. Schröter, 'What is Americanization? Or About the Use and Abuse of the Americanization-Concept', in D. Barjot, I. Lescent-Giles and M. de Ferrière le Vayer (eds), *Américanisation en Europe au XXe Siècle: Économie, Culture, Politique. Americanisation in 20th Century Europe: Economic, Culture, Politics*, vol. 1, Lille: Centre d'Histoire de l'Europe du Nord-Ouest, Université Charles-de-Gaulle Lille 3, 2002, pp. 41–57; E. Moen and H.G. Schröter, 'Americanisation as a Concept for Deeper Understanding of Economic Changes in Europe,

1945–1970', in E. Moen and H.G. Schröter (eds), *Entreprise et Histoire*, 1998, no. 19, pp. 5–13, here p. 6.

8 M. Kipping and O. Bjarnar (eds), *The Americanisation of European Business. The Marshall Plan and the transfer of US management models*, London: Routledge, 1998.

9 M. Gloor, 'Ausblick auf zukünftige Distributionsformen', in M. Gloor *et al.* (eds), *Neuzeitliche Distributionsformen*, Bern: Paul Haupt, 1963, pp. 103–115, here p. 104.

10 See H.G. Schröter, 'Perspektiven der Forschung: Amerikanisierung und Sowjetisierung als Interpretationsmuster der Integration in beiden Teilen Deutschlands', in E. Schremmer (ed.), *Wirtschaftliche und soziale Integration in historischer Sicht*, Stuttgart: Steiner, 1996, pp. 259–289, here p. 260.

11 *Statistical Yearbooks.*

12 E.g. M. Kipping, 'American Management Consulting Companies in Western Europe, 1920 to 1990: Products, Reputation, and Relationships', *Business History Review*, Summer 1999, vol. 73, no. 2, 190–220; H.G. Schröter, 'Advertising in West Germany after World War II. A Case of an Americanization', in Schröter and Moen (eds), *Entreprise et Histoire*, pp. 15–33.

13 K.-H. Henksmeier, *Die wirtschaftlichen Leistungen der Selbstbedienung in Europa*, Köln: Verlag für Selbstbedienung, 1961, p. 11.

14 For the following figures as well: Anon., *Dynamik im Handel*, Special edition '50 Jahre Selbstbedienung', 1988, no. 10, p. 11 and p. 36 f.

15 H. Eklöh, 'Der Siegeszug der Selbstbedienung', in *Neure Aspekte der Selbstbedienung*, Rüschlikon: Stiftung 'Im Grüne', 1958, pp. 9–19.

16 H. Jakubik, 'Der Umbruch zur Selbstbedienung bei Management und Mitarbeitern', in *Dynamik im Handel*, 1988, no. 10, pp. 204–217, here p. 204.

17 M. Nixdorf, 'Der Lebensmitteleinzelhandel in den USA', in Rationalisierungs-Kuratorium der Deutschen Wirtschaft (ed.), *Der Einzelhandel im Konkurrenzkampf. Eindrücke einer Studiengruppe deutscher Genossenschafter über Ein- und Verkaufsmethoden im amerikanischen Handel*, Munich: Carl Hanser, 1955, pp. 34–43, p. 34.

18 Quoted from: Henksmeier, *Selbstbedienung*, p. 11.

19 Eklöh, 'Siegeszug', p. 15.

20 Ibid., p. 12 f.

21 *Dynamik im Handel*, p. 22.

22 Both quotations: Eklöh, 'Siegeszug', p. 17.

23 *Dynamik im Handel*, p. 14.

24 B. Tietz, *Konsument und Einzelhandel. Strukturwandlungen in der Bundesrepublik Deutschland von 1950 bis 1975*, Frankfurt/M: Lorch, 1967, p. 358, Table 92.

25 Henksmeier, *Selbstbedienung*, p. 17. The numbers include *all* self-service shops, not only food.

26 T. Deutsch, 'From "Wild Animal Stores" to Women's Sphere: Supermarkets and the Politics of Mass Consumption, 1930–1950', *Business and Economic History*, Fall 1999, vol. 28, no. 1, pp. 143–153; Nieschlag, *Dynamik*, p. 13 ff; K.-H. Henksmeier, 'Der Supermarkt – seine technischen und organisatorischen Probleme', in Gloor (ed.), *Distributionsformen*, pp. 34–43.

27 See Chapter 13 by Takaoka and Kikkawa in this volume.

28 I. Lescent-Giles, 'The Americanization of Food Retailing in Britain and in France since the 1960s', in M. Kipping and N. Tiratsoo (eds), *Americanization in 20th Century Europe: Business, Culture, Politics*, vol. 2, Lille: Centre d'Histoire de l'Europe du Nord-Ouest, Université Charles-de-Gaulle Lille 3, 2002, pp. 291–308.

29 H.G. Schröter, 'Konsumpolitik und "Soziale Marktwirtschaft". Die Koexistenz liberalisierter und regulierter Verbrauchsgütermärkte in der Bundesrepublik

der 1950er Jahre', in H. Berghoff (ed.), *Konsumpolitik*, Göttingen: Vandenhoek & Ruprecht, 1999, pp. 113–133.

30 Anon., 'Supermärkte 1962', *Selbstbedienung und Supermarkt*, 1962, no. 10, pp. 6–10, here p. 6.

31 *Edeka Handels-Rundschau*, 1975, no. 21, p. 8.

32 H.G. Schröter, 'Der Verlust der "europäischen Form des Zusammenspiels von Ordnung und Freiheit". Vom Untergang der deutschen Konsumgenossenschaften, *Vierteljahrschrift für Sozial- und Wirtschaftsgeschichte*, 2000, vol. 87, no. 4, pp. 442–467.

33 Henksmeier, *Supermarkt*, p. 42 f.

34 Anon., Supermärkte in den USA, *Selbstbedienung und Supermarkt*, 1975, no. 8, pp. 40–44, here p. 42; Eklöh, 'Siegeszug', p. 14; Nixdorf, 'Der Lebensmitteleinzelhandel in den USA', p. 35 f.

35 K.-H. Henksmeier, 'Den Konsumwünschen nachkommen – doch mit der nötigen Vorsicht', *Selbstbedienung und Supermarkt*, 1962, no. 10, pp. 11–12, here p. 11.

36 *Dynamik im Handel*, p. 24.

37 '... für unsere Begriffe artfremder Artikel wie Frischfleisch ...' (Nixdorf, 'Der Lebensmitteleinzelhandel in den USA', p. 34).

38 H. Eklöh sen. and H. Eklöh jun., 'Ein heißes Eisen: Selbstbedienung bei Frischfleisch', in *Dynamik im Handel*, pp. 140–144, here p. 142.

39 Ibid., p. 142.

40 Eklöh, 'Siegeszug', p. 13.

41 Ibid, p. 141.

42 H. Nixdorf, 'Zweckmäßiger Sortimentsaufbau', *Selbstbedienung und Supermarkt*, 1962, no. 10, pp. 12–13, here p. 12.

43 *EDEKA-Handelsrundschau*, 1975, no. 20, 3; ibid., 1975, no. 21, 5.

44 K.-H. Henksmeier, 'SB-Center und SB-Warenhäuser am 1.1.1975', *Selbstbedienung und Supermarkt*, 1975, no. 5, pp. 10–19, here p. 10.

45 K.-H. Henksmeier, 'Kosten und Leistungen von SB-Center und SB-Warenhäuser 1973', *Selbstbedienung und Supermarkt*, 1975, no. 1, pp. 2–8, here p. 1.

46 Anon., 'Die Bedeutung der Kettenläden im amerikanischen Einzelhandel', *Marktinformationsdienst der Bundesstelle für Aussenhandelsinformation*, December 1956, no. A/133, 2.

47 They grew quickly. One year previously they obtained 52 per cent (ibid.).

48 The figures were given for 1980 (B. Tietz, 'Die Fachmärkte – ein neuer Betriebstyp des Einzelhandels', *Marketing ZFP*, November 1981, vol. 4, pp. 241–250, here p. 242.

49 Tietz, *Konsument*, p. 510 f.

50 D. Brandes, *Konsequent einfach. Die ALDI-Erfolgsstory*, Frankfurt/M: Campus-Verlag, 1998.

51 B. Tietz, 'Typologie und Bedeutung des Franchising', *Blätter für Genossenschaftswesen*, 25 June 1969, vol. 115, pp. 193–196.

52 H. Fink, *Amerikanisierung in der deutschen Wirtschaft. Sprache, Handel, Güter und Dienstleistungen*, Frankfurt/Main: Lang, 1995; '"Know-How" and "Hi-Fi": Zum Verständnis englischer Ausdrücke in der deutschen Werbesprache', *Muttersprache*, 1975, no. 85, pp. 186–204; H. Galinsky, and B. Carstensen, *Amerikanismen in der deutschen Gegenwartssprache*, Heidelberg: Winter, 1963.

53 H. Weinhold, 'Distributionsleistung und Distributionsform', in *Neuzeitliche Distributionsformen*, pp. 9–33, p. 9.

54 C. Hundhausen, 'Geleitwort zur deutschen Ausgabe', in R.D. Crisp, *Absatzforschung, Marketing Research*, Essen: G. Girardet, 1959, p. 6.

55 Eklöh, 'Siegeszug', p. 14, Nieschlag, Betriebsformen.

56 B. Tietz, *Die Tendenzen im Lebensmitteleinzelhandel*, ms. (Hamburg 1982), p. 80.
57 K. Jarausch and H. Siegrist (eds), *Amerikanisierung und Sowjetisierung in Deutschland 1945–1970*, Frankfurt/M: Campus, 1997; A. Lüdtke, I. Marßolek and A. von Saldern (eds), *Amerikanisierung. Traum und Alptraum im Deutschland des 20. Jahrhundert*, Stuttgart: Steiner, 1996.
58 M. De Bernardi, 'International tätige Handelsunternehmen', *Selbstbedienung und Supermarkt*, 1975, no. 12, pp. 47–51, here p. 47.
59 'Wir müssen alle lernen, uns miteinander besser zu vertragen' (*Versandhandel*, 1953, no. 12, p. 5).
60 Paul Erker criticized Volker Berghahn's periodization of an Americanization of business elite as wrong, and pointed out the fact that it is based on only a handful of case studies. According to Erker the change in the heads of managers took place in the second half of the boom, rather than in the first; V. Berghahn, *The Americanization of West German Industry, 1945–1973*, Cambridge: Cambridge University Press, 1986; P. Erker, 'Einleitung: Industrie-Eliten im 20. Jahrhundert', in P. Erker and T. Pierenkamper (eds), *Deutsche Unternehmer zwischen Kriegswirtschaft und Wiederaufbau. Studien zur Erfahrungsbildung von Industrie-Eliten*, Munich: Oldenbourg, 1999, pp. 1–18.
61 H.G. Schröter, 'Cartelization and Decartelization in Europe, 1870–1995: Rise and Decline of an Economic Institution', *Journal of European Economic History*, 1996, vol. 25, no. 1, pp. 129–153; 'Der Verlust'.

13 American influences and Japanese innovation in the distribution industry

Changes of supermarket system from the 1950s until the 1970s

Mika Takaoka and Takeo Kikkawa

Introduction

Japan's post World War II distribution system has recently become a focus of international scholarly attention. The issues concerning the Japanese distribution system can be divided broadly into two categories: those related to the distribution structure, and those pertaining to trade practices. A number of researchers, both Japanese and non-Japanese, have explored the determining factors behind the Japanese distribution structure, in which small-sized stores take up an excessively large share in the total number of retail stores, if not in the total size of the retail business, while wholesaling activities go through multiple stages.[1] Many other scholars have researched into the historical and social backgrounds of Japanese trade practices – including the return of unsold goods, dispatched salespersons, payment of rebates, resale price maintenance, and non-price vertical restraints – and have suggested how these practices are rational for the parties concerned.[2]

It can be safely said that the distribution structure and the trade practices mentioned above are peculiar to Japan. But this fact does not mean lack of American influences on Japan's postwar distributive industry. For example, supermarkets and convenience stores, two new and important business models for Japan's postwar retailing industry, were introduced from the United States of America. Supermarkets are the area in which the American system was most systematically applied to Japan. Both supermarkets and convenience stores, however, experienced Japanization after Americanization. Their Japanization has been closely connected with the peculiar aspects of Japan's distribution system. This chapter will examine changes in the supermarket system in Japan from the 1950s till the 1970s. It was the middle of the 1950s when the first supermarket store appeared in this country. And, until the 1970s, the supermarket system became one of the most important business systems in Japan's distributive industry.

The growth process of Japan's supermarkets during the period between the 1950s and the 1970s can be divided into two phases. The first is Americanization in the 1950s and the 1960s, and the second is Japanization in the 1960s and the 1970s. That is to say that in the 1960s Americanization of the supermarket system and its Japanization stood side by side in Japan. The next section of this chapter surveys the historical background of supermarkets in Japan. The following section makes clear the process of Americanization, and the final section examines that of Japanization, followed by a conclusion.

Historical outline of supermarkets in Japan

It was the middle of the 1950s when the first supermarket appeared in Japan. After that the supermarket business grew very rapidly for a quarter of a century. Several causes can be adduced as the principal environmental factors that favoured Japan's supermarkets in the period from the mid-1950s to mid-1970s. These include:

1   an improvement in consumer standards;
2   the establishment of a mass production system;
3   the Westernization of lifestyles;
4   the sudden increase in suburban populations and the increase in the number of households;
5   the beginnings of motorization;
6   tightness in workforce supply and demand and the expansion of the part-time workforce; and
7   the enactment of the Large Scale Retail Stores Law only in 1973 (i.e. the absence of any regulation of supermarkets until then).[3]

Of all the above environmental factors, the one that had an extremely important and multifaceted significance for the business expansion of supermarkets in the high-growth period was the Westernization of lifestyles. Limiting our discussion of the Westernization of lifestyles to foodstuffs, which is what this study tries to focus on, we can further subdivide it into two factors: 'the Westernization of food materials' and 'expanded consumption of processed foods'. The point that needs to be noticed here is that, during Japan's period of high growth, the rapid progression of Westernization in matters of food was accompanied by the strong survival of traditional food consumption patterns, and this had a huge impact on the distribution system. While Westernization in matters of food on the whole provided supermarkets with business opportunities, at the same time the traditional consumption patterns of a strong predilection for freshness in food and a high frequency in trips to buy food remained in place, with the result that a long period of time was required before supermarkets could carry out a systems reform in regard to the sale of fresh foodstuffs – and in fact this reform did not become a reality until the mid-1980s. This was also to be the factor that led to the totally unexpected increase in the number of small retail shops (the majority of them food stores) that went on for many years until numbers started dropping in the mid-1980s.[4]

During the period from the mid-1950s to the mid-1970s, Japan's supermarkets were able to take advantage of these factors to forge ahead with aggressive growth behaviour. Table 13.1 was compiled from *Serufu sabisuten tokei* [Self-service shop statistics] compiled by the Ministry of International Trade and Industry or MITI,[5] the only public material that makes it possible to grasp supermarket trends during the period in question. As can be seen from the table, while the percentage of increase in supermarket sales in Japan for the 2-year period 1964–66 was slightly under 50 per cent, for the 2-year period beginning in 1966 and ending in 1976 the percentage of increase consistently exceeded 50 per cent.

This rapid growth in supermarket sales in Japan from the 1960s through to the mid-1970s showed up, naturally enough, as a change in the share of the consumption pie held by the sources where goods were purchased. Table 13.2 gives the shares of that pie held by the various sources where goods were purchased, broken down by types of goods, as calculated from the *Zenkoku shohi jittai chosa hokokusho* [Report on a survey of actual conditions in national consumption], prepared by the Statistics

Table 13.1 Sales figures, employees and floor space in supermarkets

	No. of stores	Sales (million yen)	Permanent employees	Floor space (1,000 m²)	Floor space per store (1,000 m²)
1964	3,620	392,373	89,429	1,342	0.37
1966	4,790	581,146	105,083	1,557	0.33
1968	7,062	1,028,570	142,896	2,780	0.39
1970	9,403	1,612,459	173,072	4,188	0.45
1972	10,634	2,447,583	207,119	5,587	0.53
1974	12,034	4,253,531	268,698	7,890	0.66
1976	14,543	6,750,221	329,600	10,110	0.70
1979	19,172	10,937,733	455,028	14,225	0.74
1982	22,217	14,600,948	568,343	17,055	0.77
1985	25,221	14,765,585	574,731	17,515	0.79

Sources: Annual editions of *Wagakuni no shogyo* (The Nation's Trade), published by the Research and Statistics Department, Minister's Secretariat, MITI, and *Serufu sabisuten tokei* (Self-Service Shop Statistics) (1983) and *Shogyo tokeihyo-gyotaibetsu tokeihen* (Trade Statistical Tables (statistics by form of business) (1987), both also published by the same department of MITI.

Notes
The figures for the years up to 1982 are based on *The Nation's Trade* and *Self-Service Shop Statistics*. We included only those retail shops that had a floor space of at least 100 m², of which at least 50 per cent was used for a self-service format.
The figures for 1985 are based on *Trade Statistical Tables*. Of the shops treated as self-service retail stores in the original sources, we left out any 'convenience stores' and 'other supermarkets' that had less than 100 m² of floor space.

Bureau of the Prime Minister's Office. From this table we can see that the share held by supermarkets was only 5.4 per cent of total consumption expenditure in 1964, but it had risen by 6.4 points to 11.8 per cent in 1974, a movement that was in stark contrast to the 0.6 points drop of the department stores and the large drop by 10.6 points of the general retail stores. When we look at foodstuffs in particular, we can see that supermarket share rose from 9.8 per cent in 1964 to 24.4 per cent in 1974, or an amazing rise of 14.6 points. During the same period, the share of department stores in expenditure on foodstuffs fell 0.4 points, while that of general retail stores fell a huge 22.9 points. From this we can readily see the conspicuous improvement in the position held by supermarkets as sources for the purchase of foodstuffs, as compared with other retailing bodies. These trends basically continued from the latter half of the 1970s through to the first half of the 1980s, though with clearly much less momentum.[6] In other words, as can be seen from the table, even though the amount of increase in supermarkets' share as a source where goods were purchased rose by the considerably large sum of 11.2 points in foodstuffs in the period from 1974 to 1984, their share of total consumer expenditure rose no more than 2.1 points in that period.

Table 13.2 Retailer share of consumer expenditure, by items (per cent)

	Supermarkets			Department stores			General retail shops		
	1964	*1974*	*1984*	*1964*	*1974*	*1984*	*1964*	*1974*	*1984*
Total consumer expenditure	5.4	11.8	13.9	6.4	5.8	5.3	47.2	36.6	25.8
Food expenditure	9.8	24.4	35.6	2.9	2.5	3.2	78.4	55.5	36.3
Clothing expenditure	6.0	14.1	15.5	29.4	30.4	35.9	44.2	41.1	35.1
Housing expenditure	2.0	6.3	10.3	7.0	6.2	7.1	32.9	33.0	28.1

Sources: *Showa 39-nen zenkoku shohi jittai chosa hokoku dai 6-kan – konyusaki hen* (1964 Nation-wide Consumption Fact-finding Survey Report, vol. 6: Place of Purchase), *Showa 49-nen zenkoku shohi jittai chosa hokoku dai 6-kan – konyusaki hen* (1974 Nationwide Consumption Fact-finding Survey Report, vol. 6: Place of Purchase), and *Showa 59-nen zenkoku shohi jittai chosa hokoku dai 2-kan – hinmoku hen* (1984 Nationwide Consumption Fact-finding Survey Report, vol. 2: Items Purchased).

Notes
The surveys are limited to average urban households consisting of two people or more.
Besides supermarkets, department stores, and general retail shops, the other categories were 'Co-ops,' 'Others' (this includes itinerant traders, street stalls and train platform kiosks), and 'Service charges, etc.' (this includes the costs of eating out, laundry, transportation, communications and repairs).
The 'housing expenditure' for 1984 is the total of 'housing' and 'furniture and household goods' and 'educational-use/recreational-use durables.'

Americanization in the 1950s and the 1960s

The appearance of supermarkets

It is said that Kinokuniya opened the first supermarket in Japan at Aoyama, Tokyo, in 1953. Certainly Kinokuniya was a grocery store with 135 m² sales space and introduced self-service operations, but about 40 per cent of its total sales were on credit and it did not always pursue low prices. Therefore, some scholars of commercial science consider Maruwa Food Centre of Kitakyushu, Fukuoka prefecture, which was founded by Hideo Yoshida in 1956, to be the first real supermarket in Japan. Maruwa Food Center was a grocery store with 396 m² sales space and adopted self-service operations, cash sales and low price selling.[7]

For most Japanese in the 1950s, the appearance of supermarkets symbolized the emergence of America into Japan's distributive industry. The most important point of the first step of Americanization was the appearance of supermarkets, in the introduction of self-service operations. The people in Japan's distributive industry in those days defined supermarkets as large-scale grocery stores with self-service operations based on the definition of supermarkets in the United States of America.[8]

The application of chain operation theories

It was the 1960s when Americanization of the supermarket system in Japan made full-scale progress. We can find the essence of the second step of Americanization in the application of chain operation theories. A lot of Japan's supermarkets without chain operation became bankrupt in the 1960s. For Japan's supermarkets, application of the chain operation theories was a secret weapon for not only survival but also rapid growth. The advantages of moving into developing chains were:

1   the possibility of slashing sales expenditures by means of standardization; and
2   the possibility of realizing low-price mass procurement of commodities and achieving a reduction in the cost of purchasing stock (bulk discounts), by separating purchasing and sales and setting in place a concentrated bulk purchasing system.

It was Shun'ichi Atsumi who introduced into Japan the chain operation theories that had taken a firm foothold in the United States, and who had a large impact on supermarket circles in the 1960s as the president of the Pegasus Club, a chain store management research group founded in 1962.[9] Atsumi, who was born in 1926, studied business administration in commerce as a newspaper reporter for Yomiuri in the latter half of the 1950s. He visited the USA again and again, made case studies on Sears,

Roebuck, JC Penny and so on, and absorbed information about the chain operation theories.

Atsumi's Pegasus Club is very famous as the greatest contributor to the introduction of the American style chain-store operation into Japan. The club attached importance to two methods, visiting America and exchanging members' experiences. It may safely be said that the activities of the Pegasus Club were a kind of productivity movement imported from America to Japan's distributive industry, and that Shun'ichi Atsumi, the opinion leader of the club, was an apostle of Americanization. Table 13.3 shows the main members who joined the Pegasus Club at the time of its foundation. The names of representative supermarket managers in Japan, for example, Isao Nakauchi of Daiei, Masatoshi Ito of Ito-Yokado, Takuya Okada and Hidenori Futagi of Jusco, and Yukio Nishibata and Tsuneo Okamoto of Nichii Chain, can be found on the list. It is said that Kohei Ueno of Seiyu Store also began to receive Atsumi's guidance in about 1965.[10]

It was the late 1960s when the influence of the Pegasus Club reached its highest level. If we look at the top supermarkets in Japan and see the growth in the numbers of their stores in the 5-year period from the end of 1968 to 1973, we find that the number of Daiei stores shot up from 28 to 108, that of Seiyu Store from 31 to 105, that of Ito-Yokado from 14 to 43, and that of Nichii Chain from 21 to 147.[11]

Table 13.3 Main members of Pegasus Club in 1962

Manager	Company	
Isao Nakauchi	Daiei	
Masatoshi Ito	Ito-Yokado	
Takuya Okada	Jusco	(Okadaya)
Hidenori Futagi		(Futagi)
Yukio Nishibata	Nichii Chain	(Self-Hatoya)
Tsuneo Okamoto		(Akanoren)
Yoshio Otaka	York-Benimaru	(Benimaru-Shoji)
Zenbei Otaka		
Hisanori Takagi	Uny	(Hoteiya)
Toshio Nishikawa		(Nishikawaya)
Mitsuharu Wada	Izumiya	
Akio Wada		
Takashi Onishi	Onishi-Iryo	

Source: S. Atsumi, *Chen sutoa keiei no mokuteki to genjo/kaiteiban* (Purposes and the Present States of Chain Store Management), rev. ed., Tokyo: Jitsumu Kyoiku Shuppan, 1996, p. 115.

Note
Company names in parentheses are those in 1962.

Japanization in the 1960s and the 1970s

Dependence on turnover variance funds

The movement of Americanization by the Pegasus Club, however, had to change its course under the special circumstances in Japan. When supermarkets adopted the chain operation strategy, with its requirement for the aggressive opening of new stores, they were dogged by the large sums needed for plant and equipment investment funds. Even those supermarkets that had achieved rapid growth were no bigger than small-to-medium businesses or even small businesses in the 1960s, so they could not get whatever they wanted from the banks or the stock markets, and as a result they were not able to obtain sufficient funds.[12] In this aspect, Sears, Roebuck and JC Penny in America, who gathered lots of money from stock markets, were not their teachers. To sum up, Japan's supermarkets had to find a new way of fund raising.

The first step in the Japanization of the supermarket system came about from inside the Pegasus Club. In order to adapt chain-store operation to the financial situation in Japan, Atsumi himself could not help emphasizing a new fund raising method that was totally different from the American one. This was turnover variance funds which were utilized as traditional trade practices within the Japanese wholesale system. According to Atsumi, 'turnover variance funds' are 'funds that are left over when the accounts payable turnover period is delayed and the time it takes to turn goods into cash occurs earlier'.[13] From the retailer's point of view, it means surplus funds can be made available when the period for paying a wholesaler the money for goods purchased is longer than the period of selling the goods for cash to consumers.

During the period of high growth in the Japanese economy from the middle of the 1950s to the early 1970s, by means of such differences in settlement periods, wholesalers were fulfilling a financing function in regard to supermarkets that were expanding their chains by, in effect, lending them turnover variance funds. Looking back at that period, Atsumi emphasizes that turnover variance funds, the consequence of the wholesalers' financing function, were 'directed towards fixed investment'[14] in chain stores.[15]

According to archive materials, in 1961 the settlement allowance for foodstuff wholesalers was 60 days, while the turnover time for processed foods in supermarkets was 9.3 days.[16] According to a Kyoto Chamber of Commerce and Industry survey published 8 years later in 1969, the turnover time at supermarkets for processed foodstuffs was almost unchanged at 9.6 days, whereas the turnover time for processed food at small general-foodstuff retailers was more than double that, 20.1 days.[17] Unfortunately, Kyoto Chamber of Commerce and Industry does not deal with the question of the settlement allowances of foodstuff wholesalers, but it would seem fairly clear that the financing function of wholesalers by means of turnover variance funds operated heavily in favour of supermarkets rather than small retail shops.[18]

On the basis of interviews the authors of this paper have carried out, wholesalers did not, during the period of the high growth of the Japanese economy, make any distinction between traditional small retail shops and supermarkets in regard to settlement allowances. Still, the existence of turnover variance funds was extremely attractive to the supermarkets. The reason for this was that, if they raised the rate of goods turnover through managerial effort, while the wholesalers' settlement allowance remained unchanged, it was possible to increase the amount of turnover variance funds.[19] In other words, turnover variance funds became a type of incentive for supermarkets, and there was a situation in which a revolutionary retail system (supermarkets) was able to use to its advantage a traditional wholesale system that had been formed in order to handle a traditional retail system (small retail shops).[20]

The development of general merchandising stores

In parallel with the first step of the Japanization of the supermarket system, i.e. dependence on turnover variance funds, the second type of Japanization progressed in the period from the mid-1960s to mid-1970s. This was the development of general merchandising stores (GMS) which sold not only foods, but also clothes and sundry goods. These were peculiar to Japan and differed from the American style chain-store supermarkets where food was the main commodity. It is said that the main players of Japan's supermarket chains, which developed rapidly during the latter half of the high economic growth period, were GMSs as 'false department stores'.[21] Daiei, Ito-Yokado, Seiyu Store and Nichii Chain all expanded their sales in a short period through opening department store type shops in the suburbs of large cities. The shocking shift of Japan's biggest retailing firm with regard to sales base from Mitsukoshi to Daiei in 1972 symbolized the fact that 'false department stores' surpassed real department stores.

In Japan the share held by GMS sales was only 11.4 per cent of total supermarket sales in 1964, but it had risen by 31.9 points to 43.3 per cent in 1974, a movement that was in stark contrast to the 12.2 points drop in grocery supermarket sales (from 68.1 per cent to 45.9 per cent) and the 7.5 points drop of clothes selling supermarkets (from 17.6 per cent to 10.1 per cent).[22] Table 13.2 shows that the amount of increase in supermarkets' share as a source where goods were purchased rose not only in foodstuffs (from 9.8 per cent to 24.4 per cent) but also clothes (from 6.0 per cent to 14.1 per cent) and housing goods (from 2.0 per cent to 6.3 per cent) in the period from 1964 to 1974. These facts reflect the development of GMS in that period. Since the middle of the 1970s, however, the growth of GMS had lost momentum because of the enactment of the Large Scale Retail Stores Law in 1973 and later amendments to the law. The main players in Japan's supermarkets shifted from GMS to grocery supermarkets after the mid-1970s.

Why did GMS develop rapidly in Japan in the period from the mid-1960s to the mid-1970s? Here, it is important for us to bear in mind the observations made by Satoshi Azuchi, the pen name of Shin'ya Arai, President of Summit K. K.[23] He pointed out the following two reasons for the development of GMS:[24]

1   rapid progress of urbanization in the suburbs of existing large cities; and
2   the passive attitudes of existing department stores towards opening new shops.

It is not always correct to understand that the negative policies of department stores for opening shops came from regulations based on the Department Stores Law of 1956. Because, even under the Department Stores Law, existing department stores could open GMS as 'false department stores' in the suburbs of large cities until the enactment of the Large Scale Retail Stores Law in 1973. Actually Seibu Department Store developed Seiyu Stores, one of the biggest GMS chains in Japan. Most of the existing department stores except Seibu, however, took passive attitudes towards opening new shops. Azuchi emphasizes the conservatism of department stores as the reason for their negative policies. According to his argument, the Department Stores Law protected existing department stores from new entry by their rivals through regulating the opening of new shops in the large city centres where existing department stores already had their own shops. Stable earnings from protected shops in the centre of cities led the department stores to avoid new plant and equipment investments. Conservatism of department stores resulted in enlargement of business chances for supermarket firms to develop GMS as 'false department stores' in the suburbs of large cities.

System innovations of perishable food sales

The wave of Japanization in the supermarket system affected not only general merchandising stores (GMS), but also grocery supermarkets in the 1970s. Kansai Supermarket of Itami, Hyogo Prefecture, preferred systematization of perishable food sales[25] to chain-store operation. The company succeeded in pre-packaging its vegetables, meat and fish in the middle of the 1970s. This was an epoch making issue which announced the birth of Japanese style grocery supermarkets.

In the period of high growth in the Japanese economy from the middle of the 1950s to the early 1970s, while Westernization occurred in the style of foods, the traditional consumption patterns survived. In Japan, in contrast to America, a strong predilection for freshness of food and a high frequency in trips to buy food remained in place. Westernization was in favour of the development of both GMS and grocery supermarkets. Traditional consumption patterns, however, with a strong consumer predilection for freshness of food, consequently restricted development of grocery supermarkets. The supermarket system could only be successful with the pre-package system, because it is centred on self-service operations. At that time, grocery supermarkets did not have the skill for pre-packaging perishable foods. Therefore, it was not until the early 1980s that grocery supermarkets began to establish competitive advantages over traditional meat shops, fish stores and so on, by establishing their system for pre-packaging perishable foods.

Next, let us look at how the grocery supermarkets overcame their lack of skills. When grocery supermarkets were introduced in Japan, they had two options with which to compensate for their lack of pre-packaging skills. One was employment of workers for selling the perishable foods, and the other was the introduction of a tenant system. Both of them were in-person selling, or giving up the establishment of their pre-packaging system. In the early years of development, grocery supermarkets selected the tenant system, because the artisanship of workers engaged in the handling of perishable foods did not match supermarket operations. On the other hand, the tenant system chosen by them in the first stage had the following problems. First, the tenant enterprises avoided opening shops in more than two or three supermarket stores, with the result that it was difficult for grocery supermarkets to keep the goods at a standardized quality. Second, the tenant enterprises behaved in their own family-business way. Consequently, the grocery supermarkets in the period of high growth in the economy had to grapple with the problems of establishing a pre-packaging system of perishable foods.

It was the late 1970s when the pre-packaging system of perishable foods was established. The outline of the establishment of the pre-packaging system, was based on the example of Kansai Supermarket, which played a central role in system innovations of grocery supermarkets in Japan.[26] The invention of a pre-packaging system of perishable foods consisted of inventions both in hardware and software. First, in hardware, the introduction of the equipment for maintaining the freshness of the perishable foods and the improvement of the back area of the store were important. When the All Japanese Supermarkets Association (AJS) held 'The First Training in Hawaii and America' in 1967, Yuji Kitano, the president of Kansai Supermarket, was greatly astonished to see the Times Supermarket in Hawaii, because the perishable foods were displayed in an open refrigerator. Following this training session, he introduced the open refrigerator into his shops, and at the same time began to develop a new open refrigerator, which would be suitable for perishable foods in Japan. Japanese weather differs from American weather because of high humidity and a large seasonal difference in temperature. There are lots of block-type meats, few greenhouse vegetables and very few fish in American supermarkets. By contrast, Japanese supermarkets are abundant in sliced meat, greenhouse vegetables and fish. Kitano had to develop a new open refrigerator suitable for the Japanese conditions. In 1967 he was successful. For hardware innovations, the following factors were also important: the development of a cart and a sink for the preparation of food, removing gutters in a backyard, providing a flat floor for the refrigerator, and the introduction of an automatic packer. These improvements were aimed at ways to utilize part-time workers efficiently. Grocery supermarkets had to use part-time workers more and more because of the rise in wages since around the recession in 1965.

Now, let us consider software innovations, which progressed simultaneously with the hardware innovations. At first, Kitano adopted the scientific method of dealing with fruit and vegetables, based on a knowledge of basic botanical physiology learned from a specialist at Osaka Prefecture University. Second, he introduced new operations from the automobile and electricity industries, which made efficient use of the part-time workers due to simplification and standardization. As a result, fish could be sold within the self-service operations instead of in-person from 1970. Finally, they started selling meats without reliance on tenants in 1973, based on the knowledge and the skills learned from the Star Market in Hawaii.

As the above process indicates, the pre-packaging system at Kansai Supermarket was completed in the late 1970s. However, it took about 10 years for the pre-packaging system introduced by Kansai Supermarket to spread throughout Japan. AJS played a major role in spreading the pre-packaging system of perishable foods. AJS, which was established in 1962 for the purpose of exchange of information between managers of the grocery supermarkets, supported the introduction of the pre-packaging system of perishable foods to its members. Consequently, the pre-packaging system, which was introduced by the Kansai Supermarket, spread countrywide until the middle of the 1980s. Summit K. K. of Tokyo was one of the representative followers of Kansai Supermarket.

In the previous section, based on Table 13.2 we said 'even though the amount of increase in supermarkets' share as a source where goods were purchased rose by the considerably large sum of 11.2 points in foodstuffs in the period from 1974 to 1984, their share of total consumer expenditure rose no more than 2.1 points in that period'. The relatively high growth of foodstuff sales during the period reflected diffusion of the pre-packaging system of perishable foods within Japan's supermarkets. The innovation in the pre-packaging system enabled grocery supermarkets to expand their business and to establish competitive advantages over traditional meat shops, fish stores and so on. This innovation was one of the underlying factors of so-called '1985 shock'.[27]

Japan's distributive industry experienced a violent change, or what is known as the '1985 shock'. The shock is so called because the number of retail stores began to decrease in or around 1985, contrary to the long-held belief that Japan's distribution system was characterized by the presence of an excessive number of retail stores. The '1985 shock' manifested itself in the form of a decline in the number of small-sized foodstuffs and beverage stores. The pre-packaging system of perishable foods enabled grocery supermarkets to establish competitive advantages over traditional meat shops, fish stores and so on. Thus, the system innovations of perishable food sales were one of the most important causes of the '1985 shock'.

Conclusion

The chapter has examined changes in the supermarket system in Japan from the 1950s until the 1970s. It is possible to divide the growth process of Japan's supermarkets during the period into two phases. The first is Americanization in the 1950s and the 1960s, and the second is Japanization in the 1960s and the 1970s. That is to say that in the 1960s Americanization of the supermarket system and its Japanization stood side by side in Japan.

In the phase of the Americanization of Japan's supermarket system the following two facts were important:

1   appearance of supermarkets following American models (especially, introduction of self-service operations); and
2   application of chain operation theory.

And, in the phase of Japanization of Japan's supermarket system there were three noticeable factors:

1   dependence on turnover variance funds based on the financing function of wholesalers;
2   development of general merchandising stores; and
3   system innovations of perishable food sales.

For Japan's distributive industry after World War II American impacts have consistently been significant. In almost all cases, however, Americanization led to Japanization as a process of adaptation to specific conditions in Japan. For example, waves of Japanization in the convenience store system, which had originally come from America, spread to America.[28] The case of supermarkets is never exceptional in that sense.

Notes

1 See Y. Tsurumi, 'Managing Consumer and Industrial Marketing Systems in Japan', *Sloan Management Review*, vol. 24, no. 1, 1982, pp. 41–50; T.K. McCraw and P.A. O'Brien, 'Production and Distribution', in T.K. McCraw (ed.), *America versus Japan*, Boston: Harvard Business School Press, 1986, pp. 77–116; T.C. Bestor, *Neighborhood Tokyo*, Stanford: Stanford University Press, 1987; H.T. Patrick and T.P. Rohlen, 'Small-scale Family Enterprises', in K. Yamamura and Y. Yasuba (eds), *The Political Economy of Japan 1: The Domestic Transformation*, Stanford: Stanford University Press, 1987; E. Batzer and H. Laumer, *Marketing Strategies and Distribution Channels of Foreign Companies in Japan*, Boulder, CO: Westview Press, 1989; D. Flath, 'Why are There So Many Retail Stores in Japan?', *Japan and the World Economy*, vol. 2, no. 4, 1990, pp. 365–386; S. Kuribayashi, 'Present Situation and Future Prospect of Japan's Distribution System', *Japan and the World Economy*, vol. 3, no. 1, 1991, pp. 39–60; M. Shimaguchi, 'New Development in Channel Strategy in Japan', in M.R. Czinkota and M. Kotabe (eds), *The Japanese Distribution System*, Chicago: Probus Publishing Company, 1993, pp. 173–190; T. Nariu and D. Flath, 'The Complexity of Wholesale Distribution Channels in Japan', in M.R. Czinkota and M. Kotabe (eds), *The Japanese Distribution System*, pp. 83–98; T. Kikkawa and M. Takaoka, 'A New Perspective on the Japanese Distribution System: Structure and Trade Practices', *Social Science Japan Journal*, vol. 1, no. 1, 1998, pp. 101–119; M. Takaoka, 'Japan's "Distribution Revolution" and Chain Store Supermarkets', *Japanese Yearbook on Business History* 15, 1998, pp. 75–101; and M. Takaoka, 'Globalization of Distribution Structure and the "1985 Shock" in Japan', *ISS Joint Research Project Discussion Paper* 7, 2000, Institute of Social Science, University of Tokyo, pp. 1–20.

2 See Tsurumi, 'Managing Consumer and Industrial Marketing Systems in Japan'; L. Pelligrini, 'Sales or Return Agreements versus Outright Sales', in L. Pelligrini and K. Reddy (eds), *Marketing Channels: Relationships and performance*, Lexington, MA: Lexington Books, 1986, pp. 59–72; D. Flath and T. Nariu, 'Returns Policy in the Japanese Marketing System', *Journal of Japanese and International Economics*, vol. 3, no. 1, 1989, pp. 49–63; Dodwell Marketing Consultants, *Retail Distribution in Japan*, Tokyo: Dodwell Marketing Consultants, 1991; T. Suzuki, 'Trade Connections and Trade Practices in the Japanese Distribution System', in Czinkota and Kotabe (eds), *The Japanese Distribution System*, pp. 219–230; M. Takaoka, 'Sengo fukkoki no nihon no hyakkaten to itaku shiire: Nihonteki torihiki kanko no keisei katei (Japanese Department Stores and Their Consignment Purchases during the Postwar Reconstruction Period: The Formative Process of Japanese Trade Practice)', *Keiei shigaku* (Japan Business History Review), vol. 32, no. 1, 1997, pp. 1–35; and Kikkawa and Takaoka, 'A New Perspective on the Japanese Distribution System'.

3 More detailed discussions on the environmental factors favouring supermarkets in the period can be found in Y. Suzuki, 'Wagakuni ni okeru supa no shokiteki tenkai (The Early Stages of Supermarkets in Japan)', *Aoyama keiei ronshu* (Aoyama Journal of Business), vol. 26, no. 2, 1991, pp. 313–323, esp. pp. 318–319; and K. Tateno, 'Wagakuni ni okeru supa no seicho (The Growth of Supermarkets in Japan)', *Nagasaki kenritsu daigaku ronshu* (Journal of Nagasaki Prefecture University), vol. 25, nos. 3–4, 1992, pp. 85–128, here pp. 87–93.

4 A detailed discussion on this point can be found in T. Kikkawa and M. Takaoka, 'Supamaketto shisutemu no kokusai iten to nihonteki hen'yo (International Transformation and Japanization of Supermarket System)', in H. Morikawa and T. Yui (eds), *Kokusai hikaku/kokusai kankei no keieishi* (Business History of International Comparison and Relationship), Nagoya: Nagoya University Press, 1997, pp. 279–304, here pp. 287–300.

5 MITI changed its name to Ministry of Economy, Trade and Industry or METI on 6 January 2001.

6 Amendments to the Large Scale Retail Stores Law are, it is often pointed out, believed to be in large part responsible for this damping of momentum.

7 These points are based on T. Yahagi, *Kouri inobeshon no gensen* (The Origin of Retail Innovation), Tokyo: Nihon Keizai Shinbun Sha, 1997, pp. 36–37.

8 Detailed discussions on the definition of supermarkets in America can be found in Y. Suzuki, *Kouri shogyo no kindaika* (The Modernization of Retail Commerce), Tokyo: Chusho Kigyo Shindan Kyokai, 1959, pp. 47 and 53.

9 Detailed discussions on the role of Atsumi and Pegasus Club can be found in S. Atsumi, *Chen sutoa keiei no mokuteki to genjo/kaiteiban* (Purposes and the Present States of Chain Store Management), rev. edn, Tokyo: Jitsumu Kyoiku Shuppan, 1996, pp. 112–117; and Yahagi, *Kouri inobeshon no gensen*, pp. 93–99.

10 See M. Tatsuki, 'Ryutsu kakumei to Seibu ryutsu grupu no keisei (The distribution Revolution and Formation of Seibu Distribution Group)', in T. Yui (ed.), *Sezon no rekishi/jokan* (The History of Saison/First Volume), Tokyo: Riburupoto, 1991, pp. 227–458, here pp. 389–390.

11 See Takaoka, 'Japan's "Distribution Revolution" and Chain Store Supermarkets', pp. 84–85.

12 Looking back at that period, Hideo Yoshida, Founder of Maruwa Food Centre, says that 'everybody who took on a supermarket went to a lot of trouble to obtain funds', in H. Yoshida, *Supa no genten* (The Starting Point of Supermarkets), Tokyo: Hyogen Sha, 1982, p. 170.

13 S. Atsumi, *Chen sutoa keiei no gensoku to tenbo/kaiteiban* (Principles and Prospects of Chain Store Management), rev. edn, Tokyo: Jitsumu Kyoiku Shuppan, 1994, pp. 38–39.

14 Ibid., p. 39.

15 Concerning the reason why turnover variance funds were considered an important source of procuring funds for fixed investment, Atsumi pointed out that 'at the time borrowed money cost 8 per cent, so turnover variance funds costing absolutely nothing were very advantageous' (in an interview one of the authors of this paper, Takaoka, conducted with Shun'ichi Atsumi on 21 May 1998 in his position as Chief Consultant for Japan Retailing Centre).

16 See Sen'i Kouri Shinbun Sha (Textile Retailing Newspaper), *Supa: sono genjo to mondaiten* (Supermarkets: Present Situation and Problem Areas), Tokyo: Sen'i Kouri Shinbun Sha, 1962, pp. 32–33.

17 See Kyoto Shoko Kaigisho (Kyoto Chamber of Commerce and Industry), *Kyoto no supamaketto* (Supermarkets in Kyoto), Kyoto: Kyoto Shoko Kaigisho, 1969, p. 29.

18 It must be noted here that, if the bill settlement allowance of processed food makers was longer than the bill settlement allowance of the foodstuff wholesalers, it would be the processed food makers, rather than the foodstuff wholesalers, who would really be shouldering the financing function burden. The bill recovery period for processed food makers in the period of the high growth of the Japanese economy is not given among the data revealed in such things as securities reports. Still, according to a securities report for Ajinomoto (70th–71st periods), a representative processed food maker in Japan, the credit sales allowance for the 1961 year was 13.5–13.6 days, or one-fourth shorter than the bill settlement allowance of foodstuff wholesalers for the same period. Strictly speaking, there are problems with making a direct comparison between the credit sales allowances of makers and the bill settlement allowances of foodstuff wholesalers, but it seems safe to surmise here that it was not the processed food makers, but the foodstuff wholesalers, who shouldered the burden of financing the supermarkets by lending them turnover variance funds.

282   Mika Takaoka and Takeo Kikkawa

19 These points are made on the basis of an interview with Shin'ya Arai (President of Summit K. K.) on 14 February 1997.

20 A detailed discussion on the extent to which supermarkets in the period relied on turnover variance funds in the expansion of their chains through new stores can be found in Takaoka, 'Japan's "Distribution Revolution" and Chain Store Supermarkets', pp. 95–100.

21 S. Imoto, 'Epirogu' (Epilogue) in Nikkei Ryutsu Shinbun (ed.), *Ryutsu gendaishi* (The Modern History of Distribution), Tokyo: Nihon Keizai Shinbun Sha, 1993, pp. 353–359, here p. 353.

22 See Tateno, 'Wagakuni ni okeru supa no seicho', p. 117.

23 Summit K. K. developed a grocery supermarket chain mainly in Tokyo.

24 The following are based on S. Azuchi, *Nippon supamaketto genron* (The Principles of Supermarkets in Japan), Tokyo: Parusu Shuppan, 1987, pp. 25–26, 105–107, and 122–123.

25 A detailed discussion on the systematization of perishable food sales can be found in Kikkawa and Takaoka, 'Supamaketto shisutemu no kokusai iten to nihonteki hen'yo'.

26 The following descriptions are based on Kansai Supermarket, *Kansai Supa 25-nen no ayumi* (The 25 Year History of the Kansai Supermarket), Itami: Kansai Supermarket, 1985, and interviews with Yuji Kitano (President of Kansai Supermarket) on 20 and 21 August 1996.

27 A detailed discussion on the '1985 shock' can be found in Kikkawa and Takaoka, 'A New Perspective on the Japanese Distribution System', pp. 105–109; and Takaoka, 'Globalization of Distribution Structure and the "1985 Shock" in Japan', pp. 4–9.

28 A detailed discussion of Americanization and Japanization of the convenience store system can be found in M. Takaoka, 'Nippon no konbiniensu sutoa no seicho katei ni okeru shigen hokan mekanizumu' (Resource Supplement Mechanism of the Convenience Store Business in Japan), *Keiei shigaku* (Japan Business History Review), vol. 34, no. 2, 1999, pp. 44–73; and Takaoka, 'Globalization of Distribution Structure and the "1985 Shock" in Japan', pp. 12–15.

Index

rules of competition 196, 200

safety standards: automobile 88
Saito Shoichi 102, 104
sales: German companies 129–30; markets
81; techniques 83
Sasaki Satoshi x; diffusion of technology 13
Sasaki Tadashi 154
SB-centres (self-service centres) 257–8
Schröter, Harm G. x; distribution 16–17
Science and Technology Administration
Council (STAC) 224
scientific management techniques 5, 6, 76
scientific quality control methods (SQCM)
see SQCM
Seiyu Store 275
self-service distribution 248–52; Germany
257–8, 262, 263–4
semiconductors 71, 122, 138, 150–6, 157–8
seminars: for top management 63–4
shampoo: synthetic neutral 228
Shibaura Seisakusho (Shibaura Engineering
Works) 138
shitauke group companies *95*, 99; car parts
suppliers 94
'1985 shock': distribution 279
shoplifting 249
Siemens 32, 41; case study 118–31;
reorganization 126–8
Siemens AG 127
Siemens-Schuckertwerke 121–2
Sihler, Helmut 200
Sloan, Alfred: General Motors 6
small series production 76
SMEs (Small and medium-sized enterprises)
59, 61, 169; RKW 47
soap manufacture 221–42, *229*
Sohyo (General Council of Trade Unions in
Japan) 61
Sony 68, 149
Soviet Union 8
SPAR: chain-store 259–60
spare parts market 99–100, 101, 113; Japan
97
Sperry Rand Corporation 144–6
SQCM (scientific quality control methods)
175, 182, 187–9, 191
STAC (Science and Technology
Administration Council) 224
stakeholders 46
standardization 76
standardized management accounting 33
Standard Oil 163, 164
standards: international 58; safety 88
Stanford Research Institute 204, 207–7
Stapf, Erwin 204
statistical management 187–8
statistical quality control methods 57
steel 5, 41; industry 60
stock ownership 224
Stoever (car producer) 76
Stokes, Raymond 164
strategy consultancies 46

strikes 5
study trips 34, 128, 129, 224–6; to USA
120–1, 248–9, 255; *see also* visits
supermarket system 17; Germany 252–7,
262, 263–4; Japan 268–79; retailer share
271, *271*; sales figures 270, *270*
supervisional training 171
Supreme Commander of Allied Forces
(SCAP) 54
surfactants 233–4
Suzuki Tsuneo x; artificial fibre industries 15
synthetic detergents 221–42, 228; *see also*
detergents and household cleaners
synthetic fibre industry 175, 180–91
synthetic neutral shampoo 228
synthetic rubber production 163
systems technology 125–6

Tacke, Gerd 127, 128
Takaoka Mika x; supermarket system 17
Takezawa Shin'ichi 55
Taniguchi Foundation xii
Tarui Yasuo 155–6
Tashiro Shigeki 182, 186, 187
tax exemptions: cars and motor bikes 77
Taylor, Frederick W. 5, 6
Technical Assistance Contracts (Class I) 64,
65, 66
technical schools 129
technological innovation: Kao 222–3, 231
technology: Kao 233–4; synthetic fibre
manufacture 191; Volkswagen 81–3
technology license agreements 7, 11, 20,
121–2; *see also* licensing
technology and management:
Americanization 22–4; skills 11
technology payment values *69*
technology tie-ups 10, 11, 104, 140–6, 241–2
see also technology license agreements
technology transfer 22–4, 64–70, 71, 81, 93,
121–6, 162–7, 172, 176, 224–6, 231–5;
direct 54
technology transfer programmes 61–2
Telecommunications Group: Siemens 125
television: advertising 85, 202, *203*, 236;
broadcasting, licensing contracts 70;
manufacturers 70
Television Promotion Association
(Terebijon Shinko Kyokai) 70
tenant system: grocery supermarkets 277
Terebijon Shinko Kyokai (Television
Promotion Association) 70
Texas Instruments 68
textile products 176, *177*; *see also* nylon
Thyssen, August 5
'Tide' (trade name) 229; synthetic detergent
225
tie-ups 104, 140–6, 241–2; *see also*
cooperative relationships
tire production 162–7, 190
Tokyo Denki (Tokyo Electric Company)
138
top management seminars 63–4

For Product Safety Concerns and Information please contact our
EU representative GPSR@taylorandfrancis.com Taylor & Francis
Verlag GmbH, Kaufingerstraße 24, 80331 München, Germany